COUNTY G
TO ENGLISH
CHURCHES

Lawrence E. Jones & Roy Tricker

COUNTRYSIDE BOOKS
NEWBURY, BERKSHIRE

First Published 1992
© Lawrence E. Jones
and Roy Tricker 1992

COUNTRYSIDE BOOKS
3 Catherine Road
Newbury, Berkshire

ISBN 1 85306 179 4

Photographs: From Lawrence Jones' collection, taken
by Alfred Proctor, with additional photographs
by Roy Tricker, Neil Skelton and George Butler.

Produced through MRM Associates Ltd, Reading
Typeset by Acorn Bookwork, Salisbury, Wilts
Printed in England by Borcombe Printers plc, Romsey, Hampshire

CONTENTS

FOREWORD

'Churches? – Once you've seen one, you've seen the lot!' If this book can go some way towards correcting this statement then it has been well worth the effort. A book like this can only whet the appetite and scratch the surface of the indescribable wealth of beauty, mystery, antiquity and atmosphere which waits to delight the visitor to every single one of England's 10,000 medieval churches. The ideal guide to England's churches would simply list the lot! We have chosen only a token sample from each county, hoping that these may tempt you to discover the rest. If asked to make a list of the most memorable churches in a county, everybody's results would be different and this is simply a selection by two people. Some of the churches have been chosen because they are outstanding, some because they are typical of the area, others because they are *not* large or famous and rarely listed in the guidebooks, but are nevertheless lovely.

Lawrence Jones – my fellow church-fanatic, brother Reader and old friend of 25 years or more – inspired thousands of people through countless lectures, excursions, sermons and books, to love, appreciate and enjoy our old churches. His handy little *Guide To Some Interesting Old Churches*, which was regarded as an essential occupant of many a bookshelf or car glove-compartment, has long been out of print and I know how overjoyed he was when Nicholas Battle of Countryside Books realised the great need for a book such as this and encouraged him to revise it. Sadly his death in February 1991 left the revised work only half-written, but it has been my joy and privilege to complete and enlarge it, as a tribute to one who did more than anybody to spread the love and lure of churches.

This book is therefore a joint effort by two crusading church-crawlers who are total fanatics! The 20 counties completed by Lawrence have received only a few minor adjustments and additions by me, although the general introduction and the county introductions are mine.

Above all, we hope that you may detect in this book a great deal of real love, and that this love for old churches may infect our readers also. These buildings have so much to tell us, such treasures with which to delight and inspire us and, in the words so often used by Lawrence, each one is 'the House of God and the Gate of Heaven in our towns and villages'.

Roy Tricker
1992

INTRODUCTION

There are thousands of people who love visiting old churches and discovering the wealth of beauty and interest to be found in every single one. They find endless fascination in these buildings which grace our towns and villages and are a feature of our English scenery and such a part of our lives, because they are part of our nation's heritage. What is more, they are indeed 'Sermons in Stone', silent and beautiful witnesses to things far beyond that which time and space can measure. Their towers and spires raise our spirits upwards and point us heavenwards, their superb craftsmanship inspires us because it was fashioned with love and skill as 'something beautiful for God' and the atmosphere of the prayer and devotion of centuries which saturates their solid and venerable walls does have a strange habit of bringing people to their knees.

Churches were built to be open for you to enter and use whenever you wish – and an amazing number, thankfully, still are. Sadly some have to be locked, and in my searches for their keys, I hear the terrible stories of why their custodians are forced to lock them. Locked churches, however, usually expect and welcome visitors and locating their keys should not be too difficult. Even if it is impossible to gain entry, the church enthusiast never loses out – because you then have more time to enjoy the outside of the building. Don't forget that by seeing the exterior, you see half the church. There is no way, for example, that you can appreciate a lovely tower or spire from the inside of the building!

Why then are our medieval churches so fascinating and so precious, and what do they have to offer us? Here are just a few points which are worthy of consideration by people of all faiths or of none.

1. The ancient church is usually (although not always) the oldest building in its town or village, and it may be anything from 450–1,000 years old, or older. Where better to be in touch with the history of the place? What stories they can tell us, if only we have eyes to see!

2. England's churches contain our greatest heritage of art and craftsmanship in wood, stone, glass, metalwork, etc from Saxon times to the present day – from medieval Old Masters to modern design and construction, each age having left its own contribution.

3. These buildings – from Grantham's soaring 282 ft spire to Waltham Abbey's great Norman nave – were constructed by folk whom we might be tempted to think of as 'primitive'; people who believed that the earth

was flat and had never heard the word computer. They did have pulleys and wooden scaffolding, but nothing mechanical. They built with love, they built by hand and they built to last – and most of the buildings *have* lasted. What a tribute to the medieval architects' and stonemasons' skill.

4. An even greater miracle is the way in which our churches have been maintained over the centuries, entirely as the result of what people have been prepared to give voluntarily. It is only recently that grants have been available and, even with their invaluable help, we still see tiny parishes successfully raising hundreds of thousands of pounds to preserve their churches. Here we are in the world of miracles and of faith moving mountains!

5. England has about 10,000 medieval churches (if you start when you are born and see a hundred fresh ones per year, and live to be 100, then you will manage to get around the lot!). Out of this total, no two churches are exactly alike. Each is a character, which is unique and, like people, each has been moulded with a great deal of love and care, and maybe a few knocks and batterings as well. There is no such thing as an 'ordinary' church.

6. An old church is not just for services and sermons. As a shrine – a holy place – it is on duty every minute of the day and every day of the year. The church can therefore be enjoyed at any time of the day or night. If you doubt this, go and see one of our lovely churches which has been expertly floodlit. You will probably discern things in it which would be missed in daylight.

7. You will find a very, very high proportion of our medieval churches still in use for the purpose for which they were built. So you will not be visiting mere museums or ancient monuments, but working buildings, which are loved and cherished by those whose spiritual homes they are. Whatever your beliefs, to visit a building which is still functioning is much more exciting. There is really no such thing as a 'redundant' church either. Even if converted to an alternative use, most of our redundant churches have still preserved some of their character. The 270 or so churches now cared for by the Redundant Churches Fund (marked in the lists as 'RCF') are only redundant parochially, but are still churches – consecrated, cared for and available for all to visit and to use for their rightful purpose.

8. Our churches have so much to teach us about people – either those in effigies upon tombs or in the fascinating records of people of the past, recorded upon memorials in church or churchyard. All this, like so much more in churches is real living history.

9. The way to really see England is to visit its churches. Hunt them out with the aid of a map and your journey will take you where the tourists rarely get to. You will see the real England at its best; you will be rewarded with glorious scenery, beautiful villages, parkland, downland, moorland, forest, and all the other wonderful features which our English countryside has to offer. In the big towns you will often need to go down the back streets and will enjoy ancient tucked-away houses, dockland scenery and other hidden parts which are loved by their residents but are often not the tourist show-places.

10. And it is all free! What more could you want! No need for membership cards, subscriptions or tickets. Of course, if you can afford to leave a contribution in the church money-box, this will help those who care for it to maintain it intact and beautiful for future generations to use and to enjoy.

In addition to the medieval churches, we have another 5,000 or so 'modern' churches, built since the Reformation in the 1500s. These include all the wonderful churches of the Classical period (designed by Wren, Hawksmoor and their contemporaries), also a kaleidoscope of churches which were erected during the Gothic Revival of the 1800s. These buildings have their own fascination, because we usually know so much more about the architects who designed them, the people who paid for them to be built or who laboured to make them living entities, and also we can trace so much more of the stories of these churches from their foundation. There is also great beauty and interest in their architecture, which too many people so easily dismiss, because they cannot help comparing them to medieval churches. I challenge anybody, however, to visit one of Wren's London churches, or St Chad's Shrewsbury, or St Augustine's Kilburn, or St Mary's Wellingborough, or even the splendid new church in the heart of Milton Keynes, and then still to say that inspiring church architecture stopped in the 1500s!

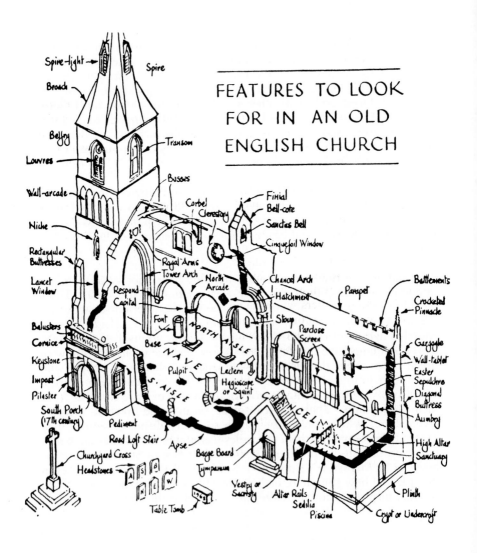

FEATURES TO LOOK FOR IN AN OLD ENGLISH CHURCH

Spire-light
Spire
Broach
Belfry
Transom
Louvres
Wall-arcade
Busses
Corbel
Clerestory
Finial
Bell-cote
Sanctus Bell
Cinquefoil Window
Niche
Rectangular Buttresses
Royal Arms
Tower Arch
North Arcade
Chancel Arch
Hatchment
Parapet
Battlements
Lancet Window
Respond
Capital
Font
Base
Stoup
Pardose Screen
Crocketed Pinnacle
Balusters
Cornice
NORTH AISLE
NAVE
Pulpit
Lectern
Hagioscope or Squint
Gargoyle
Keystone
Impost
Pilaster
South Porch (17th century)
Pediment
Rood Loft Stair
Apse
S. AISLE
CHANCEL
Wall-tablet
Easter Sepulchre
Diagonal Buttress
Aumbry
High Altar
Sanctuary
Churchyard Cross
Headstones
Barge Board
Tympanum
Table Tomb
Vestry or Sacristy
Altar Rails
Sedilia
Piscina
Plinth
Crypt or Undercroft

8

FEATURES TO LOOK FOR

Here are just some of the hundreds of features to look for when visiting a church. To catalogue everything would need a very large book indeed and would include several hundreds of items and technical terms. Please remember that you do not have to be an 'expert' in order to enjoy our churches. Just to spot something (which the experts may very well ignore as being of no interest) and to think to yourself 'Now isn't that lovely', automatically means that the church is beginning to work its spell upon you!

Never forget to enjoy the *setting* of a church and to stand back and view it as a whole in its surroundings. You may well have enjoyed some lovely scenery on the way, with very tempting *distant views* of it. The views from the churchyard may also be rewarding. This is all part of church-crawling. You may need to congratulate yourself upon actually finding the place at all! Remember that very often the more remote a church is, the more rewarding and unspoilt it may well turn out to be.

Naturalists may well gravitate to a host of plants naturally conserved in the *churchyard*. Others will hunt out ancient *headstones* and *chest-tombs* (maybe from the 1700s or occasionally earlier) or will read inscriptions about real people of the locality who have lived and died. Possibly the lychgate has medieval timbers, or is an attractive 19th or 20th century construction. The old village stocks may also have survived.

The exterior of the church building is worth examining. The *building materials* will often tell you in which part of the country you are, because local stone is often used. There are red sandstone churches, blue–green greensand churches, buff or yellow limestone churches, churches faced with thousands of small flints, or of mellow Tudor brick, or of timber.

It could be said that the *tower* stamps the character of the exterior (rather like the head or face in a human) and what wonderful constructions these often are – again reflecting local styles of building design. Devon and Cornwall have lofty towers, often with corner turrets, Somerset has magnificent and mighty creations which are a mass of stonecarving, Kent has prominent staircase-turrets rising above the parapet (as do other churches in the Home Counties), East Anglia has fine flint towers and very early round towers – to name but a few areas. Several counties (especially in the Midlands) have a host of lofty stone *spires*. These remarkable constructions are actually the tower roof carried to a ridiculous level, and the view up inside the spire from belfry level is well worth seeing if the opportunity arises. The timber towers of Essex (and elsewhere) are worth finding. Essex and most south-eastern counties also have several of those rustic and attractive timber *bell-turrets*, which perch above the roof gable and usually rest upon massive timber constructions inside.

In the body of the church itself we can admire the beauty of *windows* and *doorways* – the shape and design of which helps us to date them. A church is usually the combination of work from many different periods, as people expanded, enlarged and beautified it, using the style of architecture fashionable at the time. This often indicates that, although the windows of a particular church may be predominantly from the 1400s, the core of the structure may well date from the 11th century, with possibly a Norman doorway or a hidden blocked window to prove it, if we are lucky! Church windows themselves can be very fine, with lovely *tracery* forming patterns in the stonework of their upper sections. Where there are aisles, there are often fine sets of *clerestory* windows in the nave wall above the aisle roofs. In many English churches, the *chancel* is lower and very different in character from the nave and it is useful to remember that until comparatively recent years the rector (who was often the parish priest) was responsible for the maintenance of the chancel, whilst the parishioners looked after the rest of the church.

Very often the stonework of the exterior has much to delight us. Maybe there are carved *corbel heads* supporting the drip-stones around the arches of windows and doorways, or fearsome gargoyle faces, which throw rainwater clear of the walls, or carvings in the masonry, or little *Mass dials* scratched in the stonework (always on the south side) which were used to indicate the times of services before the days of clocks.

The church *porch* is often worthy of inspection. Occasionally it is a beautiful medieval construction in wood, stone, or brick. Some are two-storeyed (with a parvise, or priest's room, above and with a vaulted ceiling). Even the *door* by which you enter may have been opening and closing to admit worshippers and visitors for 500 years or more. It may retain its ancient ironwork, or even its sanctuary ring. Porches are often adorned with beautiful canopied *niches* externally and possibly the *Holy Water stoup* remains near the entrance, where people dipped their fingers in Holy Water and made the Sign of the Cross as an act of cleansing and rededication upon entering the sacred building. In some of our churches the stoup is still in use for this purpose.

The interior of an old church contains a kaleidoscope of craftsmanship from a variety of periods and Christian traditions, including some very tasteful work from our own times, which takes its place alongside that of past ages. We have the medieval work, from the time when the parish church itself, with its colour and carving, provided a host of visual aids to teach the Faith to the ordinary people who could not read. There may well be work from c1600–1840, when churches were furnished for the 'plain and Prayer Book' worship of the Established Church and there is nearly always work from the Victorian and Edwardian eras, when the majority of our churches were restored, and occasionally altered out of all recognition. All of this combines to create an interior of individual atmosphere and character, which is worth taking time to sit down and drink in as a whole, also to walk around and enjoy the vistas from different parts of the church.

So we come to examine some of the possible features. If there are *arcades*, these may be elegant and have fine stonecarving – some also lean precariously! The beauty of the *window tracery* can be further appreciated from the inside. Always look upwards at the *roofs*, which often contain medieval timberwork and are supported upon carved figures. Many roofs are extremely handsome and follow particular patterns of construction (tiebeam, hammerbeam, etc). If you discover a fine roof, the only way to really appreciate it is to lay flat on your back on a bench, with your head nearest the centre aisle. Try it and you will find yourself in a totally different world!

The *font* (near the west end and the doors to symbolise our entry into the Christian family through baptism) is very often medieval and is usually a beautiful piece of stonecarving. A few fonts have preserved their medieval wooden covers or canopies. Original *benches* may be seen, either with poppyhead ends (as in East Anglia) or with flat-topped ends, but splendidly carved (as in the West Country). Some churches have ancient *stalls* in the chancel, with tip-up seats (misericords) with intriguing carvings on their undersides. Occasionally one finds a medieval *pulpit*, but more often a handsome 17th century pulpit, which is sometimes a two or three-decker. A few churches have managed to keep some of their 17th or 18th century furnishings, including box-pews, and western *galleries* for musicians, also *Communion rails* of the period and maybe also a *Communion table*. Sometimes the old pre-Reformation *altar stone* (or mensa), thrown out in the 1500s, has been found, rescued and restored to its proper use. In many churches we see the *Royal Arms* (usually 17th or 18th century), put up to remind people of the position of the Monarch as temporal head of the English Church.

Look for the *parish chest*, where church and parish valuables were stored. Some are bound with iron strapwork, some have been hollowed out of massive pieces of timber and nearly all have very thorough locking systems. Medieval *lecterns* are rare, but well worth finding. Some have double bookrests, but most are in the form of an eagle, to remind folk that the Word of God must not only be read, but spread! Most lecterns were made during the past 150 years, but many of these were inspired by medieval originals.

Notice the 'holes in the walls' of our churches. These recesses usually served various purposes and are often lovely pieces of stonecarving which remind us of medieval church life. There could be canopied *niches* for statues, *aumbries* (cupboards) where valuables were stored, a *piscina* near an altar, with a drain for the disposal of water, *sedilia* forming wall-seats in the sanctuary, also maybe an *Easter Sepulchre* on the north side of the sanctuary, or a *squint*, to give a view of an altar through an expanse of wall.

The walls of our churches were once covered with *wall-paintings* and many of these have been discovered and revealed under later plaster. A favourite was St Christopher, carrying the Christ Child over the water.

Before the Reformation, every church had its carved and painted *rood-screen*, dividing the chancel from the nave. This was surmounted by a rood-loft (or gallery), above which stood the great Rood (Christ, crucified and flanked by His Mother and St John). All Roods and their lofts were destroyed in the 1500s (though a very few lofts have survived), but many screens, or parts of them, remain, also *rood-loft staircases*. Some screens are still magnificently painted with the Apostles and other characters.

It was thanks to the Puritan 'purge' in the 1640s that most of the *medieval glass* was smashed up, but many churches have preserved a little ancient stained glass in their windows, although often this is only mere fragments. Most stained glass in churches is Victorian and tends to exclude the light, creating an atmosphere of 'devotional dusk' (or Holy Gloom), but some of this glass (especially that by the firms of William Morris, C.E. Kempe, Clayton & Bell and others) is very good of its kind. The 20th century has also produced some very beautiful stained glass.

Many people visit our churches to enjoy the wealth of *monuments* which they contain. Monuments are one of the few adornments to churches which were erected to the glory of man rather than of God, but how truly splendid these are, and what a tremendous amount of history they show us – from magnificent effigies recumbent upon alabaster tomb-chests to humble wall-plaques with amusing epitaphs and strange spelling from years gone by. Look in the floors for stone *coffin-lids*, *burial slabs* and *leger slabs* and on the walls for *plaques*, *cartouches*, fine monuments with *effigies*, lozenge-shaped *hatchments* and beautifully carved *tomb-recesses.* Several burial slabs have effigies or inscriptions in *brass* (brass-rubbing is an infatuation in itself). Discover in our variety of monuments and memorials, knights and their ladies, priests, lawyers and people from many walks of life, and take a step back into history.

There is much, much more to discover in churches. There are those features which are not always easily accessible to visitors, but which are specialist studies in themselves. The *organ*, for instance, with its thousands of individual pipes and the unique tradition of Anglican choral music. The *bells* (sometimes weighing a ton or more) and England's very own tradition of change-ringing. Most churches are equipped with precious and beautiful Communion *plate*, also *registers* of baptisms, marriages and burials (now mostly available for inspection at County Record Offices), often dating back to the 1500s.

There are other things, which some of the 'standard works' do not mention. Notice for instance, how the vast majority of our churches are beautifully cherished and cared for, and how some reflect particular traditions within the Church of England. Anglo-Catholic churches are often exquisitely furnished and have specially devotional interiors, with flickering lights, superbly adorned sanctuaries and many aids to devotion. Many Evangelical churches, although less ornate, have a tremendous feeling of life and vitality, and signs that they are powerhouses of Christian activity.

The smell of a church is a feature often ignored, but is very much a part of its character. Some still smell of paraffin lamps, because they still use them – others are bathed in the odour of incense from a previous service. Then there is that very special 'C of E' smell, found in many small churches. This is hard to describe, but it seems to be a glorious cocktail of straw from rotting hassocks, green from damp walls, maturing and silvering timbers in roof and benches, mouse-chewed and greening cassocks in the vestry, mouldering hymn-books, decaying parish magazines of yesteryear, stuffed behind radiators, and maybe also a few disintegrating bats' droppings of some antiquity – all combining to make an odour which is not at all unpleasant, but which you may only find in an old church!

But all this and much, much more in our churches has to be experienced by actually visiting them, and they are all around you, whichever corner of England you may visit. They are there for you – whatever your interests or beliefs may be. Treat them with tenderness and care. Respect their sanctity and treat them with the reverence due to a Holy Place, because they are sacred to those who maintain them. Above all, if you can spare something for the offertory box, please do so, because then it will be thanks to you that generations yet unborn may enjoy them also.

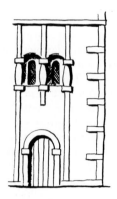

Saxon.

Norman.

E.E.

Dec.

Perp.

Saxon to 1066
Norman 1066 to 1189
Early English 1189 to 1280
Decorated 1280 to 1377
Perpendicular 1377 to 1547

STYLES OF ARCHITECTURE

We can date craftsmanship in churches by looking at the architecture which determines their construction and shape, especially in windows, doorways and arcades, which usually conform to the distinctive style of architecture in use during a particular period. We must remember, however, that architecture gradually evolved over the centuries, as different styles became fashionable, and so the dates given are only very approximate. What follows is only the briefest outline which will hopefully show how easy it is to identify the different styles. Church architecture brings with it a language of technical terms, a few of which are mentioned here. Do not be put off by them; most guide books (and books like this one) have to use them, but usually (unlike most modern jargon) if you stand and look at what is being described, you will soon see and understand what the term means and after a little experience of looking at churches, it will all become very familiar to you. The main styles of architecture used in churches are as follows:

1. **SAXON (or PRE-CONQUEST). Before 1066.** Compared with Norman work, windows and doorways often appear rather rough and crude. Arches are ROUND-HEADED or TRIANGULAR-HEADED. A DOUBLE-SPLAYED WINDOW is nearly always Saxon. LONG AND SHORT WORK in an external quoin (corner) is clear indication of Saxon work.

2. **NORMAN. c1066–1190.** ROUND-HEADED ARCHES always in windows, doorways and arcades, but much more neatly and elaborately constructed. The arches of Norman doorways are often embellished with moulded patterns (eg zig-zag, billet, cable, stars, beak-heads) and rest upon stone SHAFTS which are topped by CAPITALS (often cushion-capitals or scalloped capitals). Occasionally the semicircle made by the arch of a doorway is filled by a carved stone TYMPANUM. Other beautiful stonecarving is sometimes seen in a CORBEL-TABLE at the top of an external wall, beneath the roof.

3. **EARLY ENGLISH (EE) c1190–1280.** The first style to use the POINTED (GOTHIC) ARCH. Windows are still usually quite small (but with wide internal splays) and are SINGLE. The point of the arch is usually very sharp (hence they are called LANCET windows). Sometimes these single windows are grouped in threes or fives. Doorways have pointed arches, with stone shafts each side, which have moulded

15

capitals, sometimes embellished with carved foliage. Look for the DOG-TOOTH ornament, which was a favourite ornamental motif of this period. The arches of windows and doorways from the EE period onwards are usually framed by HOOD-MOULDS (sometimes called DRIPSTONES) which usually rest upon carved CORBELS.

NOTE HOWEVER that there is always a transition period between styles of architecture, as one style evolves into another. The blending of Norman and EE is often seen and we call this architecture TRANSITIO-NAL (c1170–1200) – possibly seen in features like a doorway with Norman style capitals and decoration, but using a pointed arch.

As we follow the transition from EE to Dec, we see single windows gradually getting larger, or pairs being placed very close together – ready to develop into double, triple or larger windows. With the advent of Dec we have these larger and more elaborate windows, which are divided vertically by stone bars called MULLIONS into two or more LIGHTS and made complete and beautiful above the lights by patterns called TRACERY.

4. **DECORATED (DEC). c1280–1377.** Here we see windows and their tracery starting simply but becoming more elaborate and delicate, as the early PLATE TRACERY and 'Y' TRACERY develops into GEOMETRICAL TRACERY, FLOWING TRACERY and RETICU-LATED TRACERY. The arches are not as sharply pointed as EE and the OGEE curve is sometimes used. Arches are often embellished (especially internally and around niches and tomb-recesses) with CROCKETS, FINIALS and PINNACLES. The tracery of the windows becomes very imaginative and in the tops of the window-lights and the tracery we see CUSPING, made up of lobes, called FOILS – making TREFOILS (three lobes), QUATREFOILS (four), CINQUEFOILS (five), etc. A favourite decoration of this period is BALLFLOWER ornament.

5. **PERPENDICULAR (PERP). c1377–1547.** Whilst the basic ske-leton of all Dec tracery is of curved arcs, the skeleton of Perp tracery is based upon vertical (perpendicular) lines, usually reaching to the top of the arch. As the style progressed, windows and doorways developed arches which became less and less sharply pointed and Perp doorways often have square hood-moulds. Between c1450–1600, brick became a popular building material and Perp architecture in brick is most attractive and is often known as TUDOR architecture.

6. **RENAISSANCE AND CLASSICAL. c1603–1840.** A return to the styles of architecture used in the early (pre Christian) buildings of Classical Greece and Rome. Windows and doorways are rectangular or round-headed (but could never be mistaken for Norman or Saxon), and there are porticos, pediments, domes, etc. Where a church in the 1600s was built or restored still using Gothic, we call this GOTHIC SURVIVAL. Where Gothic begins to appear again in the late 1700s and early 1800s, we see the precursors of the Gothic Revival; some of the more flowery work of this time is known as 'GOTHICK'.

7. **GOTHIC REVIVAL. c1840–1914.** A deliberate return to church design inspired by medieval architecture, using the Norman, EE, Dec and Perp styles, but very often developing them, embellishing them and adapting them for the new building materials used in the Victorian period and later. This is therefore very much a style (or rather a multiplicity of styles) in its own right and must be seen as such, rather than just 'a poor imitation of the real thing'.

Abbreviations used in this book:

Sax	Saxon	W	west
Norm	Norman	E	east
Dec	Decorated	N	north
Perp	Perpendicular	S	south
EE	Early English	SE	south east
Trans	Transitional	NE	north east
Jac	Jacobean	SW	south west
C/Cs	century/centuries	Mon(s)	monument/monuments

17

AVON

This modern county is made up of what was northern Somerset and southern Gloucestershire, with the river Avon itself at its centre, flowing through its two great cities, Bristol and Bath. The Cotswolds reach down into north-east Avon, where there are pretty Cotswold villages. On the west it is bounded by the broad Bristol Channel, with its resorts of Weston Super Mare and Clevedon. The Avon valley has fine scenery; it becomes a gorge at Clifton. There are high places like Dundry Hill, Cleeve Hill, Bleadon Hill, the downs around Bath and views to the Mendips across the southern border. There is great beauty here, in coombes and woodlands, parkland and agricultural countryside. There is also beauty in its 150 or so medieval churches (roughly 90 from Somerset and 60 from Gloucestershire). Several of the churches have fine Perp towers, but mostly of the north Somerset type, with prominent stair-case turrets and spirelets, and a little less elaborate than those in the south. Lovely stonecarving abounds in this area, where Cotswold stone and Bath stone are so convenient. Touring churches is great fun here because the scenery is so beautiful. Some (like Dyrham and Great Badminton) are set beside their manor houses, some in very pretty villages, and even those in Bath and Bristol (where we have a variety of interesting post-medieval churches) are in cities of great beauty and interest, although so very different in atmosphere – Bath the regal spa town and Bristol the bustling port, whose conurbation has swallowed up several surrounding villages. Bristol has the feel of a metropolis, with its noble cathedral presiding over it, whilst Bath, with its glorious architecture, has its stately abbey church.

ALMONDSBURY. A substantial cruciform church with a central tower and lead-covered spire, also a 14th century two-storeyed and vaulted porch. St Mary's has a Norman doorway and Norman font, also much EE work and some interesting monuments in this very rewarding church.

St Mary's *Olveston* has a Norman central tower, a two-storeyed porch and much to see inside.

BANWELL. St Andrew's, has almost everything one can find in an old church. It is all Perp. The tower with pierced parapets is one of the grand ones, common in this neighbourhood. Inside, note the wagon roofs. The rood-screen is glorious with colour and its coving and cresting remain (and can be dated 1522). The font is Norm, but carved with plants in the 16th C. The old benches have poppyhead ends (very rare in the West Country). The stone pulpit with blank tracery is Perp and of a type common round here. The glass is nicely arranged with some old work and there are several brasses.

Churchill's St John's has a good tower, benches and monuments; *Locking's* St Augustine's tower is also fine and here we see a Norman font and medieval pulpit. *Christon's* St Mary's has a pretty Norman church, with a central tower.

BATH ABBEY. St Peter and St Paul's is one of our latest Perp churches. The central tower is noble and the exterior seems to be all glass with its large windows. The fine W front has little ladders with angels ascending and descending. Inside are fan-vaults (that of the nave 19th C). There are many monuments but mostly late and minor: Bartholomew Barnes and wife and children 1605; Lady Wallarhus and two children, 1633; Bishop Montague 1618.

Amongst the variety of later churches, do find St Mary's Bathwick (c1820 by John Pinch and chancel 1873 by Street) – a fine Anglo-Catholic interior here, also at nearby St John's (C.E. Giles 1861 and A. Blomfield 1871). Pinch designed St Saviour's Walcot, which has a fine reredos by Sedding, whilst St Swithin's Walcot (1780) is Classical and has many memorials.

BRISTOL. A wonderful city this and, before the Second World War, third in England for the number of its old churches but now three are in ruins. The cathedral is worth visiting, although its nave and west towers were rebuilt by Street (1868–88). Grandest of all the parish churches is St Mary Redcliffe. This is one of England's grandest churches, which fortunately escaped the bombing of Bristol. Tower and spire (292 ft) are impressive as also is the N porch, early 14th C, which is hexagonal; its doorway is almost oriental (possibly due to Bristol trade with India in medieval times). The interior with its large windows (mainly Perp) gives a splendour almost unknown elsewhere. In fact Queen Elizabeth I called the church 'the fairest, goodliest and most famous parish church in England', and there is a wooden monument of the Queen in the church. There are vaults throughout with a vast number of bosses. In the S transept is a mon to William Canynge the Younger (he was Lord Mayor five times and completed the church) and wife 1465, and another mon to him (after ordination as Dean of Westbury 1474). There are some other mons and brasses.

Amongst the medieval churches, do hunt out St John's (RCF) in Tower Lane, set above St John's Gate, but with its own tower and spire. There are lovely 17th century fittings here and a particularly fine Communion table of 1635. We have here also to see William Frampton's lovely effigy (1388) and to drink in the atmosphere.

St Stephen's is a large and imposing city church, with a fine tower and monuments. St Mark's, College Green (the Lord Mayor's Chapel and owned by the Corporation) has splendid medieval glass and a wonderful array of monuments.

St James' is a large church with Norman work. St Philip and St Jacob's is EE and Perp, with much to see inside, including a Norman font with 1630 cover. This is a very lively Evangelical church. St Nicholas', with its tall spire, was rebuilt in 1769, but has a 14th century vaulted crypt. Classical Christ Church was totally rebuilt in 1786–91. All Saints', Corn Street, has a tower of 1711–16, but the rest is Norman and Perp. There are good memorials here. St Thomas' (RCF) has a medieval tower and the rest was rebuilt in 1792–3. Some lovely 18th century furnishings inside. The Temple Church is a splendid ruin, with a 114 ft leaning tower.

Amongst the later churches outside the city centre, for Classical do find Redland Chapel (1740–3) for a real treat, and for 18th century Gothick St Paul's, Portland Square (1789–94). At Clifton is All Saints', Pembroke Road (originally by Street 1868 but rebuilt in 1967) which is Anglo-Catholic, and Christ Church, Clifton Down Road, which grew between 1841–85. It is EE, extremely large and commodious, has a tall spire and is Evangelical.

CAMELEY. What a contrast to a large Somerset church, but St James' (RCF) homely, pleasing interior can hold its own with any church. The tower is of red sandstone with a pierced frieze. Inside the clear glass lights up the wagon roof and 17th and 18th C woodwork-galleries, pulpit with sounding-board, reader's desk, family pew, and altar-rails. The font is Norm and some of the benches are Perp.

CONGRESBURY. St Andrew's tower is not of Somerset standard, but it has a fine parapet stone spire (not uncommon in this area). The church seems to be entirely Perp, but there is some earlier work. There is a fine S doorway. The wagon roof of the nave has bosses. The wooden screens have stone bases.

Puxton church dedicated to the Holy Saviour, with its leaning tower, is beautifully furnished with a medieval stone screen base, box-pews, old benches, pulpit, reader's desk etc.

DUNDRY. The tower of St Michael's on the top of Dundry Hill is a landmark for shipping in Bristol, and it was indeed erected in 1484 by the Merchant Venturers of Bristol for that purpose. The parapet and pinnacles of the tower are exceptionally elaborate. The church itself has been rebuilt.

GREAT BADMINTON. Beautifully positioned, right beside the great mansion of 1608, is this fine Classical church, of St Michael and All Angels, of high quality, by Charles Evans, built in 1785. What an interior! There are 18th century box-pews and pulpit in a tunnel-vaulted nave, with classical arcades leading to aisles which have small saucer domes. The chancel and apse of 1875 were tastefully furnished in 1908 by Temple Moore. On the south side of the chancel is the huge monument to the 1st Duke of Beaufort, which is by Grinling Gibbons and rises 25 ft, showing the Duke (who died in 1699) in his Garter robes. Rysbrack made the monument to the 2nd and 3rd Dukes in 1754, also that to the 4th Duke, who died in 1756.

HAWKESBURY. A remote and rural setting for a perfectly delightful church, whose attractive and inviting exterior is crowned by a beautiful tower of Cotswold stone. St Mary's is a mainly Perp building, but we also see Norman and EE work here. The north porch is two-storeyed and delightful. Inside are two fonts (one Norman and the other 17th century), a 15th century nave roof and stone pulpit and some interesting memorials.

At St James the Elder *Horton* is a vaulted two-storeyed porch, an elegant Perp exterior and a spacious interior, with a 17th century font-cover and pulpit.

IRON ACTON. The churchyard here is graced by a most elaborate and beautiful 15th century memorial cross. The fine tower (built by Robert Poyntz, who died in 1439) is fan-vaulted inside. The Perp exterior is lovely and there is a two-storeyed porch. The prayerful interior has 15th century wagon roofs, 16th century benches, a pulpit of 1624, a reredos of c1930 and other woodwork by F.C. Eden and some interesting monuments.

ST. CATHERINE. St Catherine's church is worth seeking out. It adjoins the fine Court. The church was enlarged by Prior Cantelow in 1490 but the lower part of the tower is Norm and the font is EE. The attraction here, however, is the old glass – depicting the usual Crucifixion group with St Mary and St John the Evangelist, and also St Peter. Below St John is the kneeling figure of the Prior with an inscription.

Magnificent 15th century craftsmanship in stone at Wrington, seen in fine windows and parapets and in the superb 'Somerset' tower.

WELLOW. St Julian's is a real delight outside and in. The tower is strong-looking with a higher stair-turret. The fine S door with tracery lets us into the church. There are good roofs, a font of 1300, a rood-screen and side screen, benches with poppyheads and a wall-painting of Christ and the Twelve Apostles. There is also an effigy of a priest and a mon to Dorothy Popham 1614.

Hinton Charterhouse has an interesting church with Norman work, also the remains of a Carthusian priory.

WINSCOMBE. St James' has one of the fine Perp towers. The font is 13th C but it is the old glass here which is notable. In the E window of the N aisle is a splendid Perp Crucifixion group with St Mary and St John the Evangelist and also St Anthony, with kneeling donors below. In a S window are the Virgin, St Catherine and St John the Baptist, of about the same date, and from a little later in a N chancel window are the three Peters in yellow stain – the Deacon, the Apostle, and the Exorcist. The glass in the three lancets (rebuilt) at the E end is early work of William Morris and his firm.

WRAXALL.   All Saints' has a fine Perp tower with large pinnacles. The font is also Perp. The Victorian glass makes the church dark but one must see the fine monument to Sir Edmund Gorges and wife 1512 with recumbent figures, and on the front a big coat of arms between two angels with smaller coats of arms.

Nailsea has a fine Perp church, Holy Trinity, with a lovely tower and a 15th century stone pulpit. There is much to enjoy at *Clapton-in-Gordano* St Michael's church, with its monument to Edmund Wynter (1672).

WRINGTON.   All Saints has one of the best Perp towers with two long belfry windows. Pierced parapets predominate. Note the sanctus-bell turret on the E gable of the nave. As usual the tower arch is panelled and the tower vaulted. The font and screen are Perp.

YATE.   St Mary's has a fine Perp tower with double belfry windows, pierced parapets and pinnacles. The font is 15th century, and a small part of a St Christopher wall-painting remains. A brass of 1590 commemorates Alexander Staples, his two wives and eleven children.

YATTON.   The unusual truncated spire of St Mary's central tower will be the first thing to be noted. The W front is very fine, as also is the S porch with panelling. If you are interested in vaulting, the porch has a lierne-vault and the tower has a tierceron-vault. The interior is impressive, Dec and Perp. The roofs should be noted. There are two effigies of 1325, as well as Sir Richard Newton and wife 1475 with angels, and Sir John Newton and wife 1498 with a relief of the Annunciation on the back wall.

BEDFORDSHIRE

This must be one of our least known and least promoted counties, but it should by no means be dismissed. It is small and people often drive through it rather than come to it, but it is so fascinating to get to know. Parts of it clearly incorporate some of the characteristics of its neighbours – rolling Chiltern scenery from Buckinghamshire, stone villages from Northants, the pastureland and arable countryside of Hertfordshire and the fields of Cambridgeshire. We see this also in the 120 or so medieval churches here – flint and clunch churches from the Chilterns (especially the special clunch known as Totternhoe stone), Hertfordshire spikes, limestone churches from Northants, cobblestone churches from Cambridgeshire, etc.

Despite this, Bedfordshire does have a character and features of its very own. Its countryside is beautiful, variable and largely unspoilt, despite the occasional quarry or brickworks. Its hills are picturesque (as around the Dunstable Downs, the dramatic hills at Shillington, or Sharpenhoe, or around Billington). It has its very own dark brown limestone, seen in many of its churches, and its greensand gives parts of the churches of Husborne Crawley and Aspley Guise a really green colour.

There is a lovely assortment of Bedfordshire towers – many have staircase-turrets rising above their parapets, several are distinguished by handsome sets of double belfry windows and some have beautiful soaring spires. All periods may be enjoyed here – Saxon at Clapham, Stevington and Bedford St Peter, Norman at Elstow, Dunstable and Bedford St Mary, EE at Felmersham and in a series of lovely arcades with stiff-leaf capitals, splendid Dec at Wymington, Swineshead and several churches near the Northants border and Perp at Odell, Willington and many of the larger churches.

The little church at Hulcote (Holcot) is a complete period-piece of 1590 and an endearing little Classical church survives at Whipsnade. Of 19th century architecture, the work of Henry Clutton (architect to the 8th Duke of Bedford) may be seen in several Bedfordshire churches – his mighty church at Woburn being perhaps his most memorable.

These churches have many treasures and lovely medieval woodwork, glass, monuments and brasses may be discovered in the county.

BEDFORD. The busy county town, with a beautiful stretch of river and several fine buildings, has four medieval churches. St Paul's, the large and noble 'main' church, has a fine central tower and 166 ft spire and is a joy to visit in order to enjoy the 15th century roofs, 16th century stonework in the pulpit, a splendid screen and other adornments by G.F. Bodley. It is spacious, beautifully cared for and delightfully situated. South of the river is the cruciform St Mary's, with its notable Norman work and St John's, where Bunyan worshipped. St Peter de Merton has preserved both Saxon and Norman work and also has a delightful situation.

COCKAYNE HATLEY. This brown cobblestone church of St John the Baptist shows work of the EE, Dec and Perp periods and has a fine pinnacled tower. Its remarkable interior will never be forgotten for the array of richly carved 17th century woodwork which was 'imported' here from Belgium – a tower screen from Louvain, rails from Malines, the sumptuously carved stalls from Aulne Abbey and the magnificent pulpit from Antwerp. The wonderful 14th century glass in the north aisle is also an import, but only from Yorkshire!

Potton St Mary's church is worth a visit, also St Peter's *Wrestlingworth*.

COLMWORTH. A splendid Perp tower and spire and grand Perp windows, which create a fine interior. St Denys' is worth a visit if only to discover the lovely monument to Sir William Dyer (1641) and his family.

There is much to see inside *Bolnhurst* St Dunstan's church and a visit to St Nicholas' *Wilden* is worthwhile to admire its fine tower and the 15th century ironwork on its south door.

DEAN. All Saints' is a wonderfully atmospheric church, with a pretty 14th century tower and spire and Perp embattled nave and aisles. The interior is an absolute delight, with 15th century roofs, pulpit, three screens and benches. There is a little old glass here, also a canopied tomb-recess, other treasures and much atmosphere.

For a really unspoilt and unrestored church, you must find nearby St Mary's *Shelton*. You will always remember it because it is full of interest, with its original stone floors and such an air of antiquity – worth travelling miles to see! St Mary's *Yelden* is also beautiful, its pulpit is similar to that at Dean, and *Melchbourne* has a delightful Georgian church of St Mary Magdalen which retains its medieval tower.

DUNSTABLE. The wonderful nave of the former priory church of St Peter rises majestically above its surroundings. Here we see superb Norman and EE work. The west front has spectacular doorways of each period and there is a north-west tower which is typically Bedfordshire. Internally, the vast building has been brought to life most sympathetically by Bodley in 1890 and Felix Lander in 1962. The arcades and font are Norman and there is a Perp screen, also monuments, brasses and much else. The choir or eastern half of the church used by the priory disappeared at the Reformation, but the nave has remained as it was used by the parish. The second storey of the grand Norman nave was originally the blind storey, but is now open and filled with tracery. The original wooden rood-screen remains. There are some brasses and some 18th C monuments, but a rare treasure is a 15th C embroidered cloth, the Fayney Pall.

Do go to *Totternhoe*'s embattled church of St Giles, with its fine Perp roofs, to St Mary's *Studham*, in its lovely setting, to St Mary Magdalene *Whipsnade*, which is largely Classical and to the large and stately All Saints' church at *Houghton Regis*.

EATON BRAY. St Mary's nave arcades are a wonder of the EE period with carved foliage on the capitals. The font is of the same date, as is also the ironwork on the S door. There is a fine 16th C altar table. The handsome late Perp reredos remains in the S transept, and an angle-piscina in the chancel. A brass inscription to Lord Bray 1539 has on the back part of a brass to a bishop or abbot of about 1450.

ELSTOW. John Bunyan worshipped at the fine church of St Mary and St Helen, with its detached tower (which has a Beds staircase-turret and a Herts spike). The setting is superb and we may enjoy good Norman and EE work in this former abbey church, which was restored by Sir T. Jackson in 1881. Note the small Norman figure of Christ with St Peter and St John above the north door. The pulpit and font are Perp and the altar rail 17th C. Notable brasses are Margery Argentine 1427, and Elizabeth Herwy, Abbess of Elstow 1527. A brass of an abbess is very rare.

FELMERSHAM. St Mary's is a monumental EE church in a magnificent setting – all built between 1220–40. Here is a church where we may luxuriate in the beauty of architecture and design – from its incomparable west front to its lovely chancel, its double piscina and its noble crossing beneath the central tower. Perp craftsmen added the clerestory and some of the windows and there is also a magnificent screen.

Lovely churches hereabouts include All Saints' *Odell* (fine tower and superb Perp architecture), St Peter's *Sharnbrook* (elegant spire, screen and brasses), St Peter's *Pavenham* (with its array of 'imported' Jacobean woodwork) and St Peter's *Harrold* (another lovely spire and full of interest and atmosphere).

HOUGHTON CONQUEST. All Saints' is a church full of interest. A fine Perp tower, and indeed most of the church is of that period. The nave roof is Perp with carved bosses. There are some original pieces of old glass in many windows, stalls with good poppyheads and figures, and some Perp benches. On the chancel arch is a 14th C Doom with Christ in Glory and angels, and over the N doorway a 15th C St Christopher. Brasses to Isabel Conquest with husband and son (both look the same!) 1493, and Richard Conquest and wife, 1500. Monument to Thomas Archer, 1629, shown preaching.

LEIGHTON BUZZARD. An enormous (191 ft) spire rises from All Saints' EE tower, above a venerable cruciform church, wonderfully reordered after a disastrous fire in 1985. The 15th century roofs have been well restored and the rare 14th century eagle lectern, together with the 1638 pulpit, 14th century misericord stalls and Bodley's panelling and reredos in the sanctuary, have thankfully all survived. Much of the stained glass is by C. E. Kempe. Look for the graffiti of the Dec window and the two medieval characters carved into the southern piers of the crossing, also the remarkable ironwork of c1294 on the west door.

LOWER GRAVENHURST. A charming building (RCF) of dark ironstone – just a single cell and a tower with a Beds stair-turret. St Mary's was built by Sir Robert de Bilhorne c1360 and the windows are mostly Dec. A small church with a great character! The interior is atmospheric and devotional, with its original king-post roof, Jacobean pulpit, Perp screen and old benches. Look for Benjamin Pigott, his two wives and 14 children, all effigied in brass on their monument.

St Mary's *Meppershall* has a Norman tower and transepts and an EE chancel.

LUTON. St Mary's (182 ft long) is Bedfordshire's largest church. It is enormous, and much of its Perp exterior is faced with flint and stone chequerwork patterns. It is well worth walking round the outside and giving yourself plenty of time to enjoy all that the inside has to offer. The traceried south door is 14th century and some of the arcades rest upon 13th century stiff-leaf capitals. The 14th century Easter Sepulchre survives in the chancel and there is old screenwork and stalls. The amazing

27

Mellow ironstone seen in the tower at Lower Gravenhurst. The staircase turret and belfry windows are typical of this county and the short spike reminds us of nearby Herts.

feature here is the vaulted stone canopy over the Purbeck marble font – both of the 14th century. The Wenlock Chapel has superb Perp stonework, as does the tiny vaulted Barnard Chantry. The 14th century sacristy is also vaulted. This is a church rich in monuments and brasses.

Later churches worth visiting include St Saviour's (Micklethwaite & Somers Clarke 1897–1905), All Saints' (Caroe 1922) and St Andrew's (Sir Giles Gilbert Scott, 1931).

MARSTON MORTEYNE. St Mary's massive detached tower is of an early date, possibly built for defence. The fine nave is Perp. Note the roof with its carved bosses and angels. The chancel is Dec with a priest's chamber at its NE end with a piscina in the room below and a fireplace in the room above. In the N of the chancel arch a stairway climbs to the roof; climb this to see the sanctus bell etc. The lower panels of the screen remain with coloured figures of prophets. On the walls were a Doom and St Christopher paintings. The font is Perp. There are several brasses and a monument to Thomas Snagge, Speaker of the House of Commons, with his wife and children, 1594.

NORTHILL. This ironstone church of St Mary the Virgin has a handsome exterior, with pleasing Dec and Perp windows and a 72 ft western tower with staircase-turret, also a two-storeyed and vaulted porch. Henry Woodyer restored it in 1862 and the interior, with its lofty 14th century arcades and narrow aisles, has much which is of taste and beauty. The collegiate stalls are of c1404 and the screen also incorporates 15th century woodwork. Most remarkable of all here are the two stained glass windows of 1664, made by John Oliver for the Grocers' Company. There is also glass by Kempe and Clayton & Bell.

The exterior of *Old Warden* St Leonard's church gives little indication of the great treasures to be found inside – a feast of carved woodwork, mostly imported from the Continent. Medieval woodwork, brasses and monuments await us at *Cople* All Saints' church and *Willington's* embattled and very distinctive Perp church of St Lawrence has much to interest us.

OAKLEY. The base of St Mary's tower is Norman, and the upper part Perp. There is a fine font of the latter period, but the special feature of the church is the rood-screen with its beautiful coloured coving with Christ on a rainbow, and the traceried front of the loft. Only about twelve such fronts remain in the whole of England. There is a complete set of old bench-ends.

PODINGTON. A lovely stone village with a church of great character. It has an elegant stone spire and we see here work of most medieval periods. The font is Norman and the traceried south doors Tudor. There are medieval benches here and the interior is atmospheric and devotional.

Tiny St Michael's *Farndish* (RCF) has a beautiful doorway of c1210 and much atmosphere also.

SHILLINGTON. All Saints' tower is 14th C with a brick top of 1750. Under the chancel is a vaulted 13th C crypt. There is a rood-screen and several screens with tracery and some old benches. There is a fine brass to a priest in a cope, Matthew Asscheton 1400, and a brass of another priest, late 15th C. The church is delightfully situated on a hilltop with fine views.

TODDINGTON. A noble cruciform church of Totternhoe stone, crowned by a 90 ft central tower. St George's stands high and has a fine setting across a green. In the embattled exterior we must not miss the remarkable frieze of carved creatures beneath the parapets. The interior's crowning glory is its splendid roof, with bosses and carved angels, which gives shelter to a host of treasures of many periods, including a beautiful reredos (1949) by Christopher Webb, wall-paintings which are up to 600 years older and some fine monuments.

Chalgrave's lonely church of All Saints has an amazing array of wall-paintings of c1310, also a good EE nave and a pleasantly unrestored atmosphere.

TURVEY. There is something to interest everybody in this fascinating building. We have Saxon work here, also EE, Dec and Perp. The 15th century roof of All Saints' is studded with bosses and adorned with a dozen angels, the font has been in use since c1200 and the south door by which we enter may well be 13th century. Look for the 14th century Crucifixion painting in the south aisle, four superb Mordaunt monuments and three brasses. The chancel (1852) is the creation of Sir Gilbert Scott and the four-manual organ (which is enormous for a village church) is a fine instrument by Hill & Son.

WOBURN. A delightful area of Bedfordshire and a charming little town, in the shadow of the vast Woburn Abbey estate, with its safari park. What is left of the old church stands in the middle of the town. The present church of St Mary stands slightly aloof and in a quiet setting – but what a church! It is an enormous Bath stone building of 1856–8 and is an almost overpowering essay in neo-12th century architecture.

Everything here is larger than life and is the creation of Henry Clutton, who was commissioned by the 8th Duke of Bedford. The bold tower once had a spire which soared 200 ft. The vast vaulted interior feels rather like a French church. The chancel culminates in a magnificent reredos, made in Oberammergau in 1903 to the designs of W.D. Caroe. Look for the St Francis window (1938) which shows no less than 60 birds. The Dukes of Bedford are much in evidence in this church which was built by their family. Clearly they spared no expense here!

Clutton also designed St Michael's church at *Woburn Sands* (1868), whilst J.D. Sedding rebuilt the delightful St Mary's church at *Pottesgrove* (RCF), using medieval materials and retaining the 14th century screen and some fragments of 14th century glass. All Saints *Ridgemont* (1854) is by Sir Gilbert Scott and has a prominent spire, whilst St Peter's *Milton Bryant* has Norman work and St Mary's *Husborne Crawley* must be seen, if only to enjoy the remarkable green colours in its fine tower.

WYMINGTON. St Lawrence's has a charming exterior and interior, almost all 14th C. The top of the tower and attractive spire are Perp. The S porch is lavish with a vault with a Green Man boss. The piscina and sedilia are 14th C, and the side screen and pulpit are Jacobean. A faint 15th C Doom painting can be seen on the chancel arch, and a 14th C Trinity on the E wall of the S aisle. All the brasses are notable. That to John Curteys, Mayor of the Staple of Calais and builder of the church, and his wife, 1391, is the earliest brass in Bedfordshire. There is also Sir Thomas Brunflet, Cup Bearer to Richard II, and wife, 1430, and John Stokys, rector, in Mass vestments holding a chalice, 1510.

BERKSHIRE

A long, narrow county, sandwiched horizontally between Oxfordshire and Buckinghamshire to the north and Hampshire to the south, and bisected by the M4. Travelling westwards, we may start in the planned and planted royal splendour of Windsor Great Park at one end and finish up in the rural wildness of the Wiltshire Downs at the other. This is very much 'The Royal County of Berkshire' and therefore a great deal of the beauty here has been planned, landscaped and conserved. There are grand houses, schools and public buildings, leafy private drives, many signs of affluence and much sophisticated scenery. There is also the lovely Thames valley along the northern border, where Nature and human planning combine gloriously as it travels through Streatley, Pangbourne, Wargrave and Bray. We have the lovely downs around Lambourn and in the north-west the bracing hill-country around Chieveley and the Illsleys. There are the pretty villages along the Kennet and Lambourn rivers and in the county's delightful wooded heart, lovely places like Yattendon, Hampstead Norreys, Stanford Dingley, Aldermaston and many others. There are grand old towns like Newbury and Hungerford – and Reading, although now very big and busy, is full of history. This is an incredibly beautiful county – full of trees, satisfying scenery, and villages and hamlets of great charm.

Of almost 150 medieval churches, the county lost 60 or so when its northern part was absorbed into Oxfordshire. Berkshire's churches are lovely – some are very small and they remind us that much of what is now residential was once tiny villages. Several have little wooden belfries and flint rubble walls – rustic and simple. So many were enlarged to accommodate the people who came to live in their parishes during the past 150 years and there is much restoration in Berkshire's churches, although somehow a great deal of this has been tasteful and on occasions has added charm and character. There are a few great Perp churches (Lambourn and Newbury being good examples), but good examples of all medieval styles may be found, especially EE. We see considerable use of brick in towers, porches and for restoration and, although the county is not too rich in brasses, there are some splendid monuments.

There are almost 100 post-medieval churches, several of which are fine works of good architects – G.E. Street and Henry Woodyer being particularly well represented.

ALDERMASTON.   Known not only for its anti-nuclear marches but also for its shingle-spired church of St Mary, which has Norman and EE work, a medieval chancel roof, an Elizabethan pulpit, some 13th century (and therefore very early) glass, wall-paintings and a fine 16th century monument to Sir George and Lady Forster.

Nearby *Wasing* St Nicholas' church is a charming character which should be seen – a lovely blend of medieval and 18th century work. *Padworth* has a small and complete Norman church of St John the Baptist, with a later timber belfry.

AVINGTON.   St Mark and St Luke's is entirely Norm. There is a three-stepped E window, two W windows, one above the other, and also a S doorway with zig-zag. The chancel arch has capitals of beasts. Norm sedilia. Other doorways are EE. Also a Norm font with eleven narrow arches and 13 figures.

Hungerford has a large and much-pinnacled church of St Lawrence of 1816, whilst at *Kintbury* St Mary's are monuments by the Scheemakers.

BISHAM.   All Saints' church is on the edge of the Thames. The tower of chalk is Norm, otherwise the church has been rebuilt, except the Hoby Chapel which is 16th C. There are the Royal Arms of George III, and a 16th C reredos in the N chapel. The E window of the Hoby Chapel is filled with armorial glass of the early 17th C. Interesting mons to Sir Philip and Sir Thomas Hoby 1566, two recumbent figures, their feet on a hoby or falcon (note the poem on the monument), and also to Lady Hoby 1609, in a black robe with large headgear and a coronet. Facing her is her eldest daughter in a red cloak and coronet and behind her are three more daughters and two sons, but note the little infant boy in front of Lady Hoby, only shown by the black soles of his feet within a red gown. Margaret Hoby 1605 has an obelisk crowned by a red heart, and below are four lifelike swans. Also a kneeling Eton boy aged 14, with a spaniel, 1904.

Hurley's St Mary's Norman church is delightfully set and has much of interest. Holy Trinity church in beautiful *Cookham* has work of all periods and interesting brasses.

CHIEVELEY. St Mary's broad 13th C tower has a Perp belfry-stage and a bell-turret. A very fine EE chancel, the E wall of which has three lancets with shafts with stiff-leaf capitals. The side windows of the chancel are also lancets. The roof is original and supported the Lent Veil. The nave has been rebuilt, and there is a Perp font and a Jac pulpit.

Do find S.S. Teulon's eccentric Victorian church of St James (1858–60) at *Leckhampstead*.

33

EAST (OR LITTLE) SHEFFORD.   A tiny and really exquisite little shrine (RCF) in the sylvan meadows of the Lambourn valley. Its lovely setting near the river, the rustic simplicity of its exterior (with tiny wooden bell-turret) and its interior – so unspoilt and with so much to see – make this church, which is only 56 ft long, a little gem. The nave is Norman (and so is the simple tub font) and inside we may admire medieval wall-paintings and consecration crosses, texts in 18th century lettering, the Fettiplace monuments (one with effigies of c1442 and another with brasses of c1524) and a great deal more. Above all we have the lovely atmosphere here, produced by 900 years of prayer and greatly aided by careful conservation in our own times.

In the area are the round-towered churches of St Mary, *Great Shefford* and St Gregory, *Welford*, also *Wickham* St Swithin's, with its Saxon square tower and amazing Victorian interior. *East Garston* has a Norman church of All Saints and, further up the river, is *Lambourn* itself, with its stately cruciform St Michael's church, showing work of most periods, also good monuments and brasses.

LANGLEY MARISH.   St Mary's is a most interesting church. The tower is of brick of 1609, and the chancel and N chapel are Dec. Piscina and sedilia. Also brick is the Kedderminster Chapel with a six-light window and the gabled Kedderminster Library to the W of the chapel; the library was housed in 1631. The N arcade is of wood. There is a Perp font, a Jac gallery in the tower, also a gallery to the N aisle, a Jac pulpit, and a Perp rood-screen. There is a Jac screen in the Kedderminster Chapel with obelisks and strapwork and painted, and the chapel is also painted.

NEWBURY.   St Nicolas' is a complete Perp church, all built between 1500 and 1532 as a result of the wealth of the wool trade. The fine tower is impressive with double belfry windows, four prominent pinnacles and four small intermediate ones between them. Large Perp windows and clerestory all completely embattled. The lychgate is largely old. Fine Jac pulpit. The gates to the chancel are of iron 1704. Brass to John Smallwood and wife and children 1519, and a mon to Griffith Curteys 1587.

St John's by S.E. Dykes Bower (1955–7) is a large red-brick church, with a lofty, bright and devotional interior. St George's at Wash Common (begun 1933) is a memorable building with a campanile and an Italian feel. It was created by F.C. Eden.

The delightful little Norman church at Padworth, with its rounded apse and timber belfry. Many of the country's churches were once like this.

READING.   The medieval St Laurence's and St Mary's have distinctive Perp towers with polygonal buttresses and plenty to enjoy inside. St Giles' (medieval, but much rebuilt by J.P. St Aubyn) has a grand Anglo-Catholic interior and an extremely tall spire. For a real surprise, find the church of the Most Holy Trinity, in Oxford Road, built in 1826 and with the simplest of exteriors. Inside is a treasure house of fittings which are 'ultra' Catholic (there is not very much 'Anglo' here)! It is glorious. The spacious interior of this former 'preaching-box' now shimmers with colour, beauty and mystery which would rival any continental shrine. The 18th century pulpit and organ from All Saints' Oxford fit beautifully here, also Baroque altars from Nashdom Abbey and St Paul's Oxford, some craftsmanship imported from the continent and, dominating everything, Pugin's mighty gothic screen from the Roman Catholic

35

cathedral in Birmingham. At the other extreme is St Mary's, Castle Street, which is unashamedly Protestant and Evangelical and is still a Proprietory Chapel. Entering beneath its Grecian portico we find a preaching-house of the Prayer Book Evangelical tradition, beautifully furnished and with tremendous atmosphere. Amongst the later Victorian churches in Reading, do find the stately All Saints, Devonshire Square (by St Aubyn, 1865–74) and Henry Woodyer's Christ Church (1861), with its tall spire, traceried chancel arch and Hardman glass.

SHOTTESBROOKE. St John the Baptist's is cruciform with a central tower and a spire higher than the tower, and is of the 14th C. Flowing tracery windows with an E window of five lights. Piscina and sedilia. Fragments of glass and a font of c1400. Two 14th C tomb-recesses, fan-vaulted, for Sir William Trussell and wife.

There is Norman evidence in *Waltham St Lawrence*'s pretty church, also the fine monument to Sir Henry Neville 1593.

TIDMARSH. The church of St Lawrence has a fine Norm S doorway with zig-zag, with a large head in the apex. There are 13th C W lancets, chancel lancets and a polygonal apse with stiff-leaf capitals. An apse at this date is extremely rare. There are old timber supports of the bell-turret and a shingled pyramidal roof. Also a recut Norm font, a partly-old pulpit and 18th C altar-rails. Brasses to Margaret Wode 1499, and Henry Leynham 1517.

Scott's opulent and memorable church of St Mark at *Englefield* (1857) has interesting earlier monuments and a lovely parkland setting. *Theale* has noble Holy Trinity church (E.W. Garbett 1830–2) which is a real individual, reproducing EE in a fascinating way.

WARFIELD. St Michael's has a Perp tower with a small recessed timber spire. The N aisle is EE, the remainder mainly Dec. Elaborate Flowing tracery windows in the chancel. Piscina and sedilia with foliage, and remains of an Easter Sepulchre. There are 14th C roofs to the N chapel and nave, and a 15th C screen and rood-loft to the N chapel (very rare). Fragments of old glass. Mons to Thomas Williamson 1611, kneeling figures, and John Walsh 1797, with a lifesize female figure.

WINDSOR CASTLE. St George's Chapel is a most glorious Perp building finished by 1511. It has large windows, flying buttresses, pinnacles and Tudor porches. Inside, the high arcades reach up to the wonderful lierne-vault (the aisles being fan-vaults). The stalls, 23 on each side, are an amazing sight. They are in three tiers, the topmost tier occupied by the Knights of the Garter, and the Dean and Canons: the colourful banners are above. The carvings on the poppyheads and desk fronts should be noted. The Garter stall-plates are a wonderful heraldic record. Each stall has a misericord with a most interesting carving.

The Chapel of Edward IV with its fine iron grille of 1483 has become the royal pew, with its oriel windows. The ironwork on the door to Henry III's former chapel is even older, 13th C. A large E window of 15 lights is filled with Victorian glass. There is an early 16th C brass lectern of two desks. There are nine chantry chapels within the building, all most attractive, sometimes with grilles, vaults, paintings and colour, such as the Beaufort, Urswick, Hastings and Oxenbridge Chantries.

St John's church (1822, with a chancel enlarged by Teulon 1873) has much to interest visitors, who may find here 17th century woodwork by Grinling Gibbons, a lovely 17th century painting of the Last Supper and a host of memorials. Woodyer's devotional Anglo-Catholic church of St Stephen Clewer (1874) has an impressive interior, with a striking Gothic reredos.

BUCKINGHAMSHIRE

John Betjeman called it 'leafy Bucks' – and so it is! Probably the very best time to see it is in the autumn. What an incredibly beautiful corner of England – and yet so near to London. The lovely Chiltern hills stretch right across it and divide the county into two parts. To the south of them, Buckinghamshire has a very 'Home Counties' feel, and here we have the towns of High Wycombe, Beaconsfield, Amersham and Chesham and the lovely valleys of the Chess, Colne and Wye and, at the very south, the glorious Thames overlooked by Cliveden and Marlow. Suburbia, development and 'Metro-Land' have reached parts of south Buckinghamshire, but they have by no means destroyed its beauty. Chiltern-land in Buckinghamshire is exquisite – the Chiltern Hundreds above Chesham, the Hambleden Valley, Bledlow Ridge, the Hampdens, the Kimbles and scores of other delightful villages (and churches) must be visited. North of the Chilterns is the Vale of Aylesbury and above this the countryside changes as we go west to Oxfordshire, north to Northants and east to Bedfordshire and Hertfordshire. Villages and churches share some of the features of these neighbouring counties. Near the top is Milton Keynes, which has absorbed several villages and churches. There is no other 'city' in England like it and many church enthusiasts will dip into its network of boulevards, roundabouts and communities in order to see the lovely churches which now hopefully have a new lease of life. Buckingham itself, in the north-west corner, has great charm and is surrounded by fascinating villages, and at the very top of the county we see the splendid soaring spires of Hanslope and Olney.

There is never a dull moment in Buckinghamshire, with its varied landscape and varied churches, built often of limestone in the north and west, white clunch around the Chilterns, flint and rubble in the south and with much use of brick and timber. In the 170 or so medieval churches there is much for the lover of architecture – premier Saxon at Wing, Norman at Stewkley, EE at Chetwode and Haddenham, Dec at Olney and Perp at Maids Moreton and Hillesden (to give some of the best examples). Classical may be seen at Gayhurst, West Wycombe and Willen and there are several good 19th century churches and many 19th century restorations. We need to keep our eyes open for the Norman fonts around Aylesbury and for medieval glass and wall-paintings which occur in several Buckinghamshire churches. This county of stately homes has a fine selection of monuments and memorials and the amazing collection in the Bedford Chapel at Chenies is unmatched anywhere. This is a county where every church has something to interest us, despite the fact that few are mighty or magnificent.

BLEDLOW.   A good setting and lovely views here for Holy Trinity, also a church of individuality and character, with a little Norman work remaining, 13th century arcades, tower, fine south doorway and door, also an early Dec chancel and porch. Here is a superb 'Aylesbury type' Norman font, and fragments of 13th and 14th century wall-paintings, including Adam and Eve above the south door. Note the 18th century reredos in the south aisle.

Horsenden's little church of St Michael has a medieval screen. At St Mary's *Princes Risborough* we see the work of J. Oldrid Scott (tower and spire, 1908) and Sir. A. Blomfield (restoration, 1867–8) in the medieval church, whilst St Dunstan's *Monk's Risborough* has a screen, brasses and Norman font.

BROUGHTON.   The church (RCF) and a few houses now stand in a quiet cul-de-sac on the edge of Milton Keynes. St Lawrence's stone exterior, with elegant 15th century tower, is attractive, but the interior is wonderful, because the nave walls are covered with wall-paintings which were discovered in 1849. Here we may admire exquisite scenes of the Last Judgement, a Pieta and two people playing backgammon on one side and St Helena, St George and St Eloi (with farmers' tools) on the other. The dark but intimate chancel has two windows by Kempe and there is much else to enjoy here.

The tiny old village of *Milton Keynes* has a beautiful church of All Saints' in coursed limestone, with fine Dec windows, a sturdy north tower, the brass of a priest and much atmosphere. In the new town centre is the spanking new Church of Christ the Cornerstone – an ecumenical church of cathedral proportions, consecrated early in 1992. This is a modern church of great dignity, its mighty (120 ft) central dome, crowned by a lantern and splendid cross, dominating its surroundings at the heart of this strange city.

CHICHELEY.   St Lawrence's church is in a lovely setting near the early 18th century brick mansion. The Classical chancel is a rebuild of 1708, but the handsome central tower is Perp and the nave Dec. We enter the chancel through a screen of Tuscan columns and wrought-iron gates. It has a lovely plaster ceiling and fine c1708 furnishings. The area beneath the tower was refurbished by Comper, who designed the rood-loft. The nave is furnished with box-pews which are raised at the west end. There are two lovely monuments here – to Anthony Cave (1576) and Sir Anthony Chester (1635).

Sherington has a pretty church of St Laud with a 13th century central tower, also good Dec work and a beautiful 15th century font. St Firmin's *North Crawley* has a fine 15th century screen, old benches and a font cover of 1640. Do also see the large and noble church of St Peter and St Paul *Newport Pagnell*, which is well worth a visit.

CLIFTON REYNES. St Mary's tower is Norm with a 14th C top. There is also a 14th C font, with the Virgin, Trinity and saints. Mons include a knight and lady of oak 1300 (two), and a knight and lady of stone, with eight mourners on each side, 1380. There are brasses to Sir John Reynes 1428, and a man and woman in shrouds 1500.

The handsome 1851 spire of St Peter and St Paul's *Olney* is seen for miles. There is lovely Dec work in this impressive church which presides over the pleasant little town where William Cowper and John Newton ministered.

DORNEY. St James's, by Dorney Court, has a tower of brick which is early Tudor. The porch is also of brick, 1661. There is a Norm window S of the chancel. The great charm of the interior is due to modest and complete furnishings. These include a Norm font, a 17th C pulpit and altar-rails, the remains of a screen, stall fronts, 16th C benches, a W gallery of 1634 and a family pew of the 18th C. A wall-painting of the Annunciation and a mon to Sir William Garrard and his wife and children 1607, complete the picture.

DRAYTON BEAUCHAMP. In a picturesque setting, St Mary's is embattled throughout. There is a Norm font. The 15th C glass in the E window depicts ten Apostles, and the W window has two restored figures. Brasses commemorate Thomas Cheyne 1368, and William Cheyne 1375, and a priest 1531. Mon to Lord and Lady Newhaven 1732.

EDLESBOROUGH. St Mary's (RCF) was built on an isolated hill with fine views. It has a 14th C tower. The E window is a good example of Geometrical tracery (early 14th C). The Perp wood pulpit has the rare feature of a tall canopy, and there is a rood-screen. Stalls with misericords show an owl, a mermaid and a bat, and of the brasses, one is like a rose window.

FINGEST. Set in one of the most beautiful corners of England, St Bartholomew's massive Norman tower with double saddleback roof would tempt anybody to stop and explore this charming church. There are EE lancets in the chancel, also a 14th century font and the Royal Arms of Queen Anne. Despite a thorough restoration in 1866, this is an atmospheric church which people love to return to.

This is an area of lovely villages and churches. *Turville* must be the perfect English village, deep in a Chiltern valley, with an adorable church which has lots to see. *Ibstone* is rustic Norman and EE, with a Norman font and 15th century roof and pulpit. Southwards is *Hambleden* – another beauty spot amidst sylvan scenery. Its church is Victorianised, but very attractive, with a Norman font and splendid D'Oyley monument. Way down to the south-west is *Fawley*, with two amazing mausoleums in the churchyard, a chancel of 1748, splendid furnishings from the chapel of the Duke of Chandos and Sir James Whitelock's monument of 1632.

GAYHURST. The church (dedication unknown) and Elizabethan house make a charming scene. The whole church is a perfect specimen of c1720. The tower has a cupola and the interior has fittings of that date – wall-panelling, box-pews, pulpit and reredos. The Royal Arms are Stuart (from the previous church) altered in Georgian times. The mon to Sir Nathan Wright and son, 1728, is notable.

Do find *Tyringham*'s parkland church of St Peter (much rebuilt 1871) and never try to resist the 'pull' of St James the Great *Hanslope*'s mighty spire, visible for miles – the church is wonderful.

HILLESDEN. All Saints' is an entirely Perp church, not common around here. The exterior is all embattled with large windows. The N vestry has a lovely top of flying buttresses and the N porch has a fan-vault. The chancel has a row of stone angels below the roof. There is also a rood-screen with coving, a 17th C family pew, and 18th C paintings of Moses and Aaron. In the S transept E window, glass of the life of St Nicholas is early 16th C, and many saints from the late 15th C can be found in the tracery of the E window. Mon to Thomas Denton 1560.

In this remote corner of western Buckinghamshire, hunt out St Mary and St Nicholas *Chetwode*, remote and lovable, where we see the best EE work in the county, also good 14th century glass.

HITCHAM. St Mary's has a Tudor brick tower but the nave is Norm and the chancel Dec, with a circular window – a rarity. Old door with ironwork, 17th C pulpit and tester. There is some 14th C glass in the chancel, including angels on wheels, and some 14th C tiles in the chancel floor. Mons commemorate Roger Alford and wife 1580, and Sir William Clarke, his wife and children 1624.

IVINGHOE.   Mostly 13th and 14th C, St Mary's has a central tower with Perp top and a Herts spike. There is a Perp clerestory, W porch and roofs with angels. The N doorway is 14th C, and the W doorway 13th C, with EE stiff-leaf capitals, as also the arcades. The E bay of the nave roof is elaborated to form a canopy of honour over the rood. Completed by an ornate Jac pulpit and tester, poppyhead bench-ends, and a brass to Richard Blackhed and wife 1517.

Do find *Pitstone* St Mary's church (RCF) with its secluded setting and wonderfully atmospheric interior.

LITTLE MISSENDEN.   St John the Baptist's has a 15th C tower and timber porch, but Sax-Norm nave arcades and chancel arch, and an EE chancel. There is also a Norm font. The wall-paintings are notable – a large, late 13th C St Christopher, and five scenes from the life of St Catherine – note the spokes of the wheel on which she was martyred, flying off.

MAIDS' MORETON.   As at Hillesden, St Edmund's is a complete Perp church, with large windows typical of that period. The belfry windows show some unusual features. Both porches have fan-vaults, the sedilia have vaulted canopies and there is a wall-painting of the Last Supper on the wall. There is also a Norm font, a screen, a N door with tracery, and a Jac bread cupboard.

Buckingham   St Peter and St Paul's church is a mixture of 1777–81 and 1862 (Sir Gilbert Scott) with a stone spire and a few medieval benches. Go north to St Nicholas' *Lillingstone Dayrell* (Norman and EE, also brasses and monument) and the church of the Assumption at *Lillingstone Lovell* (saddleback tower, nice Dec, pulpit, box-pews and brasses).

PENN.   Holy Trinity stands high on the Chilterns, with splendid views. It is connected with the Penn family. The short tower is early 14th C and there is a fine Perp nave roof, a 15th C door, and an 18th C pulpit. The treasure of the church is, however, the 15th C Doom painting on boards, originally above the rood-loft: Christ in Majesty on a rainbow with angels carrying Instruments of the Passion, the Virgin and Apostles below. There are also some mons to the Curzon family and some late brasses.

Little Missenden – a beautiful church in a beautiful Chiltern setting. There is so much to see here, including fine wall-paintings inside.

STEWKLEY.   St Michael's is one of the most perfect Norm churches, date c1150. The W front is ornate, with a doorway with a tympanum. The S doorway has zig-zag and dragons' heads. At the top of the central tower are intersected zig-zag arches. The pinnacles are Perp. Inside, all the windows are surrounded by zig-zag and the central arches have beakheads and zig-zags. The chancel has a quadripartite vault.

STOKE POGES.   Known the world over as the scene of Gray's *Elegy*, St Giles' is a Norm church, altered in the 13th C by the transeptal tower (19th C pyramid roof) and chancel (E end) and aisles. The fine timber S porch is Dec. The Hastings Chapel of brick is c1560 and has 17th C heraldic glass. There is a fine nave roof. In Flemish glass at the W end a satyr sits on a bicycle – one of the earliest examples. A 14th C tomb-chest

43

stands in the chancel, and there is a mon to Nathaniel Marchant 1816 with a medallion of George III on horseback. A brass commemorates Sir William Molyns and wife 1425.

Wexham has a tiny Norman church with a wooden belfry.

WEST WYCOMBE.   What a setting – remote, high and lifted up! A 13th century chancel and 14th century tower – but we tend to forget this when we look up to the tower top, with its great golden ball (fitted with seats inside) and the Classical nave built in the 1700s by the remarkable Sir Francis Dashwood. The interior is incredible, with its Corinthian columns, magnificent ceilings and Classical fittings – the font, lectern and stalls are unusual to say the least. But one cannot help loving this amazing building.

High Wycombe's mighty church of All Saints' has much to see, especially the monument to the Earl of Selborne. Do journey through the lanes to the north-west to find rustic and atmospheric *Radnage* – there is so much beauty here, not least in the 13th century wall-paintings.

WING.   Outside All Saints' appears medieval, but it is a large Sax church. The Sax polygonal apse has below it a low crypt with an ambulatory round it. It can be seen through one of its windows. The chancel arch is Sax, and the arcades are no more than unmoulded arches cut into the wall. Later work is the Dec S aisle and Perp tower (with a tall tower arch), clerestory, S porch, roof and chancel windows. The Perp font depicts angels and Instruments of the Passion. There is a rood-screen with coving, and a Jac pulpit. Brasses include those to a civilian and wife 1470, and Harry Blackwell and wife 1460, but the most noteworthy is that of Thomas Cotes 1648, porter at Ascott Hall, shown kneeling in a high-crowned hat with his porter's staff and key, and an interesting inscription. The mon to Sir Robert Dormer 1552 is one of the finest of this date. Other monuments include Sir William Dormer and wife, two recumbent effigies, 1590; the 1st Lord Dormer and wife and children, 1617; Lady Anne Dormer 1695; and Henry Fynes 1758.

CAMBRIDGESHIRE

Now it is not only the old county of Cambridge and the Isle of Ely, but also includes Huntingdonshire to the west and the Soke of Peterborough to the north-west. The original county has a fascinating variety of landscapes and churches, with the gentle hills and valleys in the south, the miles of flat fenland in the north and the 'horsey' downs towards Newmarket in the east. The c170 medieval churches are exciting and varied, with very high quality work of the EE, Dec and Perp periods to be found here. Many of the churches are faced with local brown cobblestones and we see chalky clunch often used for windows and doorways, also ashlar facing in the greater churches. Several features have crept over the borders – Herts spikes in the south, East Anglian characteristics in the east (including two round towers, at Bartlow and Snailwell), also stone spires from Huntingdonshire and Northants (but usually not quite so ambitious and usually set behind parapets) and, in the far north, the great Marshland churches. Yet Cambridgeshire does have a character of its own, with charming villages and churches full of character and individuality. Go to Melbourn, Haslingfield or Guilden Morden, for example, to see some of the fine characteristics of the county's churches. Cambridge itself is a city supreme in architecture, with fine buildings everywhere, including lovely churches and college chapels. Ely, the Island City of the Fens, has a wonderful cathedral which is visible for miles and miles across the flat fenland.

Cambridgeshire now of course has a second cathedral (although it mostly serves Northants and Rutland). Glorious Peterborough, which is set in the small area (about ten miles by 15) once known as the Soke of Peterborough and which was ruled by its abbots and bishops. Here are 20 village churches – all of interest and built of Barnack limestone, with many features which we find in Northants and south Lincolnshire.

What was Huntingdonshire has 90 or so medieval churches and there is tremendous beauty here which should by no means be dismissed. These churches are very fine indeed and are very different in character from the real Cambridgeshire – 32 have stone spires (many of these being as lovely as the best in the Midlands) and several others have beautiful and stately towers. Every architectural period has noteworthy examples amongst these churches and they display a wealth of beauty in roofs, screens and furnishings.

ALCONBURY. A perfectly lovely village setting (yet so near the A1) for St Peter and St Paul's church, of great architectural quality, with an EE tower and spire and a superb EE chancel, both of which show so well the dignity of this period. We can appreciate the chancel from inside, where we also have 15th century roofs and plenty to enjoy.

An even more wonderful tower and spire, visible for miles around, may be admired at nearby All Saints' *Buckworth*.

BALSHAM. Holy Trinity's tower is 13th C, the chancel 14th C, and the aisles and arcades 15th C. Unusually both nave and chancel have a clerestory. The Perp rood-screen has ribbed coving. There are 26 stalls and the arm-rests have two projections, one above the other (for kneeling and standing), with human figures or animals carved upon them. Misericords display human heads, beasts and monsters. There is a Sax coffin-lid with a cross and two fine brasses. John Sleford, rector 1401, is depicted in a cope with figures of saints and a fine canopy, while John Blodwell, rector 1462, is shown under a broad canopy with figures of saints and further small saints on the cope.

In this area of interesting churches, do be sure to discover Holy Trinity *Hildersham*, with its 14th century wooden effigies and its superb brasses.

BARNACK. Stone from the quarries here may be seen in many churches. The Saxon tower of St John the Baptist's is also known far and wide; about 1200 they heightened it with an octagonal belfry and spire. Inside, the tower arch is also Saxon and there is an 11th century sculpture of Christ in Majesty. Of the 13th century is the porch, font and south arcade, whilst the south aisle windows and chancel are 14th century and the Lady Chapel 15th century. There is much to see here.

Nearby All Saints' *Wittering* also has noteworthy Saxon work.

BUCKDEN. St Mary's is a handsome building with an elegant 15th century tower and spire and a mainly Perp exterior, set beside the Tudor brick great tower and gatehouse of Buckden Palace. The vaulted two-storeyed porch shelters an EE doorway with 15th century doors. The bright interior has elegant arcades, lovely 15th century roofs and interesting woodwork in the pulpit and clergy stalls.

Diddington St Lawrence's church must also be seen, for its roof, medieval glass and superb brasses.

BURWELL. St Mary's is a grand Perp church, the arcades, windows and roofs showing the style at its best. There is a wheel-window above the chancel arch and the N porch has a fan-vault. The earliest part is the base of the tower – Norm but Perp above, having changed to an octagonal form with an open lantern with spirelet. The large brass to John Lawrence, Abbot of Ramsey 1542, shows him in a cassock, surplice and almuce, having been altered from Eucharistic vestments on the reverse. Mon to Thomas Gerard and his wife 1613.

Fordham St Peter's church is huge, with a lovely Dec Lady Chapel. *Swaffham Prior* has two churches in one churchyard – both are real characters, with unusual towers. St Mary's is the parish church, whilst St Cyriac's is cared for by the RCF.

CAMBRIDGE. A wonderful city for churches – 13 of them are medieval and there are some good 19th and 20th century ones. Most of the ancient churches are within easy walking distance of each other – as are the College Chapels which are also worth seeing. King's shows us some of the finest Perp anywhere, Pembroke is by Wren, St John's by Sir Gilbert Scott and Queen's by Bodley, whilst Jesus (part of what was the monastic church of St Radegund) delights us with the beauty of EE.

A taster of the churches must include:
St Bene'ts, with its wonderful Saxon tower and tower arch. Holy Sepulchre – the Round Church, with its distinctive circular Norman nave. Great St Mary's – the stately Perp University Church, where we can get a bird's eye view of the rest from its tower. St Botolph's, a lovable building of great character, with a 15th century screen and a remarkable font, with 17th century wooden casing and cover. St Edward's, with its linenfold pulpit of c1510. Little St Mary's, which has beautiful Dec windows and a spacious barnlike interior with delightful Anglo-Catholic fittings. St Mary Magdalene (way out east, along the Newmarket Road) – the former Leper Chapel and delightfully unaltered Norman, of great interest and value. Holy Trinity, where the great Anglican Evangelical, Charles Simeon, was incumbent. St Giles' – a vast brick church by Healey of Bradford (1875) but preserving two 12th century arches in its lofty and mysterious Anglo-Catholic interior. St Peter's (RCF), a tiny church with a stone spire and a Norman doorway. All Saints' (RCF) – this is the finest of the 19th century Anglican churches. It is by Bodley (1864) and is very largely unaltered. The broad tower, set above the chancel, has an almighty spire. The interior shows the work of C.E. Kempe, William Morris & Co and others in its stencilled walls, its furnishings and its magnificent glass.

Within three miles of Cambridge are *Cherry Hinton* (EE at its very best in the chancel here), *Grantchester* (lovable and atmospheric country church, immortalised by Rupert Brooke) and *Trumpington* (noble 14th century church, restored by Butterfield, and famous for the fine military brass of Sir Roger de Trumpington, c1289).

CASTOR. Cruciform, gloriously set and with the most amazing and spectacular Norman central tower (crowned by a 14th century spire), this church of St Kyneburgha shows interesting craftsmanship of all periods. Inside we see intriguing 12th century carvings on the capitals of the crossing-piers, a double piscina adorned with EE dogtooth, medieval roofs, a 14th century wall-painting of St Catherine and a Saxon carving which may be as early as the 9th century. A wonderful and exhilarating church.

The little church of St John the Baptist at *Upton*, remote across a field, is a real character, with a lovely monument to Sir William Dove (1633) and his two wives.

CONINGTON. A mighty and stately late Perp church (RCF), dominated by a lofty and magnificent tower with prominent turrets at its corners – yet it is remote (but beautifully set) and with hardly any village. All Saints took its present shape c1500 and its embattled exterior, with fine windows and pretty rood-staircase turret, is worth standing back to enjoy. Inside are good Perp arcades, good sedilia and piscina, original nave roof and chapel screens and interesting seating which dates from 1841. The monuments are interesting here – they include the effigy of a Franciscan tertiary of c1300 in Frosterley marble and fine monuments of the 16th and 17th centuries to the Cotton family.

Although some miles away (near Fenstanton), the other *Conington* should be discovered, to see its 14th century tower and tall stone-ribbed spire and its atmospheric Classical nave of c1737. A real character this, and beautifully cared for.

CROYDON. A peaceful setting on a ridge (fine views eastwards) for the weathered and timeworn church of All Saints which simply oozes charm, antiquity and rustic beauty. A timber-framed porch which is simplicity itself admits us to one of the county's most atmospheric interiors, which has really got to be seen and 'felt' in order to be really understood. Leaning walls, pamment floors and rustic furnishings (including a square Norman font and 17th century benches) all bathed in light from the clear glass.

Here we may easily reach St Nicholas' *Arrington* (lovely c1300 chancel), St Peter and St Paul's *Bassingbourn* (good porch, roofs, screen, benches and Dec chancel) and *Wimpole's* Classical church of St Andrew, with its medieval glass and glorious monuments.

ELLINGTON. We see All Saints' soaring spire from a considerable distance and in the exterior we also admire the fine gargoyles, the 15th century north porch (sheltering a late 13th century doorway) and the late 13th century chancel. Inside all is light and airy, with a grand 15th century roof, two 17th century chests and much else – a wonderful Huntingdonshire church, but one of several.

To really see Hunts spires at their best we need only to divert slightly from the road to Thrapston in order to find St Peter's *Easton*, St James' *Spaldwick*, St Leonard's *Catworth* and St John the Baptist's *Keyston*. *Brampton* St Mary's church is full of treasures (screen, stalls, etc) and at lovely St Mary's *Leighton Bromswold* the saintly George Herbert refurbished the large EE church in the 1630s – and it's all still there!

GLINTON.   England has no other spire like it – it dominates lovely St Benedict's church in an attractive setting. Do look carefully at the gargoyles on the south side of the clerestory, especially the eastern one, which leaves little to the imagination! A bright and colourful interior here, with a Norman font and a tastefully furnished north chapel, where John Clare received his education.

Nearby *Northborough* St Andrew's church has lovely architecture and great character, St Pega's *Peakirk* has Norman work and 14th century wall-paintings, St Stephen's *Etton* is an EE period piece and St Botolph's *Helpston* has much to interest us, especially its associations with John Clare.

HASLINGFIELD.   All Saints' has perhaps the best tower in the county. It is Perp with double belfry windows (Northants type), a Norfolk square air-hole, four turrets (based on Ely Cathedral) and a Herts spike. Most of the church is Dec including the lovely cross on the E gable of the nave. The curved roof of the S porch is dated 1746, and the aisle roofs are important. Perp pulpit, Jac font-cover, and mons to Thomas Wendy, two couples kneeling, 1612, Elizabeth Wendy 1658, and Sir Thomas Wendy 1673 (an early example of a standing figure). Note the recent beautiful kneeler in front of the altar-rails showing the church and village.

Harlton church, dedicated to the Assumption of the Blessed Virgin Mary, must be seen, with its grand 14th century east window and medieval stone reredos beneath it, also a stone screen, original roofs and stalls and a fine monument to Sir Henry Fryer and his parents.

ICKLETON.   At St Mary's the central tower of c1300 with a lead spire with an outside bell will first be noticed. The interior is an amazing sight – early Norm arcades and clerestory, the former resting on Roman monolith columns and stone pillars. The W doorway is Norm with a

49

Perp window above. The crossing arches are partly early Norm. The S aisle, S doorway and S porch with a vault with bosses are 14th C. A recent fire has revealed wall-paintings of Christ's Passion; the Last Supper and the Betrayal can be made out.

Duxford has two Norman churches worth seeing, especially St John's (RCF) which is rustic, unspoilt and full of treasures, including an amazing series of wall-paintings, some still waiting to be conserved.

ISLEHAM. St Andrew's tower, with a tiled pyramid roof, is modern. The nave has 14th C piers but above them the fine Perp work begins with tall clerestory windows and a tiebeam and hammerbeam roof. The S porch is Dec with blank arcading inside it. Perp sedilia and stalls with misericords with heads. The poppyhead bench-ends include a pelican, lion, camel etc. Medieval brass eagle lectern and Jac altar-rails. Brasses to Thomas Peyton and two wives in butterfly head-dresses and fashionable dresses, 1484, under three canopies; Sir John Bernard and wife 1451; and Sir Richard Peyton and wife 1518. Mons to Barbarie Themilthorpe recumbent 1619; a bearded 14th C knight; Sir Robert Peyton 1590 and Sir John Peyton 1616. The lychgate is late medieval.

LITTLE GIDDING. A cul-de-sac lane leads to this adorable little shrine in the middle of nowhere. Here the saintly Nicholas Ferrar founded a small religious community in 1624 and beautified the church of St John the Evangelist in 1625. John Ferrar gave it a pretty Classical west front and reredos (incorporating the 1625 Commandments, etc) in 1714. The splendid glass was installed when Henry Clutton restored it in 1853. The interior is unforgettable with so much to see in a tiny place, and so very devotional.

There are good spires at St Michael's *Great Gidding*, St Andrew's *Steeple Gidding*, All Saints' *Winwick* and St Swithin's *Old Weston* (also much else to see), whilst All Saints' *Hamerton* has fine 15th century roofs, font and tower and *Glatton's* noble and embattled church of St Nicholas has poppyhead benches and a wall-painting of St Mary Magdalene.

MARCH. St Wendreda's stands at the S end of the town. The tower has a Flowing window and a stone spire. Everything is 14th and 15th C, the latter being lavish, including the S porch and clerestory and sanctus-bellcot. But everything is overshadowed by the most splendid double hammerbeam roof with angels with outspread wings in three tiers. Brasses commemorate Andrew Dredman and his wife 1501, and

Anthony Hansard and wife 1507, scrolls from them leading to an Annunciation.

Go north to *Guyhirn* on the A47 to see the humble and rustic little chapel built during the Commonwealth period and opened in 1660. It is a period-piece, furnished with simplicity for Puritan worship.

MARSHLAND CHURCHES. Mighty Fen churches punctuate the north of the county, near its border with Lincolnshire and Norfolk. Every one is an absolute gem and should not be missed. *Wisbech* St Peter and St Paul's is a broad and complicated building, with work of many periods and much to see. Its fine free-standing north tower has superb stonecarving and many pinnacles. There are two grand 17th century monuments and the seven ft figure of a knight (1401) in brass. All Saints' *Elm* has a fine EE tower, clerestory and chancel and a 15th century double hammerbeam roof. St Leonard's *Leverington* has a superb exterior. Its lovely EE and Dec tower and spire reach 162 ft. There is a fine 14th century south chapel and a vaulted porch. The roof, Perp font, 15th century lectern and an amazing window showing the Tree of Jesse, which is partly 15th century and has 61 figures, are just a few of the treasures inside. St Mary's *Whittlesey* has one of the finest 15th century towers and spires to be seen anywhere – with flying buttresses linking spire and pinnacles. The church is largely Dec and Perp and is a most impressive building.

OVER. St Mary's is an ornate church both outside and inside. The tower and spire are Dec, as also are the S porch and S aisle with its gargoyles and frieze of ballflower ornament and battlements taken round both. The nave arcades and roof with niches below and the beautiful chancel are Perp. Perp also are the font, rood-screen and stalls with six misericords. The very tall pulpit is Jac with an ogee-dome as a tester. The nave and chancel are harmonious which is unusual, as old churches were usually built by two different bodies which is why both parts are usually so different; the nave (and tower) were built by the parishioners and the chancel by the rector (not necessarily the incumbent), or by the lay-rector, such as an Oxford or Cambridge college. Here the parish is fortunate in having had Ramsey Abbey originally, and now Trinity College, Cambridge as patrons.

Swavesey's large and impressive church of St Andrew has a grand exterior with elegant Dec windows and fine tower. Inside are Perp benches, roofs and a Dec chancel, piscina and sedilia. St Martin's *Witcham* has a 15th century stone pulpit.

This is a county of surprises, as here at Bottisham, where the great western 'galilee' porch of its predominantly early 14th century church rises above the Village Street.

ST. IVES. All Saints' riverside setting is charming and the 151 ft tower and spire are very graceful and elegant. Inside we find a Norman font, an EE double piscina and so much that is interesting and beautiful. Comper designed the chancel screen and placed statues upon the medieval stone brackets along the arcades. This is a large but very prayerful church.

St Margaret of Antioch *Hemingford Abbots* and St James *Hemingford Grey* (in a well known riverside setting) are nearby, also St Peter and St Paul's *Fenstanton* (superb Dec chancel), St Mary's *Godmanchester* (tower and spire, noteworthy Mass dial, stalls, etc) and *Huntingdon's* two churches of St Mary and All Saints. Each of these is worth a visit.

ST. NEOTS. A large, stately and majestic town church, St Mary's mostly 15th century exterior is dominated by a glorious 128 ft tower, completed c1535. The 158 ft long interior has good 15th century roofs and parclose screens, much Clayton & Bell glass and noble proportions.

Nearby St Mary's *Eynesbury* has Norman and EE work, some old bench-ends and a notable 17th century pulpit. St Mary's *Eaton Socon*, with its noble tower, has been sensitively restored (by Sir A. Richardson) after a disastrous fire in 1930. Do go north-west in order to see the Saxon Holy Trinity church at *Great Paxton*.

SOHAM. St Andrew's Perp tower is splendid with ornate stepped-battlements with flushwork and pinnacles. There was an earlier church with a central tower and parts remain inside. The W crossing arch has late Norm and EE decoration. The chancel and S doorway are Dec, and the N porch, clerestory and roof with hammerbeams and tiebeams are Perp. The screen to the N chancel chapel is Perp, as also are the poppyhead bench-ends with animals, etc.

SUTTON. The rather unusual tower of St Andrew's, which is a landmark for miles, was completed by 1400. The top stage has two octagons based on the Ely octagon. The remainder of the church is fine Dec work, including the vaulted S porch and clerestory. The Perp tower has a tierceron-vault and a tall tower arch, and there is a Perp font.

Coveney church of St Peter ad Vincula has an unforgettable Anglo-Catholic interior, containing lovely furnishings, several of which were procured for it by Athelstan Riley.

THORNEY. The church of St Mary and St Botolph was originally a Benedictine abbey, but the E half and the aisles have been destroyed. What remains, however, is most impressive. This is the grand W front, largely Norm with a Perp window. The interior with two-staged Norm arcades remains of the former abbey.

WILLINGHAM. The tower and spire of St Mary and All Saints' are Dec. The spacious chancel is of that period and indeed most of the church, with a large S doorway. There is a curious sacristy on the N of the chancel. A Perp clerestory and complete roofs, that over the nave being double hammerbeam. Some wall-paintings have been preserved: on the N side of the nave is St Christopher, on the chancel arch the Doom, and on the S side of the nave the Visitation. There is also a Perp font, screens and pulpits. The N parclose screen is one of the earliest, with green popinjays on a red background.

YAXLEY. The glorious tower and spire of St Peter's dominate the countryside south of Peterborough. They draw us to one of the county's largest and finest churches. There is majesty here in the exterior and interior, with lovely Dec and Perp architecture. The interior is full of treasures, including wall-paintings of the 14th and 16th centuries, a pulpit of 1631 and a fine screen of c1500, above which is a gallery and organ case designed by Temple Moore in the early 1900s. Two little hands holding a heart mark the burial place of the heart of William de Yaxley, who died in 1293. The 15th century stalls were carefully restored by Temple Moore and Comper designed the glorious painted reredos.

When you go to *Peterborough* to enjoy its wonderful cathedral and Perp parish church of St John the Baptist, remember that Temple Moore also built a very beautiful church, dedicated to All Saints, in Park Road. It was built in 1894 in the Dec style and, like all churches by this architect, is well worth a visit.

CHESHIRE

It is hard to remember amidst the industrial creations at Ellesmere Port, Runcorn, Stanlow oil refinery and other parts of the Mersey estuary, that Cheshire is really a very beautiful, very rural and very agricultural county. It borders both Greater Manchester and the Derbyshire Peaks at one end and North Wales at the other. Much of the Wirral Peninsula, with its splendid views across the Dee and the Mersey, and including Birkenhead and Wallasey, is now in Merseyside, but do venture into it to see several fine churches, including medieval gems at Woodchurch, Eastham and Bebington, also Pearson's sumptuous village church at Thurstaston. To explore Cheshire and visit its churches, is to discover the beauty of the Peckforton Hills and Delamere Forest, to stop in quiet villages with black-and-white houses, get distant views of manor houses and enjoy refreshing pastoral scenery.

The churches (just over 80 medieval ones) are often very well sited and positioned and many are built of red sandstone. Several were over-restored in the 19th century, when a great many new ones were also built. The handful of timber-framed churches are of unique beauty and interest. Although we may get very used to embattled and pinnacled Perp towers with triple belfry windows, we soon find that every church here is an individual, which may well surprise us with something extra special, although we may need to allow ourselves time and patience to locate the key.

Cheshire has several interesting Classical churches (like Congleton, Knutsford and Christ Church Macclesfield). Victorian churches here tend to present us with quantity rather than quality, but there are some gems, like Christleton (Butterfield), Crewe St Michael's (James Brooks), Eccleston (Bodley – and glorious), Norley (Pearson) and J.K. Colling's remarkable and very eccentric church at Hooton. Of more local architects, we see the work of Paley & Austin at St Barnabas' Crewe and elsewhere, while John Douglas of Chester produced several imaginative and interesting churches in Cheshire, the Wirral and North Wales.

ASTBURY. The tower and spire are Dec as are the N and S sides of St Mary's church, but it is the Perp period that counts here. Nave and chancel are one with a splendid clerestory and marvellous roofs with bosses and pendants. The S door is 15th C as is the three-storeyed W porch. The rood-screen is original and there is also a parclose screen. The fine font-cover and the pulpit are Jacobean. The old wooden eagle lectern is 16th C, and the box-pews 17th C. There is a 14th C figure of a knight, and a mon to Lady Egerton 1609.

Nearby *Congleton* St Peter's church is a period-piece of 1742, with 18th century glass, many original fittings and a central pulpit.

BADDILEY. The timber–framed chancel of St Michael's remains, possessing a perfect interior with nearly all its original furniture. The tympanum (possibly medieval) has the date 1663 and the Creed, Lord's Prayer and Ten Commandments, and the Royal Arms. There is a three-decker pulpit, box-pews, altar-rails and a W gallery of about the same time. Mon to Sir Thomas Mainwaring 1726.

BUNBURY. St Boniface's appears to be Perp but there is much Dec work – the chancel, lower part of the tower and S porch (with old door). The battlements and pinnacles and the upper part of the tower, and inside the arcades and large windows, are Perp. The screen to the SE chapel is dated 1527 and coloured. The font is dated 1663, while the altar-rails are of 1717. The mon to Sir Hugh Calverley 1394 has its original grille, and there are other monuments to Sir George Beeston 1601 and Sir Ralph Egerton 1527.

CHESTER. A lovely city, with its city walls, its 'Rows' and the venerable cathedral at its very heart. Some of its churches have been put to new uses, but do visit St John's, where we see the county's finest Norman work in this massive church, externally but a shadow of its medieval glory, but internally so dignified and with grand 12th century work. St Peter's at the Cross has a fine position and much character.

GAWSWORTH. There is nothing quite like Gawsworth anywhere else. The Old Rectory and Old Hall, both black-and-white half-timbered medieval houses, and the parish church, with a lake between them, make an unforgettable scene. St James' is completely Perp with a handsome tower with eight pinnacles and a large S porch. The Fitton mons are fascinating. Francis Fitton 1608 is shown as a figure above and a skeleton below. Sir Edward Fitton and his wife have their children kneeling below, 1619. Dame Alice Fitton 1627 is wearing widow's garb and is seated with children kneeling in front of and behind her. Sir Edward Fitton completes the picture with his wife and one little girl, 1643.

GREAT BUDWORTH. The setting of St Mary's is most attractive. The N transept and E window are Dec, otherwise all is Perp. All embattled, and the tower has double belfry windows. Last of all came the clerestory and a window over the chancel arch. It has a good nave roof. The font is Perp and there are some 13th C stalls. Mon to Sir John Warburton 1575. In the churchyard is an 18th C sundial.

LOWER PEOVER. St Oswald's stone tower is Perp, otherwise all is black-and-white half-timbered of the 14th C and a splendid example of that material. The nave roof is original with mighty timbers. The large font has a Jac cover, and Jac also is the main screen and those to the N and S chapels, the pulpit and the lectern. On display is a large 13th C dug-out chest and there are simple box-pews. Mons to Godfrey Shakerley 1696, and Katherine Shakerley 1725.

MALPAS. St Oswald's is mostly Perp but some Dec remains in the lower parts of the chancel (with piscina and sedilia) and lower part of the tower. All the remainder is Perp with gargoyles and large windows, including the arcades, clerestory and tower (with vault) and S porch. The Perp nave roof is glorious with many bosses and angels and is character-istic of the county. The vestry is of 1717 brick. There are stalls in the chancel and S chapel and three misericords, screens to the N and S chapels, box-pews and a fine medieval ironbound chest. Mons include an incised slab to a rector of 1495, Randle Brereton and his wife 1522 with statuettes, and Sir Hugh Cholmondeley and his wife 1605 with their children (one baby in swaddling clothes).

MARTON. St James and St Paul's is all black-and-white (except the E end). It has a timber belfry and spire in the Essex tradition, and amazing timber arcades and roof. It is 14th C and one of the earliest of its kind. The ladder in the belfry is also original. The pulpit is of 1620, while the paintings of Moses and Aaron are 18th C.

Nearby All Saints *Siddington* is a charming timber-framed church, with a medieval screen and a pulpit of 1633.

MOBBERLEY. St Wilfrid's has a broad Perp tower. The arcades and piscina are Dec, otherwise the church is Perp. Typical fine roof with tiebeams and panelling. Over the rood-screen is a rood-celure; it is one of the best Perp rood-screens and still retains its coving. There is a St Christopher wall-painting and a painted board of a figure in a shroud, 1665.

NANTWICH. The octagonal central tower (Dec) of St Mary's dominates the town. The whole church shows a change from Dec to Perp. In the chancel the piscina and sedilia are Dec, as also its lierne-vault with bosses carved with scenes from the life of Our Lord. The S porch is

Perp, also with a lierne-vault. The Perp work should be easily detected. Among the furnishings, first and foremost come the stalls. They are late 14th C and have gorgeous canopies. Twenty of them have misericords – St George and the Dragon, wrestlers, a mermaid, Samson and the lion, a woman beating her husband with a ladle, a fox pretending to be dead, the Virgin and Unicorn, several dragons etc. There are two pulpits – a fine Perp one of stone with panelling which is in the crossing, and the other one is in the nave, Jac of wood, dated 1601. There is only one mon – a 14th C alabaster figure.

NORTHWICH (WITTON).   St Helen's is very much restored, but Perp outside and partly Dec inside. Visitors however come for the gorgeous nave and chancel roofs of 1525. They are panelled with big and small bosses, and above all, beautifully coloured. The tower is Perp with double belfry windows.

OVER PEOVER.   The tower is of 1739, and the remainder of the church is brick of 1811. There are two chapels at the sides, the N chapel of 1650 having a coat of arms on the ceiling. There is a Perp font and a Jac pulpit. St Lawrence's church is noted for its mons – John Mainwaring

Mellow red sandstone in this typical Cheshire exterior at Shotwick.

and wife 1410; Randle Mainwaring and wife 1456; incised alabaster slabs to Philip Mainwaring and wife 1573 and Sir John Mainwaring and wife 1586; William Littleboys 1624, a painted panel with a skeleton; and Philip Mainwaring and his wife 1647.

SHOTWICK. This red sandstone church of St Michael near the border with Wales is a gem, though little known. It has a quiet setting in a small community and it oozes atmosphere and interest. The tower is Perp, but the south doorway indicates a Norman church. A 15th century nail-studded door admits us to a fascinating interior, with box-pews, churchwardens' pew of 1709 and three-decker pulpit, also the Annunciation in 14th century glass in the north aisle.

TARVIN. A bold and lofty Perp tower to this interesting church of St Andrew, with a short avenue of limes leading to its west doorway. Inside we admire the wonderful nave roof of 1650, with its hammerbeams, and the south aisle roof, which is 300 years older, as is the south chapel screen. There are figures of c1500 in the reredos and two windows by Kempe in the chancel.

WARRINGTON. What a landmark and how breathtakingly elegant is the 281 ft spire of St Elphin's. A fine church this, successfully combining genuine 14th century work with 19th century rebuilding (mostly 1859–67 by F & H Francis). Wonderful things inside also.

Winwick's high-set medieval church of St Oswald has a chancel (1848) by A.W.N. Pugin. This alone makes it extra-special, but there is much else to see here. Look for the Winwick pig in the west wall.

CLEVELAND

A very small area containing the old south-east corner of County Durham and the north-east corner of Yorkshire. It includes the towns of Hartlepool and Middlesborough. In its few medieval churches, we see Saxon work at Billingham, Hart and Norton on Tees (all formerly in Durham) and in the more modern churches we may appreciate the excellent designs of Temple Moore at such places as Carlton, Middlesborough (St Cuthbert's and St Columba's) and St Michael's Norton.

EGGLESCLIFFE. Rather unusually the tower and most of the church of St Mary is Perp. The south doorway, however, is Norman, and the chancel arch 13th century. The church is noted for its 17th century woodwork in Cosin style: roof, pews, screen, stalls, pulpit and font-cover. There is some Saxon sculpture and two cross-legged effigies.

HARTLEPOOL. Grand and majestic EE St Hilda's, the ancient parish church, stands on a small headland near the sea. Here is work of c1200–1250 at its grandest, although there are later additions also – including Caroe's rebuilding of the chancel, completed in 1927. Outside is a feeling of tremendous strength, inside are noble proportions and superb architecture and this also includes Caroe's chancel.

KIRKLEATHAM. One cannot resist stopping at this Classical church of St Cuthbert which was built in 1763 (although the core of the tower is medieval) by a local architect, Robert Corney. Attached to it is the most amazing octagonal mausoleum of the Turner family, designed by James Gibbs (1740). Here we must stand back and view it as a whole in its setting, especially from the east. Inside the original pews and pulpit have been lowered but are still here. The font is 18th century but the lovely cover may well be 16th century. The roof is supported upon Tuscan columns and a 16th century ironbound chest survives. There are brasses and monuments to the Turner family in the church and more in the mausoleum.

LIVERTON. St Michael's is in a country setting with a view to the sea. The church with its bell-turret is a rebuilding of early in the 20th century, but the sumptuous Norman chancel arch remains.

CORNWALL

The Duchy of Cornwall is special and has a character of its very own – it is 'in' England, but not quite 'of' it. There are deep and richly-wooded river estuaries, wild and undulating moorland, glorious and dramatic coastlines and miles of tiny country lanes, high banked and hedged, which lead through lush countryside to a host of villages, many of which are named after the early Celtic saints who first brought the Faith there. Later communities have grown up near the main roads, or around where the tin or china clay was mined, leaving the 'Church Town', with the medieval church, hidden away in the lanes.

Cornish churches are sturdy and windswept and are usually built of grey and very durable granite. Most have three long roof-gables, which emphasise the height of the tall and elegant granite towers. Churchyards have slate headstones with well-preserved lettering upon them, also ancient Celtic crosses remain in some. There are coffin-rests beneath lychgates and usually views worth pausing to enjoy.

Inside the churches, many of which were refashioned in the 15th century, we see tiny crystals in granite arcades shimmering as they catch the light. Long, tunnel-like interiors, beneath rounded wagon roofs (their woodwork intricately carved and studded with bosses), abound in magnificent late 15th or early 16th century flat-topped West Country bench-ends. Occasionally a medieval screen straddles the entire width of the church. John Betjeman, who loved Cornwall and is buried here, cycled along these lanes in search of Norman fonts – and there are over 80 of these to discover.

Cornwall has few notable Victorian churches, although its cathedral at Truro must be one of the finest 19th century creations in the land. Restorations of old churches (many of these by J.P. St Aubyn) could be very scathing on the medieval interiors. The county has just over 200 medieval churches, the majority of which are open to welcome you.

ALTARNUN. A lovely setting above the stream and old bridge, for this church of St Non with its long Cornish roof-gables and tall, thin and elegant tower. Inside we are treated to a splendid Norman font, a well-restored screen straddling the interior, Communion rails of 1684 which also extend across both chancel and aisles and have an inscription, and 17th century panels on the east wall with texts and pictures. Above all,

61

we come here to enjoy 79 medieval bench-ends, deeply carved with Christian symbols, scenes of sheep grazing on the local moors, a fiddler and a jester with his cap and bells. Robert Day carved these benches between 1510 and 1530 and has left an inscription upon one of them which tells us so.

BLISLAND. There is no way in which you could ever forget this adorable church, dedicated to St Protus and St Hyacinth, on the edge of Bodmin Moor, set in a pretty village, with its venerable old tower stuck on the north side. This Norman church, much altered in the 15th century, has one of the most atmospheric interiors anywhere, with a leaning arcade, glorious wagon roofs, two fonts, a Royal Arms of 1604 and a few old bench-ends. It is however the skill, devotion and sensitivity of Frederick Charles Eden who restored this church from 1894 onwards, which makes it so memorable. He gave it a grand new screen, which looks old and is a blaze of delicate colour, an 18th century style pulpit, and furnished the chancel and its flanking chapels exquisitely and devotionally. There is so much here, but above all, this is a church for praying in.

BODMIN. St Petroc's, Cornwall's largest parish church (its runner up is Liskeard), has one of the grandest of the Norman fonts, also the 12th century reliquary (of painted ivory), which contained the bones of Cornwall's precious St Petroc. There are wagon roofs here and, although much 19th and 20th century restoration has taken place, including the re-ordering of the chancel by Sir Charles Nicholson in 1932, this is a most rewarding church. Look for Thomas Vivian, with his mitre and crozier, on his tomb of black Cataclewse stone, to the north of the High Altar.

FALMOUTH. The parish church of King Charles the Martyr is an interesting post-Reformation structure, built in 1662 and combining Classical and Gothic architecture and fittings. It was altered and beautified in later years. Its odd little tower was added in 1684 and was later heightened. There are interesting 17th and 18th century furnishings, also stained glass and memorials in this building, which has a definite 'Civic Church' feel about it.

All Saints' church is one of Cornwall's best Gothic Revival churches, designed by J.D. Sedding and built in 1888–90. Its interior is lofty and spacious, with a splendidly adorned east end.

GUNWALLOE. If you must spend your holidays on beaches, then come here! This is a delight to find. It is set all on its own, right beside the beach in a small cove. There are the usual three roof-gables, but St Winwallow's tower is away at the top of the churchyard, built partly into the rock. (If you want to see other detached towers in Cornwall, go to *Feock*, *Gwennap*, *Lamorran*, *Mylor* and *Talland*.) The interior has great character and is very welcoming. The High Altar, of granite, was designed by Sir Ninian Comper, there is a Norman font and some beautiful woodwork may be enjoyed here. The view from the porch as you leave is glorious.

KILKHAMPTON. Kilkhampton's glorious tower broods over the large church of St James the Great, which is rather dark inside, thanks to much Victorian glass. We enter through a massive Norman doorway and there is much to see inside. There is a full set of 15th century benches with richly carved ends, a pretty granite font, a fine wall-plaque to Sir Bevill Grenville which is surrounded by carved weapons and flanked by a real helmet and gauntlets, an imposing set of Royal Arms and an organ, part of which was once in Westminster Abbey.

LANEAST. A secluded village, unspoilt and pretty, which possesses a very typical Cornish church at its best. The churchyard and setting are lovely, the exterior is dignified and well-proportioned and the interior is bright and full of interest. It is essentially Cornish, with old wagon roofs, medieval woodwork in the screen, 38 old bench-ends, fragments of 15th century glass, a pulpit made in the 1500s (from which John Wesley preached) and a plaque to the man who discovered the planet Neptune in 1845. For a further treat, go to *St Clether*, the next village, to see another lovely church, St Clederus and to walk the lonely footpath round the base of a nearby hill, to St Clether's Holy Well and its little medieval chapel.

LAUNCELLS. A secluded and very picturesque setting, with plenty of trees surrounding its atmospheric churchyard. We come here to St Swithin's mainly to see its bright and unspoilt interior which just breathes antiquity and beauty. Supreme amongst the many treasures here are some 60 medieval bench-ends and a chancel floor which is paved with medieval tiles, with various designs on them. The granite arcades have fascinating carvings and the wagon roofs are splendid. Here we have a fine set of Royal Arms of Charles II, made in plaster, as are so many in this part of the county. The Norman font has a 17th century cover and we see Sir John Chamond (died 1624) clad in his armour on his monument. There are box-pews in the north aisle and an unusual reredos of 1720.

LAUNCESTON. The wonderful feature of St Mary's is that the walls of its granite exterior are a mass of stonecarving, probably done during the early 1500s and quite an amazing achievement. Inside is an early 16th century pulpit, the Royal Arms of King George I and several interesting monuments, including one to Granville Ryder (1717) and Richard Wise (1726) who were close friends. There is a good 20th century screen, and a reredos, showing the Transfiguration, by Hems of Exeter.

MORWENSTOW. Known worldwide as 'Parson Hawker's church', and we may still feel the effect of this wonderful scholar, poet and eccentric in and around what he loved to call 'My Saxon Shrine'. The figurehead from the *Caledonia* in the churchyard reminds us of the many shipwrecked sailors whom he brought here for burial. His vicarage, with its odd chimneys in the shape of church towers, still stands, and the glorious view out to the open sea may still be enjoyed. St John's itself has Norman doorways and arches, a crude Saxon font, medieval wagon roofs and bench-ends and much which is curious and interesting. Look, for instance, for the upside-down lettering at the tops of some of the piers in the south arcade.

MULLION. St Melina is a medieval church, beautifully restored by F.C. Eden, who gave it a lovely screen. The bench-ends are superb and are the originals and, entered by old doors and set beneath old roofs, we have a house of prayer which is dignified and devotional. There is a set of Royal Arms of Charles II and the brass of a rector who was thrown out during the Commonwealth period and reinstated in 1660.

NEWQUAY. The mighty parish church of St Michael of this seaside resort is a most worthy product of our own century, built in 1911 to the designs of Sir Ninian Comper, who tried to reproduce the design of a medieval Cornish church. It is a fine building and is most handsomely furnished with work of great quality and with tasteful use of colour. The tower was added in 1968.

PROBUS. Few could fail to miss Cornwall's tallest and most magnificent tower, which makes us feel as if we are in Somerset. It is a truly wonderful piece of design and craftsmanship from the 1520s. G.E. Street restored this church of St Probus and St Grace and there is much to enjoy here, particularly the impressive arcades and windows, and the fine proportions of the building. Look for the Wolvedon brass (1514) in the south aisle, Charles I's Royal Arms, old woodwork in the base of the screen and stalls and an Easter Sepulchre.

ST BURYAN. We are almost at Land's End here, and the mighty tower of St Buryan's, which is set on high ground, can be seen for miles. It is probably the superb 15th century screen which we remember most from this stately collegiate church. There is also a good 15th century font and one of Cornwall's best porches.

ST ENODOC. It is well worth the walk over the golf links to hunt out this unusual little church with its odd, slightly twisted and curiously beckoning spire. The church has a lovely and isolated setting and, although it was thoroughly restored in 1864, it is full of atmosphere, with a simple Norman font and the base of its 15th century screen. Betjeman loved the place; he wrote a poem about it. His mother is buried here and the great man himself has a beautifully inscribed slate headstone marking his grave near the entrance to the churchyard.

ST JUST IN ROSELAND. A place-name like this would attract anybody to discover it. The setting of this unassuming little church above its idyllic creek has been described as perhaps the most beautiful in England. St Just's churchyard, once called 'a Garden of Eden that cannot be described in pen or paint', has such a variety of trees, shrubs and flowers that one could spend a day exploring it. Then the church itself – so welcoming, prayerful and delightfully cared for. The benches and pulpit were installed by a 19th century rector who was also an architect. There is a brass of a priest (c1520), a 15th century font with a 17th century cover, also tasteful work of our own times.

ST MAWGAN IN PYDAR. A superb setting and a grand and elegant exterior with a fine tower on the south side. The interior is full of interest and here we may enjoy 40 or so Cornish bench-ends, a 15th century screen and font, a pulpit made in 1553, the brass effigy of a priest (c1420) and much else besides. The village is known for its RAF station, as was nearby *St Eval*, whose lonely St Uvelus' church's bold tower may be seen for miles. This church is remote, rugged and windswept, but how the folk of its small community care for it. We have Norman work here and much evidence of its importance to the personnel of the RAF station nearby.

ST MICHAEL PENKEVIL. A picturesque 'estate' village well worth finding, and a handsome church, containing interesting medieval work, but restored and partly rebuilt in 1862 by G.E. Street. The original foundation stone of 1261 is a rare survival in the north-east corner of the chancel of this cruciform church, which is dominated by its bold western tower. Here we may see monuments and brasses to the Boscawen

County of tall granite towers, with prominent corner pinnacles, rising above long, low roofs: – as we see here at St Cleer.

family, also the brass of John Trembas, the rector (who died in 1515) dressed in academic robes.

ST NEOT. A village of great character at the foot of Bodmin Moor, with a noble and stately church from the 15th and early 16th centuries. St Neot's fine tower and handsome pinnacled exterior tempt us inside to bask in the light from one of the finest collections of medieval stained glass in southern England. Here is early 16th century glass in all its beauty, which has been enhanced by careful restoration and renewal where necessary by John Hedgeland in 1830. There are 15 windows to enjoy. One shows the Creation and Fall of Man, another shows in fascinating detail the life and legends of St Neot himself, and the north aisle west window has twelve scenes from the life of St George.

ST WINNOW. Another delectable riverside setting, with the river Fowey alongside the churchyard wall. There is evidence of Norman and 13th century work here and J.D. Sedding tastefully restored the church of St Wynnocus. The exterior blends beautifully with its surroundings and completes the idyllic rural scene. The interior is delightful, with much to reward the visitor. There is glass of c1500 in the east windows – the Lady Chapel window having much to teach us about the dress of the period. Thirty three bench-ends from the 1500s and 1600s survive (look for the Cornishman wearing his Cornish kilt). The pulpit is a rare Elizabethan one (c1590) and the screen is about 50 years earlier, although it has been tastefully restored.

TREMAINE. Do try to find this tiny church dedicated to St Winwallo in the lanes, about four miles north of Laneast. There is nothing large or grand here, nothing world famous. It is simply a small and largely unknown Cornish church – unassuming, cared for by its diminutive community and thoroughly adorable! Humble exterior with leaning walls and pretty tapering pinnacled tower. A Norman north doorway and lovely views from the churchyard. Inside, this single-celled church is sheltered by its medieval roof and has seating accommodation (chairs) for 22 people! Tremaine people enter their church by an ancient door, they are baptised in a simple Norman tub-font, as they have been for 900 years, but their Eucharist is offered at a tasteful stone altar which is a product of our own century.

CUMBRIA

This county of the far north-west stretches from the Solway Firth at the top to Morecambe Bay at the bottom, and embraces the former counties of Cumberland and Westmorland, as well as the Furness and Cartmel peninsulas which were once in Lancashire. Here we have English scenery at its most dramatic and spectacular, including the glorious Lake District, and a landscape punctuated with wonderful hills, 'pikes' and fells. It is lovely to look at at any time of the year, but most memorable of all in autumn.

Cumbria has just over 100 medieval churches and nearer 200 later ones or rebuilds. The local stone of which they are built varies according to the area. There is plenty of tough Westmorland slate, also old red sandstone of varying hues, new red sandstone and limestone. Magnificent architecture comes in small doses in these churches. There are few Saxon remains (Morland has the only Saxon tower), Norman is a little more frequent, especially in the larger churches and monastic remains. The county has its handful of those long Perp churches, with their continuous roofs, which we find in the north (as at Hawkeshead, Bowness, Beetham, Crosthwaite and Greystoke). Some interesting 17th and 18th century rebuilds and new churches may be enjoyed here; Whitehaven, Wigton and Carlisle St Cuthbert and the village churches at Witherslack, Ings, Brougham Ninekirks and Mungrisdale are a few examples. This is also a good county in which to see 18th century furnishings and several complete interiors survive from this period, while 19th century restorations and rebuildings are widespread, although most of this new work is not by architects of national repute.

The cathedral city of Carlisle is worth a visit. The cathedral is all the more endearing because only the stump of its nave survives, contrasting with a chancel which is entire and magnificent. The parish church of St Cuthbert dates from 1778.

It is really the little churches, especially the former 'Fell Chapels', which are simple, rustic and quaint, with their rugged walls, bellcots and idyllic settings, for which we remember Cumbria. These churches have little grandeur and seem to have simply grown out of the landscape – but they are so homely and so very charming and satisfying.

ABBEY TOWN. In this village not far from the Solway Firth is a curious church which has been assembled out of what is left of the great abbey of Holme Cultram. St Mary's is actually part of the nave (without its aisles) and the western porch. Much of the reconstruction that we see today is work of 1727–39, but a porch of 1507 shelters the mighty western portal – a glorious Norman doorway, with four orders of shafts each side. One of the bells in the double bellcot dates from 1465 and inside we can get some feeling of the glory which has departed and the atmosphere which still very much survives.

APPLEBY. A market town of great atmosphere on the river Eden. Its noble parish church of St Lawrence has a largely Perp exterior (fascinating gargoyles here) but has EE and Dec work inside. The unusual memorial cloister, by Smirke, was erected in 1811. There are 15th century screens to the chapels and a Corporation Pew with 18th century woodwork. Splendidly set at the west end is the oldest organ still in working order in any English church – parts of it date from 1542–7. In the north-east chapel is the recumbent alabaster effigy of Margaret, Countess of Cumberland (with her metal coronet) fashioned in 1617. Another monument commemorates her daughter, Anne (died 1676) who restored this church in 1655. She also restored St Michael's church, east of the river.

Ormside church of St James has a sturdy fortified tower, stonework of the 11th century, 15th century roofs and 17th century furnishings.

BROUGHAM. Two churches here, both restored by Lady Anne Clifford of Appleby. St Ninian's (or Ninekirks) (RCF) was rebuilt by her in 1660. Its structure is Gothic Survival and, when we enter, it is as if we are still in the 1660s because all the furnishings are still in place. What a period-piece – benches, family pews, screen, pulpit and sounding-board, rails, and even a poor box dated 1666. The setting above the river for this remote gem of a church is sylvan and is thoroughly therapeutic in itself.

St Wilfrid's chapel is not very far from Brougham Castle and could not be more of a contrast to St Ninian's, although Lady Anne restored it two years earlier. Inside this long rectangular chapel (with a medieval core and such a plain exterior) is a profusion of carved oak, mostly imported from the Continent. This amazing and magnificent collection of wood-carving includes a screen of c1500, collegiate stalls, believed to be French, and part of a Flemish triptych of c1520. Its finest treasure – the glorious Flemish reredos of c1490 – is now on display in the north transept of Carlisle Cathedral.

CARTMEL. A little town of great charm, full of antiquity and presided over by the mighty form of its priory church of St Mary. The massive exterior is crowned by a central tower which is unique because its 15th century belfry stage is set diagonally above the stage below. The glory of this splendid church has survived and here we see impressive work of all periods between the 1100s and 1400s. The 15th century stalls (with their carved misericords) are set beneath Jacobean canopies of 1618; the Renaissance screenwork is also of this date and is very fine. There are noteworthy monuments here too, and much else.

CARTMEL FELL. A simple, low and endearing upland chapel, built in 1503, with a quaint saddleback tower. The hillside setting is charming and the interior of St Anthony's (with sloping floor) is full of atmosphere. The Cowmire Hall pew was made in 1571 out of the old chancel screen. There is a three-decker pulpit of 1698 and lovely glass of c1500, showing St Anthony, St Leonard and the seven sacraments (St Anthony of Egypt is the church's Patron Saint; he is usually seen with his pet pig, wearing a bell around its neck). This little church is the proud possessor of one of only two original rood crucifixes remaining in England; this, needless to say, is now in safe-keeping.

Do go to *Witherslack*, to see St Paul's church, built by a 17th century Royalist Dean of St Paul's.

CROSTHWAITE. A long North Country church, with aisles running the entire length from east to west. St Kentigern's was rebuilt in 1523 and displays sets of external and internal consecration crosses, marking the spots where the Tudor bishop anointed the walls with holy oils at its consecration. The 14th century north chapel survives from the original church, also the beautifully carved font of c1400. Sir Gilbert Scott restored the church in 1844 and the glass in the east window is by Kempe. The poet, Robert Southey (died 1843) has a white marble effigy and an epitaph by Wordsworth. Sir John (1527) and Lady Ratcliff, who had this church rebuilt, are effigied in brass and another couple have stone effigies here.

Keswick's 19th century church of St John the Evangelist has good 1889 glass by Henry Holiday. St Mary's *Threlkeld*, set at the foot of Blencathra, is a lovable little church of 1777, with a quaint little tower and much atmosphere.

GRASMERE. Pilgrims flock here to venerate Wordsworth's simple grave and his memorial plaque inside the church. Church-crawlers will also fall in love with this funny old pebbledash church of St Oswald, with its plain but substantial tower and its roof which embraces both nave and Langdale aisle. Inside are crude and rustic arcades, one above the other (the lower of 1563 and the upper of the 17th century). Of 1563 also are the remarkable roof timbers. This is such a distinctive interior, with the le Fleming hatchments and pew in the chancel, godly texts of 1711 in the nave and an expressive modern Madonna and Child by Ophelia Gordon Bell.

Here we are in the heart of Lakeland, within a few miles of *Hawkshead*'s Perp church of St Michael, and St Martin's of *Bowness in Windermere* (1483), with its medieval glass from Cartmel Priory, also Sir Gilbert Scott's (1850–4) lovely Gothic Revival church of St Mary at *Ambleside*.

GREYSTOKE. For a Cumbrian village, this is a most noble and venerable church, which is predominantly Perp but contains some 13th century work. It was once collegiate and retains not only a 15th century screen, but also 20 canons' stalls, with carved misericords. Lovely 15th century glass in the east window taught medieval folk about St Andrew, the Patron Saint, and brasses and alabaster effigies beautifully portray to us past people of Greystoke.

Do find St Kentigern's *Mungrisdale*, with its lovely name, lovely views and lovely tiny church of 1756, with three-decker pulpit and box-pews. *Penrith* has a grand red sandstone church of St Andrew of 1720–2 (but with a Norman tower).

ISEL. A perfect setting by the river Derwent for St Michael's small and simple towerless church. (The nearby hall is much more spectacular, and has a pele tower). It is a Norman church of c1130 (with a fine chancel arch), but there are three Saxon stones with very interesting carvings, including a swastika and a triskele, also Saxon cross fragments. One 15th century chancel window has three Mass-dials carved in its stonework.

Bridekirk's church of St Bridget was mostly rebuilt in 1868, but has two genuine Norman doorways, and an amazing font of the mid 1100s which is absolutely covered with the most fascinating sculptures.

KENDAL. This church of the Holy Trinity is Cumbria's largest parish church – and vast it certainly is, with double aisles each side of the nave and chancel, making a perfect rectangle, embracing the fine (80 ft) western tower. The rectangle measures 140 ft by 103 ft. We admire here a stately embattled Perp exterior and an unforgettably broad interior, punctuated by arcade after arcade! What vistas here, through what has been described as 'a forest of pillars'. There is much to see – a 15th

71

Simple Cumbrian exterior at Isel, in an unforgettable setting. Typical of so many in this county, and full of beauty and interest.

century font of black marble, the roof with its angels, the 16th century Bellingham brasses and several memorials. What is also noteworthy is the 19th and 20th century work, including the font-cover, the Belling-ham Chapel roof, the screens (made by local craftsmen) and the glass, by Warrington, Ward & Hughes and other noteworthy firms.

KIRKBY LONSDALE.   In a small town in the Vale of Lune, but with views from the churchyard which are reckoned to be amongst the finest in the county, stands St Mary's church with two grand Norman doorways and part of what must have been a magnificent Norman north arcade. All medieval periods are represented here and there is much to admire, including a pulpit of 1619 and Jacobean stalls.

LANERCOST PRIORY.   A sequestered and scenic spot in the well-wooded vale of the river Irthing, and magnificent EE architecture to be enjoyed (c1210–20) in this great church, where we have the nave and north aisle forming the parish church and the rest of the abbey church is a stately ruin. The west front is splendid, with its great doorway, tall stepped lancets and a rare 13th century statue of St Mary Magdalene in the niche above. Inside the lofty church (whose east wall was made in 1740) is further delightful and dignified EE work and we may enjoy treasures ranging from part of a Saxon cross-shaft to glass by William Morris and Burne Jones. The complete church was 178 ft long and the ruined choir and transepts, etc, are worth exploring – again lovely EE.

More Morris and Burne Jones glass may be seen at St Patrick's *Bampton* – a distinctive church by Philip Webb (1874–8).

RAVENSTONEDALE. St Oswald's is a wonderful 18th century church for atmosphere – its tower was rebuilt in 1738 and in 1744, re-using old stonework in the south porch and chancel arch. But what an interior – an excellent place in which to see 'plain and Prayer Book' furnishings which have been totally untouched by the Oxford Move-ment. The box-pews face inwards, like a college chapel, with the three-decker pulpit (and sounding-board) halfway down the north side. The Commandment Boards are noteworthy, also the coffin-tables and Com-munion rails. The east window is interesting – it commemorates 'the last female martyr burnt at Tyburn for the cause of the Protestant Religion, 1685'.

Kirkby Stephen's large and stately church of St Stephen, with its fine Perp tower, has much to admire, including some good monuments.

ST BEES. St Mary and St Bega's cruciform priory church of sand-stone, set in a village near the coast, was greatly restored by William Butterfield in 1855–68. It still preserves its magnificent Norman door-way of c1160, EE arcades and Perp clerestory, but the church ends abruptly only one bay into the chancel. The rest of the lovely EE chancel is now part of St Bees School. Butterfield renewed the crossing tower and designed the tall wrought-iron screen.

Whitehaven's church of St James (1753) has what has been described as the finest Georgian interior in the county, whilst the striking Gothic Revival tower of what was the church of St Nicholas (1883) is a feature of the town centre.

WABERTHWAITE. There are views to the Lakeland fells from this lonely and lovable little church of St John near the estuary of the Esk. A double bellcot of 1796 crowns a simple building, the core of which is probably Norman and its red sandstone font may also be 12th century. Earlier still is the churchyard cross-shaft with its Saxon carving. The interior feels lived in and is most appealing. The pulpit dates from 1630.

To the north-east are pretty lanes leading to glorious scenery and small idyllic churches, like St Catherine's *Eskdale* (at Boot), *Lower Wasdale* (at Strands) where we see 17th century woodcarving from York Minster, and the tiny, tiny chapel at *Wasdale Head*.

DERBYSHIRE

In the north of the county we have the incomparable scenery of the Peak District, with its moors, peaks and dales, from whence the lovely rivers Dove and Derwent flow southwards through the county to join the river Trent. More and more people are coming to this beautiful county, to discover such places as Darley Dale, Matlock and other dramatically scenic spots, also fine old towns like Bakewell, Tideswell and Ashbourne, great houses like Chatsworth, Hardwick, Haddon and Kedleston, scenic villages, several of which dress with flowers their Holy Wells, and of course the churches (in the region of 145 medieval ones) which always delight us – even those in the bits of the county which have been scarred by power stations, coalfields and too much industry.

Derbyshire is rich in building materials, with varieties of limestone and sandstone, also its wonderful alabaster which has given churches in other counties some of their finest monuments. There is much to see in the churches here, although there is not a great abundance of really mighty churches. Saxon, for instance in Repton's crypt and Wirksworth's carvings of cAD 800, Norman at mighty Melbourne and tiny Steetley, EE in Doveridge and Ashbourne chancels, Dec (and here the county really excels) at Chesterfield, Norbury, Chaddesden and many others, and Perp (which is comparatively scarce) is seen at its best in some of the fine towers, like Tideswell and Youlgreave, also Derby Cathedral (the remainder of which was rebuilt by James Gibbs in 1723–5). Church interiors have a variety of fittings of quality, including several interesting Norman fonts, a few fine screens, some excellent medieval glass and, above all, monuments of great beauty and quality. Unfortunately this is a county where one often has to search for the address of the key in order to see inside a church.

ASHBOURNE.   This grand church is dominated by its central tower, with a spire rising 212 ft. The chancel of St Oswald's is glorious EE with lancets, but the seven-light E window is now Perp. The remainder of the church is mainly Dec with foliage of that period on some of the capitals. Both transepts have E aisles. In the chancel, note the sedilia. The monuments are numerous.

ASHOVER. All Saints' church is typical of Derbyshire, Perp with a recessed spire. The S doorway is 13th C, and then the remainder of the church is Dec and Perp. Note the long squint from the S to the chancel. There are not many Norman lead fonts in England, but this is one of them, with standing figures under arcades. An early 16th C screen and a late 17th C pulpit. Brasses to James Rolleston and his wife and children 1507, also a priest c1510. There is a very fine alabaster monument to Thomas Babington and wife 1518 on a tomb-chest with saints, angels and mourners.

AULT HUCKNALL. Very handy for visitors to Hardwick Hall. St John the Baptist's is a fascinating building, where small 11th century arches (the eastern one possibly Saxon) support the central tower. The north arcade is Norman, as are some carvings in the west wall. A most atmospheric interior, with 14th century nave roof, a crucifixion scene in 1527 glass in the south aisle, also the tomb of the first Earl of Devonshire's wife (1627).

BAKEWELL. In the churchyard is the stump of a Saxon cross. All Saints' has a Dec central tower and octagon and recessed spire (rebuilt). There are a number of Sax and Norm fragments. The W front is Norm, the W doorway showing beakheads. The S transept with E aisle is EE with lancets, and the chancel only a little later with fine double piscina and sedilia. The font is Dec with figures. There is a reredos of wood, and some stalls have misericords. Look also for the aumbry with fleurons, the 15 C rood-screen, and a number of foliated crosses. The mon to Sir Godfrey Foljambe and his wife 1377 shows alabaster half-length figures. In the Vernon Chapel (S transept) there are monuments to Sir Thomas Wendesley 1403, John Vernon 1477 with small figures, Sir George Vernon and two wives 1567, Sir John Manners and wife 1584 kneeling at a prayer-desk with children below, and Sir George Manners 1623 with children under arches upon which are verses from the Bible.

Ashford on the Water is a pretty village and its Holy Trinity church has a Norman tympanum, beautifully carved.

CHESTERFIELD. St Mary and All Saints' is known far and wide for its leaning and twisted spire (228 ft tall), which is of lead and has warped in the sun. It is on a central tower. The plan of the church is complicated: it is flanked by chapels and the one on the S is again flanked by another one, a most unusual arrangement in England. This is all due to the wealth of the Guilds. The W window is Dec as is most of the church, with some work of the 19th century. There is a Norm font, a Jac pulpit, several old side screens and a fine organ case. There are several mons, the earliest being the effigy of a priest of the 14th C. Henry Foljambe and wife 1510 have a tomb with mourners at the sides, and Sir Thomas Foljambe as a boy kneeling on top. Then there are Sir Godfrey Foljambe and wife 1585, Geoffrey Foljambe, incised slab 1588, and Godfrey Foljambe and wife and children 1598. That of Sir James Foljambe, with his children below, 1558, depicts a figure in a shroud with a figure of Death and bones and a shovel. There is also a brass to Sir Godfrey Foljambe and his wife and children 1541. Lovely work by Temple Moore and J Harold Gibbons makes the interior here colourful and devotional. There is also fine glass by Comper and others.

DALE ABBEY.   Not the great church that we would expect from a name like this, but the infirmary chapel (and half church, half house) of the former abbey – but what a character and what a delightful sylvan setting in a pretty valley for this tiny (26 × 25 ft) church. Most of what we see in the fabric dates from a reordering of 1480, but around 1634 the interior was refurbished, since when it has remained virtually unchanged. The pulpit and reading desk stand behind the little altar table (which is equipped with cupboards!) and the place is filled with box-pews, even in the little gallery. Older than all this are the wall-paintings, including a scene of the Visitation, which are probably early 14th century. This is a little gem, which will not be easily forgotten.

EDENSOR.   Those who visit Chatsworth must also see its nearby estate village, planned by Sir Joseph Paxton, with its picturesque houses, lovely views and (of course) its crowning glory – Sir Gilbert Scott's stately and compelling St Peter's church (of 1869), with its soaring spire and grand interior. From its predecessor has been preserved the mighty monument to Henry and William Cavendish (died 1616 and 1625), where we see Henry as a skeleton and William in his shroud.

Nearby *Baslow* is one of Derbyshire's truly lovely villages and its riverside St Anne's church, with a pretty broach spire, is well worth a visit.

EYAM.   St Lawrence's possesses a fine Sax cross with its cross-head, of the early 9th C. Perp tower, nave roof and clerestory. The chancel is EE and there is a Norm font and an 18th C pulpit. William Mompesson was rector when the Plague was brought here from London in 1665. He persuaded the villagers to seal Eyam off from the outside world in an effort to contain the infection, and the story of their sufferings and self-sacrifice has become justifiably famous.

Stoney Middleton nearby has an unusual octagonal church, St Martin's, of 1759.

HADDON HALL. This most beautiful medieval house has an equally beautiful medieval chapel like a village church. The font of St Nicholas' is Norm, with a Jac cover. One pillar on the S side of the nave is 13th C, the N of the nave is a little later, and the chancel and clerestory are of 1427. The fine woodwork is 17th C – roof, screen, benches, and three-decker pulpit. The 15th C reredos of Nottingham alabaster has been imported. Much remains of wall-paintings; St Christopher, a skeleton from the Three Living and the Three Dead, and groups from the lives of Christ and the Virgin. The old glass is also about 1427. In the E window is Christ crucified with St Mary and St John (the usual rood group), and in a N window St Michael, St Anne and the Virgin, and St George.

HORSLEY. St Clement's is on a hill with a splendid view to the E. All embattled, as usual in this county. The tower has a broach spire, indicating a 13th or 14th C date, the latter being the main date of the church, including the sedilia. The window above the chancel arch is unusual. There is a Perp font – and note the gargoyles.

MELBOURNE. St Michael and St Mary's is a most impressive church with a central tower and two W towers uncompleted, but it is even more impressive inside and completely Norm. The nave arcades have tall circular piers; the arches are decorated with zig-zag and the capitals are scalloped. The crossing-arches and the three tiers of openings above them are remarkable. A porch at the W end with vaulting is unusual.

MORLEY. St Matthew's is noted for its glass and monuments. The S arcade is Norm, the N arcade slightly later, the chancel arch, chancel and S porch are 14th C, and the remainder is Perp. The tower has a recessed spire. There are many 14th C floor tiles, and much medieval glass – scenes from the legend of St Robert of Knaresborough and stories from the Invention of the Holy Cross, and also of St William of York and St John of Bridlington. There is one original figure in the E window – St Ursula. There is a fine mon to Katherine Babington 1543 with kneeling figures, four 17th C incised slabs to Sacheverell children, and monuments to Jacynth Sacheverell and wife and their kneeling children 1656, and Jonathan Sacheverell and wife 1662. Several brasses include John Stathum and wife 1453, with St Christopher above; Thomas Stathum

Derbyshire has a variety of churches, some spectacular and some comparatively unassuming – as here, at Ashford In The Water.

and two wives 1470, with scrolls leading to St Christopher, St Anne, and the Virgin and Child; Henry Stathum and three wives and children 1480; John Sacheverell on Bosworth Field and wife and children 1485; and Henry Sacheverell and wife 1558.

NORBURY.   Noted for its monuments and beautiful 14th C chancel with windows with unusual tracery, the remainder of St Mary's with its tower on the S side is mainly Perp. The font and screen are 15th C. The chancel seating has some poppyheads with tracery on the fronts. There are fragments of two Sax crosses, and some medieval glass, mostly grisaille; in the SE chapel, three saints and kneeling donors below. Mons include an incised slab to a woman; an incised slab to Henry Prince, rector 1500, with chalice; a cross-legged 14th C knight, Sir Henry Fitzherbert; and Nicholas Fitzherbert 1473 with standing figures. On that of Sir Ralph Fitzherbert and wife 1483, with standing figures, the feet of Sir Ralph are on a lion, and under one of his soles crouches a tiny bedesman. The brass is to Sir Anthony Fitzherbert, wife and children, 1538.

REPTON.   The late Sax crypt remains complete with vaults on four columns – a wonderful survival. In it one can easily imagine that Repton is still the capital of Mercia. The 14th C tower has a fine recessed spire rising to 212 ft. St Wystan's is 13th and 14th C with Perp clerestory, roof and porch. Mons to an alabaster knight 1400, incised slab to Gilbert Thacker and wife 1563, and Francis Thacker 1710.

Do discover St Saviour's *Foremark* – a wonderful little church of 1662, gothic, with lovely original fittings including a three-decker pulpit, box-pews, screen, altar and wrought-iron rails. A real period piece.

SANDIACRE.   St Giles' has some rich Norm and Dec work. The Norm is the S doorway, chancel arch, and two windows. The fine Dec work is the long chancel with its varied windows. The piscina and sedilia have rich canopies. The tower has lancet windows and a broach spire, 13th C. The small clerestory is Perp.

SAWLEY.   All Saints' is a rewarding church. The chancel arch is Norm, the chancel is late 13th C with two stone screens to chantry chapels, and the nave is Dec. The tower with recessed spire and cleres-tory are Perp, the screen is also of that period, and the pulpit is Jac. There is a medieval effigy of a priest, and an alabaster effigy of John Boothe, Treasurer of Lichfield Cathedral, 1496 (in the Boothby Chantry Chapel). Brasses to Roger Boothby and wife and children 1467, Robert Boothby and wife 1478, and Richard Shylton and wife 1510.

STEETLEY.   Steetley chapel is a fine and complete Norm church. It consists of three parts – nave, chancel and apse, with elaborate arches between each section. The apse is vaulted, and has three small windows. The chancel arch capitals display St George and the Dragon, Adam and Eve, and animals. The roofs are supported by a corbel-table.

TIDESWELL.   St John the Baptist's is one of the grandest churches and called the Cathedral of the Peak. Most unusually it has all been built about the same time, 1350, as indicated by the Flowing tracery of the windows. The chancel, possibly slightly later, is particularly grand, with its piscina, sedilia and many niches for figures. The tower is Perp, with a large W window and eight pinnacles, the four corner ones being octagonal turrets with crocketed pinnacles upon them. The tower arch is a great height. The nave roof is original. Perp font. Mons include two stone figures of the 13th and 14th C; Sir Thurstan de Bower 1423, an alabaster figure; and Sampson Meverill 1462. Of the brasses, John Foljambe 1383 is one of the finest. A brass of the Trinity is on a modern tomb-chest with a stone cadaver underneath. Brasses also to Sir Robert Lytton and wife 1483, and Bishop Pursglove 1579.

WHITWELL.   At St Lawrence's the church enthusiast will discover two main periods – Norm and Dec. The former is shown in the tower (lower part with doorway), clerestory (rare in Norm times), and corbel-table above in nave and chancel. The nave is also Norm and the chancel arch leads to the Dec period – chancel and transepts, the former with sedilia and opposite possibly an Easter Sepulchre. The upper part of the tower with pinnacles is Perp. There is a Norm font and Jac panelling in the chancel. Mon to Sir Roger Manners 1632.

YOULGREAVE.   All Saints' has a broad tall Perp tower, with double belfry windows and eight pinnacles. The arcades are late Norm. The windows are mostly Perp (the E window of five lights). The font is c1200 with a rare projecting basin, and there is a Norm sculpture of a man. The chancel E and S windows are by Burne Jones. One mon shows a cross-legged knight holding his heart in his hands c1325, another a small alabaster figure of Thomas Cockayne 1488 on a small exquisite tomb-chest with angels. There is also a fine alabaster panel to Robert Gylbert and wife and children 1492: the Virgin and Child are seated in the centre surrounded by husband and wife and the 17 children. Mon also to Roger Rowe and wife and children 1613. There is a small brass to Frideswide Gylbert 1603.

DEVON

'Devon – glorious Devon'! Holidaymakers flock to its two coastlines (north and south) and to the many beauty spots of this large and lovely county. There is wonderful scenery everywhere we go, with fascinating Dartmoor, splendid river estuaries and harbours, pretty villages with cob cottages, and so much to see. The church enthusiast will take his life into his hands as he drives up innumerable hedged and narrow winding lanes in search of the parts which tourists rarely reach, to find churches with elegant pinnacled towers and long low rooflines (usually three gables and no clerestory) which complete the village scene. With the administrative reorganization of counties, which Devon escaped, this is now our largest county and there are over 430 medieval churches for us to visit. What splendid churches they are and what a wealth of fine craftsmanship awaits us.

Many Devon churches are built of durable granite and some of Ham Hill stone from nearby Somerset, but perhaps the most exciting of all the building stones here is the new red sandstone which we find in the south, creating fields of red soil and really red (and this is no exaggeration) church buildings.

Devon has 100 or so Norman fonts and some examples of Norman, EE and Dec, but it is Perp here which is so prolific and so magnificent. So many Devon churches were rebuilt or enlarged during this period, and so we look for an abundance of large Perp windows, lovely stone-carving in parapets, arcades and their capitals, also the wonderful wood-work for which Devon is justly famous. Here we see a host of wagon roofs, exquisitely carved and studded with bosses and often filled in with plaster panels. Here also a wealth of glorious screens – a mass of beautifully carved Perp openwork tracery, some with their ribbed coving still at the top and many gloriously painted and gilded. Then come the medieval pulpits – of stone and wood – again beautifully carved and sometimes painted. There are the sets of bench-ends (especially in the north of the county), which are usually flat-topped, but full of intriguing carvings.

Finding Devon churches is not usually difficult because of their superb tall and pinnacled towers, often with prominent corner turrets crowned with spirelets, or with stair-turrets rising above the parapet. Several in south Devon have the unusual local feature of the staircase-turret rising the full height of the tower, but at the centre of one side – as at Ipplepen and Ashburton.

Exeter has Devon's lovely cathedral and is also a city of churches, including some good Victorian ones. To see more of the better 19th century work in the county, an exploration of Torquay and Plymouth will reveal several gems.

Devon deserves a much longer list of selected churches, but this small sample will hopefully lead you to many others.

ASHTON. Situated high above the Teign valley, St Michael's is completely Perp with a fine tower. The treasure of the church is the rood-screen with 32 panels of painted figures of saints. They are the best-preserved panels in the West Country and as they are so important, here is a complete list of the figures from N to S: Saints Gregory, Jerome, Ambrose, and Augustine of Hippo (these are the four Latin Doctors). Sitha, Michael, Dorothy, Clement, the four Evangelists – Mark, Matthew, Luke and John the Evangelist. Leonard, a female with scimitar, Stephen, Sidwell, Blaise, Catherine, Thomas of Canterbury, Margaret, John the Baptist, Virgin and Child, George, Mary Magdalene, Anthony, Ursula, Leger, Apollonia, a bishop, Lawrence, Sebastian and Winifred. There are, however, an even more remarkable series of paintings on the backs of the screen at the N end, demi-figures of prophets with scrolls, the Annunciation, and Visitation. The church has wagon roofs, a Perp font, and a Jac pulpit and tester. Some bench-ends with tracery, and 17th C altar-rails. The S door is original and the heraldic glass is medieval. There is a wooden mon to Sir George Chudleigh, 1657.

ATHERINGTON. St Mary's tall tower with prominent stair-turret, set on a hill, can be seen from miles around. The church is mostly Perp with old wagon roofs and a Perp font. The old bench-ends are poppy-heads. The screen of the N aisle retains its rood-loft, a very rare feature. Note the detail of the carving on the cornice and canopies. Mons to a cross-legged knight of c1250 and a 14th C knight and his lady. Brass to Sir John Basset and his wife and twelve children, 1538.

High Bickington St Mary's has a lovely Norman font, also the largest collection of medieval bench-ends in the county – a wonderful array of 70 of them!

BOVEY TRACEY. St Thomas of Canterbury's has a tall Dec granite tower, but the church is mostly Perp. It has a vaulted S porch, wagon roofs, and a Perp font. In the church is a wonderful trio of medieval work – the screen with cornice and painted panels of Apostles and prophets, the stone pulpit coloured with all its original figures of saints (the four Evangelists, St George, St Margaret, St Peter, St Paul, St Andrew and St James the Less), and the 15th C brass eagle lectern. Mons to Nicholas Eveleigh 1618, of stone, and to Elizeus Hele with two wives and a son, 1636, of alabaster.

St John's church, by Carpenter, was built in 1852. Its interior is beautiful and devotional, with a reredos by Salviati and many lovely fittings.

BRADNINCH.   St Dionysius' has a tall Perp tower and an interior typical of Devon. The splendid screen runs right across the nave and aisles. It has the usual fan-vaulted coving and cornice, and all is beautifully re-coloured. The painted panels show the Apostles and prophets, the four Latin Doctors, St Christopher, the stigmata of St Francis, St Adrian and other saints and sibyls (as often in Devon), the Annunciation, and the Expulsion from Paradise.

BRAUNTON.   The tower on the S of St Brannock's is Norm with a lead broach spire. What a difference from a Somerset tower. Even the bell-openings are in the spire. The church is of the medieval styles. It has wagon roofs, a Norm font, a 17th C pulpit and reading desk, a Perp screen and 17th C altar-rails. The great feature is, however, the large number of medieval bench-ends with fronts and backs. They depict particularly the Instruments of the Passion: there is also one showing St Brannock.

CHITTLEHAMPTON.   St Hieritha's Perp tower (125 ft) is the finest in Devon and was probably built by Somerset masons, as many of its features occur in the grand towers of that county. The S porch has its original door. Inside one feels beauty all around. In the transepts are original timber roofs. There is a medieval stone pulpit with little figures. Brass to John Cobleigh and two wives 1490, and mons to Grace Giffard 1667 and John Giffard with figures 1666.

CHIVELSTONE.   The Perp tower of St Silvester's has a mid-stair turret common in this area, but unknown anywhere else. The screen is beautifully coloured and has figures of Apostles, Evangelists and the Latin Doctors. The pulpit (also beautifully coloured) is hollowed out of one huge piece of wood. It has heraldic shields.

COMBE MARTIN. St Peter ad Vincula's has a fine Perp tower with prominent pinnacles. It is almost entirely Perp, which overshadows the chancel with its lancets. The wagon roofs throughout are very beautiful with bosses and colouring. The rood-screen, with beautifully painted figures of Apostles and other saints, is the only one in N Devon with such painted panels. There is also a parclose screen and some bench-ends, and a Perp font. Mon to Judith Hancock 1634.

Berrynarbor St Peter's church has a 96 ft tower, a Norman font and a good monument to Richard Berry (1645).

CREDITON. Holy Cross is a large church with a central tower, all built in beautiful red sandstone. The earliest parts are the crossing arches, which are 12th C, followed by the Lady Chapel. The remainder is mostly Perp, with the very rare feature for Devon of a clerestory. The sedilia are backed by a tomb-chest with a minute lierne-vault. The oak chest is 15th C, and there is a Norm font. Mons to Sir John Sully and wife 1387, Sir William Peryam and family 1605, and John and Elizabeth Tuckfield and son, 1630.

CULLOMPTON. A complete Perp red sandstone church, St Andrew's wealth was largely due to the wool trade (hence the ships and sheep-shears carved outside on the Lane Chapel). The tower is fine with figures of the Crucifixion above the W window. Inside, the coloured roofs and medieval screen are gorgeous, and the stone fan-vault over the Lane aisle is superb. The rocks, skulls and bones which originally supported the Rood are still in the church, and the original rood-beam is still in position high up. A clerestory is a rarity. Also a Jac W gallery and an ironbound chest.

DARTMOUTH. One enters St Saviour's in the S porch, through a door with 14th C ironwork: two leopards and leaf-scrolls. As so often, the medieval screen and pulpit make the church. The former has perfect vaulting and cornice and is beautifully coloured. The stone pulpit is also beautifully coloured and has massive leaf foliage. In place of the pre-Reformation saints, in the 17th C were inserted in the niches little figures of wood – a portcullis, lion, rose, thistle, fleur-de-lis and harp. There is also a Communion table of 1588, a W gallery of 1633, and piscina and sedilia. Large brass to John Hawley and two wives, 1408.

St Petrock's church has a lovely position, near the castle, overlooking the river Dart.

DITTISHAM. St George's is beautifully situated above the river Dart. It has a tall Perp tower with a prominent stair-turret, and most of the church is Perp. The S porch is vaulted. Norm font. Much of the original rood-screen remains, and the later parclose screens. The medieval stone pulpit is, however, the real delight. It is perfectly proportioned on a slender stem and it is beautifully coloured. It retains all its original figures under canopies.

DODDISCOMBSLEIGH. St Michael's is a typical Devon Perp church with a tower, having an odd arrangement of its buttresses. It is for the medieval glass that the visitor comes here. In the N windows are some saints, St Christopher, St Michael and St Peter, and the Trinity in which the Three Persons are crowned. The real treasure is, however, the window showing the Seven Sacraments, for it is the only one in England remaining complete on that subject. Even so the figure of Christ is modern (but such a medieval figure can be seen not far away at Cadbury). Blood streams issue from the Wounds of Christ to each Sacrament, which are charming little scenes. The bedroom scene in Extreme Unction is particularly attractive. In the side light is the Eucharist, Matrimony, Confirmation: in the centre light, the figure of Christ with Confession below, and in the other side light Ordination, Baptism and Extreme Unction.

Do find *Dunchideock*'s beautifully set church of St Michael and All Angels, to see a lovely Devon screen, medieval bench-ends and the 18th century monument of Stringer Lawrence.

EXETER. In a picturesque setting at the foot of a steep hill is St Mary Steps. The small red sandstone tower has its clock of early 16th C date with three jacks above. The quarter-jacks hold a pike in one hand and in the other hand a hammer with which they strike the bell under the little platform on which each stands. The central figure, obviously more elderly, remains seated and he has a rigid rod in his hands; all he can do is to nod his head at each stroke of the hour. There are fine coloured ceiled wagon roofs and a beautiful rood-screen with painted panels of the Apostles, the Latin Doctors, St Blaise and other saints. The font is Norman.

Do take time to explore not only the cathedral but also the eight charming medieval city churches – some of them small and very red and all of them with delightful characters. Of the later churches St David's, by W. D. Caroe (1897–1900) is a magnificent and stately building, with a dominating north-east tower, and is considered by several people to be the finest 19th century church in the county.

85

Sabine Baring – Gould's beautiful church at Lewtrenchard – so very typical of Devon's smaller churches.

HARBERTON. St Andrew's has a tall tower with a prominent mid-stair turret. The S porch is vaulted and the interior is typical of Devon. The rood-screen panels have new paintings. The medieval coloured stone pulpit with a number of canopies is one of the finest anywhere: the figures in white are 17th C. The font is Norm.

HARTLAND. The village is situated near Hartland Point, the N.W. tip of the county with its grand coastal scenery. The tall Perp tower of St Nectan's, with prominent pinnacles, is 144 ft high and the highest in Devon, a landmark for shipping. It has its original figure of St Nectan on its E side. There is a tall tower arch into the church. The church is mainly 14th C and has a variety of wagon roofs. The coloured rood-screen is one of the finest in the county. The highly decorated font is Norm. The Perp tomb-chest came from Hartland Abbey.

HONEYCHURCH. (Now part of Sampford Courtenay). The name says everything! St Mary's is tiny, remote, rural, rustic and thoroughly adorable. In this county of grand Perp churches, how lovely to enjoy a taste of 'small is beautiful'. A little Norman church with a Norman font and two fascinating Norman carved heads. A fine old door admits us to one of those interiors which time has mellowed and which people have never bothered to 'improve'. It oozes antiquity and atmosphere and amongst its treasures are simple medieval benches (some made into box-pews), 17th century rails and font-cover and an Elizabethan pulpit. A little unknown church which is one of the most memorable of all.

Sampford Courtenay St Andrew's church has a fine tower and roofs and a Norman font.

IPPLEPEN. St Andrew's has a tall Perp tower with mid-stair turret and the whole church is embattled. There is a small Norm doorway on the N side, otherwise all is Perp. Perp font, and a coloured Perp rood-screen with figures of the Apostles and prophets. The medieval wood pulpit is also coloured.

KENN. A typical Devon church with a Devon tower, St Andrew's is all red sandstone and embattled. Almost completely Perp, it has a Norm font and some old bench-ends with tracery. It is, however, the rood-screen that will be particularly noticed. The beautifully painted panels show the Apostles, the Evangelists, the Latin Doctors, and St Sebastian, St Roche, St Francis, St Hubert, St Barbara, St Mary of Egypt (very rare), St Genevieve, and other saints.

KENTON.   A large Perp church, All Saints' is all of one piece. A tall tower, two-storeyed S porch embattled, and embattled aisles. The beautiful restored coloured wooden pulpit has modern paintings of West Country saints Boniface, Walburga, Aldhelm, Sidwell and Petrock. The fine medieval rood-screen still retains its original painted panels of the saints, Apostles and prophets, St Agnes, St Cecilia, St Anthony, St George, St Lawrence, St Barbara, St Stephen, and other saints. The rood-loft above is modern. Mon to Dulcebella Hodges 1628.

LAPFORD.   The tower of St Thomas of Canterbury's seems different from most Devon towers as it lacks pinnacles. The S doorway is Norm, with an old door, otherwise it is mostly Perp. Wagon roofs and a particularly rich celure above the rood-screen, the latter being one of the grandest anywhere. It has Renaissance details between the ribs of the vaulting, and a complete cornice with four strips of carving and cresting. There are numerous medieval bench-ends with profile heads and Renaissance ornament, also a figure with a scourge and another one shows heart, feet and hands to symbolise Christ's Passion.

   Do discover tiny and remote St Bartholomew's *Nymet Rowland*, with its Norman font, its old bench-ends and its rare wooden arcade.

MOLLAND.   St Mary's tower also lacks pinnacles, but the visitor comes here for the interior of the church. Old wagon roofs and furnishings, with box-pews and a three-decker pulpit with tester. Above the screen are wooden boards upon which are painted the Royal Arms and Ten Commandments. The altar-rails are of about the 17th or 18th C (and all left alone by the Victorians). The font, however, as so often is Norm. The 15th C capitals of the arcade have typical W Country foliage of large leaves. Carving of foliage on capitals in the Perp period is almost confined to the West Country. Some of the windows are very homely. There are some epitaphs to the Courtenay family.

OTTERY ST MARY.   St Mary's is one of England's greatest churches. The two towers at the ends of the transepts are Norm and are similar to those at Exeter Cathedral. The N tower has in addition a small lead spire. The remainder of the church is almost entirely 14th C, the window tracery being graduated lancets. The vaults are noteworthy and of great variety. In the chancel the curvilinear spirit of the 14th C has entered into the vault. The vaults elsewhere in the church consist of straight lines forming crosses and stars. The ribs are beautifully coloured. The bosses of the vault in the Lady Chapel deserve notice – Bishop Grandisson, St John the Baptist, St Anne and the Virgin, the Annunciation, the Virgin and Child, the Assumption, the Coronation of the

Virgin, and the Last Judgment. A 14th C reredos, restored, and sedilia in the chancel (as also in the Lady Chapel). Some 14th C stalls with misericords in the Lady Chapel. The 14th C parclose screens of wood remain (and are early examples). The S porch is 16th C and also the lovely Dorset aisle with its fine Perp window and beautiful fan-vault with remarkable pendants: three are straight but one is of spiral form. There is a 14th C clock and a 14th C wooden eagle lectern, coloured and gilded (one of the earliest and there are only about 20 in England).

PAIGNTON. A popular seaside resort and a large red sandstone church with a big tower. The re-set W portal shows some Norm work (red sandstone and white Beer stone), there is a little EE and a 14th C S porch and door, otherwise all is Perp. The great interest of this church of St John the Baptist is the Kirkham Chantry. The screen consists of two Tudor arched openings with tomb-chests, each with two effigies. All openings are fan-vaulted with pendants. The sides of the tomb-chests have mourners. At the heads of the effigies are reliefs of the Visitation and St Anne, and the Mass of St Gregory, with angels and Instruments of the Passion. There are statuettes surrounding the door of the chantry. A Norm font of red sandstone and a medieval pulpit of stone with a rood group under canopies. A roof boss in the nave shows three rabbits sharing three ears between them, yet each rabbit has two. In the Kirkham Chapel are two kneeling figures facing each other (in addition to those mentioned above). There is also a cadaver in a recess.

PARRACOMBE. Fortunately the church is away from the village, which is why the Victorians built a new church in the village and left the old church of St Petrock alone! There is an early medieval tower, a 13th C chancel and a Perp nave, but the charm of the church is inside, where all remains as it was in the 18th C – a screen with tympanum above painted with the Royal Arms, the Ten Commandments, Creed and Lord's Prayer. There is an old three-decker pulpit with tester, plain 16th C pews, and 18th C box-pews, and even the hat-pegs remain. Norm font. The church is vested in the Redundant Churches Fund.

PILTON. In this suburb of Barnstaple, St Mary's tower, rebuilt in 1696, is on the N side of the church towards the E (not uncommon round here). The stair-turret has a spirelet. This part of the church is its earliest and it was part of the former Benedictine priory. The beautifully coloured 16th C font-cover is suspended from a backpiece and tester with Renaissance details. A medieval stone pulpit, as always beautifully proportioned: an arm of sheet-iron protrudes from it holding an hour-glass. Here is one of the grand Devon medieval coloured rood-screens and a parclose screen. Elizabethan altar-rails. Mons to Sir John Chichester 1569, no figures, and Sir Robert Chichester 1627 with life-size kneeling figures.

The lovely town of *Barnstaple* has a medieval church of St Peter and St Paul, with a 17th century lead-covered spire, old wagon roofs and several 17th century monuments. Holy Trinity church, with its tall and impressive tower, is mostly by William White (1867).

PLYMTREE. St John the Baptist's tower is Perp and so is much of the church. An interior like this one with rood-screen, square-headed bench-ends, 15th C carved foliage on capitals, and wagon roofs can only be in Devon. Perp font and 18th C pulpit. The great glory is of course the medieval rood-screen, well preserved with many painted panels of saints including the Annunciation, the Magi, St Catherine, St Roche, St Margaret, St John the Baptist, St Mary Magdalene, St Dorothy, St Michael, St Sidwell, St Sebastian, St Helen and other saints. A number of bench-ends with tracery, and 17th C altar-rails.

SWIMBRIDGE. The tower is the oldest part (lacking windows as usual) and covered by a fine lead broach spire. Otherwise St James' is mostly Perp. The interior has almost its complete medieval furnishings. The capitals of the arcades have 15th C foliage, sometimes with figures in them. There is variety in the wagon roofs with bosses, and the rood-celures are particularly elaborate with blue colour and gold stars. The font is completely enclosed in a 17th C wood casing with Renaissance carvings: above it is a canopy with stars on the ceiling. The stone pulpit is medieval with figures of the four Evangelists. The medieval rood-screen is one of the finest even in Devon, the panels with carved leaf-scrolls instead of painted panels. Where the screen crosses the arcade an opening is left for a side-altar and above it is a curved coving also with leaf-panels.

TAWSTOCK. Anyone interested in church monuments will come here to St Peter's. The church is situated in the grounds of and below Tawstock Court. The top of the central tower is Perp (a central tower is rare round here), and much else is Dec. The wagon roofs should be noted. The rood-screen and parclose screens are of an unusual type. The family pew is completely panelled and ceiled. The sun-dial on the S porch is of 1757, and the hour-glass is held in an arm of sheet-iron attached to the pulpit. Mons to a lady of the 14th C in wood; Frances Lady Fitzwarren, recumbent, 1589; Sir John Wray 1597, kneeling figures; Thomas Hinson and wife 1614, kneeling figures facing each other; William Bourchier, 3rd Earl of Bath 1623, recumbent figures (note the figures at the feet) and four children below (the little girl in pink is particularly attractive) and all beautifully coloured with coats of arms. This is one of the finest monuments anywhere. Also Mary St John 1631, kneeling figure; William Skippon 1633, kneeling figures; Henry Bourchier, 5th Earl of Bath 1680, four seated dogs supporting the sarcophagus; and Lady Rachel Fane, wife of the 5th Earl of Bath, 1680, a standing figure in white marble.

TIVERTON.   St Peter's has a tall Perp red sandstone tower. There are gargoyles and grotesques everywhere. A limestone S porch and S aisle are decorated lavishly with the ships, woolpacks etc which brought the Tiverton merchants their wealth, John Greenway being the richest, and he was responsible for the S porch and the aisle adjoining. The S porch has coats of arms under canopies, of the Duchess of Devon, daughter of Edward IV, the Drapers Company and Greenway. Inside the porch is a vault and above the inner doorway are figures of the Assumption, flanked by the kneeling donor and his wife. At the top of all this lavish work on the aisle, and to complete it, are 21 little scenes from the life of Christ (to identify these, the photographs inside the church will be a great help). The date of this Greenway work is 1517 and it has recently been beautifully cleaned and restored.

TORBRYAN.   Holy Trinity (RCF) has a tower with a mid stair-turret, a S porch with a fan-vault, and a Jac font-cover. The pulpit has some old coloured wooden panels. Coloured rood-screen with painted panels: St Victor, St Margaret, St Lawrence, the Coronation of the Virgin, the four Evangelists, Apostles, St Dorothy, St Vincent, St Helen, St Catherine of Siena and other saints.

TORQUAY.   The old church of St Saviour at Tor has been much Victorianised, but has interesting monuments. Of the 19th century churches St John's (by G. E. and A. E. Street) with its bold 140 ft saddleback tower, its William Morris glass and its handsome interior, has a prominent and elevated position. All Saints' is by Pearson and has his usual dignity and fine proportions. All Saints' Babbacombe is by Butterfield and is a very original and enjoyable example of his work. St Marychurch (by Hugall, 1852–61) is a large and splendid church with a 137 ft tower, which has been wonderfully rebuilt after war damage. It has a beautifully carved Norman font and a spacious, colourful and devotional interior. Tourists flock to the pretty nearby village of *Cockington* to see its charming and delightfully set Perp church, which has a fine pulpit, also a medieval screen, stalls and some glass showing saints.

TOTNES. St Mary's is a beautiful Perp red sandstone church with a fine tower (120 ft) with prominent pinnacles, mid stair-turret and niches with figures. The S porch has ribs and bosses and its original S door. Wagon roofs, but the most notable feature is the fine stone screen which runs right across the church and also provides two parclose screens for the side chapels. The rood-stairs survive. Perp font and pulpit of stone.

WEMBURY. What could be a finer setting for any church? St Werburgh's faces the open sea and its tower lines up with Great Mew Stone. It is 14th and 15th C with two fine monuments. On that to Sir John Hele and family 1608, he is propped up on one elbow and below and in front of him is his wife with their little daughter in a chair; there are kneeling figures of the other children. The other monument is to Lady Narborough 1678. The sarcophagus is supported by four white lions, and on it kneels the small figure of the deceased.

WIDECOMBE. In this popular beauty spot surrounded by Dartmoor, St Pancras' church has a magnificent Perp Devon tower with prominent pinnacles. The arcades are of granite. The base of the screen remains, with painted figures of the Apostles, Latin Doctors and other saints. There are also paintings of Moses and Aaron. The interior is surprisingly spacious and is tastefully adorned. Do look up to the roof with its carved bosses – especially the one with the three rabbits.

WOLBOROUGH. St Mary's is the Mother Church of Newton Abbot. A somewhat plain tower and all is mostly Perp. It is, however, for its interior that it is notable. The arcades show the West Country 15th C foliage to perfection. Norm font. The 15th C rood-screen and parclose screens round the side chapels are show-pieces and are brightly coloured in red, green and gold. There are over 60 panels of painted figures, including the Apostles, St Ursula, St Helen, St Sidwell, St Catherine, St Dorothy, St Cosmas and St Damian, St Adrian, St Leger, St Victor and other saints. The brass eagle lectern is 15th C. Mon to Sir Richard Reynell 1634 with his wife and daughter and baby, also figures of Justice and Time.

St Luke's church *Milber* is one of the most interesting 'modern' churches anywhere. It is an exciting and devotional building, and its very original design is believed to have been revealed to its priest, the Rev W. Keble Martin, in a dream. It grew between 1931 and 1963.

DORSET

For a south coast county, Dorset really is incredibly unspoilt and surprisingly undiscovered. The scenery here is glorious, with the Purbeck Hills, the Vales of Blackmore and Marshwood and the chalk downlands in the county's heart. And what a fascinating coastline with Chesil Beach, Lulworth Cove, Portland Bill and other remarkable features. Dorset is still very rural, with many small villages and small and homely churches (about 200 medieval ones), also a good selection of stone manor houses. It has its very own Purbeck stone (which becomes Purbeck marble when polished and is seen in fonts in many parts of England) and Portland stone, which was used so much in the 17th and 18th centuries, especially in London. Dorset towns are full of character and interest, as at Sherborne, Shaftesbury, Dorchester and Wareham, and even some of its seaside resorts, like Swanage and Weymouth, have preserved their historic atmosphere.

Dorset churches are rich in variety and interest and there are good examples of all periods of architecture – Saxon at Wareham St Martin and Canford Magna, Norman at Studland, EE at Whitchurch Canonicorum, Dec at Milton Abbey and Perp at majestic Sherborne, in fine towers such as Beaminster and Bradford Abbas and in a host of features throughout the county. There are several noteworthy 17th and 18th century churches, like Folke (1628 and Gothic), Portland St George and Blandford Forum. The 19th century is represented in some lovely village churches, like Cattistock, Kingston and Bryanston. For a real 19th century feast, we must go to the Bournemouth and Poole area, which must be second only to Brighton for the quality and variety of Victorian and later church architecture.

ABBOTSBURY. St Nicholas' has a Dec N porch and N aisle, otherwise all is Perp or 17th C. The E part of the nave roof has a decorated plaster tunnel-vault. Perp font, reredos of 1751, Jac pulpit and tester, and a W gallery of 1808. There is a carving of the Trinity over the W door, and the Crucifixion over the N door. Also the figure of an abbot in a chasuble, early 13th C. The abbey tithe barn and St Catherine's Chapel on its hill are also well worth a visit.

Portisham church is worth seeing, also Holy Trinity *Swyre* (brasses) and St Mary's *Puncknowle* (memorials and Norman font).

BEAMINSTER. St Mary's Perp tower is the finest in the county, with its pinnacles, niches, and display of sculpture. The church is all about the same date. There is a 13th C font, a Jac pulpit and mons to Thomas Strode, Serjeant-at-Law 1698, and George Strode and wife, 1753.

BERE REGIS. Known to readers of Thomas Hardy as Kingsbere. The church of St John the Baptist is late 12th C and later, with the usual Perp tower, here with stone and flint chequer work. The roof is one of the finest anywhere. It appears to be hammerbeam, but it is in reality tie-beam, with huge bosses and large figures of the Twelve Apostles, all beautifully coloured. St Peter in a mitre has a key, and St James looks like a fire-watcher in the Second World War in a dressing-gown and steel helmet with a stirrup-pump! The font is Norm with intersecting arches. Against the back wall of a mon are brasses to John Skerne and family 1596. The S chapel is the Turberville Chapel, a family also known to readers of Thomas Hardy.

BLANDFORD FORUM. A great Georgian church (1733–9), St Peter and St Paul's was created by the local architects and builders, who rejoiced in the names of John and William Bastard! Inside, mighty classical columns of Portland stone rise to a vaulted ceiling. The galleries, reredos, font and cover, box-pews and most of the furnishings here, also the special seat for the Mayor, are original and unaltered. The Bastards almost certainly created the delightful Classical church of St Mary at *Charlton Marshall* (1713), which also has fine furnishings, especially the very handsome reredos. Set near *Bryanston* School is the 'old' church of 1745 (Classical and delightful) and the 'new' church of St Martin by E.P. Warren (1895–8) which is remarkably stately and ambitious.

BOURNEMOUTH AND POOLE. The 202 ft spire of G.E. Street's St Peter's beckons us to the mighty and majestic main church of Bournemouth, which is Dec and has so much to enthral us. Not very far away are the towering walls and turrets of Pearson's stately vaulted EE St Stephen's, with its colourful and cathedral-like Anglo-Catholic interior. J.D. Sedding designed St Clement's *Boscombe*, with its magnificent tower and glorious interior. St Alban's is by Fellowes Prynne, St Ambrose's by Hodgson Fowler, St Michael's (what a tower here) and St Swithun's by Norman Shaw – and this line-up of architects gives only a taster of some of the larger churches. We have Butterfield at St Augustine's, Sir Charles Nicholson at St Mary's, and St Francis *Charminster* must be one of the most memorable Italianate churches which 20th century

England produced. Towards Poole we find Bodley's lovely church of St Aldhelm's *Branksome*, Pearson's splendid St Peter's *Parkstone* and the amazing Byzantine church of St Osmund Parkstone (1913–16) by E.S. Prior. There are many other churches – and it appears that most of them were built with absolutely no expense spared.

BRADFORD ABBAS.   St Mary's has the usual fine Perp tower with a number of niches. The church is also mainly of that period. The roofs should be noted. The rood-screen is rather unusual, being of stone. Perp font with figures, a Jac pulpit and some linenfold bench-ends.

A trip northwards is worthwhile, to St Michael's *Over Compton* (Perp, with good Jacobean pulpit and Goodden memorials), St Nicholas' *Nether Compton* (another fine pulpit, also benches and stone screen), and St Andrew's *Trent* (a treasure house with so much to see – spire, wonderful screen, pulpit, lectern, font-cover, bench-ends and monuments).

CERNE ABBAS.   A fine Perp tower with a figure of St Mary, and a higher stair-turret. The church is mainly of that date with a 13th C chancel, but has a Perp E window with 15th C shields. The interior has been beautifully restored. There is a medieval stone rood-screen, Jac altar-rails and pulpit with tester, and some wall-paintings in the chancel. Don't miss the abbey gateway at Abbey Farm, the 14th C tithe barn, and the Cerne Giant cut in the downs, possibly about AD 190.

CHALBURY.   All Saints' is a little gem. The three medieval periods can be traced, but it is the 18th C that predominates in its charming white-washed interior – the baluster font, the three-decker pulpit, the squire's pew, box-pews and W gallery. How fortunate the Victorians didn't know about it!

Horton St Wolfreda's is a fascinating 18th century church, full of beautiful things. *Hinton Martell* St John the Evangelist (mostly rebuilt 1870) is a much loved Anglo-Catholic shrine.

CHARMINSTER.   As usual, it is the Perp tower that is all important. It has double belfry windows under square hood-moulds and triplets of pinnacles at the corners. The stylised T's inside and outside refer to Sir Thomas Trenchard who built the tower early in the 16th C. Amongst the Perp windows of St Mary's clerestory are four Norm ones, and late Norm work seems to predominate inside. The chancel is modern. Jac pulpit. There are two Purbeck marble mons without figures, and a kneeling figure of Grace Pole, 1636.

95

Dorchester's church of St Peter is Perp, with much to see and *Fordington St George* has a fine tower, a 16th century pulpit and much else.

CHRISTCHURCH. At Holy Trinity church, of Christchurch Priory, broadly speaking, Norm and EE covers the earlier work. Outside, the N transept is the showpiece. The N porch is also splendid and is 13th C. Fourteenth C work (as often around here) is almost non-existent (except for the reredos), but Perp gives the lovely tower. It has double belfry windows, battlements and pinnacles and its original figure in a niche. The E parts are also Perp – the chancel and Lady Chapel. The latter has large windows and a curious upper chamber. There are three crypts, all rib-vaulted and before 1100. A lierne-vault covers the chancel.

The chancel reredos is one of the finest pieces of Dec sculpture in England. There are seated figures of Daniel and Solomon with Jesse reclining between them. In the tier above is the Adoration of the Magi. The stalls, in two tiers, are 16th C and have a full set of misericords – jesters and tumblers seem to be the favourites. They also show a rabbit warren, bat, ape, greyhound and eagle, a man with an axe, a fox wearing a cowl, and a pair of fishes.

MELBURY BUBB. A charming group of church, cottages and manor house in lovely country. St Mary's has a small Perp tower on the S side and most of the remainder is modern, but visitors come to see the font and old glass. The former is amazing: it is a Sax cross-shaft turned upside down. If you stand on your head, you will see that the animals on it then make sense! The good 15th C glass is in two N windows – the Annunciation, Christ showing His Wounds, and the Sacrament of Ordination.

Melbury Sampford church is near the great house in the park. It has one of the finest collections of monuments in Dorset, whilst St Edwold's *Stockwood* (RCF) is tiny (30 ft by 12 ft 8 inches) and enchanting.

MILTON ABBAS. Milton Abbey is a great church with chancel, transepts and central tower. The nave was never built. The E half is Dec and the grand tower Perp. Both transepts have lierne-vaults – the large S window 14th C Flowing, and the N window Perp. In the chancel is a reredos, a wall of niches with canopies, and a wooden pyx tabernacle with spire (the only other being at Wells). The sedilia are typically Dec. The pulpitum is a solid wall of the 14th C. The stalls are partly original and there are some misericords. The font is modern with two large angels. The two painted panels of King Athelstan and Queen Egwyma come from a 15th C screen. Mons to Sir John Tregonwell 1565, with a brass, Mary Bancks 1704, and Lady Milton and her husband (who built the house) 1775.

Milton Abbas village church of St James was built in 1786 and extended in 1889. It is set in a picture postcard village. St Mary's *Winterborne Whitechurch* has a Perp pulpit and All Saints *Hilton* has a grand Perp north aisle, well worth seeing.

PUDDLETOWN.   The lower part of St Mary's tower is 14th C and the upper part with pinnacles Perp, as indeed is most of this charming church. The chancel is modern. Note the roof of the nave. The Norm font has a Jac cover. There is a 17th C W gallery, pulpit with tester, box-pews, altar-rails (three-sided) and some bold painted inscriptions. Mons include a cross-legged knight and his lady of 1300, a 14th C knight, two recumbent figures 1470, an alabaster figure 1420, and many 17th C tablets. Brasses to Roger Cheverell 1517, Christopher Martyn 1524, kneeling with Trinity above, and Nicholas Martyn and family, kneeling figures, 1595.

Tolpuddle, Affpuddle, Piddlehinton and *Piddletrenthide* have irresistible names and lovely churches – all worth seeing.

SHERBORNE ABBEY.   This great church of St Mary has minor early work (Sax at the NW corner and Norm N & S crossing arches and S doorway with a 14th C one set in it), but the church was almost entirely encased in the Perp style. The fine central tower and the fan-vaults with bosses throughout are superb, and there are several lierne-vaults also with bosses. The large Perp clerestory windows are splendid. The stalls are Victorian, but have their old misericords – a man whipping a boy, a woman beating a man, the Last Judgment, a hen hanging a fox, a chained monkey, an archer, and some others. Laurence Whistler glass can be seen in the Lady Chapel. There are many mons and tablets, but note Sir John Horsey and son, 1564; John Leweston and wife 1584; and John Digby, Earl of Bristol and two wives, 1698.

Folke (three miles south-east) has a little gem of a church, St Lawrence's, beside its manor house – a period-piece of 1638, furnishings as well!

STUDLAND.   St Nicholas' is a perfect complete Norm church (but one should take away some of its windows and the S porch). A sturdy central tower, a corbel-table of faces etc along the walls of the nave, and N and S doorways with tympana. The tower space and chancel have rib-vaults.

WAREHAM. The Sax work in St Martin's is seen in long-and-short work at the NE and SE angles of the chancel and the NE angle of the nave, and the chancel arch. The tower on the S side with a saddleback roof is 16th C. Mon by Eric Kennington to T.E. Lawrence of Arabia, 1935. Lady St Mary church is also worth a visit. A lovely interior, but the nave very much altered, a beautiful 14th C E window and a Norm lead font.

WHITCHURCH CANONICORUM. St Candida's (or Wite) is nearly all EE. The S doorway is however Norm and the S porch Perp. The arcades are EE with stiff-leaf foliage and trumpet-scallop capitals. The fine tower has eight pinnacles and is Perp. Norm font with intersecting arches, 16th C stalls (French), and a Jac pulpit. There is also the shrine of St Candida (very rare). Mon to Sir John Jeffery, 1611.

WHITCOMBE. A perfect rural setting for this small Dorset church (RCF) – simple but yet so unspoilt, with a Norman nave, EE chancel and pretty Perp tower. Inside are parts of a Saxon cross-shaft, a 13th century font of Purbeck marble and a superb wall-painting of St Christopher. William Barnes, the 19th century Dorset poet and writer, preached here, also at nearby *Winterborne Came* (RCF) where (having first found St Peter's church, near the great house) we may admire a 16th century

So many of the smaller churches here are so appealing and unspoilt, as we see here at Whitcombe.

screen, a pulpit of 1624 and monuments to the Miller family. In *West Stafford* St Andrew's church are a roof and furnishings dating from 1640, when the church was restored.

WIMBORNE MINSTER. St Cuthberga's two towers will be noted, the central one Norm and the W one Perp, with a clock-jack on the N side and a sundial dated 1636 on the S side. Norm crossing arches and Norm nave. At the E end it is mainly 13th C, but the piscina and sedilia are Dec. The sacristy has the famous Chained Library of c1350. The old clock of the 14th C also remains. The stalls are of 1610. A Flemish Jesse Tree glass is in the middle of the E window. Brass eagle lectern 1623, and a Norm font. There is a dug-out chest and another one with six locks.

WIMBORNE ST GILES. A delightful village setting, with the green, the almshouses and the bold Classical church (it was rebuilt in 1732), with its sturdy tower. After a fire in 1908, Comper refurbished the interior, which is full of beauty, colour and atmosphere. He designed the tall screen, the reredos, the pulpit, seating, font-cover, most of the glass and several other fittings. Amongst the monuments to be enjoyed here is the superb tomb of Sir Anthony Ashley (1627).

WINTERBORNE TOMSON. Situated in a farmyard, what a contrast to Sherborne Abbey and Wimborne Minster, but St Andrew's (RCF) can hold its own. The nave and chancel are in one with an apse at the E end. It is all Norm, with a charming little bell-turret. Inside are all its 18th C fittings – pulpit with tester, box-pews, altar-rails, and W gallery. The front of the latter may well be the original rood-loft. Perp font. A charming plastered wagon roof whose arches include the apse.

There are ten Winterborne churches, plus two Winterbourne churches. Try discovering the lot!

WORTH MATRAVERS. St Nicholas' is another complete Norm church – the corbel-table round the nave and chancel proves that. The tower and chancel arch follow suit and also the S doorway with a worn tympanum of the Coronation of the Virgin. The E window is Dec.

Kingston has a wonderful church of St James of 1873–80 by G.E. Street, with a bold central tower which is a landmark for miles, and a fine High Victorian interior. It really dominates its surroundings. Further north is St Edward's *Corfe Castle*, much rebuilt by T.H. Wyatt and containing lovely furnishings by Martin Travers.

DURHAM AND
TYNE AND WEAR

There are less than 70 medieval churches in this little-explored county, the western part of which is predominantly moorland and much of that which is most travelled through is punctuated by pit-heaps and the remains of closed mines. Yet the countryside here has so much to offer – lovely rolling hills and beautiful valleys, also fascinating towns like Barnard Castle and Bishop Auckland, and the wonderful city of Durham, with the incomparable setting of its splendid cathedral, above a dramatic gorge of the river Wear.

For the church enthusiast it is an important county, with its wealth of Saxon work in early churches and the remains of Saxon crosses. We must however go into the north-east of the county (now Tyne & Wear) in order to see the wonderful Saxon churches of Jarrow and Monkwearmouth and thus to tread in the footsteps of St Benedict Biscop and the Venerable Bede. It is also worthwhile crossing the Tyne to enjoy the city of Newcastle, with its fascinating stretch of river, its Perp cathedral and interesting churches.

COUNTY DURHAM

BRANCEPETH. St Brandon's is in the grounds of the castle. The tower is Norm below, and then EE with pointed twin windows. The nave arcades are also EE, but heightened by the Perp clerestory. The transepts are also EE. In the 14th C some Dec windows have been added with Flowing tracery. The chancel is Perp, the nave roof is 15th C and the chancel roof 17th C, both the latter having bosses. The N porch is in Jac style. The person responsible for the porch and for all the glorious woodwork of that time was John Cosin, rector from 1626, and Bishop of Durham in 1660. It was Gothic Revival in the middle of the 17th C. His earlier work is seen in the pews, pulpit with tester, and roof, and later, more sumptuous in the font-cover with a spire, rood-screen (richest of all), choir stalls, and family pews. The Communion table and altar-rails are also 17th C. There is a fine Flemish chest with tracery and monsters, and a defaced figure of Christ on a chancel buttress. Mons to Robert Neville, cross-legged 1319, and to Ralph Neville, 2nd Earl of Westmorland and his wife 1484, of wood. Brasses to Thomas Claxton, knight 1403, and Richard Drax, demi-figure of a priest 1456, with symbols of the four Evangelists at the corners.

CHESTER-le-STREET. St Mary and St Cuthbert's tower and spire will be the most remembered – the tower is EE and it has an octagon and spire of c1400. The W end of the N aisle was replaced by an Anker House with a curious window on the street and a squint into the church. The piscina and sedilia in the chancel are EE. There is a 15th C font, a Roman inscription, and fragments of Sax carving and cross-shafts remain. There is a brass, Alice Lambton 1434, and an effigy of a priest 1300. There are also 14 effigies of the Lumley family placed against the wall of the N aisle. To fit them in, sometimes the feet had to be cut off. From the E, the third, fourth and tenth are 14th C and the remainder are mostly Elizabethan.

DARLINGTON. St Cuthbert's is an almost complete EE church, with central tower (rebuilt) and many lancet windows. The piscina and sedilia are a little later in the chancel (also rebuilt). There is a fine W doorway. The stone rood-screen is later 14th C, and the Easter Sepulchre and stalls with poppyheads and misericords, one showing the Flight of Alexander, are the only Perp additions. The spire-like font-cover is 17th C, of Cosin style. A female effigy is late 13th C.

Do find St Andrew's *Haughton le Skerne* (to the north-east) and enjoy a lovely medieval church in a delightful village, where Bishop Cosin refurnished the interior in the 17th century, leaving us much to admire and enjoy.

DURHAM. A city not to be missed and never to be forgotten, with its castle and Norman cathedral set high on the rock, also its five medieval churches. St Giles' has a good position, also Norman and EE work for us to see and the wooden effigy of John Heath (c1591). More Norman work awaits us in St Margaret's and late 12th century work at St Oswald's, where the west window (1864) is by Ford Madox Brown. St Mary le Bow was rebuilt in 1685 and is equipped with fine furnishings (including a screen of 1707) in the Bishop Cosin tradition. J. Pritchett's 1857 church of St Nicholas, with its tall spire, stands nobly across the Market Place.

ESCOMBE. This small church will never be forgotten by those who visit it. St John the Evangelist's is completely Sax of about the 7th C.

Here is one of the County's gems, at Staindrop – beautifully set, and containing so much to delight us.

Long-and-short work can be seen at the angles, and by the chancel arch.

Bishop Auckland has two medieval churches – the substantial St Andrew's and the small St Helen's, both with 13th century work of interest.

LANCHESTER.   All Saints' has splendid examples of Norm and EE. Of the former, note the chancel arch, nave, and S doorway. It is EE in the chancel with lancets, a small carving of Christ seated, and corbel-heads. The tower is early Perp (with a vault) as is the clerestory and nave roof. Note the medieval stalls and Jac altar-rails. There is a Roman altar in the porch. There are three fine pieces of 13th C glass – the Flight into Egypt, Annunciation to the Shepherds, and the Adoration of the Magi. Also a 14th C figure of a priest holding a chalice.

SEDGEFIELD.   St Edmund of Canterbury's tower is Perp, with prominent pinnacles. The nave is EE with fine stiff-leaf carving on the capitals of the arcades. Some window tracery is Dec with Flowing tracery, rare in this county. The 17th C woodwork by Bishop Cosin is notable – rood-screen, stalls and panelling. The organ-case and font are slightly later. A brass of 1630 shows the skeletons of husband and wife bundled up in shrouds.

STAINDROP. There was a Sax church here, as proved by the walls of the nave above the arches. Then comes the tower up to the corbel-table, Norm, completed in Perp times. Mid-13th C is St Mary's N transept and chancel with its excellent sedilia with stiff-leaf capitals. Perp also the clerestory, nave roof, screen, font and stalls. The Communion table is 17th C. There is an ironbound chest, and the S aisle has some splendid gargoyles. Mons are numerous: the 13th C effigy of a lady; Ralph Neville, Earl of Westmorland and two wives 1425; Henry Neville, 5th Earl of Westmorland, 1564, of oak; John Lee, 1792, with bust; Henry, 2nd Earl of Darlington, 1792, and also a few later ones.

TYNE and WEAR

CULLERCOATES. One of J.L. Pearson's noble and dignified churches, built in 1884. St George's is stone faced, stone vaulted and has a splendid tower and spire. The east end terminates in an apse and in its high-set windows we admire glass by C.E. Kempe.

HOUGHTON-le-SPRING. That there was a Norm church is proved by one window on the N of the chancel, and a doorway with a tympanum near it. Most of St Michael and All Angels is 13th C – note the lancets. There are, however, some large windows of the next century with interesting tracery. The top of the central tower is 19th C. Mons include a cross-legged knight with his helmet covering his face, 13th C, another cross-legged knight of c1300, and Bernard Gill, rector, 1583, but no figure. Brass to Margery Belassis with kneeling figures 1587. The detached chapel is the Chapel of the Guild of Holy Trinity, late 15th C.

JARROW. St Paul's was founded by Benedict Biscop in AD 684. The dedication inscription still remains. The tower and chancel with windows and doorways are that church. Tall and narrow, it is typically Sax. Some Dec windows have been inserted. The Saxon tower is now central and the present nave is 19th C. There are some pieces of cross-shafts. There are stalls with poppyheads and a chair called Bede's Chair but this is 14th C.

MONKWEARMOUTH. The monastery here was founded by Benedict Biscop in AD 675. The W porch of St Peter's (with a tunnel-vault) and the tower above it, 9th C, is that church. Tall and narrow nave and 14th C. chancel.

NEWCASTLE.   The parish church of St Nicholas, with its distinctive crown-like spire, became the cathedral in 1882. St Andrew's church has a fine Norman chancel arch and arcades, also a 15th century font-cover. Another fine font-cover may be seen in St John's, also a grand 17th century pulpit. This is an appealing church, with a devotional interior, with 20th century furnishings by Sir Charles Nicholson and S.E. Dykes Bower. All Saints' is a singular and impressive Classical church of 1786–96, by David Stephenson. It is oval in shape, with a tall tower on the south side, which is quite a feature of the Newcastle townscape. Although now it serves a new and useful purpose outside parochial life, it deserves a visit.

SUNDERLAND.   Holy Trinity (RCF) is a large Classical church of 1719, with an unusual apse (with a Venetian window) of 1735. The western screen is equipped with seats for churchwardens etc, the font has an elaborate and beautiful cover and great Corinthian columns support the nave roof. There is much to see here, not least the Rev Robert Gray's memorial in the west porch (1838) showing him in gown and bands, sermon in hand.

St Andrew's *Roker* is a superb Edwardian church (E.S. Prior, 1906–7) – refreshingly original in design and a showplace for lovely Arts and Crafts decoration and furnishings, including works by Ernest Gimson, Eric Gill and Morris & Co. Everything here is of the highest quality and in its own way it is a premier church.

ESSEX

There is never a dull moment for the lover of scenery or for the lover of churches who comes to this county of many facets. The coastline is delightful, with marshes, creeks and estuaries, there is the beautiful Constable country around the Stour valley in the north, the hill-country in the far north-west, the rural Hertfordshire borderland, the lovely Epping Forest and, of course, the industrial Thames-side and the sprawling suburbia of London-over-the-Border. The heart of this county is as beautiful and appealing as anywhere could be, with trees, green lanes and villages of great character and beauty. Of the towns, Colchester is steeped in history, from the Romans onwards, Chelmsford has the cathedral, created in 1914 using its large Perp parish church, and then there are attractive market towns like Thaxted, Dunmow, Saffron Walden and Coggeshall – all with lovely churches. Where else in England could you find our one medieval triangular tower (All Saints Maldon), over 100 churches which incorporate reused Roman bricks and tiles, the chapel built in AD 654 by St Cedd, who brought the Faith here (St Peter on the Wall, Bradwell), our only Saxon wooden nave (c AD 845, at Greensted juxta Ongar), more wooden effigies than in any other county and villages with names like Messing, Mucking, Ugley and Shellow Bowells!

Every period of architecture from AD 654 to the present is well represented here. There are over 350 medieval churches and these display a variety of building materials – we see ragstone from Kent and septaria from the coastal marshes, with pudding-stone conglomerate and flint rubble being common in the churches. Two other materials make Essex special, however. It must surely hold the record for the use of timber in churches, seen in eight complete towers, over 80 of those charming little belfries, two detached bell-houses (at Wix and Wrabness, near Harwich), a font at Mark's Tey and an arcade at Shenfield, to say nothing of porches, doors, chests, about 50 screens and over 100 medieval roofs. Essex also excels in Tudor brickwork (also some examples of earlier brickwork, as far back as the 13th century). Here we find over 30 brick towers, 20 porches, brick parts of churches, a clerestory at Great Baddow and brick arcades at Blackmore and St Osyth, also complete brick churches at East Horndon, Woodham Walter and Chignal Smealy.

In addition we would mention that about 50 Essex churches have wall-paintings, many have monuments of note and about 150 contain interesting brasses. What a county – yet it is still so little known and little admired, although not, of course, by those who have discovered its churches.

BLACKMORE. St Lawrence's has one of the most remarkable of all Essex timber towers and spires. Inside, its supports are posts arranged like a nave and aisles. The nave is Norm. The N aisle is 14th C and the S aisle 16th C with piers and arches of brick. The 17th C dormers enhance the church. Mon to Thomas Smith and wife 1594.

BRADWELL-juxta-COGGESHALL. Holy Trinity is just a nave, chancel and timber belfry, small and charming. The doorways and several windows are Norm. The S porch is of timber, there is a 15th C screen and a 17th C font-cover. The wall-paintings are 14th C – in jambs of the S window is Doubting Thomas and a saint; in a N window the Trinity and Resurrection. Mon (behind the altar) to Anthony Maxey and wife, and their son and his wife, at prayer-desks, 1592.

Coggeshall's grand church of St Peter ad Vincula was gutted in 1940 but has been imaginatively restored to life by S.E. Dykes Bower, a wonderful spacious building with great dignity and the brass of Thomas Paycocke (1580), whose lovely house may be visited in the town.

BRIGHTLINGSEA. All Saints' grand Perp tower dominates the church and the countryside. Some 13th C work remains, but the church is mainly 15th and 16th C. S porch with flushwork, a Perp font, numerous brasses to the Beriffe family and a large 18th C mon to Nicholas Magens.

CASTLE HEDINGHAM. A fine 16th C brick tower and the clerestory is also of brick. On entering St Nicholas', one gets a surprise, for it is a fine late Norm church, the chancel even more sumptuous with a rare wheel-window with eight columns as spokes. The fine screen is 15th C, as also the stalls with misericords. The N and S doorways are Norm with old doors. Zig-zag is prominent on the chancel arch. The roof of the nave is a fine Perp double hammerbeam roof. Mon to John, 15th Earl of Oxford and wife 1539, and four kneeling daughters (the four sons on the other side are not now visible).

Nearby *Great Yeldham* St Andrew's has a fine tower and much of interest, St Mary's *Gestingthorpe* has one of the finest brick towers, *Great Maplestead* St Giles is a Norman church with fine monuments, whilst *Little Maplestead* St John the Baptist's is a 14th century round church, the only one of the four in England which is not in a town.

CLAVERING.   St Mary and St Clement's is a completely Perp church in a beautiful setting. The roofs are original. There is a 13th C Purbeck marble font, 15th C screen and benches and an Elizabethan pulpit. Fifteenth C glass in the N windows depicts the life of St Catherine, including disputing with the philosophers. There is a 13th C Purbeck marble knight, some 17th and 18th C mons, and some brasses.

COLCHESTER.   People rightly flock to see the wealth of interest in Britain's oldest recorded town. The nine medieval churches are worth seeing also, although some have been put to new uses. All Saints', with its handsome Perp tower, and Holy Trinity which has a Saxon tower of considerable importance, are both museums, so you can see inside them. St James', set nicely above the road on the East Hill, is a large and spacious Perp church which is Anglo-Catholic, whilst St Peter's, prominently set on the North Hill, has a brick tower of 1758 and much evidence of its Classical re-ordering, and is Evangelical. St Leonard at the Hythe (RCF) has an impressive exterior and inside we look up to a fine hammerbeam roof in the nave and an earlier (14th century) roof in the north aisle. There is much tasteful 19th and 20th century work in this devotional building, including glass by Heaton, Butler & Bayne. Although now 'in retirement', this church has a wonderfully cared-for feeling.

Another RCF church, north-west of Colchester, is St Mary's at *West Bergholt*, which is idyllically set beside the Hall and is beautifully unspoilt and rustic, with many items of interest.

COPFORD.   St Mary's has a timber belfry and spire on the nave roof. It is still a complete Norm church with apse. There is a 13th C Purbeck marble font and a 14th C ironbound chest, but the church is famous for its wall-paintings of the 12th C (restored). In the apse is a painting of Christ in Glory, and between the windows are Apostles (mostly modern). On the chancel arch are signs of the zodiac. On the N of the nave from the E is the healing of Jairus's daughter, and a Virtue. On the S, two angels and at the W, a seated figure on a throne and two Virtues.

Some lovely small churches hereabouts, like St Albright's *Stanway* (Norman, with Roman brick), St Edmund's *Easthorpe* (Norman and EE) and St Andrew's *Mark's Tey* (tower of brick and wood, Norman work, font of medieval oak).

DEDHAM.   A beautiful small place and a beautiful church. The fine tower with octagonal buttresses and pinnacles is Perp as indeed is most of St Mary's, with plenty of flush-work outside, particularly on the N side. There are two porches and a clerestory. The N door is old with tracery,

107

and there is a Perp font. Mons to Thomas Webbe 1500 with an indent of his family above, and John Roger 1636, a demi-figure in a niche.

Do find *Lawford*'s church of St Mary in its remote and sylvan setting. The views over the Stour valley are glorious, the atmosphere unforgett-able and the Dec work in the chancel is fit to grace a cathedral.

EPPING. Bodley & Garner created this majestic church of St John the Baptist which is so much part of the Epping townscape, its east end set right beside the attractive main street, above which a magnificent clock projects from the 96 ft tower. It was consecrated in 1891 and completed in 1909. It is stately outside and colourful and impressive within and, like most of Bodley's churches, gives the impression that no expense has been spared to produce the very best. Just look here at Bodley's wonder-ful screen and carved pulpit, his sumptuous triptych reredos and truly magnificent organ-case.

The mother church of All Saints, at *Epping Upland*, is beautifully set and has a Tudor brick tower, 18th century rails and some old benches. *North Weald* St Andrew's church, which is right away from the centre of its village, also has a brick tower. There is an interesting screen here and a colourful and devotional interior.

FINCHINGFIELD. A picture-postcard village – much visited and photographed. Crowning the scene (and, of course, making it!) is the bold and sturdy tower (with 17th century cupola) of the parish church of St John. The tower has a grand Norman base and doorway and the south door by which we enter is medieval and traceried. Inside are medieval roofs, a 15th century screen (one of the finest in the county) and an earlier screen in the south aisle. Much of interest here.

This is an area of picturesque villages with above-average churches, *Great Bardfield* St Mary's has a late 14th century stone screen (as does Stebbing, near Dunmow) and some lovely Dec windows. *Little Bardfield* St Katherine's has Saxon work and a beautiful organ of c1700, *Little Sampford* St Mary's is full of character and charm and *Great Sampford* St Michael's is noted for its glorious Dec architecture.

GREAT BROMLEY. St George's has a fine Perp tower with stepped battlements, common in E Anglia. A tall clerestory. The S porch has flush-work. The S arcade is 14th C and the N arcade 15th C. The former has capitals carved with leaves and figures, one with his tongue out, and a frog biting a dragon. The N and W doors are of c1500, as also the wonderful double hammerbeam roof of the nave. There is also a splendid brass to a priest, William Bischopton in Mass vestments, 1432.

Elmstead church of St Ann and St Laurence, at the end of a long cul-de-sac lane, is small, humble, rustic and thoroughly rewarding, with box-pews, two-decker pulpit, old glass and a timber effigy.

GREAT CANFIELD. In a charming setting, St Mary's has a 15th C timber belfry and spire, otherwise it is mostly Norm, as is the S doorway with ornamented capitals. The chancel arch is Norm, the upper part of the S capital having Sax carving (use the mirror to see it). The centre E window has a wall-painting of c1250 of the Virgin and Child, one of the most beautiful in the whole country (switch on the light to see it). A small lancet window has lovely modern glass showing the flowers in season on each of St Mary's festivals. There are some small brasses and a mon to Sir William Wisemen and wife, demi-figures holding hands, 1684.

Whilst in the area why not try to see all of the seven *Roding* churches – Abbess, Aythorp, Berners, High, Leaden, Margaret and White Roding, also St Mary's at *Hatfield Broad Oak*, with its magnificent tower and many treasures.

GREENSTED. Is this the most famous church in England? St Andrew's has the oldest wooden walls in the country, for the nave is built of Sax split oak-tree trunks (just think when the trees must have been planted). The body of St Edmund rested in this nave in 1013. The tower and spire are also of timber.

Stanford Rivers St Margaret's church has a wooden belfry and much to see inside. St Martin of Tours at *Chipping Ongar* has an atmospheric interior and incorporates ancient brickwork and St Mary's *High Ongar* has a glorious Norman doorway.

INGATESTONE. St Edmund and St Mary's has a fine tall brick tower. There is some Norm work, but it is mostly Perp with a brick arcade to the brick Petre Chapel, and a Perp font. Mons to Sir William Petre, Secretary of State and wife, 1572; Robert Petre 1593; John Troughton 1621; John, Lord Petre and wife and kneeling children, 1613.

At nearby St Mary's *Fryerning* is a Norman nave, incorporating Roman bricks, and a sturdy Tudor brick tower.

MARGARETTING. St Margaret's is essentially Perp. There is a timber porch and timber tower and spire (note its amazing construction inside). Equally amazing is that the tower has four medieval bells. Perp font. Dado of screen. The E window has a complete 15th C Tree of Jesse (restored – showing the genealogy of Christ) – four medallions with two

109

figures each in the side lights and Jesse and three medallions and the seated Virgin in the centre light. Brass to a knight and lady, 15th C.

The tiny church of St Mary *Buttsbury* is rustic and atmospheric, whilst All Saints' *Stock* has a complete wooden tower, a pretty setting and a colourful and devotional Anglo-Catholic interior.

NEWPORT. In the very pretty street, St Mary's fine tower is of 1858 and the large church, 14th and 15th C. There is a 15th C S porch and nave clerestory and a 16th C brick clerestory of the chancel. Also a 13th C font, 17th C Communion table, parts of a 15th C screen and a remarkable 13th C chest with paintings inside the lid – a Crucifixion group and St Peter and St Paul (probably used as a portable altar). Some 14th C glass, St Catherine and St Michael.

SAFFRON WALDEN. St Mary's church is in a commanding position on a hill. The stone spire was added in 1831, otherwise the church is entirely 15th and 16th C, apart from the crypt and some arcades. The tower has polygonal turrets, as also on either side of the clerestory. The spandrels of the easternmost bay of the N aisle have figures of King David, St John, St Thomas, St Mary, the Scourging of Christ, and the Agony in the Garden. All the roofs are original and the font is 15th C. All the brasses are on the N wall and there is a mon to Lord Audley, Lord Chancellor 1544.

Nearby *Littlebury* Holy Trinity contains a font which is enclosed in Elizabethan linenfold panelling, with a carved canopy and several brasses. *Hadstock* St Botolph's church has important 11th century Saxon work, also a 15th century lectern, chapel screen and benches. *Radwinter* St Mary's interior is a lavish paradise of exquisite Tractarian craftsmanship, all part of a restoration begun by Eden Nesfield and finished by Temple Moore.

ST OSYTH. St Peter and St Paul's stands just outside the lovely priory gatehouse. The nave is early 16th C with brick piers and arches, and the chancel is 13th C. The S aisle and S porch are also of brick. The tower is 14th C. The nave has a hammerbeam roof, and note the altar-rails. Two wall-mons, facing each other, commemorate the 1st and 2nd Lord Darcy and wives, 1580. Also a 17th C mon with recumbent figures of husband and wife, and one to John Darcy 1638.

Not far away is *Clacton on Sea*, with its Norman mother church of St John the Baptist at *Great Clacton* and Temple Moore's exciting (but unfinished) church of St James (1913), with its High Altar magnificently high!

County of timber belfries and wonderful timber towers like this one at Stock.

STEBBING. The whole church is 14th C. The tower is tall with a small lead spire, but the notable feature of St Mary's and most unusual is the stone rood-screen filling the chancel arch. It is intricately carved and is typical of the 14th C. Altar-rails of the 18th C. Brass of a widow 1390.

Lindsell's curious, but picturesque, church of St Mary the Virgin is full of interest and atmosphere and at *Little Dunmow* St Mary's church is the Lady Chapel of a once glorious priory church. Its beautiful 14th century windows, the blank arcade beneath them and the 15th century Fitzwalter monument will be remembered here.

THAXTED. A glorious church in a delightful small town with its 15th C Guildhall. The whole of St John the Baptist's appears to be Perp at its best, but it is built around 14th C arcades, and that is the reason why the aisles are so wide. The tower and stone spire with flying-buttresses are noble, the spire having been rebuilt (it was struck by lightning). Both porches are fine, the N with a lierne-vault and bosses and its original door with tracery. The reredos on the E of the N transept is medieval. All the roofs are original and the tall clerestory will be noted. The font case and cover are 16th C and completely hide the font. The pulpit, altar-rails and screens are 17th century. There are fragments of old glass, including Adam and Eve, and a 15th C brass to a priest. The spaciousness and colour indeed make this church the House of God.

THEYDON GARNON. All Saints' brick tower has the date 1520 and the brick N aisle 1644. Its arcade is entirely of timber. There is an 18th C pulpit with tester, and 17th C altar-rails. The Royal Arms and numerous hatchments have recently been restored. Brass to William Kirkeby, rector in a cope, 1458. Mon to William Eyre Archer 1739, with a medallion of the deceased.

Do find *Lambourne*'s small and remote church of St Mary and All Saints (near the village of Abridge), with its Norman nave and chancel and remarkable early 18th century reordering which makes the interior fascinating and charming. The brick church of St Michael (1611–14) at *Theydon Mount* is a period-piece, with good monuments.

TILTY. Little-known, but this is a treasure. It was the chapel at the gate of the monastery. St Mary's nave is EE with lancets and with an 18th C belfry and cupola. The chancel is sumptuous Dec with splendid E window with Flowing tracery and two side windows of the same style. Note the piscina and sedilia. Brasses to Gerard Danet and wife 1520, George Medeley and wife 1562, and Margaret Tuke, kneeling figures, 1590.

112

Chickney's lovely Saxon church of St Mary (RCF) has a 14th century font with a 16th century cover, a medieval altar-slab and bags of atmosphere, whilst *Little Easton* St Mary's is noted for its wonderful wall-paintings, 17th century German glass and an incredible array of monuments.

WALTHAM ABBEY. The E half of the abbey church disappeared at the Reformation, and what remains at Holy Cross is a Norman nave with massive columns grooved somewhat like the columns in Durham Cathedral, a blind storey, and a clerestory, all early 12th C. The Lady Chapel is 14th C. The W end of the nave was then rebuilt and the W tower added in 1558. The E wall with its wheel-window is 19th C.

There is a 12th C Purbeck marble font, a 17th C pulpit, and a 14th C screen in the N aisle. The ceiling of the nave, based on Peterborough Cathedral, is modern. The modern E window glass is by Burne-Jones. Mons to Sir Edward Denny and wife 1599, Captain Robert Smith 1697, and James and Hester Spilman 1763. The abbey gatehouse and the bridge leading to it are 14th C.

WENDENS AMBO. The church makes the perfect ending to the pretty village street. St Mary's tower is Norman with a W doorway with Roman bricks. It has a Herts spike. The tower arch is also Norm. The S doorway and S arcade are EE, the N arcade is slightly later and the chancel c1300. There is a 16th C domed font-cover, a 15th C pre-Reformation wooden pulpit and screen, and several old benches, one with a tiger looking into a mirror. Some wall-paintings depict the life of St Margaret. Brass of a knight c1415.

WILLINGALE DOE & WILLINGALE SPAIN. An example of two parish churches sharing the same churchyard (no doubt for geological reasons). St Andrew's (to the S) is the older church. It has Norm windows and doorways, the chancel is 15th C as also is the timber belfry with spire on the nave roof, the door has 12th C ironwork and there is a 14th C font. St Christopher's (to the N) has a tower but the church has been much restored. Perp font. Mon to Robert Wiseman and Richard Wiseman and his wife 1641, and a brass to Thomas Torrell, knight, 1442.

Shellow Bowells has a tiny church of 1754, St Peter and St Paul's, now converted into a house, but delightful externally. *Fyfield* St Nicholas' has a Norman nave and central tower (with an odd timber top) and a Dec chancel, with good sedilia and piscina.

GLOUCESTERSHIRE

County of the glorious Cotswolds – at their wildest in the north-east around Stow on the Wold and at their most dramatic in the south, around Stroud and Painswick – but everywhere beautiful. The Forest of Dean lies in the south-west and the broad valley of the Severn has Gloucestershire scenery on both sides. This county delights the visitor wherever he chooses to explore and the way to search out its scenery is to pursue its churches – about 300 medieval ones, until 60 or so were taken into Avon. The Cotswold churches are famous, with their warm golden (and sometimes almost white) oolitic limestone, which both weathers and carves so well, and was easily obtained from these hills. West of the Severn, in the Forest of Dean, we could be in a different county – with fewer medieval churches and a totally different, but nevertheless very appealing, character.

There are Saxon churches here – from Deerhurst's amazing Minster Church to diminutive Duntisbourne Rous, and much Norman work. Early English abounds, with some very high quality design and a few beautiful bell-turrets of the period. The Dec period provided several Gloucestershire churches with very tall and sleek broach spires (as at Painswick, Standish, Saintbury and Shurdington) and Perp, as in East Anglia, produced most of the county's 'big guns' in their present form – magnificent structures like Chipping Campden, Northleach, Fairford, Winchcombe and Cirencester.

It is however the tiny churches of all periods which are unforgettable here – including those which are little known or publicised. Time and time again we find a hidden gem beneath a bellcot or a saddleback tower – churches with limestone walls, roofs and even belfry-louvres, set in green churchyards, often with parts of their churchyard crosses remaining (go to Ampney Crucis to see one of the best of these), and with those wonderful 17th and 18th century chest-tombs and headstones, bathed in lichen. These places in hot weather even give off a distinctive smell externally.

Interiors here are full of surprises. Fonts are of high quality (with many Norman examples), several stone pulpits survive, also wall-paintings and glass. Much 17th and 18th century woodwork may be seen (including a few largely unspoilt interiors) and monuments and brasses abound. It is difficult to suggest common features to look for, as the joy of

Gloucestershire interiors lies in their infinite variety.

Occasionally we stumble upon a Classical church, or part of a church and there are several high quality Gothic Revival village churches (eg Highnam, Selsley, Daylesford and Toddington), whilst the town of Cheltenham provides us with a wide spectrum of church architecture from the past 200 years.

BERKELEY. A fine setting near Berkeley's splendid castle for this noble church of St Mary, with a pure EE west front and arcades, Dec aisles and lower part of the porch, and Perp Berkeley Chapel and its stone screen. There is Norman work here, seen particularly in the font, pillar piscina and a reused doorway. The nine-light east window is filled with Hardman (1873) glass and the walls are rich in medieval wall-paintings, including a consecration cross and the remains of a Doom painting. Several good monuments to the Berkeleys may be seen in their chapel and there is much else to delight and interest the visitor. The tower (a fine Gothic structure, although it was built in 1753) stands on its own, about 50 yards from the church.

BIBURY. A Cotswold village, unspoilt and beautiful, with a church of St Mary which shows work of all architectural periods from its Saxon cross-shaft, now set in the chancel wall, to the Norman north doorway and the EE, Dec and Perp windows. The south porch and doorway are Transitional Norman/EE. More Saxon work may be seen supporting the 13th century chancel arch. The square font was made c1200 and the nave has a sturdy medieval roof. The large and spacious chancel is equipped with no less than nine aumbries and its tiny south-east window contains original glass of the 1200s. This is a church where the architectural detective may have fun piecing together its development. It is also a church which has been treated sympathetically by its 20th century restorers. The churchyard, with its Cotswold tombs and headstones, is delightful also.

To the south-west, along the Coln valley, we may enjoy *Coln St Aldwyn*'s church of St John the Baptist, with Norman and EE work, *Hatherop*'s rebuilt church of St Nicholas (1854, by Henry Clutton and William Burges) and *Quenington* St Swithin's two magnificent Norman doorways, each with a carved tympanum.

CHIPPING CAMPDEN. A lovely country town, dominated by its truly magnificent golden Perp church of St James, in a setting which shows off well its 120 ft tower and the noble proportions of its embattled and pinnacled exterior. The interior is graced by large windows (including one over the chancel arch), elegant arcades with tall, concave-sided piers and almost flat roofs. There is a rare 15th century falcon lectern, a fine pulpit of 1612, altar hangings of c1500 and a cope of c1400 – and much, much more. There are some excellent monuments and brasses to the 15th century wool-staplers by whose generosity this great building took its present shape.

To the west of Chipping Campden is *Saintbury*'s hillside church of St Nicholas – wonderfully positioned and so attractive, both from a distance and close-to. This little-known church is a 'must'.

CIRENCESTER. At the heart of its busy town rises this sumptuous and truly enormous church of St John the Baptist – Gloucestershire's largest and one of England's finest. It has been lavishly designed and exquisitely fashioned. The stonework (in panelling, parapets and pinnacles), the mighty windows (almost creating walls of glass), the stately and elegant 162 ft tower and the amazing three-storeyed south porch (a complete building in itself and at one time used as the Town Hall) all combine to create a breathtaking exterior. Inside we are aware of its great height and tremendous area as we survey the richly panelled walls of the nave, the soaring arcades and the great Perp windows. In the chancel is earlier work, mainly of 1200–1300, but in its five-light east window has been set an array of 15th century stained glass. St Catherine's Chapel has a fan-vaulted ceiling and wall-paintings of St Catherine and St Christopher. The Lady Chapel contains the elaborate 17th century monument of Humphrey Bridges. Holy Trinity Chapel has a fine collection of brasses and a medieval reredos of canopied niches. The wineglass pulpit is exquisitely carved (c1450), the great rood-screen survives, also a medieval screen in the south aisle. All this is but the beginning of what would be a long list of features, furnishings and monuments which adorn this premier church.

COLN ST DENNIS AND COLN ROGERS. Two adjoining villages on the river Coln, both with delightful churches of very great age. Coln St Denis St James' is Norman, with an endearing exterior (nave, central tower and chancel), and several Norman features remaining. At Coln Rogers St Andrew's, the nave and chancel are Saxon, where we see pilaster strips, long and short quoins and other Saxon features. From the 15th century comes the stone pulpit and the figure of St Margaret in stained glass.

Chedworth St Andrew's church (to the north-west) has another fine stone pulpit, also more Norman work and grand Perp windows.

DEERHURST. In a peaceful setting beside a farm and not far from the river Severn, is this remarkable Anglo-Saxon minster church of St Mary – one of the best Saxon churches in England. It was founded c AD 800 and was reordered in the late 900s. Here we may see Saxon doorways, masonry, windows and carvings in abundance. The font is a wonderful piece of stonecarving of the 800s – a cylindrical bowl covered with patterned motifs. Of the later work here, look for St Catherine and St Alphege in stained glass of the early 1300s, eight 15th century benches, a stone coffin, and Terri – Sir John Cassey's dog on his splendid brass, the only brass which commemorates a dog by name! The sanctuary furnishings are arranged in the 17th century fashion, with communicants' seats around the Holy Table on three sides.

As if this feast of interest in a tiny village isn't enough, 200 yards away is the Anglo-Saxon Odda's Chapel – another gem, which was dedicated by Earl Odda on 12th April 1056, in memory of his brother Aelfric.

Here we are only a few miles from *Tewkesbury*'s might abbey church of St Mary, with its wonderful Norman nave and tower, 14th century choir, chapels and glass, splendid monuments, and much else. There is as much to see here as in many cathedrals.

DIDMARTON. The great joy of this little medieval L-shaped church (RCF) is that the Victorians left it entirely alone. (Instead, they built another church, St Michael's, in 1872). The old church of St Lawrence is therefore furnished as it would have been in the 1700s, with its Georgian three-decker pulpit and box-pews. There are medieval features as well in this little church of great character.

DUNTISBOURNE ROUS. So tiny, so simple, yet so memorable, is this little gem, built against a slope. Because of the rise in the churchyard, the Norman chancel of St Michael's is so tall that there is a little crypt chapel beneath it. The nave is Saxon, with herringbone masonry, long-and-short western quoins and two Saxon doorways. The unspoilt interior has 17th century box-pews and pulpit in the nave, 15th century stalls with carved misericords in the chancel, and an atmosphere which is delightful.

The Norman church of St Peter at *Duntisbourne Abbots* is also worth a visit, but *Daglingworth* Holy Rood is a must, with its Saxon sundial and three wonderful Saxon sculptures.

EASTLEACH MARTIN and EASTLEACH TURVILLE. Two delightful Cotswold villages (where John Keble was curate) and two delightful Norman churches either side of the little river Leach. Turville St Andrew's, with its saddleback tower, has a superb Norman doorway,

117

Lovely Fairford – a late medieval masterpiece in Cotswold limestone – its windows filled with original glass.

with Christ in Majesty carved in its tympanum, also a lovely EE chancel and 17th century woodwork inside. Martin St Michael and St Martin's (RCF), with its short, stone-capped tower, EE chancel and beautiful Dec north transept, has Norman piers supporting its chancel arch, a Jacobean pulpit, 15th and 17th century seating and some old glass remaining. The atmosphere in both churches is wonderful.

John Keble was later curate at nearby St Peter's *Southrop*, which has one of the finest Norman fonts in the county.

ELKSTONE. Within a mile of the Roman Ermine Street rises Elkstone's fine Perp tower – but the church of St John behind it is superb and unspoilt Norman of the highest quality. Christ in Majesty greets us from the south doorway, with the hand of the Almighty above. Look for the upside down figure grasping the snouts of its neighbours in the arch moulding. Sturdy Norman arches inside once supported a central tower. The vaulted chancel and sanctuary show the real dignity of Norman architecture. The nave roof and font are 15th century; the pulpit, rails and reading desk are 17th century.

Winstone St Bartholomew's and *Syde* St Mary's churches, with their saddleback towers, both have interesting work of the 11th century.

118

FAIRFORD. Glorious Fairford (it is indeed 'fair'), St Mary's showing latest Perp in all its richness, was rebuilt c1490–1500 by John Tame, a wool merchant, and his son. The golden exterior is imposing and rising from its centre is a magnificent tower, adorned with niches and fascinating sculpted figures and coats of arms. Entering (by means of an original door beneath the fan-vaulted roof of the porch) we find ourselves surrounded by the finest collection of 15th and 16th century stained glass in any parish church in the land. There is about 2,000 square ft of it in 28 windows – a wonderful set of visual aids to teach the Faith of the Church. Also wonderful are the 14 intriguing and hilarious misericord carvings in the choir stalls, the Perp screenwork, the 69 angels supporting the roof, Geoffrey Webb's Lady Chapel reredos (1913) and Comper's dignified High Altar (1920).

HAILES. A tiny, humble companion to the ruins of the abbey nearby – but what a gem! It was begun in 1300 and has a sanctus bell-turret and a timber-framed bell-turret. It is the unspoilt interior which will be remembered here, with its wall-paintings of c1300, its nine Apostles in 15th century glass and its furnishings – Elizabethan benches, 15th century screen, 17th century pulpit and one box-pew, chancel panelling, stalls and Holy Table (with medieval stone altar-slab beneath it).

Wonderful Cotswold villages hereabouts, like St George's *Didbrook*, St Michael's *Stanton* and St Peter's *Stanway* – all with charming churches. Also do try to find G.E. Street's (1873) grand estate church of St Andrew at *Toddington*.

KEMPLEY. St Mary's amazing church of the Norman period, with a tower of the late 1200s and a timber porch of the 1300s, has a fine south doorway, showing the Tree of Life and framing a very old door. The glory of this place is its amazing frescos of c1130–40 which adorn the chancel and which are more or less complete. How lovely our churches must have looked when their walls were covered with these wonderful teaching aids. St Edward's church, in the village, is a fascinating example of the Arts and Crafts Movement, designed by Randall Wells and built in 1903. It should not be missed.

In this corner of the county, St Mary's *Dymock*, St John's *Pauntley* and St Mary's *Newent* are among the many churches which will reward a visit.

LITTLE WASHBOURNE. A simple, humble, rustic little church (RCF) in an orchard. The chancel arch of St Mary's declares it to be Norman, but the 18th century furnishings are complete and extremely beautiful, creating an atmosphere which is incomparable and just as wonderful as the greatest cathedral. It is an unspoilt and largely undiscovered gem!

NEWLAND. This great church of All Saints, near the Welsh border, is nicknamed 'The Cathedral of the Forest'. We are drawn by its distinctive tower, with its array of corner turrets and spirelets, to a handsome and spacious building which was tastefully restored by William White in 1861. It is distinguished by its wide aisles and noble proportions, but there are many treasures, not least the pretty font of 1661, the stone mensa slabs on the chapel altars, the 18th century chandelier and the medieval floor-tiles in the south chancel chapel. Newland is noted for its monuments, especially the series of recumbent effigies and the miner's brass, showing a miner with his pick and hod and his candle-stick held in the mouth.

Whilst in the area, find the churches of St Mary at *St Briavels* and St Mary at *English Bicknor*.

NORTH CERNEY. Wonderfully set in the valley of the Churn. An enticing exterior to All Saints' with a saddleback tower (the base of which is Norman). Look for the graffito of a lion with a man's head in the south transept wall. Inside is sheer unadulterated beauty, with a Norman chancel arch, stone pulpit of c1480, 15th century roof and glass all combining successfully with F.C. Eden's brilliant and sensitive restoration here in the 1920s. He designed the rood-loft, rood, altar, reredos, etc which have made this interior so very colourful and devotional.

Bagendon St Margaret's nearby has a Norman saddleback tower and arcade. *Rendcomb* has a perfect smaller example of a late Perp church of the 1500s, St Peter's, with lovely architecture, a fine screen and a beautifully carved Norman font from earlier times.

NORTHLEACH. Another magnificent wool church of the 15th century. St Peter and St Paul's superb exterior features one of the grandest porches in England, also a noble tower rising 100 ft above us and, again, the nearest that the builders could get to walls of glass. A lofty and light interior here, with elegant arcades (the piers have concave sides), vaulted tower ceiling and fine canopied sedilia, also a 15th century pulpit and a nine-light window above the chancel arch. In this church is a collection of ten brasses to local wool merchants. The interior was reordered in 1964 and was reseated to the designs of Sir Basil Spence.

ODDINGTON. When the new church was built in 1852, the church of St Nicholas was left untouched – later to be conserved so that we can now marvel at the delights of a very atmospheric building, with EE and Decorated work in its structure, a 15th century roof and, above all, a wonderfully unspoilt interior. Here we see a grand Jacobean pulpit and canopy, and other 17th and 18th century features. Supreme amongst all the treasures here is the 14th century Doom painting on the nave wall; look for the person climbing the battlements of the heavenly city, also the damned, being hung on a gibbet or boiled in a cauldron.

Here we are not far from a host of delightful villages and churches, including the *Swells*, the *Rissingtons*, the *Slaughters*, *Daylesford*'s 19th century church of St Peter by Pearson and St Edward's *Stow on the Wold*.

STANDISH. A lovely churchyard, with the medieval church house and the gateway to Standish Court nearby, also one of those tall graceful spires which adorn several church towers in this part of the county. Decorated architecture predominates at St Nicholas', seen at its best in the east window. The interior is equipped with a pulpit and pews from the 1700s, but the choir stalls, the handsome altar, the west gallery and the organ-case are 20th century, designed by S.E. Dykes Bower. There are 180 carved bosses in the nave roof and Sir Henry Winston (1609) whose monument is here, was an ancestor of Sir Winston Churchill.

A few miles to the north is *Gloucester*, with the county's wonderful cathedral. Look out here for the five churches of medieval foundation, including St Michael's of which only the tower now stands.

TETBURY. The lofty tapering spire of mighty St Mary's is visible for miles. The vast church was designed and built by Francis Hiorn of Warwick in 1781 (the medieval tower and spire were rebuilt in 1890). This huge auditorium has to be seen to be believed – and it is all Gothic, with mighty windows and an array of thin timber-faced iron columns rising to support the vaulted plaster ceiling way above. An unusual feature of this unique building is the low ambulatory passage which surrounds it. The pews and galleries have gothic panelling and two huge chandeliers (for 36 lights each) hang in the nave.

By contrast, St Saviour's (RCF) was built in 1848 to be 'a little church for the poor'. S.W. Daukes designed it, but he collaborated with A.W.N. Pugin and John Hardman, whose work may be enjoyed in this church which was built for Tractarian worship.

HAMPSHIRE AND
THE ISLE OF WIGHT

To many people Hampshire is England at its loveliest and most English, in its rolling chalk downs, its clear rippling rivers, like the Itchen, the Test and the Meon and others which flow through its gentle green valleys, in its wooded hills along the border with Sussex, in its lovely small towns, like Alresford, Alton, Petersfield and Romsey, and in its collection of 200 or so medieval churches, so many of which are small, homely and very special. People who really explore Hampshire fall in love with it before very long, as they discover the wonderful woodland of the New Forest, as they travel the lanes to search out its villages (and what lovely villages so many of these are, with delectable names like Stoke Charity, Farley Chamberlayne, Itchen Abbas, Brown Candover and Abbots Ann), as they ascend into the hill country in the north-west and even as they explore the great cities of Southampton, Portsmouth and wonderful Winchester (once described so accurately as 'A lovely city, set in a green valley').

For the church enthusiast what a wealth and what variety here – not in any great abundance of mighty structures, as in East Anglia (although the county's few 'big guns' are indeed quite something), but in small (and often quite unassuming) churches, which the Philistine might dare to describe as 'ordinary', because they do not immediately strike one as spectacular. We have wonderful examples of Saxon work here, plenty of Norman and, like Sussex, much EE. Dec and Perp are not so prolific as in some counties, but there are plenty of pleasing examples from these periods. There are a few Classical churches of great interest (mostly in the villages), also several brick towers or tower restorations of the period, which is quite a Hampshire feature. The 19th century has also given Hampshire some very good quality work, especially in its glass, but also in new or rebuilt churches – again, many in the villages, although the very best places to enjoy 19th and 20th century churches are Portsmouth and area, also Southampton.

There is much to enjoy in the furniture and fittings of Hampshire's churches and there are plenty of monuments, although in this county it is the atmosphere and character of each individual church which is so worthwhile.

To these we add just over 20 medieval churches on the Isle of Wight and even in this small number there is the widest possible scope of things to see in architecture, fittings and monuments – and here is a place where one could actually set out to see the lot and maybe a few of the Victorian ones as well.

AVINGTON.   St Mary's is all brick and a perfect example of an 18th C church (1771) with its interior furnishings complete and unspoilt – reredos, three-decker pulpit with tester, pews and family pews, font, gallery and altar-rails. Even the barrel-organ still works. The tower is splendid and the E window is Venetian. The coved plaster ceiling should also be noted. There are some monuments of that period.

Within a few miles are several delightful churches including St Mary's *Itchen Stoke* (1866 by H. Conybeare, a lovely Victorian church), St Mary's *Easton* (church of c1200 with unusual tower top), and lovely St Swithin's *Headbourne Worthy* with its important Saxon work and great atmosphere.

BOARHUNT.   Set in a very rural area and with no village, St Nicholas' is a complete Sax church (c1064) and unaltered except for the later bell-turret. The N and S doorways have been blocked, but the chancel arch is the best feature and a good example of Sax work. There is a pilaster-strip on the E wall. The window on the N of the chancel (also blocked) has a double-splay which is an infallible proof of late Sax work. Most of the windows are 13th C lancets. There is a three-decker pulpit, squire's pew, and W gallery. The font may well be Sax. A monument to the Henslowe family 1577. There is a large yew tree in the churchyard.

Nearby *Fareham*'s church of St Peter and St Paul is a wonderful mixture of good craftsmanship of several eras – Saxon, EE and other medieval periods may be identified, also a Classical tower of 1742, 19th century work by Blomfield and 20th century work by Sir C. Nicholson – and this is only the structure! A fascinating church.

BRADING.   (Isle of Wight). This is the largest medieval church on the island. St Mary's 13th century tower has processional arches and a spire. Most of the rest of the church is Perp, including the lovely Oglander Chapel, with its superb monuments and hatchments. In the chancel is the incised slab in memory of John de Cherewin (c1441).

The 180 ft spire of All Saints' *Ryde* crowns the island's finest Victorian church. It was designed by Sir Gilbert Scott and was built in 1869–72.

BRAMLEY.   St James' has a 17th C brick tower, but a Norm window proves the age of the church. Perp E window. The S porch is 18th

123

century and the brick Brocas Chapel of 1801 is surmounted by two great Moorish head crests as weathervanes. It is for its fittings that the church is noted. There is an elaborated rood-celure over the former rood-loft, a Norm font, a pillar piscina, an 18th C pulpit, a Perp rood-screen of five-light divisions, an 18th C W gallery and 17th C altar-rails. Some of the bench-ends are medieval. The 13th C wall-painting of the murder of St Thomas a Becket shows him in outdoor clothes, which is probably correct as this painting was executed so near the time. Opposite the S door is a large 15th C painting of St Christopher (note the mermaids), and N of the altar is a wall-painting of St James. There are some fragments of old glass. In the Brocas Chapel there is a window with 16 panes of early 16th C Flemish glass. The Royal Arms are those of Charles I when still Prince of Wales. There are two brasses and a large monument to Bernard Brocas 1777.

Pamber's wonderful EE church must be seen, also St Mary's *Silchester* (all periods, with a Perp screen and Jac pulpit) and the eccentric Classical parkland church of St Mary (1745 and with so much to enjoy) at *Stratfield Saye*.

BREAMORE. In a charming setting, St Mary's is a complete Sax church of about 1000. It is cruciform in plan as usual at that time but the windows have been altered. The S transept is completely Sax with a tall narrow arch above which is inscribed (translated) 'Here the Covenant becomes manifest'. Also above the S doorway (in the porch) is a great Sax Rood (the body is bent by suffering and the arms are raised). Above the doorway is a Norm medallion of the Lamb and Cross. On the W wall of the porch, Judas is hanged. Sax long-and-short work can be seen. There are also several Mass dials on the S side. Hatchments inside, and a fine yew tree in the churchyard. The crossing arches are 14th C with large leaves.

The church of St Mary in the pleasant town of *Fordingbridge* has some good EE work in the chancel, a two-storeyed Perp porch and a lovely hammerbeam roof in the north chapel. Much of interest here.

CORHAMPTON. Another Sax church, dedication unknown, and within a quarter of a mile of Meonstoke church. Long-and-short work and pilaster-strips will be noticed. The chancel arch is typical of the period. Outside should be seen the Sax sundial. There is some 13th C wall-painting in the chancel, a Norm font, and a Jac pulpit. A huge yew tree stretches over the churchyard.

St Andrew's *Meonstoke* has much EE work and a pretty tower with a timber top. *Droxford* St Mary and All Saints has work of most periods, including Norman, some worthy furnishings and the effigy of a 13th century lady.

DUMMER.   All Saints' has a most interesting interior. The nave is Perp (but there is a blocked Norm S doorway). The chancel and chancel arch are EE. There is a timber belfry with a sanctus-bell hanging outside. The unique feature inside is the 15th C panelled canopy coloured with bosses against the E wall of the nave over the chancel arch, and which was a canopy of honour for the Rood, which would have originally stood beneath it. The medieval wooden pulpit of c1380 is also a great treasure. The W gallery dates from the reign of Charles II (his Arms are above). Go up to this gallery for a good view of the Rood canopy. A set of 17th C Ringers' Rules are painted on the wall above the W window. The altar-rails are also 17th century. Note the palimpsest brass, hinged so that both sides can be seen – Robert Clerk c1500 reused for Allys Magewik 1591.

EAST MEON.   All Saints' is set under the Downs and at the end of the village street. It is cruciform Norm with a fine Norm central tower with three belfry windows with zig-zag on each side and circular openings in the top stage, and all surmounted by a large lead spire. The W doorway (with zig-zag) and S doorway are also Norm. The crossing arches E and W go with the tower. The great treasure is the Norm black Tournai marble font (as in Winchester Cathedral). On the N side is the creation of Adam and Eve, recumbent, and the Temptation, and on the E side the Expulsion from Paradise and an angel showing Adam how to dig and Eve with a distaff. On the other sides are arcading and a frieze with dragons, birds and animals. The pulpit dates from 1706.

A few miles to the north is Holy Trinity *Privett*, whose 160 ft spire is visible for miles. The church (RCF) is a large and splendid building of 1876–8 by Sir Arthur Blomfield – stately and satisfying both outside and in.

ELLINGHAM.   St Mary's, mostly 13th C but restored, has a timber belfry and spire. The brick S porch is of 1720, upon which is a large painted sun-dial. There is a double piscina. The church is fully furnished, with a Perp screen with hour-glass and above it a plaster tympanum with the Creed, Lord's Prayer and Ten Commandments, and the Royal Arms of Charles II 1671, a Jac pulpit, reredos c1700 at the W end, family pew, Perp font and 18th C altar-rails. The roof of the nave is 15th C barrel-vaulted.

125

Ringwood church of St Peter and St Paul, a large and noble building by F. & H. Francis (1853–5) with a central tower, incorporates items from its predecessor, including an EE piscina and a fine brass of c1416.

FARLEIGH CHAMBERLAYNE. An isolated and lovable little bell-turreted downland church – and what a character! St John's doorway tells us that it is Norman, but the 18th century refurbished it and gave it its present windows, also the font, pulpit and rails. What atmosphere inside, with rustic timberwork in the king-post roof and beneath the bell-turret, also a lovely monument to William St John (c1600).

FROYLE. The church of the Assumption is delightfully set near the manor house. The brick tower was built in 1722 and the brick nave in 1812, but the chancel is late 13th century, with an elegant east window of c1330 (its reticulated tracery still filled with original heraldic glass). Other chancel windows have glass by C.E. Kempe, which illuminate an exquisite interior, magnificently and devotionally furnished with beautiful things, in the Anglo-Catholic tradition.

St Lawrence's at *Alton* is mainly Perp, but its tower stands upon Norman arches. Amongst the treasures inside are 15th century misericord stalls and a splendid 17th century pulpit. A few miles to the north is the grand Norman and EE church at *Crondall*.

GODSHILL. (Isle of Wight). One of England's beauty spots, with the church tower above the roofs of the thatched cottages. The top of the tower with its eight pinnacles is early 16th C, whereas most of St Lawrence's is 14th C. The S transept has a 15th C plastered wagon roof. In this transept is a 15th C wall-painting of Christ crucified on a lily plant. The large Rubens-school painting is of Daniel in the Lion's Den. The altar-rails are 17th C. Mons to Sir John Leigh and wife 1529, Sir James Worsley and wife 1536 (note the figures at the feet), and Sir Robert Worsley and his brother 1747.

IDSWORTH. A tiny chapel (with 18th century bell-turret), remote and isolated in a downland field. St Hubert's is basically Norman but was altered in the 1500s. What a delight it is, with box-pews, Jacobean pulpit, plastered chancel ceiling and the most important set of wall-paintings in Hampshire, depicting the life of St Hubert. This little shrine was greatly enhanced by its sensitive 1912 restoration by H.S. Goodhart Rendel.

So many villages and churches of real character here, including this one at Headbourne Worthy, part of which is Saxon.

MINSTED. All Saints' in the New Forest is second only to Whitby in its wealth of 17th and 18th C fittings. The tower is of red brick 1774, the N porch 1683, and S transept 1825, with gables and a variety of windows giving a homely effect. The interior is even more homely. The N doorway and chancel arch are 13th C. The font is Norm and carved with the Baptism of Christ, two eagles, Agnus Dei and two lions with a joint head. It is, however, for the post-Reformation furniture that one comes here: a double W gallery, pews, two squire's pews, one with a fireplace, a three-decker pulpit and even hat-pegs, all giving the atmosphere of that period.

The New Forest has some delightful churches. St Peter's *Brockenhurst*

127

has Norman and c1300 work and a tower and spire of 1761, and St Michael's *Lyndhurst* (by William White 1858–70) has a massive tower and spire and a colourful interior with polychromatic brick walls, a fine painted reredos (by Lord Leighton 1864), glass by Morris, Kempe and Burne Jones, and interesting 19th century memorials.

PORTSMOUTH AND ENVIRONS. St Thomas' church – now the cathedral – has grown from 1185 until it was finally finished in 1991! The number and variety of parish churches here will keep you happy for ages. Some have been beautifully resurrected following bomb damage. The Royal Garrison church is excellent EE of c1212, St Anne's Dockyard church is Classical, of 1785 and amongst the later churches St Alban's *Copnor* (1914, by Sir Charles Nicholson) and Holy Spirit *Southsea* (by Micklethwaite, 1904, with later work by Nicholson and S.E. Dykes Bower) should be high on anyone's list of priorities. They pale into insignificance, however, when compared to Sir Arthur Blomfield's gigantic St Mary's *Kingston* (1887–9). It is enormous, sumptuous, Perp and breathtaking outside and inside – 210 ft long and with a great tower reaching 165 ft.

Just off the peninsula is *Portchester*'s castle and amazing Norman church, which is such a gem and has an unforgettable situation, also St Philip's *Cosham* – a masterpiece by Sir Ninian Comper (1938) whose exterior gives little hint of the glory within. Do also go to the top of Portsdown Hill for a wonderful panoramic view of the whole area and beyond.

ROMSEY ABBEY. St Mary and St Ethelfleda's was the church of the Benedictine nunnery. The whole church was taken over by the town at the Reformation (as at Tewkesbury and St Albans). The central tower is simple with small windows and a later bell-cage of 1625. It is a great Norm 12th C church and it is all very uniform (with ground storey, triforium and clerestory) with the exception of the 13th C Gothic W bay with EE lancets and 13th C capitals with heads and foliage, and the E end with four Dec windows with Geometrical tracery, two above two. The aisles have rib-vaults. The richly carved Norm capital on the right just before reaching the High Altar should be noted. It depicts a battle scene in which some angels are intervening; they are gripping the swords of the combatants whilst several heads and limbs lie below.

The SE apse has a most valuable reredos. It is Sax, of Christ crucified with two angels on the arms of the Cross and the Virgin and St John the Evangelist below, and Longinus and the Soldier with the Sponge yet lower. The very famous Sax crucifix is, however, outside on the W wall of the S transept. It is nearly seven feet high and can be dated about the first half of the 11th C. Above Christ's head the hand of God the Father shoots out of a cloud.

The large early 16th C painted board in the N transept is both interesting and instructive. It was obviously intended for a reredos. There are nine saints in the top row – St Jerome, St Francis (with St Clare at his feet), St Sebastian, St Augustine of Canterbury, St Scolastica, St Benedict, St Roche, St Armel, and St Augustine of Hippo. Below, Christ rises from the tomb with the soldiers asleep and two censing angels. The Abbess, who is the donor, appears as a small kneeling figure. In the N aisle is a large Flemish chest c1500 with Flamboyant tracery and a fine lock. One of the most recent graves, and certainly one of the simplest, is that of Earl Mountbatten in the S transept.

SHORWELL. (Isle of Wight). The tower has a recessed stone spire and a tierceron-vault within it. There is a 13th C doorway, otherwise St Peter's is mostly Perp. The stone pulpit is medieval and has its doorway; its wooden tester is dated 1620. There is a 17th C hour-glass, a fine Jac font-cover and a Flemish panel of the Flagellation of Christ. There is the usual St Christopher wall-painting with fishes and ships, but what is unusual is that small panels depict the life of the saint and only one other painting in England does that (at Hemblington in Norfolk). Brass to Richard Bethell, vicar 1518, and a brass plate to the two wives of Barnaby Leigh 1615: they together hold his heart. Mons to Lady Elizabeth Leigh 1619 – two putti with instruments of death; John Leigh and baby son nine months, both kneeling, 1629; and John Leigh 1688.

STOKE CHARITY. St Michael's is beautifully set – aloof from the rat-race, rural and very inviting. A pretty wooden belfry outside and inside a treasure house. It has a grand Norman arcade and chancel arch, an exquisite 15th century sculpture depicting the Mass of St Gregory, part of a wall-painting and lovely monuments and brasses. Above all it will be remembered specially for its atmosphere, its peace and its beauty.

Micheldever church of St Mary has a fine Perp tower of 1527 and a curious but memorable octagonal brick nave (1808) by George Dance Jr.

TICHBORNE. St Andrew's pleasing tower of brick is dated 1703. The nave is EE and the chancel older still, Sax, as proved by the double-splay windows on both sides of the chancel and pilasters. There is a Norm font, Jac altar-rails and box-pews, and a 16th C Communion table. Fragments of glass of St Andrew appear in the head of the E window, which is Reticulated Dec. In the Tichborne Chapel are monuments to Richard Tichborne 1619, and beautifully coloured, a baby of 18 months two days lying on its side; and Sir Benjamin Tichborne and wife with four sons and three daughters, 1621. The village became known during the 19th century for the long and expensive Court proceedings provoked by a bogus claimant to the estate.

Cheriton St Michael's is picturesque and has an attractive church with EE, Dec and Perp work.

WINCHESTER. St Cross, a large mainly Norm church, was begun in Norm times and finished in the following centuries, being built from E to W. This is the church of the hospital (meaning almshouse). It is cruciform with a central tower. The building ends at the W end, by then Dec as the five-light W window shows (and the clerestory). There are rib-vaults, and a number of interesting fittings. In the chancel there are some old tiles. There is a Perp stone screen and some early Renaissance stalls. In the E window is 15th C glass of the Virgin, St John the Evangelist, St Catherine and St Swithin. There is a fine brass to John de Campeden in a cope, nearly six feet long, 1410, and others to Richard Harward 1493, and to Thomas Laune 1518. Some 15th C glass of St Gregory in the N transept. In the nave is a splendid medieval wooden lectern with a parrot's head. The S chancel aisle has a 16th C Flemish triptych. The charming buildings of the hospital around its quadrangle were built by Cardinal Beaufort c1445.

The city itself is one of the most attractive in England and the cathedral is the longest (556 ft externally). Including St Cross and St Matthew's Weeke, Winchester has seven medieval churches. St Bartholomew Hyde has a Norman south doorway and north arcade. St John's has work of c1200, a beautiful Dec window in the south chapel, 13th century wall-paintings, 14th century screenwork and a Perp pulpit. Perhaps the most memorable of all is the tiny St Swithin Upon Kingsgate, which is delightful and set above the 14th century Kingsgate. It has a charming interior with an ancient roof and several features of interest. Of the 19th century churches, Holy Trinity, North Walls (1853–4) is by Henry Woodyer, with good Clayton & Bell glass; St Thomas' (by E.W. Elmslie 1845) is a stately Dec church (now the County Record Office) with a fine tower and spire; and All Saints' (1890–8) is by Pearson and contains the Norman font from the redundant church of St Peter Chesil.

HEREFORD AND WORCESTER

In Herefordshire we have one of England's most unspoilt counties – a pastoral place of great rural charm, with remote hamlets and villages, rich countryside, plenty of trees and always the sight of near or distant hills. It is a county of orchards, hop fields and agriculture; its beauty is more rustic than spectacular and so, in the main, are its churches, which are often quite small, thankfully often open, always delightfully cared for and extremely welcoming. Usually they are built of local sandstone which has a pinkish tinge (even the soil here has a reddish colour). Occasionally chunks of brown tufa mark very early work. In this county, known for its black-and-white houses, we have the occasional church tower also capped with black-and-white.

Herefordshire is a Welsh border county and in some of the churches we are reminded of this by a sturdy fortress-like tower, occasionally totally detached from the church. Here we may enjoy the most exquisite Norman sculpture and design in a multitude of fonts across the county, in tympana above doorways and in complete churches, like Moccas, Peterchurch and, above all, Kilpeck's little Norman gem. Although some good EE and Dec work (with shoals of ballflowers) may been seen here, the county largely had no share in the wealth which produced so many grand Perp churches elsewhere.

Victorian restoration hit many Herefordshire churches but, with a few exceptions, there is little spectacular 19th century work here. Sir G.G. Scott did some work in the county, as did G.F. Bodley, but in many churches we see the honest work of local architects, like Thomas Nicholson and F.R. Kempson. One 20th century creation which must be visited is W.R. Lethaby's delightful thatched Arts and Crafts church at Brockhampton by Ross.

Worcestershire, although a little less untouched than Herefordshire (it borders Birmingham on one side) also has most beautiful scenery, with lush pastures, fields and orchards, the lovely rivers Severn, Avon and Teme, and the sight of hills. From just about everywhere in Worcestershire we see hills, and what lovely hills they are! We have the Cotswolds in one corner, the haunting profile of the Malvern Hills, Bredon Hill, which rises out of nowhere, and even at the Birmingham end are the delightful Clent and Lickey Hills. It is a small county and one of differing and contrasting characters. Civilisation has brought the grand old towns of Evesham, Pershore and Malvern (all with monastic churches), spa towns like Droitwich and Tenbury and industrial towns like Bromsgrove and Kidderminster.

The churches form quite a kaleidoscope too, with lovely golden Cotswold limestone in the south-east, Herefordshire pinky-grey sandstone, brown ironstone in the north-east and some very red churches indeed (like Martley) to the north of Worcester. In this county of many black-and-white houses (often with dovecotes) there is also interesting timberwork in the churches, with a timber-framed church at Besford and towers at Warndon, Pirton, Dormston, etc. The county has a fair representation of most periods of architecture. The 18th century may be seen at Bewdley, Stourbridge, Tardebigge and, above all, Great Witley. For interesting Gothic Revival work we must go to Great Malvern and its area, also to Worcester. This is a county which is rich in monuments, and rich in variety. Every church is worth visiting for something. Sadly, so many now have to be locked.

Of Herefordshire's 200 or so medieval churches and Worcestershire's c150, a few of the latter are now included in the new West Midlands county.

HEREFORDSHIRE

ABBEY DORE.   What remains of St Mary's church is the chancel and transept of the Cistercian abbey, the nave having disappeared. It is in isolated country. The chancel is late 12th C and there is therefore little Norm work. The E window has three stepped lancets and foliage is still stiff-leaf. There was a complete restoration in the 17th C when the slender tower was located on the S side. The ambulatory ends at the E end in a double walk with four slender piers and eight shafts. There is a fine piscina in the S transept. The chancel and transepts have flat Jac ceilings of the restoration. Also of that time are the fine screen, stalls, benches, pulpit with tester, altar-rails and W gallery. The N ambulatory door is 13th C ironwork. Some bosses of interest should be seen, and there are fragments of old glass and two 13th C cross-legged knights.

AYMESTREY.   At St John the Baptist and St Alkmund's the screens are worth anyone's interest. The rood-screen is splendid with liernevaulted panels, coving, three foliage friezes and cresting. The parclose screens are plainer. The church is mainly Norm but there is a Jac pulpit.

Sir John Lingen and wife are commemorated by an incised slab, 1506. There is the base and shaft of a churchyard cross.

BOSBURY. The massive detached tower was originally built for defence. Holy Trinity is mainly EE with lancets, with a timber S porch and later nave roof. The font is EE. The Morton Chapel is 16th C with Perp windows and fan-vaulting. There is a screen with coving, and a Jac pulpit, lectern and reader's desk. Mons include a coffin-lid with crosses and sword; John Harford 1573; and Richard Harford and wife 1578. The village has some attractive black-and-white houses.

BRINSOP. The Hereford School of Norm sculpture have left their mark here, with a c11th C tympanum with St George. Also the inner and outer arches of the inner doorway have human figures, animals and angels flying down. The chancel is c1350. A Victorian bell-turret but the bells are medieval. A Perp stoup, simple screen, some fragments of sculpture, and wall-paintings of the Crucifixion above the S door. Some 14th C panels of glass, including St George and a seated Christ, and two 13th C coffin-lids. Brinsop Court with its moat is 14th C. It is of red sandstone, and later half-timbered black-and-white.

CASTLE FROME. St Michael's has a Victorian timber black-and-white belfry and a small spire. There is some Norm work in the W and S and the priest's doorway, and some windows and the chancel arch. The great Norm font is probably the finest of its kind in England, by the Hereford School of carvers. The Baptism of Christ is a wonderful scene – the ripples of the water and Christ's legs seen through them, and two pairs of fishes; then the hands of St John the Baptist and of God the Father, and the Dove of the Holy Spirit followed by the signs of the four Evangelists, angel, eagle, lion and ox, two doves on each side. Its date is c1170. As the population of the parish is about 60, the font cannot often be used. There is Perp ceilure in the chancel, a 17th C pulpit, Jac stalls, a small bust of a knight holding a heart, and fragments of old glass. Mons include a tomb-chest with alabaster effigies of husband, wife and children below, c1640; and one to Francis Unett 1656.

GARWAY. A sturdy Norman church in a lonely spot on the slopes of the hills overlooking the river Monnow, near the Welsh border. Its massive 13th century tower (70 ft high and 33 ft square) stands well away from the church and at a jaunty angle to it, although tower and church have been linked by a passage since the 1600s. This building, with its fine Norman chancel arch and EE south chapel, was founded by the Knights

133

Templar. Of special note here is the chancel roof (c1400), the medieval carvings around the chapel piscina, the sturdy benches and some good 17th century woodwork, but just to drink in this remarkable building in its setting is worth the journey down the lanes to find it.

HEREFORD.   A lovely city centre, some superb river scenery, a jewel of a cathedral and two good medieval churches, both with tall spires. St Peter's – a big town church of the 13th and 14th centuries (restored by T Nicholson in the 1880s), has a large chancel, furnished with 15th century stalls and a fine roof to the south chapel, also a splendid set of Royal Arms of William III. It is a lively Evangelical church and its spire reaches 160 ft. All Saints' is Anglo-Catholic and very devotional inside. Its 225 ft spire (completed c1330) is a wonderful sight. Its interior is full of atmosphere and beautiful things. There are lovely medieval roofs, some stalls with misericords, and a fine chest (c1300), the front of which is a mass of interlacing arches. The south chapel reredos was fashioned c1700 and the carved pulpit a few years before. There is a bread-shelf of 1683 and a collection of chained books.

Holmer St Bartholomew's church (one mile north), with its detached tower, is Norman and worth finding.

KILPECK.   A small village with a small church, St Mary and St David's, but famous throughout England for its wonderful Norman carvings – all c1170–1190 and all worth careful study. Most wonderful of all is the south doorway, then the carvings around the corbel table beneath the roofs (try to turn a blind eye to the naughty ones!), the lovely chancel arch and the delightful vaulted apse. It is all superb, and rightly famous. Some think that the holy water stoup, with its pair of hands, is Saxon.

LEDBURY.   One of those perfect market towns, with one of the county's largest and grandest churches. We are drawn by the spire (1773) on the detached tower, rising 202 ft into the air. In the noble church of St Michael and All Angels we see Norman work in the west doorway and chancel arcade, EE in the tower, superb Dec in many of the windows (especially those in the baptistry) and Perp in the east window (with glass by C.E. Kempe). The aisle roofs are noteworthy, also the 16th century stalls, but possibly the array of monuments here will be remembered most of all.

Another selection of monuments awaits you at *Much Marcle's* interesting church of St Bartholomew and *Eastnor* church of St John the Baptist is by Sir George Gilbert Scott.

LEOMINSTER. Part of what was an enormous priory church of St Peter and St Paul and it is still large, broad and spacious. Its 104 ft tower, which is Norman in its lower stages, is part of a noble west front. Work of all periods may be seen here, but the finest craftsmanship must surely be in the splendid Dec windows of the south aisle, which are covered with ballflower ornament, also the mighty Perp west window – of eight lights and some 45 ft high. Inside are massive Norman arcades, a fine organ-case (1739) and a ducking stool which was last used in 1809, amongst many interesting features. A great deal of what was once here perished in a terrible fire in 1699.

MADLEY. Lovely architecture and proportions in this stately and elegant sandstone village church of the Nativity of the Virgin from the EE and Dec periods. Beneath its apsidal east end is a vaulted crypt and in the churchyard is an original (if rather worn) cross. A noble interior here – the long nave is punctuated by EE arcades and there is a further Dec arcade to the beautiful Chilstone Chapel. The font is Norman and old woodwork survives in the parclose screen and the stalls with misericords, but it is the lovely 13th and 14th century glass in the east window which is the focal point here.

Eaton Bishop St Michael's church, nearby, also has remarkable 14th century glass.

PETERCHURCH. Delightfully set in the Golden Valley, with a 13th and 14th century tower and tall spire (195 ft), which was replaced in recent years. St Peter's itself is bold, large and unaltered Norman, of four sections and having great dignity. The general effect of the place as a whole, inside and out, is memorable. The High Altar stone is the original, and may even pre-date the Norman church.

This is a wonderful area for churches. Down the valley is St Bartholomew's *Vowchurch*, with its timbered belfry and 17th century woodwork, idyllically set by the river. To the north-east is *Tyberton*'s Classical church of St Mary of 1720 and the adorable little Norman parkland church of St Michael and All Angels at *Moccas*.

SAINT MARGARET's. Amidst beautiful countryside, lonely and isolated, is this humble little shrine, with its timber belfry and unassuming rustic exterior. Inside however is the most wonderful rood-screen of c1520, complete with its sumptuous loft – one of the handful remaining in England. It hides a chancel arch which is 400 years older. The godly texts which were painted upon the walls to edify the faithful in the 1700s have been carefully preserved.

Vowchurch, delightfully set by the river, contains interesting woodwork – notice its perky timber-framed belfry.

In *Bacton* church of St Faith (on the way back to the Golden Valley) is the fascinating monument to Blanche Parry, Maid of Honour to Queen Elizabeth I, where we see the maid kneeling before the Queen herself.

SHOBDON. What a place! A church in an idyllic parkland setting, up a drive, its Norman arches now forming a parkland ornament about quarter of a mile to the north. Onto the 13th century tower in 1756 was built a new church of St John the Evangelist – and what a church! This is what we call 'Strawberry Hill Gothic' (or 'Gothick') and here is a complete and eccentric period-piece. There are ogee arches everywhere, benches with odd-shaped ends, a stately three-decker pulpit (draped with velvet) and sounding-board, pews for the Bateman family (with fireplace) and their servants, and other 1756 furnishings – all painted in subdued colours. The worn Norman font, with its fine lions, forms a striking contrast. Even this was rescued from a new life as a garden ornament.

WORCESTERSHIRE

BREDON.   So much here which is typical of the best in the county – the haunting Bredon Hill nearby, the charming stone village, the 14th century tithe barn and a wonderful church, with its central tower and elegant (161 ft) spire. We see architecture from most periods at St Giles', together with Jacobean woodwork in the font-cover and rails, a set of 86 heraldic tiles from the 14th century, two lady saints in 14th century glass, an Easter Sepulchre and some excellent monuments – that to Sir Giles Read (1611) in the EE Mitton Chapel being of premier interest.

BROADWAY.   Tourists flock to this picture-postcard village with its old houses. Some seek out the bold tower of H. Eginton's 1839 church of St Michael. A few manage to find Broadway's ancient church of St Eadburgha, tucked away along the lane to Snowshill in its peaceful setting. Cruciform, of Cotswold stone and with a pretty central tower, it contains work from most medieval periods. There is a crude old font, and old woodwork in the chancel screen, in some of the seating and in a carved panel showing eight saints. There are 17th century rails and a palimpsest brass (1572) of Anthony Daston. Another delightful approach to a church may be enjoyed at nearby St Mary's *Childswickham*.

CROOME D'ABITOT.   The date 1763, the names of Robert Adam and 'Capability' Brown and the lovely parkland setting, will tempt many to seek this remarkable church (RCF), with its stately tower and its light and airy interior. St Mary Magdalene's stucco-covered ceiling and slender piers, its Gothick arches with ogee embellishments, its ambitious Gothick pulpit and exquisitely carved wooden font and its superb Coventry monuments – will make many very glad that they did find it!
   Nearby is St Peter's *Pirton*, with its remarkable timber-framed tower and St Peter's *Besford*, where the whole church is timber-framed.

137

ELMLEY CASTLE. Another idyllic village, set near the foot of Bredon Hill. St Mary's church stands well, at the top of a wide street, and it oozes charm both inside and out. The embattled north aisle, transept and porch, the sturdy 13th century tower and the chancel with its 11th century herringbone masonry, make the exterior worth seeing. On our way in, we must look for the strange carvings of the pig and rabbit in the porch, before enjoying the host of treasures awaiting us inside. The 15th century font bowl rests on a 12th century base, where monsters lurk, with curly tails. There are medieval benches and two truly magnificent monuments. Above all, the atmosphere is wonderful!

EVESHAM. A town with much antiquity and interest, presided over by the mighty stone-panelled bell-tower of the former abbey, with two medieval churches nearby, side by side. All Saints' (with the taller spire) has a beautiful western porch and superb Perp architecture in the Lichfield Chapel, built just before 1513. St Lawrence's (RCF) has a stately Perp interior, with superb stone panelling and a mighty east window. Here the chapel of St Clement has a fine fan-vaulted ceiling. The tower ceiling is also vaulted and the tower arch is panelled.

Find *Cropthorne*, beautifully set beside the Avon, whose church of St Michael has a Saxon cross of c AD 800, also *Fladbury* St John the Baptist's where there are splendid 15th century brasses to the Throckmortons.

GREAT WITLEY. To see Baroque in all its splendour, we must go to Germany, Italy, or Austria – or, in England, to Great Witley, whose amazing St Michael's church of 1735, with the ruined shell of Witley Court beside it, forms an unforgettable picture. A Classical exterior, with an entrance portico with Tuscan columns, hides an interior which is breathtaking in its splendour, thanks to Baron Foley, who acquired glass, paintings and fittings from the chapel of the Duke of Chandos at Canons, Little Stanmore (the church there has the other famous English Baroque interior), and set them up here between 1747–56. So here we gaze at vivid 17th century glass in the ten windows, we look up at a ceiling adorned with rich paintings by Antonio Belluci, surrounded by adornments worked in papier-mache by Pietro Bagutti – a brilliant essay in white and gold, set up, we think, under the direction of James Gibbs. The fine organ-case from Canons is here also. The white marble font has kneeling angels and the furnishings, although 19th century, blend in beautifully with their surroundings.

Abberley has a noble 19th century church, St Mary's, by J.J. Cole, also a little old church at the centre of the village, where only the chancel is roofed. St Peter's *Martley* (to the south) has a tower of very red stone and some interesting medieval wall-paintings.

HOLT. Here a Norman church and a 14th century castle stand together. A Norman church of high quality this; another may be seen at Rock, near Kidderminster. The superb carvings around St Martin's two Norman doorways and its chancel arch are worth examining. The font is also Norman, but the nave roof is 15th century, whilst the south chapel shows interesting 14th century Dec architecture and preserves a scene of the Annunciation in 15th century glass.

At *Ombersley*, St Andrew's church (with its elegant spire) was built in 1830 to the designs of Rickman.

MALVERN. Beautiful Malvern, under the shadow of those distinctive Malvern Hills – and so much for the church-crawler here. At the centre of the spa town of Great Malvern rises the glorious priory church with its stately, pinnacled exterior, tall Perp clerestory and panelled central tower. Inside are Norman arcades, a complete and fascinating set of misericord stalls, a wonderful array of 15th century glass and a fine collection of medieval tiles. Of the later churches, St Matthias', Malvern Link (Sir G.G. Scott 1844 and F.W. Hunt 1880) is large and grand, St. Peter's Cowleigh (Street 1863) is smaller and Tractarian and the Ascension (Sir W. Tapper 1903) is distinctive and devotional. There are several others. Most endearing of all, to many visitors, is Little Malvern Priory, in its sylvan setting (try approaching it from the east), whose grand tower broods over a fragment of what was once a great church, containing medieval tiles, more 15th century glass (showing Edward IV and his family) and a wonderful atmosphere which makes us feel in touch with real history.

Two lovely Victorian churches may be seen to the east of Malvern, at St Leonard's *Newland* (P.C. Hardwick 1864) and at St Mary's *Madresfield* (F. Preedy 1866).

OVERBURY. Another picturesque village, watched over by the noble Perp central tower of its parish church of St Faith. The nave has Norman arcades, the chancel has EE lancet windows in pairs, also a broad east window of eight lights and a vaulted ceiling. Parts of the nave benches are 15th century and wood from the rood screen was reused to make the present pulpit. The font is partly Norman and upon its bowl we see a carving of a priest holding a church.

In this area of grand scenery are *Beckford*, with St John the Baptist's important Norman stonecarving and St Mary's *Ripple*, where we see

139

Norman evolving into EE in a large cruciform church where the architecture is very noteworthy and the misericords delightfully portray the
labours of the months of the year.

PERSHORE.   The mighty (144 ft) tower and the eastern parts of the
abbey church dominate this lively little town. The church must have
been enormous when complete; even now St Andrew's church across the
road looks very small beneath its shadow. Inside, stonework of the 1200s
in the handsome vaulted chancel (with 41 craved bosses) and of the 1300s
in the tower, contrast with Norman work in the south transept. Sir G.G.
Scott restored it in 1863 – look up to see his 'cat's cradle' ringing platform
beneath the tower. Amongst the other treasures here are a Norman font
and some fine monuments. Here also is a great feeling of life and use, the
modern work being very tasteful. Nothing, however, can compare with
that wonderful tower – a masterpiece of the 14th century.

SHELSLEY WALSH.   A small church, beautifully situated near the
manor house. St Andrew's has a Norman nave of tufa and an EE chancel,
with a 19th century bell-turret and porch. We come here especially to
enjoy the remarkable medieval roof timbers, the medieval tiles in the
chancel and, above all, the 15th century screenwork, intricately and
exquisitely carved, with the rood beam in its original position above.
The pulpit is by Comper and Sir Francis Walsh (1596) has a monument
of wood – a great rarity. *Shelsley Beauchamp* church of All Saints has a red
medieval tower attached to an attractive Victorian church by James
Cranston (1846).

STRENSHAM.   A real character this – but aren't they all? A lonely
position near the river Avon gives atmosphere to the exterior but
it is what is inside which is really worth seeing. St Philip and St James'
nave has 16th century benches, panelling and hat-pegs. There is a family
pew and a two-decker pulpit. There are the Royal Arms and some
hatchments on the walls. The front of the western gallery was part of the
rood-screen or loft and dates from c1500. It is painted with 23 saints
(look for the delightful picture of St Anthony with his pig). There are
some superb brasses here and the tomb of Sir Thomas Russell (1632) and
his wife not only has their effigies but also a coffin underneath. Sir
Francis Russell (1705) and his wife are opposite and we witness here his
coronet being carried into the clouds.
   Nearby *Eckington* has a fine monument to John Hanford (1616) in its
partly Norman church of Holy Trinity and part of *Defford* St James'
church tower is timber-framed.

TENBURY ST MICHAEL.   People pass this great Victorian church, near a pleasant stretch of common, and wonder what it is. The answer is that it is unique in England, being built in 1856 to Henry Woodyer's designs, partly as a parish church and partly as the chapel for the adjacent choir school. Church and college were the brainchild of Sir A.F. Gore Ouseley and are a monument to English choral music. Inside the great church are soaring wood-vaulted roofs, a remarkable canopy over the High Altar, delicate iron screenwork, a 22 ft tall wooden font-cover, a superb four-manual organ (mostly by Willis) – and all this and much more bathed in light which shines through Hardman's glorious stained glass, reputed to be some of the best 19th century glass in any English church.

St Mary's *Tenbury Wells* has a Norman tower and a 14th century Easter Sepulchre, but was largely rebuilt in 1865 – again by Woodyer.

WICKHAMFORD.   What could be more endearing than the setting of this church of St John the Baptist beside the Tudor manor house, and how very charming it is inside, with its box-pews and other 17th and 18th century woodwork, the Royal Arms of Charles II and the fine monument to Sir Samuel and Sir Edward Sandys (both 1626) and their wives. There is great atmosphere and much interest here – and more at nearby St James' *Badsey*, with its monument to Richard Hoby (1617).

WORCESTER.   One needs to cross the river in order to get the much photographed view of the county's noble cathedral from the west, and also to find the 12th century church of St John in Bedwardine. The best churches in the city are the four classical ones – All Saints' (1739), St Swithun's (RCF, 1734 with Perp tower), St Nicholas' (1735) and Old St Martin's (1768). Among the more interesting later churches are St Martin's London Road (1903) by G.H. Fellowes Prynne and St George's (1895) by Sir Aston Webb. The most spectacular of all Worcester's churches is St Andrew's, where only the 15th century tower and spire (rebuilt in the 18th century) remain from what must have been a splendid Perp church. The spire reaches a spectacular height of 247 ft and is a prominent and very graceful city landmark.

HERTFORDSHIRE

'Loving, warm and homely Hertfordshire – county of pleasant hills and streams'. So it was described by one of its poets and so it certainly still is. County of the rolling Chilterns in the north, of gentle lanes and fords, of lush meadows, parkland and arable land, of many fine trees, of ancient Roman roads, of pretty villages and hamlets with old inns, plastered and weatherboarded cottages, of manor houses known here as 'Burys', of old coaching towns like Baldock, Ware, Hitchin and Sawbridgeworth, of rippling rivers with lovely names, like the Rib, Mimram, Stort, Beane, Gade and Ver. Yes – and also the county of the M1, A1, M25 and Stevenage and Watford. Hertfordshire's scenery is gentle but never monotonous and so many of its villages are picture postcard settings – try Aldbury, Braughing, Much Hadham, Ardeley, Benington, Great Amwell and Westmill for starters! Yet it is little known and its lovely churches often underrated.

About 125 medieval churches await us (and 90 or so later ones), built mostly of flint, with the occasional use of brick and timber to compensate for the lack of durable stone. There is interesting work of all periods from Saxon onwards, including several churches built in the 1950s and 1960s as new estates and new towns grew up. Most Hertfordshire churches are homely and endearing rather than mighty and magnificent, delighting us with mellow colours and textures and pretty settings, which help to shape their characters. There are treasures to be found inside them – fittings, paintings, memorials and brasses and also several surprises. The great distinguishing feature of so many of them is the 'Hertfordshire Spike' – a thin spire (covered with lead, copper or shingles), which may in some cases be medieval in origin, or 16th or 17th century. The Victorians loved them too and placed them on several of their Hertfordshire churches. They range from short stumpy terminations of pyramid roofs (but nearly always behind parapets) to slender and sometimes needle-like spires of considerable height. Several Hertfordshire towers have prominent staircase-turrets which rise above the parapets and occasionally one of these, combined with a largely embattled exterior, makes for a very dignified building.

Hertford, the county town, where four rivers meet, has great atmosphere and two Victorian churches. St Albans is larger and has the cathedral – and indeed what a cathedral! It is 550 ft long externally and has our longest nave, also an immense Norman crossing tower entirely faced with ancient bricks. Its surroundings are delightful, with Roman Verulamium hard by, where lived the saint whose venerable shrine may still be visited in the cathedral church (and city) which bears his name.

ANSTEY. We first see the lychgate, which is medieval and very rare. The lower part of St George's central tower is Norm and the upper part 14th C with its Herts spike. The chancel and transepts are 13th C with characteristic windows. There are unusual piscina and sedilia and a fine 14th C tomb-recess with canopy and pinnacles. The arcades are 14th C and the clerestory 15th C, as is the S porch. On the Norm font four mermen hold their split tails with both hands. There are also 15th C stalls with misericords (a head with tongue out, etc).

Tiny St Mary's church at *Meesden* has a superb Tudor brick porch and St Mary's *Brent Pelham* has a lovely traceried door of the early 14th century and a black marble burial slab of the 13th century, with interesting carvings.

ARDELEY. St Lawrence's has a tower with a Herts spike and the interior is of the three Gothic periods. A fine 13th C piscina and recess opposite. The nave and aisle roofs with angels and bosses are 15th C. There is no screen, but there is a modern rood-loft with coloured Rood figures of beauty (by F.C. Eden). A 14th C font. Brasses to Philip Metcalffe, vicar 1515, and Thomas Shotbolt with wife and children 1599. The mon to Mary Markham 1673 is a demi-figure, and on the ledge in front is her baby. There is also a cartouche for Henry Chauncy 1703.

Walkern St Mary's has Saxon evidence, a Norman arcade, a 15th century screen, and interesting monuments and brasses. St John the Baptist *Cottered* has good Perp windows, a tall lead spire and a fine St Christopher wall-painting.

ASHWELL. St Mary's has the highest tower in the county, crowned by an octagonal lantern and a lead spike reaching 176 ft. Both porches are 15th C, but otherwise nearly all is 14th C with Perp windows. The aisle roofs are original. The chancel has large windows with clear glass, flooding the chancel with light. Jac pulpit. Of great interest are the graffiti in the tower: old St Paul's Cathedral is accurately drawn and there are inscriptions giving useful information. The lychgate is 15th C. The village abounds in picturesque houses.

AYOT ST LAWRENCE. George Bernard Shaw lived in the lovely village – and so did Sir Lyonal Lyde, the lord of the manor who,

143

according to tradition, pulled down the medieval church because it obstructed his view, but was prevented from finishing the job by the Bishop – and so the old tower and some of the roofless walls remain, making a picturesque ruin. Sir Lyonal's Palladian replacement (inconveniently away from the village) was designed by Nicholas Revett and built in 1778. New St Lawrence's looks like something out of pagan classical Greece, with its portico, colonnades and flanking chambers containing the funerary urns of Sir Lyonal and his wife. The interior is spacious and light, with attractive ceilings, black and white marble floors and some tasteful furnishings – and there is certainly much atmosphere in this strange but memorable building.

Ayot St Peter (by J.P. Seddon, 1875) contains lovely Arts and Crafts furnishings. There is much to enjoy at St Peter and St Paul's *Kimpton*, including a 15th century screen and benches.

BRAUGHING. Here is Village England at its most delightful-picturesque houses and the venerable walls of its truly lovely church. The tall tower has an extremely lofty spike. All of St Mary's is 15th C except parts of the chancel which are 13th C. Battlements and pinnacles abound above and spandrels in doorways. There is a two-storeyed S porch with side windows, a clerestory, a rood-turret at the SE of the nave, and a fine nave roof with angels and with the two E bays beautifully coloured and gilt as a rood-celure. Brasses to a man and his wife 1480, and to Barbara Hauchett 1561. Mon to Augustin Steward 1597 and a bust to John Brograve and his younger brother 1625; an angel blows soap-bubbles (for vanity), and Father Time. Also a monument to Ralph Freeman D.D. and wife 1772, with two other Freemans and their wives, all in three medallions.

To the north is St Mary's *Furneux Pelham* (Perp with EE chancel, good roofs and lovely 15th century brass), tiny Norman St Mary's *Little Hormead* with its wonderful 12th century door surviving, and St Mary's *Westmill* (Saxon evidence, Norman arcade and 15th century benches).

DIGSWELL. The old church and manor house are still on their own, although now part of Welwyn Garden City. St John the Evangelist's has been effectively enlarged by adding a new church to its side. The old church with a 13th C piscina has a fine display of brasses: John Peryent, Steward to Richard II, and wife 1415 (very fine); John Peryent his son, 1442; William Roberts and wife (both in shrouds) and two sons, 1484; Thomas Hoore and wife, four sons and eight daughters, 1495; Robert Batyl with one son and wife and ten children, 1557.

Tewin has a small and lovable church of St Peter in a pretty setting, with Norman, EE and Perp work, and an atmospheric interior, with a monument to General Sabine (died 1739).

FLAMSTEAD.   St Leonard's is a church that has almost everything. The tower is Norm, of flint and random stone patched up with bricks and Roman tiles, and has a tall lead Herts spike. The church is mostly 13th and 14th C with Perp windows. The arcades are 13th C with capitals with stiff-leaf foliage. The chancel arch and piscina are 14th C, and there is a 15th C nave roof, a pulpit of 1698, altar-rails of 1700 and a nice Perp rood-screen. Wall-paintings have only recently been discovered. On the N side of the nave is St Christopher and on the chancel arch is Christ in Majesty. In the NE chapel are depicted stories of the Passion, in two tiers. The Entombment scene is the best-preserved. A brass to John Oudeby, rector 1414, and several mons. There is a 15th C tomb-chest with man and wife; Sir Bartholomew Fouke 1604, kneeling; and the Saunders children 1690 – five children with praying hands, placed on a ledge. The sixth child kneels on the floor.

HEMEL HEMPSTEAD.   St Mary's is a large Norm church with a central tower with Norm windows and a fine tall tapering lead spire, nearly 200 ft high. The earliest part is the chancel with a rib-vault. The nave has six bays with circular piers with capitals of great variety. The clerestory is also Norm – a great rarity. The W doorway has zig-zag and leaf motifs. The windows are mostly Dec and Perp. The only early roofs are those in the transepts, 15th C. A brass commemorates Robert Albyn and wife, late 14th C.

HITCHIN.   The largest parish church in the county, St Mary's shows commercial wealth (wool). A fine view has been opened up on the E side. The 13th C tower is low but it has its Herts spike. The S porch is fine: two-storeyed with a lierne-vault and a 15th C door. (The N porch is also two-storeyed). The Arms of the Staple of Calais appear on the S wall. Large Perp windows light the whole church. All is embattled, indicating local wealth. There is a fine series of 14th and 15th C roofs, and also of 15th C screens with a variety of tracery. The 15th C font has figures under ogee canopies, and the pulpit has restored 15th C panels. Several brasses – a priest of the late 15th C; a man and woman in shrouds, with children, late 15th C; a man, woman and children 1452; a woman of the late 15th C; and a man with three wives late 15th C. Of three 15th C tomb-chests, two have brasses on them. Brasses also to a shrouded young woman, and to a shrouded woman with children, and to a civilian and his wife of the mid-15th C.

Embattled walls and a slender Hertfordshire 'Spike', so typical of this county, are seen here at Much Hadham, one of its most beautiful villages.

Holy Saviour church (1865) is a good example of the Gothic Revival work of William Butterfield.

HUNSDON. Hunsdon House (of Henry VIII and his three children fame) and the church of St Dunstan are on their own some way from the village. The tower has a Herts spike. The windows of the chancel are late Perp. There is a fine timber N porch. Both chapels are of brick. The pulpit with tester is Jac, and the screen between the nave and S chapel is also Jac and is one of the best. The family pews have Jac decoration. The altar-rails are of 1700. A brass shows Margaret Shelley in a shroud with the Trinity above, 1495, and a brass plate to James Gray, Park-keeper, 1591 shows him aiming at a stag whilst Death (a skeleton) is aiming at him. Mons to Francis Poyntz 1528; Sir John Carey and wife 1617; and Sir Thomas Forster in his Judge's robes, beautifully coloured, 1612.

Widford St John the Baptist's church has a tall copper spire and, although much restored, has great charm. It also has a little Norman work and some lovely 14th century wall-paintings.

MUCH HADHAM. A delightful village with the church on its own. St Andrew's tower is Perp with a tall Herts spike. Perp also the S porch, E window and the roofs, which should be studied. The remainder of the church is 13th and 14th C. There is a 15th C rood-screen, stalls with panelled backs and poppyheads, two big chairs with panelled backs of 1400, and 13th C ironwork on the door to the N vestry. Brasses show a demi-figure of a priest c1420; a man and his wife 1520; Clement Newce, wife and 17 children, 1582; and William Newce, two wives and 13 children, 1610. Mons to Joane Goldsmith 1569 and Dionis Burton 1616.

Little Hadham St Cecilia's has a 15th century timber porch and a 16th century brick transept, also a medieval screen and a pulpit of 1633. The large embattled Perp church of St Michael at *Bishop's Stortford* has much to interest us, including fine roofs, screen, misericord stalls and a pulpit of 1658. Its tall tower and spire (182 ft) are visible for miles.

OXHEY. In a large housing estate at South Oxhey stands Seely & Paget's large church of All Saints (built in 1953) and beside it is the tiny chapel (RCF) which Sir James Altham built in 1612. Its walls are faced with squares of brick and flint, its windows are square-headed and gothic, its pretty hexagonal bell-turret was added as late as 1963. What a surprise inside – no humble or rustic little chapel here – it is a sumptuous ensemble, with original Baroque woodcarving framing the doorway through which we entered, furnished with stalls which face each other ('college-wise') and fit the atmosphere beautifully, although they (and the western porch) were part of a restoration of 1897 by Messrs Cutts. The wooden font and cover are 17th century and are exquisitely carved, but the whole place is dominated by a mighty altarpiece of c1690, with barley-sugar columns and an open pediment with a central flaming urn. We see the founder and his lady in their monument on the south wall. Never dismiss the occasional housing estate!

REDBOURN. St Mary's tower (with spike) and nave are both Norm but the chancel and S aisle are 14th C. The chancel chapel, S porch, clerestory and N aisle are 15th C. Brick battlements and corbel-table. The N arcade is Norm and that on the S a little later. Piscina and sedilia, and an 18th C font. There is a very fine 15th C rood-screen with tracery and vaulting, and it is the best in the county.

At *Harpenden* the church of St Nicholas has a medieval tower, font and brasses, but was mostly rebuilt by W Slater in 1862. St John's is a light and spacious church of 1908 by F.C. Eden.

RIDGE. Although only 15 miles from the centre of London, it is as quiet and peaceful here as it has always been. The small and charming church of St Margaret has also barely been touched since medieval times. It is mainly 15th C and the low tower exactly fits the church. One enters appropriately through a timber porch, although 19th C. Medieval timberwork can however be seen inside in the fine king-post roof. Very modern timberwork can now be seen on stalls, pulpit, altar-rails and Bishop's chair by Thompson of Kilburn, Yorkshire, with his trade-mark of a little mouse. There has, however, been a fairly recent discovery of a fine 15th C St Christopher wall-painting. It covers the whole height of the wall and as nearly always, is opposite the principal entrance. The saint has a long staff and carries the Infant Christ on his shoulder. Fish can be seen in the river.

ST ALBANS. St Michael's church is built on the site of the Roman Forum, and there are many Roman tiles in the church. The tower and W end are modern, but the nave and chancel walls are Sax. 10th C. The Normans added aisles, but left the Sax walls. The clerestory is 13th C with lancets. The Lady Chapel or S chancel chapel is slightly later and higher, so that part of the clerestory looks into it. This chapel has a fine E window with two lancets and a circular window between them. There is a fine 15th C nave roof, a Perp font, and a fine Jac pulpit with tester and hour-glass. On a board is part of a Doom painting. Brasses to John Pecock and wife 1330; a civilian in an ogee-foliated cross, 1330; and a knight c1400. But the monument which everyone comes to see is to Sir

Francis Bacon, Lord Chancellor 1626 – a life-sized figure seated comfortably and asleep, as after a big dinner.

This church, the cathedral and the fine church of St Peter were restored by Lord Grimthorpe. St Stephen's has Norman work and a 16th century eagle lectern. Sir Walter Tapper and Martin Travers both designed fine reredoses for St Saviour's church (1904, by William Woodward) which is Anglo-Catholic and beautiful inside.

SOUTH MIMMS. The fine Perp tower of St Giles' is a splendid example of the typical Kent tower of that date, with a prominent stair-turret at one corner and continued above the top of the tower. The nave is also Perp, the chancel 13th C and the N aisle of brick 16th C. The rood-screen is modern, but both side screens are original and beautifully carved with leopards' heads (the Frowyk badge) on the cusps. The medieval glass in the N aisle in bright colours shows the donors and families which gave the glass originally above. There is a large 13th C chest and the font is also of that period. There are two splendid Frowyk monuments – in the N chapel Henry Frowyk, the son who died before his father, and in the chancel the father who died a few years later, c1540. The interest is that the earlier monument is purely Perp, whereas the later one (but only by a few years) is purely Renaissance.

The parkland St Mary's church of *North Mimms* has good Dec work, also an Elizabethan pulpit and several monuments and brasses. The stately church of St Mary at *Potters Bar* was designed by J.S. Alder and consecrated in 1915. It has a lofty and impressive interior with tasteful and devotional fittings but, above all, here the late Lawrence E. Jones, co-author of this book, worshipped for 60 years and served as church-warden and licensed Reader.

STANDON. A picturesque village street here and a large and remarkable flint church of great interest which is built upon rising ground (climb to the top of the churchyard for an unusual view of it). The tall tower (with Herts spike) is detached (or was until the organ chamber arrived) and stands proudly to the south of St Mary's, which has an EE chancel, good Dec windows in the nave and aisles and a large and unusual western porch. What a surprise inside! Not only does the floor slope dramatically upwards from west to east, but we climb a total of 13 steps in order to reach the altar (which is indeed 'high and lifted up') and to obtain the lovely view westwards down the church. So much to discover here also, including a beautiful font of c1200, a (restored) EE chancel arch with shafts of polished marble, several brasses and two splendid monuments in the chancel to Sir Ralph (1587) and Sir Thomas Sadleir (1606).

STANSTEAD ABBOTS.   St James' (RCF) has a perfect Hertfordshire exterior and is well away from its village. A prominent 15th
century flint tower, with higher staircase-turret and Herts spike, a pretty
15th century timber porch and a north chapel of 1577 in Tudor brick.
Inside, this church is an absolute gem because the Victorians did not
bother to alter it (instead they built St Andrew's church in the village)
and so here we have the 17th and 18th century fittings and the atmosphere which goes with them. There are tall box-pews, a three-decker
pulpit (its sounding-board is now part of a door in the tower), the Royal
Arms of William and Mary and the Commandments above the east
window, with the Creed and Lord's Prayer flanking the window; there
are hatchments, brasses and monuments of interest and much else, all set
beneath a medieval king-post roof.

Do go, via the charming little church of *Stanstead St Margaret* (box-
pews here and lovely Dec east window), to *Great Amwell* to see its very
endearing Norman church of St John the Baptist, with a rounded apse
(also a 15th century tower with original west doors, 17th century pulpit,
and brasses). It is set so beautifully above the New River, with its
weeping willows, green islands and Myddleton monument. Could there
be a more charming picture anywhere? A little corner of paradise here –
do go down to look up at it.

WARE.   St Mary's is a typical Hertfordshire town church, all embattled, showing the prosperity of the place. The tower has the usual Herts
spike. The church is mainly 14th and 15th C, very much restored. There
are two transepts, unusual in this county. Most of the roofs are old. The
font of c1400 is the finest in the county, and indeed one of the finest in the
country: on the bowl are figures of St Mary and the Archangel Gabriel,
St Margaret, St Christopher, St George, St Catherine, St James, and St
John the Baptist. Between the figures are demi-figures of angels, alterna-
tely carrying musical instruments and Instruments of the Passion. There
is a 17th C pulpit, altar-rails and panelling in the S chapel, and a 15th C
door to the N vestry with three locks. Brasses to Elene Warbulton 1454;
a lady of about 1425; and William Pyrry, his wife and children 1470.

Hertford has two fine 19th century churches – St Andrew's (by J.
Johnson 1869) with an elegant tower and spire and preserving the Perp
doorway from its medieval predecessor, and grand and stately All Saints'
which is Perp, by Paley, Austin & Paley (1895–1905), looking just like
their Lancashire churches and built of red Runcorn stone – a bit of the
north-west planted in the middle of Hertford. *Bengeo* has a tiny and
complete Norman church of St Leonard (very atmospheric and with a
13th century wall-painting) and an impressive Victorian church of the
Holy Trinity (by Benjamin Ferrey 1855) with a tall spire.

HUMBERSIDE

About two-thirds of it was once Yorkshire and the rest the Lincolnshire district of Lindsey, with the broad Humber estuary still marking the natural division of the old counties and providing exciting views from both sides. The coastline stretches from Flamborough Head down to Cleethorpes and its countryside includes the Yorkshire Wolds, the plain and peninsula of Holderness (with its grand churches) and the northern part of Lindsey, where we find several Saxon churches. There are market towns like Pocklington, Great Driffield and Market Weighton to visit, larger towns like Bridlington (with its priory) and Beverley (with its wonderful, wonderful minster) and Kingston upon Hull, with one of England's largest parish churches. Churchwise there is much for us to explore here, not least the glories of Howden, Hedon and Patrington, which are nationally famous.

NORTH HUMBERSIDE

BEEFORD.   St Leonard's has a splendid Perp tower with a figure of St Leonard and a lace-like open-work parapet of Yorkshire type and eight pinnacles. Perp S porch and arcades. The long lancets on the S side of the chancel indicate a 13th C date. A 14th C effigy of a priest, and a brass to Thomas Tonge, rector in cope, holding a book, 1472.

BEVERLEY MINSTER.   Of cathedral size and magnificence. The W front with its two perfect Perp W towers was completed by 1450. The towers are oblong and have 14 pinnacles, and are the finest W towers in England (and show Perp at its best). W window of nine lights. A grand N porch. The nave and aisles are Dec; they have flying buttresses with pinnacles. The clerestory shows a change from Dec to Perp. The chancel and transepts are mainly EE with lancets (the exception being the great Perp nine-light E window and the Perp Percy Chapel). The beautiful EE staircase to the former chapter house remains on the N side. The Percy screen is exquisite Dec work which continues as the Percy tomb, which has the most splendid Dec monument in the country, probably Lady Eleanor Percy. There are pinnacles and cusps with little figures, seven knights and a lady, all with heraldry, as well as St Michael, the Virgin, Christ blessing, the Annunciation, St Catherine and the Nativity. At the apex Christ is seated holding a soul in a napkin on one side, and on the other side is Christ seated. Numerous angels are ascending and descending and holding Instruments of the Passion. Opposite are sedilia of wood equally elaborate and with little vaults.

There is a Saxon stone seat called the Frid-stool. Also stalls of 1520 with poppyheads and vaulted canopies with 68 misericords, which should be studied in detail. The large 12th C font has an 18th C cover. The church is mostly vaulted. A tread-wheel for lifting stones still remains in the roofs of the crossing and S trancept.

The Minster clock is unique. It is the only one which strikes on bells in two towers – the quarter chimes on the ten bells in the N tower and the hours on the great bell (St John of Beverley, weighing over seven tons) in the S tower.

BEVERLEY.   St Mary's is one of the most beautiful churches in England. The earliest part is the N chapel, with late 13th C Geometrical tracery. It has a fine early 16th C timber roof beautifully coloured in blue and gold with a crypt below the chapel. The E window of five lights is Perp and is flanked by turreted crocketed spirelets. Both nave and chancel have a clerestory. The splendid central tower was erected in 1530 with four-light belfry windows and 16 pinnacles.

A splendid S porch, with four windows on each side and vaulted. Perp W front with two turrets with octagonal tops. The W window is of seven lights. The N chancel aisle has a tierceron-vault and Flowing tracery: the doorway to the adjoining sacristy has a hare and a lion and it is thought that the hare gave Lewis Carroll the idea of the March Hare in *Alice in Wonderland*. The nave arcade was rebuilt in 1524, partly by the Masons Guild, who appear as a lovable group of five in blue jackets and wearing pink shoes on a capital. The nave ceiling is original. The stalls with poppyheads and 23 misericords are of 1450. The chancel ceiling, 1445, is painted with 40 English kings ending with Henry VI. There is nothing like it anywhere else. The N chancel chapel has an early 16th C ceiling with bosses. Large 16th C font.

BRIDLINGTON PRIORY.   Only the western half remains at St Mary's with two W towers – the N is Norm, EE and Dec, and the top modern, and the S tower is Perp and the top part modern, with a W doorway between the two towers. The N aisle is EE and the S aisle early Dec. The great W window of nine lights is Perp. The clerestory has large windows. The N porch is EE with fine stiff-leaf capitals. A very rare object is a stone offertory-box with a bracket for a figure adjacent. Pillar piscina and a 14th C font. A mon, a 12th C slab of Tournai marble with animals and a cat upside down. The monastic gatehouse remains.

COTTINGHAM. St Mary's is a large church with a massive Perp central tower with eight pinnacles and a prominent stair-turret. The nave and arcades are Dec with a W window with Flowing tracery. Then Perp transept end windows and chancel with a seven-light E window. Brasses to Nicholas de Luda, priest in cope 1383, and John Smith and wife 1504.

FLAMBOROUGH. The tower, chancel and S aisle of St Oswald's are modern, but the chancel arch and font are Norm. The great feature of the church is the rood-loft, only about twelve original ones still remaining in England. It has beautiful canopied niches which would have been filled with coloured figures. If one can imagine this loft front in its glory with figures, gilt and colouring, one can visualise a little of the magnificence of a church just before the Reformation.

GREAT DRIFFIELD. The glory of All Saints' is the magnificent Perp tower with large belfry windows with eight elaborate pinnacles. The arcades and clerestory are 13th C. The E windows are Perp, the S aisle windows Dec. Late 12th C font. There is a 13th C figure of a bishop on the E wall outside, and two kneeling figures remain from the Jac monument to Richard and William Spinke.

HEDON. St Augustine's has one of the most impressive exteriors in England. The grand Perp central tower has two tiers of large double windows, a pierced parapet and 16 pinnacles. The N face of the N transept shows lancets to perfection. Two N doorways. The interior of the church as it now exists is largely EE with some early Dec work. Dec font. There is the effigy of a bearded man of the 14th C, and a black marble slab with a floriated head of the 13th C.

HOLME UPON SPALDING MOOR. A wonderful hilltop site for this lovely churchyard and lovely church of All Saints – its pinnacled tower a landmark for miles around. The interior is atmospheric and beautiful, beneath a 15th century nave roof with bosses and containing a 17th century pulpit, a 17th century barrel organ in an 18th century gallery, part of a Perp screen and some godly Elizabethan texts. It was restored by the ever-sensitive Temple Moore, who also restored the nearby Classical church of St Edmund at *Seaton Ross* (1788), which contains its original pulpit and rails.

One of the stately stone churches on the Yorkshire side of the Humber at Cottingham, near Hull.

HOWDEN. St Peter's grand, tall Perp central tower has two tiers of large windows, battlements, and four small pinnacles. The chancel and 14th C chapter house (the church was collegiate) have disappeared and the chancel that remains is Dec. The two-storeyed porch is vaulted. The ruined chancel shows the beauty that has been lost. The Perp stone pulpitum remains and it now serves as a reredos: many figures are original. Dec font. There is a cross-legged knight and his lady of 1311, and a cross-legged knight on a tomb-chest 1338, with weepers. Brass to a knight c1480.

HULL. Holy Trinity is one of the largest parish churches in England by area; it is 285 ft long. The dates are early 14th C for the transepts, mid-14th C for the chancel, early 15th C for the nave, and c1500 for the 150 ft tower. The transepts of the lower part of the tower are the earliest use of brick in England. The grand central tower again makes the church outside. It has two tiers of large windows, a pierced parapet, and eight small pinnacles. The chancel is also of brick – the E window of seven lights has Flowing tracery, and the W window of nine lights is Perp.

The clerestory, both nave and chancel, has twice as many windows as there are arcade bays. Some stalls have poppyheads, and some parts remain of the Perp screen. Large Dec font. A mon possibly to Sir William de la Pole and wife 1381, and the canopied tomb of another de la Pole (no effigy).

LANGTOFT. St Peter's has a 13th C tower and the chancel arch is Perp, although the chancel is Dec with lavish piscina and sedilia. The visitor, however, comes here to see the magnificent Norm font, one of several around here. This one is carved with Adam and Eve, the Tree, St Margaret and the Dragon, St Lawrence, and the Crucifixion of St Andrew.

In *Cowlam*'s church of St Mary of 1852 is a wonderful Norman font where subjects range from the Wise Men to a couple of wrestlers!

PATRINGTON. St Patrick's is an architectural beauty. All is Dec except the lower part of the central tower (EE) and the E window and the glorious spire which are Perp. The latter rises from behind an octagonal screen of Perp panels and small flying buttresses from curious pinnacles. Both transepts have E and W aisles, which is very unusual for a parish church. The window tracery is Flowing and Reticulated, but the E window of seven lights is Perp. The great W window of five lights has Flowing tracery. The N transept has a small doorway with a stone roof on corbels of a lion and an eagle, with a small seated Christ on the keystone. There are N and S porches. The capitals of the arcades are splendid examples of Dec natural foliage (such as oak leaves and vine leaves etc and the mouldings were not so deeply cut as in the EE period).

Winestead's St German is a gem – small and secluded, with Norman work, the 17th century Hildyard Chapel sensitively restored by Temple Moore. Screens, pulpit, brass and monuments of note.

POCKLINGTON. All Saints has a fine Perp tower with a tall tower-arch, large W window and belfry windows, battlements and eight pinnacles. The clerestory is also Perp but otherwise all is late 12th and 13th C. The N arcade is late 12th C. The S arcade is 13th C as also is the S porch and doorway. Note the carvings on all the capitals. There is a 16th C Flemish altar-piece of wood, a coloured organ-case, and the head of a churchyard cross (now inside the church) with the Crucifixion on one side and the Virgin and Child on the other side. An incised slab with foliated cross to the Prioress of Wilberfoss Priory, 1512, and another incised slab to Thomas Dolman, wife and family, 1589. Robert Sothebie is commemorated by an alabaster tablet, 1594.

PRESTON. The Perp tower is beautiful, whether seen from a distance or nearby. It has a large W window and belfry windows and eight pinnacles. There is a tall tower arch. The clerestory is also Perp, the N arcade is EE and the S arcade Dec. The font has leaves on the underside. Some fragments of 15th C Chellastone alabaster altar-pieces. All Saints' has a large W window and two tall belfry windows on each side.

RUDSTON. All Saints' has a Norm tower with twin bell-openings and a tympanum of pierced circles and a Norm tower arch. The arcades are EE, the chancel arch is Dec, as also the sedilia. A Norm font ornamented with circles and octagons. In the churchyard is the largest monolith in Britain – 25½ ft high and six ft wide (apparently it is the same length underground). It is prehistoric and much older than any church or Roman work. This churchyard is circular, and a circular churchyard usually indicates a very ancient site, no doubt of a heathen temple.

Kilham's All Saints, to the south-west, has a superb Norman doorway and *Burton Agnes* has some remarkable monuments – one with three black coffins in place of effigies.

SLEDMERE. What a remarkable place – a real estate village, full of curious and lovely buildings, including its own Eleanor Cross (by Temple Moore, 1895). In the great house lived Sir Tatton Sykes who on his extensive estates built twelve new churches and restored eight others, using architects like Street, Hodgson Fowler and Temple Moore. Sledmere's St Mary's church is by Temple Moore – it is sophisticated and very beautiful, with its vaulted porch and its wonderful interior which shows work of the very highest quality in stone, wood and glass – created in 1898.

Another of Sir Tatton Sykes' churches, this one by Street (1871) is at nearby *Fimber*.

SOUTH DALTON (OR DALTON HULME). J.L. Pearson created in this tiny village one of England's grandest estate churches (1858–61). St Mary's mighty tower and spire rise 200 ft and form a glorious landmark. This is a stately and sophisticated building, its architecture based mainly upon the late 13th century style and providing a feast of wonderful stonework. The vaulted porch admits us to a soaring interior, where we may appreciate Clayton & Bell's superb glass and the fascinating monument to Sir John Hotham (1689).

Pearson also designed nearby *Scorborough* (1857–9), which is smaller, but also fascinating. We see work of all periods at *Lockington*, with its fine roofs, 18th century screen, rails and pulpit, also the Estoft Chapel, panelled in 1634 and painted with 173 heraldic shields.

SOUTH HUMBERSIDE

BARTON-on-HUMBER. St Peter's is a notable Sax church. The W part is the oldest of the church, mid-10th C, then the tower later 10th C, and the top stage of the tower 11th C. The W part has long-and-short work. The tower has arcading and triangular heads and the top stage has twin windows with mid-wall shafts. Inside are two arches with unmoulded blocks as capitals added on the E side. On the W face of the E wall is a head of Christ. There is a new nave with aisles and chancel added on the E side. On the S are 13th C three-light windows. Perp E window and clerestory of brick. The S arcade is 13th C and the N arcade Dec with Dec windows (the E window with Flowing tracery, having a Crucifixion group on the mullions). The screen is mostly original. In the E window are two panels of 14th C glass – St James and St George. This church has not been used for worship for some time.

St Mary's is very near St Peter's. It has a majestic EE tower with elaborate Perp battlements and eight pinnacles. Late 12th C arcade, fine S aisle windows and a S porch of the early 13th C. The chancel has a fine E window, early Dec. Perp clerestory, with eight windows on each side. Brasses to Simon Seman, vintner, 1433, who balances himself on two casks of wine, and the demi-effigy of a lady, 1386.

BROUGHTON.   St Mary's has a spacious Sax tower, with on its W side a staircase attachment. The doorway and tower arch are ornate. The top of the tower is Perp with eight pinnacles. The arcades are Dec and the chancel EE. The N chapel is of 1670. The aisles and clerestory are Perp. There is a Sax slab interlace. A fine monument to Sir Henry Redford and wife c1375 with two effigies, and others to Sir Edward Anderson, Lord Chief Justice 1671, a reclining figure, and Sir Edward Anderson 1676, bust. A fine brass to a knight and lady of the Redford family c1390, holding hands.

GREAT GRIMSBY.   St James' is a large, venerable and sturdy cruciform church with a superb west front and a central tower. Much restoration has taken place in the 19th and 20th centuries but it retains its 13th century core and proportions, with some fine EE architecture, including the arcades and wall passages along the clerestory. There are chapels here by Bodley (1906) and Sir Charles Nicholson (1920). There is Saxon work at Holy Trinity *Old Clee* and St Giles' *Scartho*, also much else to see in both churches.

WINTERTON.   A 19th century lamp over the gateway of All Saints announces the date 'AD 1203', but the tower here is Saxon, although heightened in the EE period, from which time come the chancel and transepts (note the lovely Dec east windows in the transepts). The interior is tastefully furnished, with much to enjoy, including the two wives of John Rudd (c1504) portrayed in brass.

At All Saints *Winteringham* are good views over the Humber and a church with Norman and Transitional arcades and an EE chancel. *Roxby* St Mary's tower is Saxon and there is pretty Dec architecture in the aisles and chancel here.

KENT

Everybody who visits this large county, which does indeed have a many-faceted character of its very own, falls in love with it. It is a beautiful corner of England and a great deal of it is still very much 'The Garden of England'. It is a county of hop-fields, oast houses, apple and cherry orchards, lush countryside, many trees and green and civilised rolling downland. To the north is the Thames estuary and then the fascinating coastline which surrounds its eastern part on three sides, where there are not only the much visited bays and the holiday resorts, but the grand old towns of Deal and Sandwich, the ports of Dover and Folkestone and the famous white cliffs, where the North Downs, which form a backbone stretching the entire length of the county, meet the sea. The Downs are broken by the Darent, Medway and Stour valleys; to the south of them are the gentler uplands of the Greensand Ridge and further south is the incredibly beautiful landscape of the Weald. Kent also offers us the marshes near the river Thames, the Hoo peninsula, and the Islands of Grain and Sheppey, while in the south-east is the haunting and mysterious Romney Marsh, with its wonderful churches. It has many fascinating towns and delightful villages, with timber-framed houses and cottages, old inns, several village greens and a fair selection of castles and manor houses. There are the charming wealden towns of Tenterden and Cranbrook, the spa town of Tunbridge Wells and Tonbridge nearby, set in hill country, as are also Westerham and Sevenoaks. There are still Dickensian streets in Rochester and Chatham, and pleasant corners in Faversham and Ashford. There is Maidstone, the capital, set beside the Medway and wonderful Canterbury, which is worth viewing from a distance from all sides – always dominated by the soaring walls of the cathedral which is the jewel in the crown of Kent and in the mitre of the Church of England! But do not ignore Rochester Cathedral (set with the castle near the Medway) which, although smaller, is venerable and delightful in its own way.

About 360 medieval churches grace this county – and they are wonderful – of all shapes and sizes, but as we get to know them, we shall become quite familiar with the sturdy Kentish towers with their taller staircase-turrets, the shingled chamfered spires, the occasional large roof embracing nave and aisles in one, the arrays of roof-gables to aisles, chapels and maybe transepts also, and the lack of clerestories. Here we have EE and

Dec work of high quality and in abundance, also a few very important Saxon examples and some splendid Norman work, but not a great deal of big-boned Perp churches. Kent will be remembered for churches in lush and lovely settings, for several interiors which have that unspoilt feel, even if not always abounding in luxurious furnishings. It will be remembered for its abundance of monuments and brasses, for its ancient but usually uncomplicated timber roofs (often tiebeams with crownposts), for its many fragments of medieval glass and for its surprises and real characters amongst the churches, its oddities, curiosities and one-offs. Kent churches come in several colours and textures – warm deep yellow or brown ironstone in the Weald, flints and clunch from the chalk downs, and rugged grey Kentish ragstone from the hills south of Maidstone, also plenty of timber in spires and belfries and a fair amount of brick.

For the best 19th century churches, we must explore the Bromley, Beckenham and Chislehurst area, also Dover, Folkestone and Tunbridge Wells. Other good examples are Bicknor (Bodley), Kingsdown (RCF, Edward W. Pugin), Kilndown (A. Salvin and others), Langley (Butterfield) and Speldhurst (John Oldrid Scott).

ADISHAM.   Holy Innocents is a fine cruciform church with a central tower capped by a tiled pyramid. Mostly EE, as proved by the lancets, particularly in the chancel with five on each side and a triplet at the E end. Elsewhere some windows are Dec. There is a Norm font, a 13th C wooden reredos originally in Canterbury Cathedral, and many 13th C tiles.

Goodnestone Holy Cross church has a pretty setting, a Perp Kentish tower and an EE Gothic Revival nave and chancel of 1839–41 by R.C. Hussey which has great distinction. A little medieval glass has been preserved, also monuments and brasses.

ALDINGTON.   St Martin's has a fine Perp tower typical of Kent, with a prominent stair-turret and a splendid view from the top. There is evidence of Sax work. In the chancel are fine sedilia and also a complete set of stalls with poppyheads and misericords. The base of the rood-screen remains. The pulpit has a panel of a Pelican in Piety, and there is a 17th C font-cover. Brass to John Weddeot and wife and three sons, 1475.

Do see the tiny churches of St Rumwold *Bonnington* (Norman chancel, timber porch, 18th century pulpit) and St Peter and St Paul *Bilsington* (setting, atmosphere, old glass), also St Mary Magdalene *Ruckinge* (atmospheric interior with old stalls, also Norman tower).

ASH-next-SANDWICH. A cruciform church with a tall Perp central tower with lead spire and prominent stair-turret. The tower is a landmark all around and for shipping in the Straits of Dover. The Perp tower arches are fine. St Nicholas' is EE and Dec. Anyone interested in medieval monuments should come here – there are some twelve monuments and brasses.

BADLESMERE. Tiny, rustic and with few airs and graces, but you must find St Leonard's for atmosphere, created by 18th century furnishings (box-pews, pulpit, altar and reredos) beneath medieval crown-post roofs. Also note two medieval bench-ends, carved with the emblem of the Trinity and the Star and Garter.

Nearby St Lawrence's *Leaveland* is tiny, charming and has a crown-post roof and a pretty monument of 1606. *Throwley* St Michael and All Angels is larger, with Norman work and interesting monuments.

BARFRESTON. St Nicholas' is a sumptuous Norm church, as fine as any in England. A wheel-window at the E end is very rare. The magnificent S doorway and parts of the church are so profusely covered with interesting sculpture which is so well-preserved, we suggest that one seeks the help of a guide-book for detailed study. On the tympanum of the doorway, Our Lord still gives His blessing after 800 years.

Eythorne St Peter and St Paul's church is attractive EE, with a lead font bowl bearing the date 1628.

BROOKLAND. St Augustine's is one of the many gems on Romney Marsh. The detached wooden steeple containing five bells will first be seen. The weathervane is a duck in flight, 1797. One enters the church through a rustic porch and the interior is delightfully unrestored, being EE and Dec (from E to W). Sedilia in the chancel. The huge lead font is Norm and is carved with the signs of the Zodiac and the occupations of the months (March to October are repeated and one should remember that the year then began in March). Three little 13th C plaques of the Resurrection have been inserted at the base of the font. An 18th C pulpit, some old bench-ends and box-pews, a tithe-pen and scales dated 1795, and weights and measures and a graveside shelter should be noticed. Some 14th C glass canopies. Brass to Thomas Leddes, vicar, in mass vestments 1503.

Do find tiny *Fairfield* St Thomas a Becket's, all on its own in the marshes (one of the most fascinating settings for a church anywhere in England). What a gem it is – timber-framed and encased in brick, containing box-pews and a three-decker pulpit.

CANTERBURY. This lovely place has nine medieval churches (mostly quite small and some no longer in use for worship) and the remains of two others. Supreme amongst them is St Martin's (on its hill to the east of the city) where St Augustine worshipped and Queen Bertha came to pray. Parts of the nave and chancel walls have been dated back to the 600s AD; 1,300 years of worship – a holy place indeed! The beautiful arcaded font is Norman – so is comparatively new! We really do become pilgrims when we visit this shrine.

CHARTHAM. St Mary's has a large Perp tower with stair-turret, but the show-piece is the chancel, so well known for its windows showing Kent tracery to perfection. They contain glass of c1294. A fine brass to Sir Robert de Septvans, originally dated 1306 but now thought to be 1322: he is cross-legged and carries a shield with his emblem – a winnowing fan. Also brasses to three priests – Robert London, rector in cope, 1416; Robert Arthur, rector in cope, 1454; Robert Sheffelde, rector in amulce, 1508.

CHIDDINGSTONE. The church harmonises with the perfect village street of old houses. The Perp tower has large pinnacles. St Mary's was restored after a fire in the 17th C, and the font and font-cover with doors are of that period. Jac pulpit, and altar-rails of 1700. The church shows well the type of Kent plan – three equal aisles separately gabled and no division between nave and chancel (and of course no clerestory). (This plan can also be found in the other tip of England, in Cornwall).

Penshurst must be seen – another lovely village, with a sandstone church of St John the Baptist, much restored by Sir Gilbert Scott, where there are several good monuments.

CHILHAM. St Mary's typical Kentish tower with stair-turret just makes the perfect village square of old houses opposite the castle. There are many fragments of medieval glass and many monuments from the 17th C up to 1858. Arthur and Edmund Hardy, two little boys, nestle affectionately together near their battledore and shuttlecock, 1858.

CLIFFE. St Helen's is a remarkable church – cruciform and with striped walls of ragstone and flints in layers. Superb EE and Dec architecture here, also wall-paintings, medieval screenwork and stalls, a 17th century pulpit, and plenty more to discover.

Nearby *Higham's* (RCF) church of St Mary, in its lovely and lonely setting overlooking the Thames marshes, also has striped walls. A grand old door lets us in and we have here a fine screen and an exquisite 14th century pulpit to admire. *Cooling* St James' churchyard contains the fascinating set of little graves which inspired Dickens' opening of *Great Expectations* and we can feel the atmosphere here still. Lovely 13th century arcading, sedilia and piscina in the chancel here, and much else to see, especially the little vestry, whose walls are lined with thousands of cockle-shells (RCF).

COBHAM.   Anyone interested in brasses will know this church, for it has the largest collection in the world. The fine Perp tower overlooks the medieval college, since converted into charming almshouses. The church of St Mary Magdalene is mainly 13th and 14th C with a grand 13th C chancel, which not only has all the brasses, but a double piscina, a later single one, and fine sedilia. There are five lancets on each side, and a triplet at the E end. A 13th C font. The main brasses (usually under elaborate canopies) represent the de Cobham and Brooke families, lords of the manor. The remainder are of priests who were masters of the college. For details of these brasses (no less than 18), reference should be made to a guide-book. A fine monument to Sir George Brooke, 9th Lord Cobham and wife and ten sons and four daughters, 1561.

Nurstead has a pretty Perp church of St Mildred, with a Kentish tower, and at *Meopham*'s noble church of St John the Baptist we see good 14th century work and a fine pulpit of 1682.

DARENTH.   Parts of the nave are Sax but the charm of St Margaret's is its early Norm chancel with three round-headed E windows and a stone roof before vaulting ribs were known. Small 13th C tower with a timber cap, 18th C pulpit and altar-rails. Large Norm font: under eight arches it shows Baptism, a man and dragon, a lion, a gryphon, Sagittarius, King David, a fantastic beast, and a man with a flabellum.

Do find *Stone* St Mary the Virgin's church, to the north and not far from the Thames. Here is wonderful 13th century work of amazing quality, also wall-paintings and a beautiful little brass of a priest of c1408.

ELHAM.   The interior of St Mary's is a treasure house of beauty, many of the fittings being recent and by F.C. Eden. The church itself is of all medieval periods, the tower being late 14th century. Modern fittings – reredos, font-cover, organ-loft and organ, parclose screens, pews and panelling. The lectern is 17th century. The 15th century alabaster reredos of St Catherine and the murder of St Thomas of Canterbury is of special importance.

Lyminge church of St Mary and St Ethelburga is basically Saxon (c AD 950) and tiny *Paddlesworth* St Oswald's is early Norman. Both are well worth finding.

163

This has to be Kent with a tower like this at Rodmersham.

FOLKESTONE. A port and seaside resort, surrounded by hills and good for 19th century churches. The mother of them all is the large and medieval St Mary and St Eanswythe (St Eanswythe's casket and remains are in the north wall of the chancel here), where we see fine EE in the chancel, a bold Perp central tower and wonderful Tractarian decorations inside, including wall-paintings by A. Henning and C.E. Kempe (also glass by Kempe). R.C. Hussey rebuilt the nave and north aisle in 1856–7. He also designed St Peter's church (1862–4), high on the east cliff, which is inviting but unassuming outside and is all-glorious within. A much-loved Anglo-Catholic shrine and the scene of 'ritual' controversy in the 19th century. Holy Trinity is large and dignified, with an octagonal central tower and spire and a fine interior with a broad nave and tasteful furnishings. It was designed by Ewan Christian and built in 1868–9. St Saviour's has a noble and very distinctive exterior in ragstone, brick and terracotta, with a curved west gable and brick bellcot, also large and elegant Perp windows. Inside, the western end has been converted into a hall, rooms and offices, but the lofty and spacious church has not lost its dignified Anglo-Catholic atmosphere and the south chapel still has its elaborate aumbry and reredos. The architects were Micklethwaite & Somers Clarke and the building grew between 1891 and 1913.

There is Saxon evidence and lovely EE work in *Cheriton*'s distinctive and interesting church of St Martin of great character. *Capel le Ferne*'s little church (RCF) of St Mary has a wonderfully remote setting far from its village, but rewards the visitor with a rare stone screen, like a small arcade, a little brass of 1526 and a great deal of charm.

GOUDHURST. St Mary's stands on top of the hill above the pretty village street, with fine views. It has become quite a tourist centre. The short Kentish tower of yellow sandstone, partly Gothic and partly Renaissance, was built in 1640. Inside, the church is mostly 13th and 14th C. Brasses to John Bedgebury 1424; Sir John Culpeper 1480 on a tomb-chest; and a knight c1520. Mon in an oriel window to Sir Alexander Culpeper and wife 1537, all wood and beautifully coloured. The armour of the knight is unusual. On the E jamb is a two-tiered relief dated 1537 with tiny kneeling figures: God in Majesty, the Virgin and Child, and St George and the Dragon with the Culpeper family, Sir Alexander, his wife and 16 children, 1599. Also a monument to William Campion and wife and five sons and four daughters, 1615.

The great Perp church of St Dunstan at *Cranbrook* is full of interest, and St Mary's *Lamberhurst* (Kentish tower and spire, crown-post roof, pulpit of 1630) and St Margaret's *Horsmonden* (fine tower, 15th century south chapel screen and fine 1338 brass of a priest) should be visited.

GRAVENEY. A delightful small church of much interest, with a simple but pleasing tower on the N side. All Saints is mainly EE and Dec but the chancel arch is Norm. It has an unusual nave roof. Sedilia and piscina, Perp rood-screen and font, poppyhead benches and box-pews, a fine 17th C pulpit, a 13th C chest and fragments of old glass. Brasses to Joan de Feversham and son, demi-figures 1360; Richard de Feversham 1381; John Martyn, shown as a Justice of the Common Pleas, and wife, 1436 (very fine).

Tiny *Goodnestone* St Bartholomew's is early Norman, whilst St Michael's *Hernhill* is Perp (Kentish tower, crown-post roof, good screen etc). St Mary's *Faversham*, although the nave is 18th century, has medieval stalls with misericords, wall-paintings of c1310 and superb monuments and brasses.

HEVER. All who visit the castle should also visit the church. St Peter's has an unbuttressed Perp W tower with a tapering shingled spire. The early 16th C N chapel has an original fireplace and chimney-piece. There is a 17th C pulpit with tester. The brasses are notable – Margaret Cheyne 1419, with angels holding a cushion for her head; Sir Thomas Bullen – the father of Queen Anne Boleyn, 1538, lies in his Garter robes, his feet on a wyvern and his head on a mantled helmet (very fine); William Todde 1585.

HIGH HALDEN.   St Mary's has an amazing timber tower and spire and W porch of the 14th C. Its interior construction is remarkable. The S porch is also a splendid example of 14th C timberwork, the entrance arch being two huge baulks and with cusped bargeboards. A 13th C font on its original plinth. The king-post roof of the chancel is Perp.

Bethersden St Margaret's is Perp, with a fine Kentish tower, and two brasses. Another fine tower at St Michael's *Smarden*, also scissorbeam roofs and an unusually wide nave, nicknamed 'The Barn of Kent'.

HYTHE.   St Leonard's stands high above the town. The chancel alone attracts attention as it is raised twelve steps over a processional route (as at Walpole St Peter, Norfolk). It has some of the finest EE work in the country. Double piscina and sedilia. The E window is the usual lancet triplet of that time. The rest of the church does not come up to the standard of the chancel. The tower was rebuilt in 1751. Dec font, and an ironbound chest. The processional path has become quite a tourist attraction as it has a bone-hole for hundreds of skulls in racks.

Lympne St Stephen's has a wonderful setting, overlooking the expanse of Romney Marsh. A Norman central tower here, and much of interest.

IVYCHURCH.   Another gem of Romney Marsh. The outside of St George's is dominated by the fine Perp Kentish tower. The two-storeyed vaulted porch is also large with a round stair-turret. The church is mostly Dec, and in it one feels transported to another world. The arcades run for seven bays without a break. Old roofs, screens and stalls. Tower screen 1686. There are also Text boards and a graveside shelter.

There is much to enjoy at St Peter and St Paul's *Newchurch*, with its Dec window tracery, screens and 14th century chest. *St Mary in the Marsh* is as delightful as any of the Marsh Churches, full of beauty and atmosphere, also very prayerful. Do find it.

LYDD.   All Saints' fine and prominent Perp tower is a landmark and is based on the towers of Ashford and Tenterden. Double W doorway. The rough walling at the NW corner is the remains of an early Sax church. The church is mostly EE and its E end has been beautifully rebuilt after war damage. Several brasses remain.

MAIDSTONE.   Mighty All Saints' is indeed worthy of Kent's county town – a great rambling Perp (and formerly collegiate) church, begun in 1395 and very grandly set, with its former collegiate buildings, beside the Medway. The 78 ft Kentish tower stands over the porch and the building is 227 ft long. Inside we realise that it is broad as well, spacious and dignified, with a 'Civic Church' feel about it. Amongst the lovely things here is a magnificent sedilia, also the collegiate chancel stalls with misericords, a screen, reredos and roofs by J.L. Pearson and some glorious monuments, including one (behind the sedilia) to John Wotton (1417) with a fascinating painting of him being presented to Our Lady by the saints.

MINSTER-in-SHEPPEY.   St Mary and St Sexburga's is built on the highest point of the island above the Thames estuary. The church is really two churches, the N being that of the nunnery, and the S being parochial. Part of the nuns' church is Sax, whereas the parochial church is EE, the sedilia being of that period. Perp font with a Jac cover, 14th C screen. Mon to Sir Robert de Shurland c1300, and behind him a horse's head rises from the waves. There are also three later medieval monuments. Two very fine large brasses – Sir John de Northwade and Joan de Northwade c1330.

Go east to *Eastchurch* to enjoy All Saints' screens, pulpit, 1622 monument and devotional interior, then further east to the small remote church of St Thomas on the *Isle of Harty* where the screen and chest are 14th century and the atmosphere and setting are wonderful.

MINSTER-in-THANET.   St Mary's tower with a lead spire and nave are Norm. The beautiful vaulted chancel with E lancet triplet is EE. Eighteen fine stalls with carved arm-rests and an old wooden chest. There is part of a 13th C sculptured Virgin and Child. A 13th C tomb-chest, and a monument to Thomas Paramore and wife kneeling, 1620.

Ramsgate's ancient church of St Lawrence in Thanet is Norman and has much to see, and St George's (1824–7 by Henry Hemsley) is Gothic and good of its period, with a very distinctive tower.

NETTLESTEAD.   St Mary's has a 13th C tower, as proved by the lancets, but we come here to see the old glass for which the large Perp windows were made. That on the S side was mostly destroyed in a gale in the 18th C, but some canopies and angels with shields survive in the tracery. The central N window of the nave, however, has all its original glass – St Thomas the Apostle, St Bartholomew and St Matthew. These formed part of a series of the Twelve Apostles with creed-scrolls. In the NW window is a small scene from the life of St Thomas of Canterbury. In the Crucifixion group in the E window, the figures of St Mary and St John the Evangelist are old. The figures of St Lawrence and St Stephen in the NW window are also old. This church will give a good idea of what every church in England used to look like before the Reformation.

East Peckham St Michael's (RCF) is isolated and wonderfully positioned, with panoramic views to the south. It is well worth a visit. So is St Lawrence's *Mereworth*, Kent's finest Classical church (1744–6) with imposing tower and spire and a superb interior with excellent brasses and monuments.

NEWINGTON-on-the-STREET.

A grand Perp Kentish tower with stair-turret. The church should be seen in the spring when the blossom is out. St Mary's is fine inside because the Dec nave has wide aisles. The chancel is EE. There are interesting roofs and red-tiled floors, a Dec S chapel screen, an old bench-end with poppyheads and little animals, a Perp and Renaissance font-cover with doors, and 17th C altar-rails. There have been wall-paintings, particularly in window splays. A 14th C tomb-chest of the shrine of St Robert le Bouser. There are six brasses and two wall monuments.

Rainham St Margaret's has a lofty Kentish tower and much to see inside, including 15th century screenwork, a 14th century chest, brasses, monuments and remains of wall-paintings.

NEW ROMNEY.

St Nicholas' is a grand example of rich Norm work expanded by rich Dec work. The W end and the tower are Norm; the latter is of five storeys enriched by zig-zag and has large pinnacles and the stump of a spire. The W doorway is very rich. The exterior of the Dec E end is a fine sight with three gabled roofs, each with a fine reticulated window. There are a piscina and sedilia in each part. The roofs are plastered and the floors of the nave have old tiles with ledger stones. There are 18th C altar-rails, and a tower screen of 1602. Brasses to Thomas Lombard 1510, and Thomas Smith, wife and daughter 1610.

OLD ROMNEY.

Another gem of Romney Marsh, the church is on its own in the middle of fields with sheep. The SW tower of St Clement's has a typical chamfered timber spire. Go into the tower to see the remarkable wooden stair-ladder with solid wooden steps, obviously contemporary. Mostly 13th C with nave and aisles under one roof (as often in Sussex). Red-brick floors. A number of squints, plastered ceilings, and many 18th C fittings – reredos with the Ten Commandments, altar-rails, gates in chancel arch, Text boards, box-pews and W gallery. Dec font. All is nicely unrestored. Brass to John Ips and wife 1526.

PATRIXBOURNE. St Mary's tower on the S with a typical chamfered timber spire has a marvellous Norm S doorway with a tympanum of Christ seated and with angels above the tympanum. There are five orders of rich Norm carving. Above the usual triplet of windows at the E end is a rare wheel-window with four of the eight spokes swallowed by beasts' heads. The priest's doorway is also rich Norm with zig-zag and carved capitals, one possibly being St Thomas of Canterbury. A 17th C S door, and a 13th C piscina. There is much Swiss glass of the 16th and 17th Cs worth careful study.

It is worth seeing the churches west of the A2, beneath Barham Downs. St Mary's *Bishopsbourne* is beautiful with much to see, including the monument of the saintly Elizabethan divine, Richard Hooker (1633). St Giles *Kingston* is small, but enjoyable, whilst St John the Baptist *Barham*, with its copper spire and crown-post roofs and more to interest us, is set in a pretty village.

ST MARGARET-at-CLIFFE. High up on the coast, St Margaret's looks down on St Margaret's Bay. A complete Norm church, with a rather low tower. Outside, the Norm clerestory is the chief feature. The fine rich W doorway should also be noted. The N doorway is late Norm. The interior is impressive with tall arches and a taller chancel arch of great width showing up the three E windows with two-light windows above. There is also a 13th C low-side window. Font dated 1663.

Historic *Dover*'s parish church of St Mary has a Norman tower, the castle church of St Mary in Castro is a wonderful late Saxon building, with the Roman pharos (lighthouse) beside it, and the church of St Peter and St Paul is a splendid Gothic Revival (1893) building by James Brooks, with an imposing and devotional interior.

SANDWICH. A most interesting town, but we come to see one of England's finest Norm towers at St Clement's. It has three tiers of arcading all round the outside and its staircase door inside has a small stag on the tympanum. The four tower arches are fine with scallops and volutes on the capitals. To the E the chancel is EE (with usual E triplet) and to the W it is Perp. Two-storeyed N porch. The roof has a number of gilded angels with outspread wings. Perp font with heraldry and a carved stem, and stalls with poppyheads. A brass to a civilian c1450, and a mon to Frances Rampton, kneeling, 1611.

Vast, barnlike St Mary's and lofty EE and Dec St Peter's are both RCF and both well worth a visit – two real characters here, with much to discover.

SHOREHAM.   St Peter and St Paul's is mainly Perp. The large tower of flint with brick trimmings was built in 1775 but the tower arch is EE. We come here for two special pieces of woodwork – the Perp S porch with tracery and a great split oak which forms its arch, and the rood-screen. The latter is the best in the county and extends the full width of the church (as in the W Country) and keeps its vaulting and cresting. The organ-case, 1730, came from Westminster Abbey, as also the pulpit. There are four monuments of 18th C date to the Borett family, with busts.

To the north are St Botolph's *Lullingstone* (an unforgettable gem – tiny, beautiful setting, 18th century pulpit and benches, superb screen, 16th century glass, wonderful brasses and monuments), St Mary's *Eynsford* (lovely village, shingled spire and good EE) and St Peter and St Paul *Farningham* (rare Seven Sacrament font and some brasses etc). To the south is picturesque *Offord* – a great character.

TENTERDEN.   St Mildred's has the finest tower in the county (Ashford and Lydd type). Perp with octagonal turrets and crocketed pinnacles, the tower arch inside is fine. Double W doorway. There has been much restoration but there is a genuine Dec S doorway and Perp font. There are numbers of coats of arms. Mon to Herbert Whitfield and wife kneeling, 1622.

Do not miss St Michael's, an attractive and well positioned Gothic Revival church of 1863 by Gordon Hills. Tiny *Smallhythe* St John the Baptist's church is brick-built, of 1516–17, beside lovely 16th century half-timbered houses. St Mary the Virgin *Rolvenden* is large, well-set and full of interest (including a family pew of 1825 – and furnished!).

TUDELEY.   A small church rebuilt in 1765, All Saints' tower is of red brick on a sandstone base with a tiled spirelet. One will, however, come here to see modern glass by Marc Chagall in nearly all the windows, put in by the lord of the manor when his daughter, Sarah D'Avigdor Goldsmid, was drowned in a sailing accident: blue therefore prevails. There are 17th C altar-rails. Brass to Thomas Stydolf and wife 1457, and a finely lettered tablet to the said Sarah D'Avigdor Goldsmid, 1963.

Capel St Thomas (RCF) is nearby and must not be missed because of its wonderful series of wall-paintings, dating from the 13th century.

TUNBRIDGE WELLS.   King Charles the Martyr is the patron of its oldest church, and the Stuarts were known to patronise the health-giving wells here. The building grew between 1676–1690 and has a charming red brick exterior with a pretty clock-turret and cupola and wonderful plaster ceilings inside, with shallow domes. We also admire the chancel woodwork here, brought from Wren's St Antholin's church in the City of London.

Tunbridge Wells (as did Tonbridge and several village churches in the area) very strongly adhered to the principles of the Evangelical Movement in the English Church, and most of the 19th century churches here have maintained this tradition. Holy Trinity is a period-piece of 1827–9, built in Gothic as a preaching house, as was Christ Church (neo-Norman in white brick, by R. Palmer Brown, 1836–41). St John's (mainly by E.E. Cronk, enlarging A.D. Gough's church of 1858) is more refined, with Dec architecture and a bold and very stately tower, but still built to hold thousands. St Mark's Broadwater Down (1864–6) is a very distinctive building by R.L. Roumieu, which is eccentric and fascinating, with an elegant tower and spire. The one Anglo-Catholic centre is the lofty and magnificently proportioned St Barnabas' (1889–93) by J.E.K. and J.P. Cutts. Inside it is lofty, sturdy, spacious and devotional.

UPPER HARDRES.   St Peter and St Paul's S tower is Norm with later lancets. Mainly 13th C, there is a timber chancel arch, an old roof in the nave, a Norm font, and an 18th C pulpit with tester. Much old glass – in the W window three roundels c1200 showing St Nicholas with the three poverty-stricken daughters, St Nicholas, and the Virgin crowned and a donor. In the two E lancets is 14th C glass of small figures in three tiers all in bright colours, ruby, green and yellow – a kneeling female, St Edmund, and the Virgin and St Elizabeth in one window, and a kneeling female, a bishop and St Anne teaching the Virgin to read in the other window. Note the quarry of a bird in a chasuble with bells on its claws. There is a well known bracket-brass to John Strete, rector, 1405, showing him kneeling at the base with his prayer on a scroll up to the stem of the bracket, on which are St Peter and St Paul. Mons to Sir Thomas Hamon 1634 and Thomas Hardres 1681.

Do find *Stelling* St Mary's church, which is EE and Dec, but is memorable for its unspoilt 18th century fittings – box-pews, three-decker pulpit, large gallery etc.

WESTWELL.   A charming village in a fold of the hills. St Mary's church has a shingled spire and a timber-framed porch, but the exterior gives little hint of the splendour within. We see a complete EE church of the highest quality and architectural beauty, where a tall and elegant stone screen of three trefoil-headed arches leads to a lovely stone-vaulted chancel, with lancet windows, arcaded sanctuary with later (14th century) piscina and triple sedilia *and* the central lancet of the east window has a Jesse Tree in stained glass, the top half of which is original 13th century. The font is Norman, there is medieval woodwork in the stalls and the whole place is exciting and very rewarding.

Some lovely churches hereabouts, including massive and fortress-like All Saints *Boughton Aluph* (with much to see and a wonderful atmosphere), remote and delightful *Challock* St Cosmas and St Damian's with its lovely 1950s wall-paintings and good Kentish tower, noble and stately *Charing* St Peter and St Paul's with so much to see and admire, including one of Kent's finest towers (another is not far away from it, at St James' *Egerton*) and St Margaret's *Hothfield*, which is lovely outside and in and has a splendid monument of 1624.

WINGHAM. In a pretty village street is St Mary's church, with delightful colouring in the walls, mellow tiled roofs and a slender green copper spire. The chancel is 13th and 14th C, and the nave and S aisle 16th C. There is some good Geometric tracery and old roofs. The nave arcade is of wood. A 15th C stone reredos shows five Passion scenes above, and the Last Supper and the Magi below. There is the base of a 15th C rood-screen, plus seven misericords, and 14th C grisaille glass in the head of the chancel S window. There are six monuments of note of the 17th and 18th centuries.

Go north to *West Stourmouth* All Saints (RCF) for a church of great character and atmosphere. Many items of interest from a variety of periods, but all blending together so successfully and creating such a memorable interior. The exterior, with its white wooden bell-turret, is also very lovable.

WOODCHURCH. All Saints' is one of the most beautiful churches in the county. Almost completely EE, and of that period are the lovely triplet of lancets at the E end of the fine tower, with its large chamfered timber spire. It is equally beautiful inside with handsome nave arcades. Double piscina and sedilia, a Norm font, a pulpit with linenfold panels and traceried heads, and stalls made up similarly. Old glass includes a 13th C medallion of the Entombment of the Virgin, and some 17th C Flemish panels. Brasses to Nichol de Gore, priest in mass vestments in a quatrefoil with a rhyming inscription 1333; and Thomas Harlakynden, kneeling, with two wives and ten children 1558. A fine village green with old houses completes a perfect picture.

LANCASHIRE
GREATER MANCHESTER
AND MERSEYSIDE

There were only about 80 medieval churches in the unreorganised county of Lancashire and now a few of these have been lost to Cumbria. The number of later churches, however, is nearer 800. Odd though it may seem, hunting out urban churches in the great conurbations around Manchester and Liverpool can be fascinating, not just for the rewards of discovering magnificent buildings by Paley & Austin (and these are all indeed truly splendid) or J.S. Crowther of Manchester, or of the great architects of national repute, but also to see the complex variety of churches built to serve local communities and very often still serving them for seven days per week. These churches have often been adapted and altered into church centres for a variety of uses by local people. Some have been replaced by exciting modern buildings. The traditions of churchmanship are well represented here and we may discover great Evangelical preaching-houses, built to hold thousands. There is St Clement's Toxteth, where the pulpit is in the centre, as it has always been, and St Saviour's Bacup, where the black preaching gown is still worn for the sermon. There are the great Anglo-Catholic centres with their glittering interiors, often built in the middle of miles of terraced houses. Occasionally you may stumble upon one which never hits the guidebooks, like Our Lady and St Thomas', Gorton, or St Stephen's Grove Street Liverpool, or St Augustine's Tonge Moor, Bolton. Sadly this is a county of many locked churches, but many are in use during the week and usually the genuine searcher for the key is made welcome at the vicarage door. There are many Classical churches too, either built in developing towns, or rebuilt in villages. Also we occasionally stumble upon the often blackened form of a medieval church, possibly the church of what was a former village or maybe one of those great buildings which are the ancient parish churches of the towns and are now the parents and grandparents of a host of others. These churches have a wonderful 'Civic Church' feel about them and, although often very restored, are greatly cherished and prized.

So much for the towns – Lancashire has much more to offer in its lovely countryside. There are moors and fells, forests and beautiful rivers, also villages of great character, and venerable churches which are steeped in atmosphere and are full of surprises. Their towers are often bold and rugged, their exteriors embattled and their walls lit by Perp windows. Occasionally we find a stately spire, sometimes crowning an octagonal belfry stage.

ASHTON UNDER LYNE. The large and impressive church of St Michael is mainly 15th century but has been altered since that time. Its magnificent (139 ft) tower was rebuilt by J.S. Crowther in 1886. Inside is a wonderful feast of carved stonework and plasterwork, under impressive ceilings. The furnishings form a stately period piece of the 1840s, with balconies, a massive three-decker pulpit and many pews – all gothic. The great treasure here is the wonderful array of stained glass, dating from c1460–1517, including a fascinating series of scenes from the life of St Helena.

ATHERTON. The grand 120 ft south-west tower of St John's draws us to one of the many fine churches in Lancashire and Cheshire by the Lancaster firm of Paley & Austin. This large, dignified and impressive church, built of Runcorn stone, was opened in 1879. This firm also created its daughter churches of St Anne, *Hindsford* and St John *Howe Bridge*.

BOLTON. The 180 ft tower of mighty St Peter's (an E.G. Paley rebuild of the medieval church in 1867–71) is a wonderful landmark, and here we have a town church, built to seat 1,200, of great splendour. Holy Trinity (by Philip Hardwick, 1823) is also large and impressive but, for real medieval Perp beauty, we must hunt out the old village church at *Deane*.

DENTON. St Lawrence's is a fascinating timber-framed church of c1531, restored in the 19th century. There is great character here, with its black-and-white exterior and its very distinctive interior.

ECCLES. St Mary's is an embattled red sandstone town church, with large Perp clerestory windows giving light to a truly magnificent 15th century nave roof. There are several items of interest here, including the Brereton monument and part of a Saxon cross-shaft.

GREAT MITTON. A pleasing exterior, with an EE nave and chancel, Perp tower and a lovely Perp chapel of 1594. Inside All Hallows there is much to see, including the medieval nave roof, 16th century

A typical Lancs medieval village church – rugged and sturdy. This one is at St Michael's On Wyre.

font-cover and 17th century pulpit. The chapel, which has an Elizabethan screen, contains some superb monuments.

HALSALL. The octagonal belfry and spire which crown the west tower of St Cuthbert's draw us to a beautiful Dec and Perp church. Outside we admire the stately pinnacled chancel, the rood-staircase turrets and the sanctus bellcot at the east end of the nave, also the gargoyles which peer out at us and, in the south-east corner, we look for the little man saying his prayers in his boat. Inside are lovely misericord stalls (look for the wrestlers here), an ancient vestry door, the effigy of a 14th century priest, and much, much more.

LANCASTER. A fine old town with much to see, graced by the glorious exterior (mostly embattled, pinnacled and Perp) and 108 ft tower of its noble priory church of St Mary. This is one of the county's greatest and best and a feast of craftsmanship awaits us inside, from the wonderful canopied stalls, with their carved misericords, to the 17th century woodcarving in the font-cover and pulpit. There are Saxon remains here and one of the monuments (to William Stratford) is by Roubiliac.

175

St John's (RCF) is a Classical period-piece of 1754–5, with a tower of 1784.

LIVERPOOL AND ENVIRONS. The Anglican cathedral here is one of the greatest 20th century masterpieces to be seen anywhere. Its massive bulk (and 331 ft tower) in Runcorn stone dominates the skyline for miles. Some of the more interesting of the many churches of all periods in this vast urban area are described below.

Our Lady and St Nicholas', Pier Head – the distinctive lantern spire of Liverpool's parish church is well known on the Liverpool skyline. The church itself (rebuilt 1952 by Edward Butler) is not only beautiful, but exercises an active ministry in the city.

Of the Classical churches, St Bride's Percy Street (1831) should be seen, also the grand and spacious Holy Trinity Wavertree (1794), with its 18th C mahogany pulpit and very tasteful alterations by Sir Charles Reilly in 1911.

The finest Gothic Revival churches must surely be the Anglo-Catholic strongholds of St Agnes', Sefton Park and St John's, Tue Brook. Of all J.L. Pearson's wonderful churches throughout the land, St Agnes' is one of the most adorable. What an interior! Amidst exquisite stonework, sumptuous furnishings and adornments, beneath vaulted roofs and through richly coloured glass, heaven and earth meet. They must meet for many also at St John's, whose magnificent interior has walls resplendent with stencilling and painting by C.E. Kempe, coloured roofs, Morris glass and splendid adornments. The building, with its prominent spire, was designed by G.F. Bodley. Paley & Austin's finest creation here is the cruciform, cathedral-like church of St Matthew and St James, Mossley Hill. Set at the top of a hill, its magnificent central tower is visible for miles, especially from the other side of the Mersey. Thomas Rickman's two churches of St George's, Everton and St Michael in the Hamlet, Toxteth must be discovered. Both grew between 1812 and 1815 and both are remarkable because so much of their structure and architecture is not in stone, but in iron! This material certainly does seem to create beautiful window-tracery and grand churches! An amazing modern conversion of a Victorian church of 1853 into a complex which serves its community in many ways can be seen at St John the Divine, Fairfield.

The modern churches and rebuilds are all worth seeing, and amongst the most interesting are St Margaret's, Anfield (rebuilt 1965 after the vast Victorian church was gutted by fire), St Philemon's, Toxteth (which is equipped with a baptistry for total immersion) and the church and community centre at St Peter's, Everton.

MANCHESTER AND ENVIRONS. So many churches have gone in central Manchester, although the cathedral preserves the feel of a richly-adorned north country big-town parish church. St Anne's is the regal Classical town centre church of 1712 and it has the atmosphere of a London city church, with its splendid Georgian interior, galleries, pews and fine pulpit. There are medieval churches at *Didsbury* and *Northenden* and a kaleidoscope of later churches, of which the following are a very small token sample.

Classical architecture may be enjoyed in Smirke's Grecian St Philip's, Salford (1825) with its odd circular tower, and at the Sacred Trinity, Salford, whose pinnacled gothic tower reminds us of the cathedral but whose galleried and beautifully furnished interior of 1751 is well worth seeing, as is its new role as a religious education centre.

There is a host of Gothic Revival churches to be enjoyed here – many of great quality and some of considerable eccentricity. The local architect, J.S. Crowther, designed several churches, including the Anglo-Catholic strongholds of St Benedict's, Ardwick, whose massive exterior and odd north-west tower rise high above this area of Manchester suburbia. Its vast interior is full of atmosphere and beauty. He also created St Alban's, Cheetwood, of similar tradition, but a very different building. Butterfield's great Manchester church is St Cross, Clayton (1866), with streaky patterns in brick over its massive exterior and an odd, pencil-like tower at one side. Inside it is nobly proportioned and Butterfield's reredos is still in place, beneath the high-set east window.

Further out of the city are two churches which are of great character and beauty. One is St Elisabeth's, Reddish, by Waterhouse (1883) – a wonderful essay in brick and stone. The other is St Augustine's, Pendlebury, which must be one of the most monumental suburban churches anywhere in England. Its vast bulk rises some 80 ft above its surroundings. There is no tower and just one great continuous roofline. What an array of glorious windows and what a truly magnificent eastern face to its oddly canted sanctuary. This is the masterpiece of G.F. Bodley and it was opened in 1874. Inside we are aware of its great height and space, with the mighty unbroken wagon roof above and the internal buttressing providing narrow processional passages at the sides. There is a blaze of colour from glass by Burlison & Grylls in the mighty windows, also a glorious oak screen and an enormous painted reredos. All this majesty, devotion and character created out of one vast rectangle.

The 20th century gave us the great church of St Nicholas, Burnage (1932) and St Michael's, Northenden, both by Cachemaille Day and Lander and both monumental churches of their period. To really see a functional and devotional building for present day ministry in a tough

177

area, do find the church of the Ascension, Hulme, built to replace a whole handful of Victorian churches in this vastly populated area.

ORMSKIRK. The exterior of St Peter and St Paul's is amazing, with its two towers – one with an elegant spire rising from an octagonal belfry and the other massive, fortress-like and pinnacled. Paley & Austin's restoration of 1877–9 is much in evidence but there is a great deal to enjoy in this grand building. We see the effigies of the Earls of Derby and their wives in the Derby Chapel, also a 17th century screen and font. The Norman window in the chancel dates this church back to the 12th century.

At nearby *Aughton* is the interesting medieval church of St Michael, again with an octagonal belfry and spire.

ROCHDALE. St Chad's is mighty, medieval and 'civic', splendidly positioned above the town centre, with a stately 95 ft tower. Much 19th century reordering took place here, but what a lovely example of a Lancashire town parish church. A noble pinnacled exterior and a spacious and dignified interior – much cherished and with much to see. St Mary's was a small 1740 church until 1909–11 when Comper created out of it a large and atmospheric building, beautifully adorned and full of colour and atmosphere. It is worth finding St Edmund's, Falinge (by J.M. and H. Taylor, 1873), which is remarkable for its links with Masonry. Built by a prominent Freemason, nearly everything here has some reference to the Masonic Craft.

SEFTON. The elegant profile of St Helen's 14th century spire rises over flat countryside, tempting us towards a church which is otherwise predominantly late Perp and is a real treasure house. Here we may marvel at magnificent 16th century screens, including one around Lord Sefton's family pew, also poppyhead bench-ends, medieval chancel stalls, a pulpit and sounding board of 1638, a font-cover of 1688 and glorious monuments and brasses.

STANDISH. A Lancashire tower with octagonal belfry and spire (rebuilt 1867) and a fine church of St Wilfrid, much of which was rebuilt in 1582–4. How very grand it is, with its embattled exterior, large windows, superb proportions and, internally, 16th century panelled roofs throughout. The pulpit was made in 1616 and more 17th century woodwork survives. The seeker after monuments will not be disappointed here.

STOCKPORT.   St George's church must surely be one of the finest of the magnificent Perp churches of Paley & Austin. It rises regal, stately and cruciform, like a great East Anglian 'wool' church but in Runcorn stone and with a glorious tower and spire (236 ft) with flying buttresses. Inside the detail, the stonework, woodwork and glass in this vast and cathedral-like building (seating 1,200) is simply glorious. It was opened in 1897.

STYDD.   A tiny and remote church, built by the Knights Hospitallers. There is Norman work here and an EE south doorway, whilst the screen and pulpit were made in the 17th century. Less than a mile away is St Wilfrid's *Ribchester* whose delightfully set EE church, with a Perp tower, has great character and much to enjoy.

TUNSTALL.   Visiting a country church like this, in its delightful rural setting, stops people imagining that Lancashire is just industry and surburbia. This lovely church of St John the Baptist was much rebuilt in 1415, but incorporates earlier work, and we enter beneath a fine two-storeyed porch, to admire 15th and 16th century glass from Flanders in the east window and much else in this atmospheric place. The medieval altar stone, cast out at the Reformation, has now been restored to its rightful use.

In this pretty Lune valley are several picturesque and interesting churches.

WHALLEY.   This is a church of tremendous interest, with good EE and Perp architecture and a glorious array of exquisite woodwork. St Mary's 15th century stalls (from the nearby abbey) are of national importance, with their delicate canopies and incredible misericords which do merit careful examination. Then there is the screenwork and the various family pews (one of 1534 is known as the Cage), the medieval roofs and the fine organ-case of 1727. Outside we must find the bronze knocker on the priest's door and the Saxon crosses in the churchyard.

LEICESTERSHIRE AND RUTLAND

People often pass through Leicestershire on the way to somewhere else. For those, however, who do really explore the county, what treasures are in store, for its scenery is beautiful – from the Wold country in the north, to the unique area known as Charnwood Forest or the delightful hill-country near the Rutland border. It is a county of meadow and woodland, of country seats and much hunting territory (for which it was renowned), where we may travel along miles of narrow (and often gated) roads to discover pretty stone villages and to visit its c250 medieval churches. These churches (many of which are well above average in beauty and interest) are usually built of limestone or warm yellow-brown ironstone towards the east and greyish sandstone as we go westwards. Other materials, obtained locally, are also used in Leicestershire churches.

There is little Saxon or Norman in these churches, but EE is very frequent and Dec reaches a very high quality here, seen in many 'good' churches which have work of c1270–1340, when much church building appears to have taken place in the county. There is plenty of Perp, although very few complete Perp churches. This is a wonderful county for towers and spires – and not just the great and lofty. It is also good for monuments and at Wanlip we have the oldest brass with an inscription in English, made c1393. The 1600s and 1700s gave Leicestershire some interesting and unusual churches and restorations, including Staunton Harold, Gaulby, King's Norton, Stapleford, Saxby and Wistow. There are interesting 19th century churches too, especially in Leicester and its environs.

Rutland is an entity in itself (as most Rutlanders will proudly tell you) and will be treated as such, despite the bureaucrats. On paper it was turned into Leicestershire in 1974 but it has a character of its very own, as anybody who has seen all of its churches will know. Also in the 1970s, some 3,500 acres of it were flooded to make Rutland Water reservoir, although the result is extremely beautiful. Rutland is a wonderful corner of England – grand countryside, lovely stone villages, rolling hills, superb views and the market towns of Oakham and Uppingham – both full of history. Above all there are its 50 churches (47 are the medieval ones), every one of which deserves a visit – and it is quite possible in this county! Towers, spires and medieval bellcots draw us to them and the quality and interest to be discovered in their fabrics and fittings is amazing. See the lot and you will automatically see Rutland in all its glory. You will also see bits of Rutland in hundreds of churches elsewhere, for limestone quarried at Ketton, Clipsham and Casterton has for centuries been used to build and restore churches in other counties.

LEICESTERSHIRE

BOTTESFORD.   Some 210 ft of soaring tower and spire draws us to this wonderful church of St Mary the Virgin in the Vale of Belvoir (sometimes known as the 'Lady of the Vale'). It is superb outside – the tall pinnacled tower and mighty spire (with its lines of crockets and elegant lucarne openings) somewhat dwarfing the largely Perp exterior of this very substantial church. The south aisle, transept and porch are good Dec and a little EE work may be detected here. What an absolute feast inside for the lover of monuments. They fill the chancel – a dozen or so splendid ones, mostly commemorating the Earls of Rutland of Belvoir Castle. There is also the five ft long figure of a priest (c1404) in brass. If any English church is remembered for its monuments, it must be this one.

Nearby St John the Baptist's *Muston* is much smaller, but has a 14th century spire, also a Perp screen and benches.

BREEDON ON THE HILL.   On the hill it most certainly is – we can see it for miles! St Mary and St Hardulph is perched some 180 ft above the surrounding countryside. Set in its walls are some of the finest Anglo-Saxon carvings in England, with delightful scrolls and patterns, mounted warriors, birds, saints and the wonderful Breedon Angel – all carved around AD 700–800. There is work of all periods here and the Perp font is beautifully carved. The Shirley Pew is dated 1627 and the other furnishings are mostly 18th century, while 16th century members of the Shirley family are commemorated in three fine monuments. Outside we admire the sturdy embattled walls (it is in fact the tower and eastern section of a large priory church) but above all we luxuriate in the lovely views from this superb vantage point.

CHURCH LANGTON.   St Peter's noble tower rises above a stately Leicestershire village church which is handsomely proportioned and architecturally very satisfying. Much Dec here, seen in the delightful and varied tracery of the windows and contrasting with the wonderful Perp in the tower and clerestory. Inside we must search for the little sculpture of a person, which could well be Norman. A font of 1662 and a fine organ case of about 100 years later grace the lofty and imposing interior.

Tur Langton has an exciting Gothic Revival church of St Andrew (1866) by Joseph Goddard of Leicester. *Thorpe Langton* St Leonard's church shows so typically the Dec architecture of c1280–1350 which is seen in many Leicestershire churches.

CROXTON KERRIAL.   A high-set village in an area which is good for views. An endearing 15th century church of St John the Baptist here, with a lovely pinnacled central tower and a chancel of ironstone. We come here to see the county's finest collection of medieval benches – a set of 42, with carved poppyhead ends.

Nearby St Cuthbert's *Branston* and St Denis *Eaton* are attractive 13th century churches. *Waltham on the Wolds* has a fine, large church of St Mary Magdalene, and grand views. *Stonesby* St Peter's is worth a visit just to look up at its splendid Perp tower.

GADDESBY.   St Luke's is one of the county's gems – a Dec master-piece of c1270–1340, and what beauty there is in the design and crafts-manship here. A perfect tower and spire, superb windows and, above all, the lavish stonecarving in the south aisle, which would easily grace any cathedral. The interior is bathed in atmosphere and in plenty of light, shining through clear glass.

There are monuments to enjoy at St Mary's *Ashby Folville*, a 12th century arcade at St Andrew's *Twyford*, a Norman font at St John the Baptist's *South Croxton* and a wonderful tower and spire at St Mary's *Queniborough*.

HALLATON.   One of several lovely villages in this corner of the county, with a memorable church of St Michael and All Angels which is mostly 13th and 14th century, although the fine tympanum with St Michael and the dragon takes us back to Norman times. An imposing tower and spire which are late EE and have dog-tooth ornament, and then we progress to Dec in the lovely aisle windows. Inside, part of a Norman arcade survives and more dog-tooth adorns the EE piscina and sedilia. Much of the glass here is by C.E. Kempe and is very beautiful.

Do find *Great Easton* St Andrew's church (lovely spire) and St Nicho-las *Bringhurst* (hill-top site and Norman work). *Stockerston* church of St Peter is lonely and so lovely, with views into Rutland over the Eye

Brook reservoir. *Medbourne* church of St Giles and village are picturesque and worth savouring, but, above all else in this area, do find *Nevill Holt*, where St Mary's church and the hall actually adjoin in a most memorable setting.

KING'S NORTON. A tiny village with a mighty church of St John the Baptist of 1757–75. It is stately Gothic and very ambitious, by John Wing the Younger of Leicester. The fine tower lost its tall spire in 1850. Inside we are treated to all the original furnishings, but the bonus is that they are arranged in the Puritan fashion, around a massive central three-decker pulpit, with the altar and its rails hidden behind.

At *Gaulby* (the next village), we see the work of Wing Senior (1741) who rebuilt all St Peter's apart from the chancel (a must for atmosphere and furnishings). St John the Baptist *Little Stretton*, St Andrew's *Burton Overy* and St Cuthbert's *Great Glen* are also worth seeing.

LEICESTER. Of the medieval churches, St Martin's is now the cathedral and All Saints' (RCF) has Norman work, a good 13th century font, a wealth of 14th century tiles and a 15th century pulpit and doors. St Margaret's is large and handsome Dec and Perp, with a very imposing tower. St Nicholas' is a fascinating building of great interest, because so much of it is either Saxon or Norman. St Mary de Castro, with its tall (179 ft) spire is probably the most fascinating of all. There is superb Norman work in its chancel (including the sedilia), also good EE and Dec work and a 15th century chancel roof. It too has some 14th century tiles, and there is much more to admire in this rather dark, but very devotional and prayerful church.

LOCKINGTON. There is much to see in St Nicholas' church of the 13th and 14th centuries, with a fine Perp tower. The interior is of great interest. There is a grand Perp screen, above which is a most spectacular tympanum, with the Lord's Prayer, Creed and Commandments and a truly magnificent set of Royal Arms of 1704. There are a few bench-ends of c1500, box-pews and rails of the 17th century, a two-decker pulpit of the 18th century and some monuments of interest.

Nearby *Kegworth*'s superb Dec church of St Andrew also has a mighty Royal Arms, dated 1684. St Edward, King and Martyr *Castle Donington* has a lofty spire, a fine brass and monuments.

LUBENHAM. All Saints is a wonderfully atmospheric church which has not been spoiled by too much restoration. A beautiful setting also, and a charming exterior. Inside it is really delightful, with old bench-

183

ends, box-pews, three-decker pulpit and much else but, above all, everything here is homely and largely unspoilt and all of it put together creates the feeling of a real country church at its best.

At All Saints *Theddingworth* we find a Norman arcade and three interesting monuments, whilst *Market Harborough*'s stately church of St Dionysius has an imposing tower and spire, also much to see and enjoy.

MELTON MOWBRAY.   Melton Mowbray's mighty and magnificent cruciform church of St Mary dominates the centre of the busy town. The exterior is so impressive – the nave has aisles, the transepts have aisles and there is a western galilee porch. The stately Perp clerestory (48 windows in all) soars above aisles which have lovely Dec windows. The climax of the exterior is the central tower (c100 ft high), with a 13th century lower stage and a magnificent Perp upper stage, parapet and pinnacles.

In the neighbourhood are several small churches of interest (St Swithin's *Great Dalby*, St James' *Burton Lazars*, *Brentingby*'s unusual tower etc); there is *Stapleford*'s parkland church of St Mary Magdalene of 1783, which is a real period-piece. Westwards is St Peter's *Kirby Bellars* with its fine steeple, screen and monuments and the pretty churches of the Wreak Valley (like St Thomas of Canterbury *Frisby*, All Saints *Hoby* and St Michael's *Brooksby*).

STAUNTON HAROLD.   A taste of paradise here – what could be more attractive than this lush parkland, the lakes, the great house and this wonderful church of Holy Trinity (cared for by the National Trust), which is entirely of 1653–1665 but shows stately and authentic looking Dec and Perp, with an impressive tower and embattled and pinnacled exterior. Inside, all its original fittings and furnishings are in place – box-pews, lectern, pulpit (complete with cushions and hangings), chancel panelling and altar. The wrought-iron screen is 18th century but is very beautiful. Most amazing of all is the painted ceiling, executed in 1665 and showing the Creation. The organ retains some of its original 17th century work and there is a lovely wooden screen beneath it.

St Helen's *Ashby de la Zouche* is a large Perp church by the castle ruins, where we may enjoy a fine 17th century reredos and several interesting monuments.

STOKE GOLDING.   A wonderful building, which breathes beauty and antiquity and is almost entirely work of c1272–1307. It is not St Margaret's size which draws people here, but the inestimable beauty of its architecture, seen in its truly exquisite Dec windows and arcade,

One of the lovely towers and spires which grace this county, at Great Easton.

which has lavishly carved capitals, with foliage, human heads of knights and ladies, and a lad sticking his tongue out. One lancet window remains from the EE church here. The font (c1330) is carved with figures of saints, the old parish chest is dated 1636 and, beneath an arched recess, is a slab with an incised sword – maybe the monument of Sir Robert de Champaigne, who rebuilt the church.

Amongst the lovely smaller churches nearby are 13th century St James' *Dadlington* and St James' *Sutton Cheney*, also St Peter's *Higham on the Hill*, with its Norman tower, *Hinckley* has a large church, St Mary's, with a very bold tower and spire.

WITHCOTE CHAPEL.   In a charming position near the 18th century hall, amidst wooded and undulating countryside. This simple embattled and pinnacled Gothic chapel of c1500–1510 (RCF) was restored and refurnished in 1744. A wonderful interior here, culminating in a Classical reredos, which is flanked by marble monuments of 1723 and 1742. The Communion rails are of wrought iron. The precious stained glass in the windows however is of c1536. In them we see ten prophets and eight Apostles. Truly a fascinating and very memorable place.

To the west is St Peter's *Tilton on the Hill*, with its splendid clerestory, Norman font and Digby monuments. The journey south to *Loddington*'s remote church of St Michael takes us past Launde Abbey, and through beautiful and unspoilt countryside.

RUTLAND

BARROWDEN.   St Peter's beautiful spire rises above the picturesque churchyard in the Welland valley. In this basically 13th and 14th century church, with Perp clerestory, tower and chancel windows, is a pulpit with ancient woodwork, 15th century figures supporting the chancel roof and the superb monument of Roland Durant (1588).

Do go and find the remote Norman church at *Tixover* dedicated to St Mary Magdalen and see the Norman work and Elizabethan pulpit at St Mary the Virgin *Morcott*, also St Mary's *South Luffenham*'s late Norman arcade and graceful tower and spire.

BROOKE.   St Peter's is a real character, with a Norman doorway, north arcade and font, but with a north aisle and chancel of 1579. It is the furnishings however which are so remarkable and rare because they are a complete Elizabethan set – box-pews, family pews, reading desk, pulpit, stalls, and even screens, are all work of the late 1500s. The lovely monument to Charles Noel (1619) still has its original colouring.

Braunston is a pretty village with a church, St Peter's, of considerable character – even to the odd position of its clock-face. *Manton* St Mary's with its 13th C bellcot and 1796 chancel, is delightful and St Mary and St Andrew's *Ridlington* preserves the musical instruments once used to accompany services before the organ was installed.

EMPINGHAM. St Peter's wonderfully imposing church presides over its limestone village near Rutland Water. Outside we admire the lofty 14th century tower and spire, the Perp clerestory and aisle windows and the handsome proportions. Inside we see the 13th century core, with EE arcades, double piscina and fine triple sedilia in the chancel.

In the neighbourhood are two wonderful churches which must be visited, St Peter and St Paul's *Exton* is set in a park, has a glorious tower and spire and the most incredible collection of monuments. St Mary *Ketton*'s incomparable central tower and spire must be as near to perfection as any; there is much of interest here. *Normanton*'s grandly Classical church of St Matthew (1826 and 1911) is now half-submerged on a little peninsula at the edge of Rutland Water and is leading a new life as a museum. It must be seen – there is no other church quite like it!

OAKHAM. Rutland's charming county town in the Vale of Catmose, with the soaring 14th century spire of its stately church of All Saints visible from far and near. Even the weathercock here is medieval. The noble exterior is mostly Perp, but inside are 13th century arcades, their capitals carved with animals, symbols and scenes from the Bible. Much of interest in this grand and spacious interior, also many signs of active life and use.

Langham also has a stately church of St Peter and St Paul, with a wonderful tower and spire, whilst *Burley on the Hill* Holy Cross church was restored by J.L. Pearson (RCF). *Hambleton*'s atmospheric church of St Andrew and village now have Rutland Water on both sides and reward a visit, St Edmund's *Egleton* has lovely Norman work in its doorway and chancel arch.

STOKE DRY. Who could fail to fall in love with this refreshingly individual building and with the views from its hillside position? There is intricate Norman stonecarving in the shafts of the chancel arch of St Andrew's and there is much work here from the 1200–1300 period, although the 15th century provided the clerestory, roof and the north porch with its oriel window. There is so much to see inside, including 15th century benches and fine screen, also several wall-paintings (including the martyrdoms of St Andrew and St Edmund) and the lovely Digby monuments. But it is the 'whole' which is memorable, including the exterior, which has few airs and graces but which is so very beautiful.

St Andrew's *Lyddington* must be seen for its fine exterior, for its screen and most of all for its Communion rails, which surround the altar on all four sides. St Peter and St Paul's *Uppingham* church porch is entered directly from the market place. The spire here is elegant, the pulpit Elizabethan and there are some beautifully preserved sculptures which are Norman.

TICKENCOTE. A curious-looking church, just off the A1, much rebuilt by S.P. Cockerell in 1792, but St Peter and St Paul's chancel is genuine and elaborate Norman, and is vaulted inside. The great feature here is the most sumptuous, most elaborate and most amazing Norman chancel arch to be found in any English church. There are five orders of it and it defies description in the space allowed here. You must see it!

Do see also St Peter and St Paul's *Great Casterton* (unspoilt and very atmospheric), All Saints *Little Casterton* (bellcot, wall-paintings and brass), St John the Evangelist *Ryhall* (fine spire and 14th century work, especially the sedilia) and St Mary's *Essendine* (bellcot and excellent Norman doorway).

WHISSENDINE. The mighty (100 ft) 14th century tower of St Andrew's is a masterpiece in design and construction. The church is large and splendid Perp. Inside, beneath a fine 15th century roof (with a dozen carved figures under canopies), is a 16th century screen from St John's College Cambridge, Kempe glass in the east window, some tasteful modern furnishings and much more of interest.

Holy Trinity *Teigh* is a small church of 1782 with a 14th century tower. Here the congregation face each other (as in a college chapel) in three tiers of box-pews, with the pulpit, reading-desk and clerk's desk at one end and the altar at the other, all beneath pretty plaster ceilings.

LINCOLNSHIRE

A very large county indeed, despite losing its top section to Humberside, and also a very varied and fascinating county, with some 70 miles of coastline forming its eastern border. At the south-east are the Fens and above them the Marshland – both areas with mighty and magnificent churches. In the north-east the Wolds stretch some 45 miles from the Humber down to Spilsby and Horncastle, whilst in a north–south line runs the (mostly very narrow) ridge known as the Lincoln Cliff, upon which the Romans built their road called Ermine Street.

Lincolnshire is a truly wonderful place for churches, with 450 or so medieval ones and many interesting later examples. A vast amount of these are built of limestone, including the county's very own Ancaster stone, and several in the Wolds are built of local greenstone. Lincolnshire is rich in examples of all periods of architecture. Over 40 churches contain notable Saxon work (including several Saxon towers) and there are some fine Norman churches, also much EE work of very high quality. Dec is seen magnificently in several Lincolnshire churches, especially in a number of fine chapels, equipped with lovely piscinae, sedilia and Easter Sepulchres, and all over the county in lovely towers, spires and windows of the period. Perp appears in splendour in the Marsh and Fen churches, and in many great buildings with fine clerestories, stately towers with double pairs of belfry windows and light and spacious interiors. Lincolnshire has some of England's largest and finest churches – enormous Louth, Grantham and Boston, also Heckington, Gedney, Tattershall, Holbeach and a good many others which are of supreme interest. The medieval churches here have plenty of treasures inside, with amazing stonecarving, delightful woodwork and plenty of monuments and brasses.

Then come the 18th century churches – several of them in villages, like Langton by Partney and Cherry Willingham, also the little Fen chapels and other village churches which were built during the late 1700s and early 1800s, and the remarkable early Victorian churches, like Raithby near Louth and Haugham. The Gothic Revival itself is widely represented in a variety of new churches and heavy restorations, but surprisingly few of national importance. A good many were the work of local architects, like the prolific James Fowler of Louth and Charles Kirk of Sleaford.

The visitor to Lincolnshire is rewarded by villages and churches in shoals, sometimes little more than a mile apart, often in lines along the roads which punctuate the county, or in little groups. Planning a church-crawl here with a map can be great fun and it is easy to spend a day seeing 20 or so but travelling within a very small area. Remember that in the north, around the Wolds, many of the churches are smaller and have much more 'plain and wholesome' work, but are of great age and beauty, whilst in the south are many churches which are large and contain work of great richness and splendour.

ADDLETHORPE.   St Nicholas' is a fine Perp marshland church with a typical tower, an embattled clerestory and aisles with pinnacles and gargoyles. Grand S porch with a cross with the Crucifixion and the Virgin and Child, and an original old door with Perp tracery and roof with bosses. Splendid nave roof. Perp font and noble screens, many poppyhead benches and some old glass. Unfortunately the chancel has disappeared.

Nearby *Ingoldmells* St Peter and St Paul's has a fine tower and some medieval benches – another grand church which lost its chancel, in 1706.

BAG ENDERBY.   A Perp greenstone church in the Wolds – not large but beautiful and with the air of antiquity. St Margaret's font is carved with the Instruments of the Passion, a Pieta scene and other subjects; there is a simple screen, some old glass and a monument of 1591.

Nearby is St Margaret's *Somersby* (Tennyson's church, with a superb 15th century churchyard cross), *South Ormsby* (much to see in this delightfully set church of St Leonard, including brasses and a lovely font), *Langton by Partney* (a classical period-piece of c1720–30, with its original fittings) and St Mary's *Harrington* (mostly rebuilt by S.S. Teulon, 1854, but with the tower and interesting monuments from the old church).

BOSTON.   St Botolph's is one of the wonders of England. Boston Stump is the highest medieval church tower in England (including cathedrals) at 272½ ft, crowned by an octagon. The base is Dec, otherwise it is Perp. The tower is open inside to the top of the second stage, 137 ft, and then comes a lierne-vault with bosses. The church itself is Dec on a huge scale. The clerestory has 14 two-light windows on each side. The 64 stalls are of 1390 with a wealth of misericords which should be studied carefully: also the poppyheads and elbow-rests. There are 18th C wrought-iron altar-rails, a 17th C pulpit and tester, and the SW and N doors are original. Mons include an incised slab, Wissel Smalenburg

1340; an alabaster knight on a tomb-chest with angels holding shields, 15th C; also a 14th C lady, with puppies eating her dress. Brasses to Walter Pescod and wife 1398, and a priest in a cope with saints on the orphreys c1400.

Fine churches all around here, including St Guthlac's *Fishtoft*, St James' *Freiston*, All Saints' *Benington*, St Helen's *Leverton*, St Mary's *Old Leake*, St Margaret's *Sibsey*, and St Peter and St Paul's *Kirton in Holland*.

BRANT BROUGHTON. The tower is Dec with pinnacles and one of Lincolnshire's most elegant spires, 198 ft high. St Helen's is mainly Perp. Both porches are show-pieces and vaulted, the nave roof is original, and there is a Perp clerestory and font. Bodley restored this church and much of its glass was designed and made by its rector, Canon Frederick Sutton.

By contrast, go to tiny, rustic St Michael's *Stragglethorpe*, with its unspoilt interior, Saxon west wall and lovely monument (c1697) to Richard Earle. *Leadenham* St Swithin's and *Welbourn* St Chad's have lovely spires, and *Caythorpe* St Vincent's spire is spectacular, whilst *Fulbeck* St Nicholas' has a fine tower and much of interest.

CLAYPOLE. St Peter's has a 13th and 15th C tower with pinnacles and a lovely recessed spire. A tall 14th C chancel with large windows, the E being Perp. Dec piscina and sedilia, arcades with foliage capitals and clerestory. Panelled nave ceiling. A fine Perp S porch with battlements and pinnacles and an old door. Dec font with tracery, a Perp wooden pulpit, and a 15th C rood-screen. The chancel arch has bracket-figures to carry the rood-beam.

CHERRY WILLINGHAM. Perhaps the finest of the village Georgian churches, St Peter and St Paul's is delightfully set and dating from 1753. It is built of stone and is small, but has great dignity. Tuscan columns flank its west doorway and there is a pretty octagonal lantern above. The interior is beautiful, with original font and good Georgian reredos. Its founder (Thomas Becke, died 1757) has his memorial here.

Fiskerton St Clement's church is worth seeing for its fine arcades (one Norman and the other EE), also its unusual Perp tower, its 13th century font and the brass of a priest.

COTES-by-STOW. St Edith's is small by Lincolnshire standards, but full of interest. An original bellcot, Norm windows in the chancel and Trans N and S nave doorways. On the N side of the chancel is an Easter Sepulchre with small figures, Christ risen and an angel. Perp rood-screen with most unusually its original rood-loft, with a central projection. There is also a Perp wooden pulpit, a Norm font, a set of old benches and a Jac family pew. Brasses to William Butler and wife 1590, and baby in swaddling bands; Charles Butler and wife and eight children, 1602. Mon to Brian Cooke, a demi-figure, 1653.

CROFT. A splendid Marsh church, All Saints is large, noble and mainly of local greenstone. What a joy to go inside, to find lovely woodwork in the old roofs, rood-screen, parclose screens and benches, also a pulpit of 1615 and a south door of 1633. There is a medieval brass lectern here, also part of a very early brass of a knight in chain mail.

Burgh le Marsh St Peter and St Paul's is also a delight, with its magnificent tower and colourful prayerful interior, where we admire fine woodwork. *Bratoft* St Peter and St Paul's is a good Perp church (tower 1747) with a restored screen and some old bench-ends.

DONINGTON. The church of St Mary and Holy Rood has a proud Dec tower and tall recessed spire, 143 ft, and a Dec vaulted S porch. The chancel is mainly Dec and Perp, as indicated by the windows. Piscina and sedilia, and a Perp clerestory with seven windows on each side.

Why not go east on the A52 to see St Swithin's *Bicker* (wonderful Norman and EE, also stalls and benches) and stately St Mary's *Swineshead* (160 ft spire, fine Dec and Perp, screen, old doors etc).

EWERBY. St Andrew's is a Dec church with tower (ten bells) and a good example of a broach spire, 172 ft. The tower is vaulted. Fine S porch, piscina and sedilia. The vault is Norm (with intersecting arches) and Dec (with blank windows). Dec rood-screen with tracery, 17th C altar-rails, a 14th C chest and an Anglo-Saxon slab. Mon to Sir Alexander Aunsell 1360.

Asgarby St Andrew's also has a handsome spire, and wall-paintings.

FOLKINGHAM. The tall Perp tower (vaulted) of St Andrew's, with 16 pinnacles, overlooks the spacious market square. The chancel is 13th C with Geometrical tracery. Dec arcades, a Perp two-storeyed S porch (vaulted), and a tierceron-vault with an upper room with fire-place. Nice rood-screen.

A very good set of bench-ends in the Dec church of St Peter and St Paul at *Osbournby* and lovely spires at St Andrew's *Pickworth* (also pulpit, benches and wall-paintings) and St Nicholas' *Walcot*. *Sempringham* St Andrew's is totally isolated – a fascinating Norman church.

There are many fine stone towers, like this one at Folkingham, in this county of splendid stonework.

GEDNEY. A splendid church all ashlar-faced (only the best being good enough), St Mary Magdalene's belonged to Crowland Abbey. The tower up to and including the original belfry-openings is c1280, and then there is a tall Perp top stage, and then the start of a stone spire never finished (a little red spike instead). The exterior up to the clerestory is all Dec. A two-storeyed S porch with Dec S door, and a chancel with Flowing E window and piscina and sedilia. The Perp clerestory is marvellous – twelve windows of three lights, battlements and pinnacles. On the E gable a sanctus bellcot. The roof has tiebeams and arch-braces alternating. There is an EE pillar piscina, a font base of 1664, a pulpit c1700 and the remains of a 14th C Jesse window. Mons include a damaged effigy of a knight and Adlard Welby and wife facing each other, and five children 1605. Brass to a lady c1400 with a puppy at her feet.

GOSBERTON. St Peter and St Paul's has a Dec central tower with pinnacles and flying buttresses and recessed Perp spire, 160 ft. The windows of the church are Dec and Perp. Perp clerestory and S porch, and a Perp crossing with a lierne-vault. Piscina and sedilia. On the E wall is an elephant gargoyle. Perp font and screen to the N chapel. There is also an ironbound chest. Mon to a 14th C knight cross-legged in his recess with censing angels; the monument to his wife also survives.

A fascinating leaning tower and spire at St Laurence's *Surfleet* and, to the north-east, splendid churches at St Mary's *Sutterton* (cruciform, fine spire and lovely architecture) and St Peter and St Paul's *Algarkirk* (stately exterior, cruciform, with imposing Dec and Perp architecture).

GRANTHAM. A large church with a conspicuous Dec tower with big pinnacles and a recessed spire, 282 ft (vaulted inside). A small piece of Norm proves that there was a Norm chancel, but all St Wulfram's is now Dec and Perp. Large windows – Perp E window of six lights and another in the N chapel with seven lights. S chapel with Flowing tracery – underneath the chapel is a vaulted crypt. Large N porch and gargoyles everywhere. Perp font. In the S porch is a Chained Library given in 1598. In a recess of 1380 is the Harrington tomb: the main cusps are angels with Instruments of the Passion. Monuments also to Richard Saltby 1369, and Lord Chief Justice Sir Dudley Ryder, seated, 1756.

To the south-west is lovely *Harlaxton*, with its amazing manor house and fine ironstone church of St Mary and St Peter.

GREAT PONTON. Holy Cross is situated beyond the Great North Road and the main railway line to Edinburgh, just S of Grantham, so that travellers by road or rail will see its glorious Perp tower. This has a beautiful top of decorated battlements and eight pinnacles, and on one of the pinnacles is the weathervane, a violin. On three faces of the tower is an inscription 'Thynke and thanke God of all', for the tower was built in 1519 by a wealthy wool merchant, Anthony Ellys. The chancel arch and arch to the N chapel and S porch are EE and all else is Perp. Sedilia. At the W end of the S aisle is a 16th C fireplace. In the N chapel are three shields of Anthony Ellys.

Little Ponton St Guthlac's has a very early chancel arch, also an EE arcade and doorway. Do also go to see the monuments at St Mary and St Andrew's *Stoke Rochford* (or South Stoke).

HECKINGTON. A grand Dec church all of one piece, St Andrew's tower with pinnacles and broach spire, 182 ft, is typical. The S porch has niches on the buttresses, as on the tower, and a band of shields, angels, kneeling figures and a figure of Christ (replaced). The S transept S window of five lights has Flowing tracery, and the E window of the chancel of seven lights Flowing, is one of England's glories in that style. The tower is vaulted. There is a clerestory, and both transepts and aisles have original roofs. In the chancel are the four features that make Heckington famous – all have exuberant ogee and crocketed work, foliations and pinnacles. The double piscina also has figures and leaf capitals. The sedilia are vaulted and have figures of Christ, the Virgin, two angels, St Margaret and St Catherine. Four scenes are all connected with feeding – a woman feeding a dove, another feeding a dog, a man on all fours eating, and a bearded man feeding someone else. The tomb recess on the N side has a monument of Richard de Potesgrave, vicar in the 14th C. The Easter Sepulchre is a show-front round a recess: below are four seated soldiers sleeping, with shafts leading to the top cornice with small figures, a mermaid, piper, and bagpipers. In sidepieces are the three Maries, and an angel. Above are angels and Christ Risen. There is also a Dec font.

Great Hale St John the Baptist's has a Saxon tower and *Helpringham* St Andrew's a splendid spire and screen.

HEYDOUR. St Michael's has an EE chancel, with three-storeyed lancets in the E wall. Sedilia, and opposite a tomb-recess. The tower is Dec with a recessed spire (vaulted). Dec arcades, the windows having intersecting tracery, the S porch is vaulted, and there is a Perp clerestory and Dec font. The chest of c1550 shows three heads in profile. In two N aisle windows is richly coloured Dec glass, one depicting St Edward the Confessor, St George and St Edmund, the other St Vincent, St Lawrence, St Stephen and some children. There are some 18th C monuments in the Newton Chapel.

HOLBEACH.   All Saints' is all Dec and has a tower with battlements and a recessed broach spire about 180 ft. The tower, vaulted, forms a porch with a large Perp W window above the fine clerestory. There is a sanctus bellcot on the E gable. The chancel windows are most elaborate with Flowing tracery. The nave arcades are late 14th C. The S door is original with reticulated tracery, and there is a Perp font. Mon to Sir Humphrey Littlebury, late 14th C, and a brass to Joanne Welby on a tomb-chest 1488.

Fleet St Mary Magdalen's has a handsome tower and spire (14th century) which stands detached from the church.

HUTTOFT.   In the salt marshes stands St Margaret's with its tall 13th C tower with lancets, plate-tracery belfry windows, and dog-tooth. The 13th C chancel arch has two fine corbel-heads. Dec arcades, Perp S aisle with gargoyles and S porch and doorway, Perp N aisle and clerestory. It is, however, for two pieces of furniture that the visitor comes here. One is the chest, 14th C and carved with Dec tracery, the other the Perp font. On the bowl are the Twelve Apostles in pairs of two, and the Virgin and Child and the Trinity. All the Apostles need a haircut. Against the underside of the bowl are angels with outspread wings and against the stem are figures of saints. Against the foot are the symbols of the Four Evangelists.

LINCOLN.   The cathedral here seems to pale everything else into insignificance – but there *is* more to see! There are three Saxon towers in this city (St Peter at Gowts, St Mary le Wigford and St Benedict). St Mary Magdalene's (near the cathedral) was rebuilt by Bodley in 1882 and St Swithin's, with its tall spire, is a large town church by James Fowler (1869–87). St Giles' is a sturdy Classical church built in a modern housing estate in 1936 – although most of it began life in the city centre in 1724 as St Peter at Arches, designed by Smith of Warwick.

LONG SUTTON.   The 13th C tower of St Mary's was originally completely detached and it has the earliest lead spire in England, 162 ft The pinnacles are little lead spirelets. The two-storeyed S porch is Perp, with a vault. On entering the church one has a great surprise: it is a complete Norm church to beyond the chancel arch with arcades of seven bays. The complete Norm clerestory is now inside the church. Perp brass eagle lectern, fragments of old glass and a Norm font.

Lutton has a very pleasing Perp church of St Nicholas in brick, with a stone spire, and a pulpit of 1702.

LOUTH. The church dominates the green valley beyond the Wolds and the marsh. St James' has the highest and finest parish church stone spire in England. Its height is 294 ft, tower and spire being the same as they should be. Most stone spires are EE or Dec, but this one is Perp – at its best. The tower itself is noble and the spire is supported by flying buttresses resting against solid turret pinnacles with spirelets themselves 52 ft high. The crockets on the spire are used discreetly. Long lines can appear hollow in the centre and so a bulge was given to a spire half-way up and here the genius who designed the spire increased the size of the crockets at that point. The window is of five lights and is very high. The clerestory is in nave and chancel. The E window is of seven lights. There are porches N and S, good angel figures on the nave roof, and the S chapel has sedilia with lierne-vaults. A high tower arch: in fact the tower is open for 86 ft, and then a lierne-vault with bosses. Perp font, side-screens, six plain stalls and an old cupboard with busts of c1500. A traceried door leads to the staircase in the W wall. Paintings of Moses and Aaron.

To the north-east the churches of St Adelwold *Alvingham* and St Mary *North Cockerington* stand together in the same churchyard. The latter (RCF) has a Saxon window and a set of box-pews.

MOULTON. All Saints' has a fine Perp W tower with crocketed recessed spire, connected to the pinnacles by flying buttresses. EE clerestory and the arcades are late 12th C. The capitals have upright leaves (on the way to stiff-leaf) and some heads. The chancel has EE sedilia and a plain 14th C Easter Sepulchre. There is an 18th C font with the Baptism of Christ, and Adam and Eve. Old roof, and the N and S doorways are EE.

QUADRING. St Margaret's has a Perp tower, considerably leaning (as often around here), and a recessed spire. It has a fine row of clerestory windows, eight three-light windows on each side. Both arcades are Perp. The rood-stair turret is placed oddly in the nave, with decoration round the doorway.

RIPPINGALE. A lovely village, presided over by the tall Perp tower of its fine church of St Andrew, where we discover an unusually long south aisle of c1300, with pleasing Dec windows. There is much to see inside, including the ribbed coving from beneath the former rood-loft and a variety of monuments, especially a rare 13th century deacon with a book, a 13th century cross-legged knight and a lady beneath a 14th century canopy.

Morton church stands grandly at the end of the village street – a fine central tower here, a noble west front, with west porch and a splendid interior. *Hacconby* St Andrew's has a graceful spire, a 14th century chest and a 15th century pulpit.

SILK WILLOUGHBY. St Denis' splendid Dec tower has a recessed spire with pinnacles and flying buttresses. The church has a Dec S porch with a doorway with ballflower, a Dec nave, Perp sedilia with a lierne-vault, a Norm font, a Jac pulpit and many poppyhead benches. There is also a 17th C painting of the Annunciation, and a Perp rood-screen and banner-stave niche.

SLEAFORD. The W doorway of St Denis', vaulted, is late 12th C and early 13th C. The W portal is Trans. The broach spire has been rebuilt. The chancel is then late Dec with Flowing tracery windows and Perp clerestory and chancel. There is much exterior decoration. The great N window of the N transept is of six lights and shows Flowing tracery to perfection. The E window of the chancel is a seven-light Perp window. There is a splendid Perp rood-screen with vault, a Dec font, 18th C altar-rails, a 17th C dole cupboard and a desk with chained books. Mons include a 14th C slab to the wife of a de Rauceby with a foliated cross and her face in a roundel. Below are her praying hands, and at the bottom her feet. Sir Edward Carre and family 1618 are commemorated, as is Sir Robert Carre, with a plain tomb-chest 1682, and next to it a bust of his son. Brass to George Carre and wife 1521.

SNARFORD. St Lawrence's small tower is 12th C below and 13th C above. The Perp font has shields referring to Christ's Passion. It is for monuments that one comes here. Sir Thomas St Pol and wife 1582 have a six-poster with two recumbent effigies and shields; on top are the kneeling children, the eldest son on his own. Sir George St Pol and wife 1613 have both effigies lying on their sides; below is an infant daughter. Robert, Lord Rich, Earl of Warwick and wife 1619 have busts in a medallion.

SPALDING. St Mary and St Nicholas' EE and Dec tower has pinnacles and flying buttresses to a recessed, crocketed spire, 160 ft. The church is mainly Dec and Perp. There is a Perp clerestory, a sanctus bellcot, Perp N and S porches, the former with a fan-vault, a hammerbeam roof and Perp W and N doors with tracery. There is a five-light window over the chancel arch.
St Paul's *Fulney* is a sturdy brick church of 1880, designed by Sir Gilbert Scott. It is EE, with a detached tower and spire, 135 ft high.

SPILSBY.   A very pleasant market town on a hill, whose St James' church has a pinnacled late Perp tower of c1529. The chancel and south aisle (1879) are by William Bassett Smith. Inside there are now three arcades, which is unusual. We come here to admire the wonderful monuments in the Willoughby Chapel. These begin with John, 1st Lord Willoughby D'Eresby in 1348 and finish with the 10th Lord (1601) and his daughter (1610). These tombs are worth taking time to examine in detail – here we are face to face with history and real people. There are brasses as well. (Why not try to discover the superb church of St Michael at *Edenham*, which is near Bourne, where there is another remarkable set of monuments to the same family – continuing the series begun at Spilsby).

In the Spilsby area, *Halton Holgate* St Andrew's has good roofs, benches and stalls, and you must not miss a visit (particularly on a clear day) to the church of St Helen at *West Keal*, not only to admire the grand pinnacled tower, the fine porch and the fascinating carved capitals on the Dec arcades, but here we are on the southern 'parapet' of the Wolds, with the most incredible panoramic view over the wide sweep of the Fens, with Boston Stump in the distance.

STAMFORD.   One of our most delightful old towns, all built of the local stone. The following can be only a summary of its marvellous churches.

St Mary's has a beautiful EE doorway with a splendid broach spire. The N chapel has a coloured panelled ceiling with bosses. Mon to Sir David Phillips and wife 1506, with the Twelve Apostles and angels. All Saints' Perp tower with polygonal turret pinnacles has a soaring recessed spire (vaulted inside). Brasses to wool merchants. St John the Baptist's has a splendid Perp tower and inside note the roof, screens and glass.

St Martin's (originally in Northamptonshire) has another splendid Perp tower (vaulted inside). There is much old glass and a Dec font. Mons to William Cecil, Lord Burghley, 1598; Richard Cecil, wife and three daughters, 1587; John, 5th Earl of Exeter 1703.

St George's is refreshingly modest after the rest, but with much to interest us, including a 15th century roof and some medieval glass, also the fine monument (1797) of Sir Richard Cust and his wife.

STOW.   This great church of St Mary was more or less the same size at the Norm Conquest. The huge crossing and transepts are Sax 10th C, while the nave is early Norm 1095 with W and S doorways with zig-zag c1140. The magnificent chancel is late Norm, also c1140. The only post-Norm work is the EE two-light windows, one with plate tracery (S wall of S transept), and others with bar tracery (S transept E, and N transept E and W), and the central tower which is Perp. EE font with carvings on nine supports, and a 17th C pulpit.

Sturton has a humble brick church, St Hugh's (1879), by J.L. Pearson.

TATTERSHALL.   Noted for its castle, but the church of Holy Trinity is equally important. The church was begun by Lord Cromwell, Treasurer of England in 1440, and finished by his executors, one being Bishop Waynflete. This church is entirely Perp. It is gaunt in the absence of ornament and all the windows are left without cusping. The large windows make the church a glass-house. The massive tower has four pinnacles and there are old roofs. Stone screen, with on its E side two stone desks (for reading the Epistle and Gospel) and on the W side two recesses for altars and a pillar piscina. The stone screen has its old door and is also the N door of the church with a wicket. Perp wooden pulpit with Jac tester. Old glass in the E window (several panels from the Seven Sacraments and the Acts of Mercy and Virtues). A number of brasses to the family and the members of the College. A number of saints also occur on the brasses.

Coningsby St Michael's church is distinguished by its splendid tower, with a huge clock face.

THEDDLETHORPE.   All Saints (RCF) is the richest of the marshland churches. Double piscina and the sedilia have late Norm capitals. The remainder is early Perp c1400. The tower (with a lead spirelet) and S porch have much pre-Reformation brickwork. Battlements and gargoyles. There is a clerestory, a Perp font, a reredos niche at the E end of the S aisle, a good rood-screen and side-screens, some old benches and Norm stones with chevrons built into the N arcade. Both aisles have medieval stone altars. Old roofs and a Jac Communion table. Brass to Robert Hayton 1424. Another beautiful reredos niche may be seen at *Theddlethorpe St Helen.*

Nearby *Saltfleetby All Saints* (RCF) has a wonderful church, with another reredos, also a screen, original roofs, leaning tower and much atmosphere.

THRECKINGHAM.   St Peter's has a fine 13th C tower with 14th C bar tracery belfry windows and a broach spire with big steep broaches. In the Norm chancel the E wall has three tall even windows. EE font, and a 14th C S porch with an old door with ironwork. The mon to Lambert de Treckingham and wife c1310 has very large figures, with two lions at his feet and two puppies at her feet.

Horbling St Andrew's church is cruciform and well worth seeing, also

Billingborough St Andrew's with its splendid spire. *Swaton* St Michael's is cruciform, with good EE and Dec, much to see and plenty of atmosphere.

WESTON. St Mary's Perp W tower has a tall tower arch. The EE S porch with stiff-leaf capitals prepares us for the glory of that style inside. The arcades are EE and have stiff-leaf capitals worthy of Lincoln Cathedral. The beautiful chancel is full of lancets (at the E end a triplet with quatrefoils above). EE also the clerestory. The aisle windows are Dec and there is an EE font. Base and shaft of a churchyard cross.

WHAPLODE. The church of St Mary has a Norm and EE tower with a later parapet and small pinnacles on the S side, almost detached. Norm clerestory. The W and S doorways are late 12th C and there is a 14th C S porch with an old door and tunnel-vault. The chancel arch is Norm with zig-zag. The arcades are Norm but there is some EE work at the W end with stiff-leaf capitals. The N chancel chapel is fully EE. The old nave roof has hammerbeams and arched braces. There is also a 17th C font and a Jac pulpit with tester. Mons include a 13th C coffin-lid with foliated cross, fragments of a 14th C lady, and Sir Anthony Irvy and wife 1625 with five kneeling children, all beautifully coloured: original railings.

WRANGLE. St Mary and St Nicholas' is a marshland church, mainly Perp. The tower is Perp, but its arch into the church shows scalloped and stiff-leaf capitals. There is a sanctus bellcot. The S doorway is EE. The N arcade is EE and the S is Dec. Dec chancel with E window of five lights. The chancel arch, aisle windows, S porch and clerestory are Perp. Double piscina and sedilia, Jac pulpit and much old glass of 1350–70, all in the gorgeous colours of that period.

LONDON

London is a fascinating oasis for the church enthusiast, especially if he is prepared to go into the parts where the tourists rarely go – along the backstreets, 'Broadways' and mews and into the boroughs where the majority of the people live and where we do really see London life. To walk from church to church is to see London properly – and what a feast awaits us. Sadly so many of the churches have to be locked, but it is often possible to find people working inside them or maybe to catch the parish priest at home.

There is not a great deal for the pure medievalist here for (if we exclude the most recent reorganisation which has swallowed up more of Essex, Kent and Surrey and the whole of Middlesex) we find about 25 medieval churches – and some of these have been reordered or rebuilt to such an extent in later periods that maybe only fragments of their medieval work remain. The later churches however do have so much to offer, because some of the finest works of the finest architects are naturally found in the metropolis, and there is a great deal which is unusual and eccentric here, embracing the widest possible spectrum of churchmanship and tradition. Visitors flock to Wren's mighty Classical cathedral of St Paul, and to Westminster Abbey, but please do not ignore Southwark's venerable cathedral of St Saviour, just south of London Bridge.

Stimulating the enthusiast's appetite for over 500 Anglican churches in London and pointing him to the real gems is no easy task, but the following suggestions are offered with the understanding that although what follows is a mere sample, if you really want to get a taste of the very best that London's churches, in their infinite variety, have to offer, then each and every one of the churches mentioned should be visited.

MEDIEVAL CHURCHES

The square mile which we call the City (which is a wonderful entity in itself) has ten churches where medieval work remains, in addition to the fascinating chapels to be enjoyed in the Tower of London.

St Bartholomew the Great, West Smithfield is magnificent and is set in a lovely environment. Here we have the chancel and transepts of a Norman priory church founded by Rahere about 1123. Look for his monument, erected some 300 years later, in the church. Inside we may enjoy the massive Norman arcade, triforium and apse, also later work of high quality, especially Sir Aston Webb's restoration. There is much to see here, including some fine monuments.

St Ethelburga's, Bishopsgate is small, delightful and atmospheric, with its west wall right beside the pavement and the rest hidden by the buildings which sandwich it. A pretty 18th century belfry here and a lovely interior, enriched by Comper furnishings.

St Helen's Bishopsgate is set in a quiet square and with another 18th century belfry. This church is of great beauty and interest, with a double nave and fine architecture of the 14th–16th centuries. Amongst the treasures in its glorious interior is a superb pulpit of 1615, stalls of the 15th century, a poor box of 1620 and a wonderful array of monuments and brasses.

The Temple Church, in its unique setting, is one of England's four round churches, consecrated in 1195. East of the circular nave is a chancel with aisles which is superb EE and inside are several 13th century effigies of knights and an exceptional effigy of a 13th century bishop, also later monuments and a reredos by Wren.

Other medieval churches in the City include *St Giles' Cripplegate* (in the Barbican), *St Andrew's Undershaft* (mostly 1520–32), *St Olave's, Hart Street*, the fine 15th century tower of *St Sepulchre's Newgate Street* (150 ft) and fragments at *St Katherine Cree*, in Leadenhall Street, which was largely rebuilt in 1628–30 and has a splendid Laudian interior, where Classical and Gothic architecture combine.

Outside the City, *St Margaret's Westminster* is a regal Perp church of the early 1500s – its east window containing fine Flemish glass of the period.

Chelsea Old Church of All Saints, Cheyne Walk, has a medieval chancel and a 17th century tower and nave and has been wonderfully rebuilt after destruction in 1941. Its glorious Tudor monuments have been pieced together and its atmosphere so successfully recreated. St Thomas More is commemorated here and the More Chapel, built by him in 1528, has survived.

In *Stoke Newington*, by Clissold Park, two churches stand opposite each other. *Old St Mary's*, with its shingled spire, was restored in 1563, when the lovely Tudor brick south aisle was built, also its brick arcade. Here we may enjoy the lovely Jacobean Dudley Monument. Across the road rises the mighty bulk of *New St Mary's* – a huge Dec church of 1858 by Sir Gilbert Scott, built to replace the village church opposite. It is 190 ft long and its stately 243 ft spire (completed by John Oldrid Scott in

1890) is a prominent landmark. (Whilst in Stoke Newington, do try to find *St Matthias'*, Wordsworth Road – a masterpiece by William Butterfield).

St Dunstan and All Saints', Stepney stands in a large churchyard. It is large and embattled, with a sturdy tower. Most of what we see outside is Perp, although inside is a Saxon carving of the Crucifixion, an EE triple sedilia and dramatic modern glass by Hugh Easton in the east window.

Other medieval churches include *St Mary's Stratford Bow*, on its island in the middle of the busy A12 and, south of the river, *St Nicholas' Deptford* (medieval tower and the rest a period piece of c1697, with contemporary furnishings), *St Nicholas' Plumstead* (much altered and enlarged) and *St Mary's Putney* (mostly rebuilt after a fire in 1977).

CLASSICAL CHURCHES

London is riddled with them and what glorious work of this period to thrill us here – not only whole buildings, but also furnishings and internal work preserved in earlier or later buildings. Supreme amongst all are the churches of Sir Christopher Wren, from the late 1600s and opening years of the 1700s, of which 24 may be seen in the City (some of these rebuilt after the Second World War), also St Clement Danes and St James Piccadilly to the west. This architecture is of course entirely pagan in origin – based upon classical Greece and Rome, and most of the churches are rectangular, with no structural chancel. But what an array of craftsmanship – a wonderful variety of towers, interiors with superb woodwork in pews, pulpits and altarpieces, beautifully adorned ceilings and, as always, each church is a unique entity in itself.

Some of Wren's finest towers may be admired at *St Bride's, Fleet Street* (226 ft), *St Mary le Bow, Cheapside* (224 ft), *St Vedast, Foster Lane* (c160 ft), *St Lawrence Jewry* and *St Clement Danes* – all these churches gloriously refurbished after war damage.

For unspoilt Wren interiors, go to *St Margaret's, Lothbury*, *St Edmund the King, Lombard Street*, *St Mary Abchurch* (a domed interior, as is also *St Stephen's Walbrook*), *St Peter upon Cornhill* (screen and reredos of note) and *St Martin, Ludgate*. *St Mary at Hill*, with the best interior of all, has recently suffered a terrible fire. *St Magnus the Martyr* has a splendid Anglo-Catholic interior with most interesting 17th century furnishings gloriously brought to life but in a style which may not have pleased Wren!

Here is classical architecture at its most stunning in Hawksmoor's St George's In The East, built between 1715–23.

To see that Wren was also competent in Gothic, visit *St Mary Aldermary*, with its lofty fan-vaulted interior and 135 ft tower. Every Wren church has its own charm – as you will see for yourself when you discover little churches like *St Anne and St Agnes, Gresham Street* or the three related (but very different) steeples of *St Stephen Walbrook, St James Garlickhithe* and *St Michael Paternoster Royal*.

Most of the London Boroughs have one or more Classical churches of the 18th or early 19th centuries. Classical architecture is seen at its most extreme in the vast churches of Nicholas Hawksmoor, which appeared after the 1711 Act to build 50 new churches in London. Hawksmoor's mighty works inspire us with grandeur, bulk, size and dignity, rather than their elegance and beauty, but they must not be missed. *Christ Church Spitalfields*, with its 225 ft spire, is simply gigantic, *St George in the East* was gutted and its eastern part made into a smaller church in 1960, but the massive walls remain intact, with their amazing and almost oriental turrets and the mighty 160 ft tower. *St Anne's Limehouse* is another massive and spectacular East End landmark – bold and Classical, and of immense proportions. In the City is *St Mary Woolnoth* (smaller but just as eccentric), further west is *St George's Bloomsbury* and south of the river is *St Alfege Greenwich* (tower by John James).

Churches by other Classical architects which must be visited include *St Mary le Strand* (1717) and *St Martin in the Fields* (1726) – both by James Gibbs and both with splendid interiors, *St Giles in the Fields* (1733) by Henry Flitcroft, also the impressive churches by George Dance of *St Botolph Aldgate* (1744) and *St Leonard's Shoreditch*. South of the river is the atmospheric and very enjoyable church of *St Mary's Rotherhithe* (1715) and the spectacular *St Paul's Deptford* (by Thomas Archer and consecrated in 1730) which has a stunning Baroque elegance. Its interior is galleried and thoroughly Classical, but yet wonderfully devotional and prayerful. Do also try to find, north of the river, *St John at Hackney* (1797), *St James Clerkenwell* (1792) *All Saints Poplar* (1823), *St George's Hanover Square* (1724) and a host of other Classical churches, which are worth stopping to see, if only to admire their exteriors. The great church of *St Pancras, Euston Road* (1822) is by W. and H.W. Inwood, who also created the very cheap-looking Gothick church of *St Mary, Eversholt Street, Somers Town* in 1824 – a building which is now adorned with splendid furnishings inside.

Supreme amongst a group of Gothic churches built before the advent of the Oxford Movement to hold vast congregations of sermon tasters is *St Luke's Chelsea* – a mighty and magnificent building, grandly set in a wide open space, with a 142 ft tower and a lavish exterior. This masterpiece of James Savage, consecrated in 1824, has a lofty interior with a stone-vaulted ceiling (some 60 ft above us) and is liberally equipped with galleries and pews, with much of interest. Savage also designed the giant Classical church of *St James, Thurland Road, Bermondsey* (1825–7), whose tower is surmounted by a fine golden dragon.

GOTHIC REVIVAL CHURCHES

Here we list a selection of the best, but do stop at any others that you see on the way. Many are made more lovely by magnificent furnishings and adornments in the Anglo-Catholic tradition and are marked 'AC'.

WESTMINSTER, ST MARYLEBONE AND PADDINGTON:
All Saints, Margaret Street (AC) (1850–9), is one of William Butterfield's finest, with church, clergy house and former choir school jammed ingeniously into a small space, with a courtyard in the middle. Soaring 230 ft spire and inside, amidst dim devotional dusk, wonderful craftsmanship may be seen in the lavish stonecarving (much marble here), pictures in tiles on the walls (by Dyce 1873), rich Victorian glass, side chapel by Comper and, filling the east wall, William Dyce's sumptuous reredos. (By contrast, walk up to *All Souls Langham Place*, where we see a lively Classical church in the Evangelical tradition which is tastefully adorned and equipped for worship in the 1990s.)

St Mary, Bourne Street (AC) by R.J. Withers (1874) and Martin Travers (1919). A small church with a simple and undistinguished exterior, but all-glorious within – a treasure house of colour and beauty, using the Baroque style in many of its lovely furnishings. *St James the Less, Thorndyke Street, Westminster* is a fascinating church by G.E. Street (1858–61) which is a must for the student of architecture, for here we have 'High Victorian' Gothic of very good quality and originality.

Holy Trinity, Prince Consort Road is Bodley's major London work and one of his last (1902). As we would expect, this is lofty, dignified and beautifully proportioned, with lovely window tracery and colour tastefully employed in the reredos, roofs and glass by Burlison and Grylls. (See *St Paul's Knightsbridge*, where Bodley added the chancel and many of the lovely furnishings.)

St Cyprian, Clarence Gate (AC) is Comper at his most magnificent in this wonderful church, built in 1902–3. Everything shimmers as a church interior would have done in the 15th century – in the sumptuous and delicate screen and loft, in the long High Altar and the tester above it and in the many beautiful things which adorn this light, airy and spacious interior.

The Annunciation, Bryanston Street (AC) is a magnificent church by Sir Walter Tapper (1912–14), with a lofty red-brick exterior, punctuated by 14th century style windows, and a tall and mysterious vaulted interior, graced by good screenwork and a glorious reredos.

At *St Augustine's, Kilburn* (AC), the exterior of this cathedral-like giant is breathtaking – EE in red-brick and stone, cruciform, punctuated by corner turrets and spirelets and dominated by a glorious tower and spire rising 254 ft. This great church is one of the masterpieces of J.L. Pearson and was built in 1880. The vaulted interior is a wonderful place of vistas, surrounded by a triforium and with so much to see, not least the stone screen of five arches, the paintings by Clayton & Bell and the host of glorious furnishings and rich glass. No visitor will ever forget it.

St Mary Magdalene's, Clarendon Crescent, Paddington (AC) is another soaring brick church (by Street) – tall and stately, with an elegant and partly octagonal tower and spire. Inside we are aware of great height and superb stonecarving in the arcades, and in the statues in their niches between the arches. There is fine glass by Henry Holiday, painted roofs by Daniel Bell, also alabaster panelling and Salviati's Venetian mosaics in the chancel. More glories lie beneath, in the crypt chapel, created in great colour and splendour by Comper in 1895.

KENSINGTON AND CHELSEA:

St Augustine's Queen's Gate (AC) is a broad, towerless church by William Butterfield (1871) with a very striking west front surmounted by a bellcot and, amongst the lovely things inside, is a magnificent Baroque reredos by Martin Travers.

St Mary Abbots is Kensington's parish church – a grand and magnificent building by Sir Gilbert Scott (1872). Here we see dignified architecture, reproducing the period c1250–1310. The ragstone exterior culminates in a tower and spire reaching 278 ft. Inside we see the 17th century pulpit from the former church and a host of memorials.

At *St Cuthbert's, Philbeach Gardens* (AC), a distinctive copper fleche draws us to one of the most sumptuously adorned interiors in England. Built in 1884–7, this church has a display of exquisite (and often larger than life) craftsmanship by eminent people. The architect was H. Romieu Gough and many of the furnishings are the handiwork of William Bainbridge Reynolds. Dominating everything is the massive reredos by the Rev Ernest Geldart (1914), which is a mass of intricate woodcarving, showing 'the worship of the incarnate Son of God with incense and lights'. There is so much here – it is amazing but also very uplifting.

In the superb Perp church of *Holy Trinity, Sloane Street* by J.D. Sedding (1890), we see the Arts and Crafts Movement gloriously represented in wonderful craftsmanship by Sir Edward Burne Jones, William Morris, Henry Wilson and other designers and artists. The huge east window has twelve lights, the pulpit is massive, the arcades are broad and the whole is vast but very satisfying. (To see J.D. Sedding in a very different context, find the church of *Our Most Holy Redeemer, Exmouth Market, Clerkenwell* 1888 (AC), which is like a 17th century church in an Italian town, both externally and in its internal furnishings – another truly amazing building.)

HACKNEY, SHOREDITCH AND STEPNEY:

The huge building of *St Mark's Dalston* by Chester Cheston was opened in 1866 and received its tower (by E.L. Blackburne) in 1877. Here is London's largest parish church, accommodating about 2,000 worshippers. The interior is vast and has wonderfully preserved its 19th century Evangelical atmosphere. Look outside for the unique barometer on the tower and inside for the stained glass in the roof at the crossing. St Mark's proclaims itself to be 'Protestant : Low Church : Evangelical – Victorian in architecture and Victorian in outlook'! It is a fascinating church and is always open to welcome you during daylight hours.

St Mary of Eton, Hackney Wick (AC) is a red-brick church by Bodley of c1890, completed by Cecil Hare in 1912 and distinguished by its noble entrance tower. As we would expect, the interior is dignified, devotional and beautifully (but not extravagantly) furnished.

St Chad's, Nicholas Square, Haggerston (AC) is the only one of four bold and imposing churches by James Brooks in this part of London which is still in use as a parish church (another of the four is the nearby St Columba's, in Kingsland Road). Built in 1868–9, St Chad's is an EE masterpiece in red-brick, with vast roof-gables, built to tower over its surroundings. Inside it is lofty, spacious and dignified, with a vaulted chancel and colourful adornments.

St Peter's London Docks (AC) is a church with a wonderful history of loving and caring for the people of Wapping by hardworking clergy and people. The brick church, by F.H. Pownall, was opened in 1866. The interior, which has a French gothic feel about it, is lofty and colourful, with some very beautiful post-war craftsmanship and glass, also much to remind us of its witness in what was once a thickly populated area of tenements.

SOUTH OF THE RIVER:

The Ascension, Lavender Hill, Battersea (AC) is another lofty and towerless church by James Brooks (1873) in his bold EE style. Inside it is beautifully furnished, tall and mysterious.

St Giles, Camberwell, an exciting cruciform church of 1844 by Sir Gilbert Scott, has a central tower and spire (210 ft), fine architecture and noble proportions. Inside are the piscina and sedilia, also some brasses, from the medieval church.

At *St Peter's, Kennington Park Road, Vauxhall* (AC) there is a very distinctive brick exterior to this church by J.L. Pearson (1863–4), but it is the noble vaulted interior which is so fascinating because it is largely unaltered by successive generations and still has the feel of a Tractarian place of worship in the 19th century, with exposed brickwork, iron screenwork, a mosaic reredos and much Clayton & Bell glass.

St John the Divine, Vassall Road, Kennington is a stately and magnificent brick church by G.E. Street (consecrated 1874) which is broad and spacious, with a dominating tower and spire of 1889 (212 ft tall). The interior has been tastefully and sensitively restored after war damage to the designs of H.S. Goodhart Rendel.

All Saints, Rosendale Road, West Dulwich – there cannot be another church quite like this one, which is set upon a sloping site, its great apsidal east end rising above the houses beneath it. The graceful and very distinctive interior has a traceried stone screen filling its chancel arch, tall east windows and much to enjoy. It was designed by G.H. Fellowes Prynne, it grew between 1888–91 and the west end is still unfinished.

Christ Church, North Brixton is an amazing Byzantine building with a strange octagonal tower above the entrance and a great dome at the centre, designed by Beresford Pite (1899–1902). It was built for worship in the Conservative Evangelical tradition and has the Lord's Prayer, Creed and Commandments emblazoned (by Eric Gill) beneath the dome, a large outside pulpit and was built to seat 1,400. Now it has been wonderfully adapted to serve the local community in a variety of ways, yet still providing an inspiring place of worship.

All Saints, Tooting Graveney was erected in 1904–6 to the impressive designs of Temple Moore, and this building in stock brick has immense dignity and grandeur outside, with its southern tower and eastern Lady Chapel. Inside we marvel at its noble proportions and a splendid array of furnishings, some of which are of the Renaissance period and have come from Italy and France, including a delightful Baroque reredos from Bologna, stalls from Como and a 16th century French altarpiece in the Lady Chapel. The organ-case, pulpit, font and font-cover were designed by Sir Walter Tapper.

MIDDLESEX

Although swallowed up by Greater London in 1965, the part of this small county which was not included in the old county of London deserves to be considered on its own. So much of it is now suburbia but there are still a few idyllic pockets of countryside and a few of the old villages also survive, although most of the churches have to be locked.

Of the 40 or so medieval churches, a handful in the south are now in Surrey and South Mimms in the north has gone into Hertfordshire, in exchange for Barnet. The rest form an interesting group – several of them are tiny, with rustic wooden belfries; some of the others have 15th century towers, with the staircase-turret rising above the parapet. These are all churches of great character, even if the hand of the 19th or 20th century restorer or extender was rather heavy at times. In this little corner of England we see all medieval periods represented. There are seven Norman fonts, also some interesting medieval roofs and a rich selection of monuments and brasses.

Of over 220 post-medieval churches, a few possess 17th or 18th century work of very high quality, but the bulk are Victorian or later – and what a splendid variety we have here. This is also a county in which we see imaginative buildings which have been created during the past century. One architect of note (but little known) who designed some 20 Middlesex churches is John S. Alder. He created (between c1895–1915) stately stone-faced churches with noble proportions and beautiful architecture. These are well worth finding. They include St Stephen's, Bush Hill Park, Enfield, St Benet Fink, Tottenham, St John Greenhill, Harrow and St Michael, Cricklewood.

BARNET.   Much of it was once in Hertfordshire, including *Chipping Barnet*, where St John's presides elegantly over the town centre. Its chequered walls, lofty tower (80 ft) and elegant fleche are all part of Butterfield's (1875) enlargement of the medieval church (rebuilt 1420) which is now the north aisle. Inside is superb 19th century woodcarving in 159 bench-ends, font-cover, pulpit and stalls, also the tomb of Thomas Ravenscroft (1630). *East Barnet* St Mary's church has a Norman nave and St James at *Friern Barnet* has kept its Norman doorway, although both have been enlarged and greatly altered. St John's Friern Barnet is a large and noble building by Pearson (1891–1902), with a spacious vaulted interior and an ambulatory passage around its tall chancel and apse. *Monken Hadley*, to the north, has a charming setting, a beacon on its tower and some good monuments and brasses.

CRANFORD. St Dunstan's has a rural parkland setting, not far from the M4. It is small and has great character, with a medieval chancel and tower, a brick nave of 1716 and a brick belfry stage to the tower. Inside is a wonderfully devotional feel, also much to admire. The marble font is 18th century and the Classical chancel arch is flanked by seated cherubs. The altar (which has a wooden frontal) is by Martin Travers, the sanctuary lamp by Omar Ramsden, the east window by Kempe and the wall painting above it is 15th century. A wonderful little chancel this. Here also we admire splendid monuments, including those to Sir Roger Aston, his two wives and five children (he was Barber and Gentleman of the Bedchamber to James I) and to Elizabeth Berkeley, who was the cousin of Anne Boleyn.

Heston church nearby has a medieval lychgate, a fine tower, a 16th century font-cover and several brasses, at St Peter and St Paul's *Harlington* is a Norman font and splendid doorway, St Mary's *Hayes* has good medieval roofs and a St Christopher wall-painting and St Mary's *Harmondsworth*, in its pretty village setting, has a Tudor brick tower, a Norman doorway and much to see inside.

EALING. St Peter's, in Mount Park Road, must be found. It is a spectacular creation by J.D. Sedding and Henry Wilson (1893). The west front, with its flanking turrets and vast deep-set west window of twelve lights, also the odd little turret pinnacles along the vast expanse of roof, help to make the exterior memorable. Inside are wide arcades, with triforium arches above and an unusual east end with three EE lancets set beneath a large circular window. The later Lady Chapel has furnishings by C.G. Hare.

ENFIELD. St Andrew's is the medieval town centre church, containing work from many periods and, upon her altar-tomb, the splendid brass of Lady Joyce Tiptoft (1446). Butterfield created St Mary Magdalene, Windmill Hill, whose spire (140 ft) is a prominent landmark, and St Stephen's Bush Hill Park (1906) is a fine church by J.S. Alder.

At *Edmonton*, the ancient church of All Saints should be seen, also St Aldhelm's (1903), which is by Caroe. *Tottenham*'s medieval church of All Hallows was restored by Butterfield and has some fine monuments.

HAMPSTEAD GARDEN SUBURB. The 178 ft spire of St Jude's on the Hill is a prominent landmark. The glorious cruciform church (total length 200 ft) is set at the centre of a remarkable environment and was designed (as was the Free Church nearby) by Sir Edwin Lutyens – a remarkable building (1908–10) of great originality. Externally we admire the bold tower and 16-sided spire, also the mighty, all-embracing nave roof, which sweeps almost to the ground. Inside we marvel at the tremendous space and height, the mysterious Byzantine decor, the beautiful furnishings and the amazing murals by Walter Starmer which cover the roofs and walls.

HAREFIELD. A charming rural setting, in a little corner of Middlesex which is still countryside, for this thoroughly 'one-off' church, St Mary's, which has so much to enjoy. The roofs are interesting, especially the chancel ceiling of 1768; the three-decker pulpit is 18th century and the altar rails, reredos and font-cover are 17th century. There is work of many periods here, but it is the monuments which we will always remember, because they are a wonderful collection. Supreme amongst these is the incredible canopied tomb of Alice, Countess of Derby (1636), who reclines in a four-poster, complete with very realistic curtains.

HARROW ON THE HILL. St Mary's spire, rising above the trees at the top of the hill, must be the county's most-seen landmark. What a splendid setting for a truly lovely church with a noble embattled Perp exterior, Norman lower parts of the tower and the elegant lead-covered spire. There is good EE in the chancel and arcades and from the 15th century comes the excellent nave roof. The pulpit and sounding-board were given to the church in 1708 and there is some good 19th and 20th century glass – the east window, by Comper, lets in plenty of light to illuminate the exemplary modern colouring on the chancel roof. The church has a remarkable collection of brasses – 13 of them, ranging from c1370 to 1613.

Other Harrow churches include Alder's stately St John's Greenhill and W.A. Kenyon's exciting church (1937) of St Alban, North Harrow. All Saints, *Harrow Weald* is mainly by Butterfield and *Pinner*'s medieval church of St John the Baptist, in its perfect setting, must also be seen.

ICKENHAM. A little 14th century church of St Giles with a wooden belfry, extended westwards in 1958. It has a 16th century north aisle of brick, a 17th century chapel and an attractive timber-framed porch. Inside are medieval roofs, a delightful 17th century wooden font and cover, three brasses and the marble effigy of a shrouded baby, whose name was Robert Clayton, died 1665.

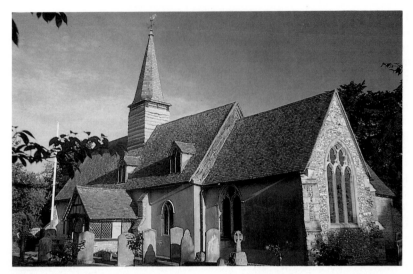

What was a tiny village church at Ickenham has been extended west-wards of its wooden belfry to cater for its growing congregation.

Hillingdon's flint-faced church of St John, beautifully positioned and with a sturdy tower of 1629, has a splendid brass of 1509 and two fine monuments. St Martin's *Ruislip* has many treasures, including fine woodwork in roofs, doors and pulpit, Norman font, wall-paintings and much else.

KINGSBURY.   Here two very different church buildings stand in the same churchyard. Old St Andrew's is a small and humble Norman church with a wooden belfry. New St Andrew's, with its graceful exterior and fine spire, was originally built in 1849 to the designs of S.W. Dawkes – but not here! It began life as St Andrew's Wells Street, in the heart of London's West End, and was moved here in 1931–4. Inside we see the work of several distinguished people. The west gallery by Alfred Bell is a textbook of saints and symbols. Pearson designed the font-cover and Butterfield the lectern, whilst Street created the font, pulpit and sumptuous Caen Stone reredos. To cap it all, the High Altar itself is by Pugin.

Kenton St Mary's is a gracious and very devotional church of 1936 by J.H. Gibbons. Do not dismiss this because of its date – it is splendid. *Hendon*'s medieval church of St Mary has one of the county's best Norman fonts.

NORTHOLT. A little oasis in suburbia! Here we have the old village church of St Mary and village green in the midst of a vastly populated parish. The nave is c1300, the chancel 16th century and there is a wooden belfry and spire. Inside are medieval roofs, a delightful font-bowl of the late 1300s and cover of 1624, the Royal Arms of Queen Anne and some interesting brasses. This is a splendid example of a church which is loved and tended and is so very tastefully adorned and furnished.

Other little medieval village churches in the area and all worth a visit are Holy Cross *Greenford* (with a large new church of 1939 beside it) and St Mary's *Perivale*, with its weatherboarded tower. St Laurence's *Cowley*, in the far west of the county, is another.

STANMORE. *Great Stanmore* has a large and imposing ragstone church of St John of 1850 by H. Clutton, with the fascinating ruin of its Classical brick predecessor of 1632 in the churchyard behind it. It is St Lawrence's *Little Stanmore*, however (sometimes called Whitchurch), which is the real gem here. The tower is 15th century but the rest was rebuilt in 1715 to the designs of John James by the Duke of Chandos. What a shock awaits us inside, because here is no bare Classical auditorium, but rather a rare and sumptuous piece of Baroque splendour, which is exciting and absolutely beautiful. Walls and ceilings are covered with paintings (including works by Louis Laguerre and Antonio Bellucci), from the Transfiguration over the Ducal Pew in the west, through eight miracles over the nave to the Adoration of Jehovah above the altar. Within this painted paradise are box-pews, a font of Italian marble, Corinthian columns and other woodwork by Grinling Gibbons and the case and other parts of an organ upon which Handel played. To the north, in a mausoleum (RCF) added in 1735 to James Gibbs' designs (and with another painted ceiling) is the truly magnificent monument to the first Duke and his two wives, fashioned some years earlier by Grinling Gibbons.

In *Edgware* church (with medieval tower) is a brass of 1599 to a tiny baby in swaddling clothes. Further east is the bold and eccentric form of John Keble church *Mill Hill*, designed by D.F. Martin Smith and built in 1936. It is an impressive, imaginative and dignified tribute to the inter-war period of church building.

TWICKENHAM. St Mary's has a picturesque setting near the river. Here we see a 15th century ragstone tower with higher staircase-turret and a Classical church of 1715 by John James. The galleried interior with its impressive ceiling contains several 17th and 18th century fittings, including the font, reredos, pulpit and metal Communion rails. There are several interesting memorials here, including one to Alexander Pope.

All Hallows, on the Chertsey Road (1940) incorporates the rebuilt tower (104 ft) and some splendid furnishings from Wren's City Church of All Hallows Lombard Street. At *Teddington*, the old brick church of St Mary stands almost under the mighty shadow of St Alban's (by W. Niven, 1889) – one of the county's most breathtaking Gothic Revival churches but now sadly no longer used for worship. To the north, and again near the river, is the noble 15th century tower of All Saints' *Isleworth*, with Michael Blee's intriguing modern church of 1969 beside it, replacing a Classical church burned down in 1943.

WILLESDEN.   Medieval St Mary's is an oasis of beauty in very indifferent urban surroundings. Inside it is devotional and beautifully adorned, with a font of c1150, a particularly fine Communion table of c1600 and six interesting brasses. Here also the pilgrim will find the Shrine of Our Lady of Willesden, much visited in the Middle Ages; the present statue, showing Mary as a Saxon peasant woman, was made in 1972.

St Andrew's Willesden Green (1887) is one of James Brooks' mighty, mysterious and very thrilling EE churches, with an impressive interior. All Souls *Harlesden* (1879) by Edward Tarver, is octagonal and has a fascinating roof.

NORFOLK

There are more medieval churches here than in any other county. The total comes out at about 650 and, when we add the many ruined churches where interesting work is visible, we cross the 700 mark, and every one is an individual, worth getting to know.

There are many features of Norfolk churches. For instance, 119 of them have round towers, of which 78 are thought to be Saxon. In this county where durable stone for the corners was scarce, these early builders simply erected towers without corners – and most of them have stood very well for up to 1,200 years! Three Norfolk towers are octagonal throughout, although many of the round towers have later octagonal belfries. Many of the square towers are stately, elegant and well proportioned, and reach a considerable height and about 95 have square apertures filled with tracery, known as 'Norfolk sound holes'.

Perhaps it is best just to give an idea of a few of the other features to be seen in Norfolk churches. Over 70 churches have good Norman doorways and an interesting group of Norman fonts may be seen in the area west of Fakenham, 25 churches have 15th century Seven Sacrament fonts, 13 have medieval font-covers and about 40 have 17th century font-covers. This is a wonderful county for woodwork, seen in glorious roofs and beautiful benches. Over 200 of the churches have screens or parts of them remaining. There are about 20 medieval pulpits and many 17th century ones. Over 100 churches have monuments which are of special note, over 120 have good brasses and about 126 contain fragments at least of their medieval glass.

The great magnitude of interest for the church enthusiast defies description and these brief notes can only begin to point you to a very small amount of what awaits you here. A very small proportion of the churches have been chosen and by no means all of the great and famous ones, but we hope that the following will give a taste of this wonderful corner of England which offers you more churches than any other county. Do take note of the additional churches after each of the examples, especially here, because so many of these are premier churches themselves.

ATTLEBOROUGH.   St Mary's is a commanding cruciform church shorn of its chancel, with massive Norman and EE tower and lovely Dec windows. Impressive interior with good roofs and dominated by one of

217

England's finest screens – mighty and magnificent – 19 ft high, 52 ft wide, of c1475 and with original painting and remains of overpainted Elizabethan texts.

All Saints *Besthorpe*, All Saints *Old Buckenham* and St James *Great Ellingham* all reward a visit.

BARTON TURF. Lovely rural setting in the Broadland and a lovely church of St Michael, with lofty tower and grand porch. Much to see inside, especially the wonderful screen paintings of angels and other figures, including King Henry VI.

The little round-towered church of *Beeston St Lawrence* has monuments to the Prestons of the nearby Hall, whilst *Irstead*'s thatched riverside church of St Michael is atmospheric, full of interest and a 'must' to visit.

BEDINGHAM. A prettily set church with a round tower and octagonal top, also good 13th century work. The interior of St Andrew's is atmospheric, containing old benches, box-pews, 17th century pulpit and rails and great character.

All Saints *Woodton* and St Margaret's *Topcroft* are round-towered churches, whilst St Peter's *Hedenham* has good monuments and *Ditchingham* St Mary's church, in its delightful setting, draws us to see it by its stately and elegant tower.

BEESTON NEXT MILEHAM. Here is a lone church in the fields – but one of the highest quality, and crowned by one of Norfolk's rare spires. Superb Dec architecture here and a wonderful interior with glorious roofs and benches, a pulpit of 1592 and lovely rood and parclose screens. Above all, the atmosphere here is very real.

Great Fransham All Saints also has a spire, and good brasses, whilst St Andrew's *Great Dunham*, with its central tower, is Saxon. All Saints *Litcham* has a good variety of interesting furnishings and St John the Baptist *Mileham* has a medieval pulpit and some fine glass.

BINHAM. Wonderful Norman and EE fragment of a great priory church. The west front is truly amazing and we must imagine what it looked like with its window complete. Inside St Mary's is a Seven Sacrament font, remains of a screen, benches and stalls. There is great atmosphere here and in the adjacent priory remains.

Do go to see the *Warhams*, (All Saints' with its Norman font and St Mary's with its wonderfully unspoilt Georgian interior), also All Saints *Cockthorpe* (monuments) and All Saints *Bale* (superb 15th century glass).

THE BURNHAMS. Six churches in this group of villages in north Norfolk (and the remains of another), all worth seeing. *Deepdale* St Mary's has a round tower and an amazing Norman font, *Market* St Mary's tower of c1310 is noted for the wonderful parapet which was added in the Perp period. *Norton* St Margaret's is probably the most memorable of all, with round tower, Norman font, screen and a glorious 15th century pulpit, painted with the Four Latin Doctors and the donor. *Overy* St Clement's has great character, and a Norman central tower. *Sutton cum Ulph* St Ethelbert's has a towerless church with a fine chancel arch of c1190. *Burnham Thorpe* All Saints, of course, draws the most visitors because here Nelson grew up and was baptized. A lovely sedilia and piscina here of the 15th century, a brass to Sir William Calthorp (1420) and much about Nelson.

BURGH NEXT AYLSHAM. We come to this idyllic riverside spot to enjoy an amazing EE chancel (sensitively restored 1876–8 by Phipson) and a beautiful Perp tower. Do go to the nearby bridge over the Bure to see St Mary's from the south. This is as lovely as any sight in England.

Aylsham's big market town church of St Michael has much for us to see. St Peter's *Brampton* is small and curious and St Michael's *Oxnead* has lovely monuments.

BURGH ST PETER. Lonely, far from its village and with views over the marshes and river is this fascinating church of St Mary, made memorable by its tower – a strange construction in brick of c1800 upon a short medieval base and looking like something built in Lego! A long single-celled nave and chancel beneath a thatched roof. Arch-braced roof inside and 14th century font. Sometimes it is nice to visit a church just because it is curious and therefore special – and this one certainly is.

In the area is All Saints *Wheatacre*, with its delightful tower of flint and brick, St Mary's *Aldeby*, which is basically Norman, St Margaret's *Toft Monks*, where the tower is octagonal and the font is noteworthy, and St Mary's *Haddiscoe*, where what must be the grandest of the Saxon round towers crowns a church of great interest.

CASTLE ACRE. A wonderful place, with a motte and bailey castle, the remains of a splendid priory and a glorious church of St James with a fine tower and much to see inside. We are treated here to superb woodwork, seen in the soaring font-cover, the pulpit, painted with the Four Latin Doctors, the misericord stalls, some poppyhead benches and the screen-base with its twelve painted panels – all dating from c1400.

Newton's attractive wayside church of All Saints is Saxon and the little church of St Andrew at *East Lexham*, set in a farmyard, has one of our very oldest round towers, which has stood here for well over a thousand years. *South Acre* St George's church has much to delight us, including a medieval font-cover over a Norman font, Sir John Harsick's life-sized brass (1384) and a fine monument (1623) to a former Lord Mayor of London.

CLEY NEXT THE SEA.   This is one of Norfolk's most memorable churches. St Margaret's exterior is superb Dec and Perp (the former seen in the clerestory and west doorway). Its interior is amazing for its architecture, its treasures and its wonderful atmosphere. It is lofty, light and airy, with canopied niches above the arcade, old floors and many vistas. A Seven Sacrament font, 15th century benches and 16th century misericord stalls, also a 17th century pulpit and an array of lovely brasses are among the host of interesting features here.

What an area for fine churches! Nearby St Mary's *Wiveton* may be seen across the river Glaven – this too is full of interest. *Blakeney*'s 124 ft tower of St Nicholas beckons us to a wonderful church of superb and majestic proportions, with an EE chancel, which has a small beacon tower. There is the Perp church of St Nicholas at *Salthouse*, which must be the lightest and airiest interior anywhere, also *Glandford*'s lavishly rebuilt and reordered church of St Martin, with lovely fittings from c1899–1906, and St Andrew's *Letheringsett*, with its round tower and beautiful interior.

EAST DEREHAM.   A fine market town, presided over by a noble cruciform church of St Nicholas with a central lantern tower and a detached bell-tower. Work of many periods may be identified in this venerable and imposing church, which has much to enjoy, including a Seven Sacrament font, a lectern of c1500 and some brasses. William Cowper has a memorial here and the well of St Withburga, who founded a convent here, may be seen to the west of the church.

Nearby is St Peter and St Paul's *Scarning*, with its grand screen, round-towered St Peter's *Yaxham*, with its beautiful font and devotional interior and All Saints *Mattishall*, whose splendid church is full of interest.

EAST HARLING.   A jewel of a church, with a lovely Dec and Perp exterior and a tower crowned by an elegant lead-covered fleche. What a feast inside St Peter and St Paul's, where we may enjoy lovely screen-work, medieval benches, misericord stalls and the most amazing 15th century glass. The 20 panels in the east window tell the story of Our

Lord's life, including the Ascension, where we see footprints in the ground and a pair of feet ascending. Wonderful monuments here too, and much else.

Bridgham church of St Mary has much of interest inside and St Ethelbert's *Larling* has a superb Norman doorway, Dec chancel and south aisle.

ELSING. A pretty village, with a church built in one piece c1330, which is a fine piece of Dec architecture and has the widest unaisled nave in East Anglia – 39½ ft. St Mary's exterior has embattled parapets and good gargoyles. The windows have beautiful tracery. The vast nave roof was renewed in 1781. The font is crowned by a 14th century cover and the base of the 15th century screen survives. One chancel window contains 14th century glass, assembled here in 1901 and including figures of three Apostles. The greatest treasure here is the wonderful brass of Sir Hugh Hastings (died 1347), the founder of this lovely church.

Bylaugh St Mary's church, in its sequestered setting, has an atmospheric interior with furnishings made in 1809, whilst All Saints *Swanton Morley's* mighty tower tempts us to a church with good early Perp architecture. To the east, through the lanes, is *Weston Longueville*, where Parson Woodforde was rector of its beautiful church.

ERPINGHAM. We see St Mary's lofty tower from the main road to Cromer. The interior here is a wonderfully colourful and devotional place, with Flemish glass in the east window, atmospheric brick floors, some old bench-ends and the superb brass of Sir John de Erpingham.

St Margaret's *Calthorpe* also has a lovely interior, with a Jacobean pulpit, St Andrew's *Blickling* (set near the famous Blickling Hall) has a fine collection of brasses and St Laurence's *Ingworth*, with the stump only of its round tower, is full of atmosphere. To the north-west, in an unforgettable setting near the great Hall, is the lovely Classical church of St Andrew at *Gunton* (RCF), designed by Robert Adam and built in 1769. It is well worth finding and enjoying.

FINCHAM. A fine Perp tower and church of St Martin, containing a Norman font, an elegant screen, old poppyheads and a little shrouded lady in brass, beneath a fine 15th century roof.

Barton Bendish has two churches, St Andrew's and St Mary's, both worth seeing. *Crimplesham* St Mary's has Norman work, St Mary's *Bexwell* has a good round tower of brown carstone and do go to Holy Trinity *Stow Bardolph*, which is a must, if only to see the monuments and particularly to have a look at Sarah Hare's life-like wax effigy, behind the doors of her mahogany case. She died in 1744.

Here is one of Norfolk's 119 round towers, at Bessingham, near Cromer. This tower, like so many of them, has stood for around a thousand years.

FOXLEY. One of the smaller churches, St Thomas' has a pretty Dec tower and a very satisfying and atmospheric interior, where we see a medieval screen, 18th century pulpit, box-pews and font-cover and much which is charming.

Bawdeswell All Saints church was rebuilt in 1953–5 by J. Fletcher Watson and should be seen because it is charming neo-Georgian, beautifully and simply furnished. St Mary's *Sparham*, by contrast is large, medieval and glorious, with a lofty tower, old roofs, pulpit, screen and benches. *North Elmham* has a superb church of St Mary of the highest quality, with much to see.

FRENZE. A tiny, tiny church in a farmyard has the most wonderful rustic beauty. St Andrew's charming interior has a Jacobean pulpit and family pew, also superb brasses to the Blennerhassets and others.

Shimpling St George's church (RCF) is remote, picturesque and delightful in every way. St Mary's *Gissing* has an early round tower and a fine 15th century roof, and *Diss* St Mary's church, in its fine position overlooking its market town, has much to interest us.

GOODERSTONE. A most interesting building, with work of all medieval periods to identify. St George's screen has twelve painted saints, and stalls at its rear side, there are superb 15th century benches and a Jacobean pulpit. We look at the Resurrection of the Dead in 14th century glass in the north aisle and we drink in the atmosphere here.

We are not far from St John the Evangelist *Oxborough*, where we may enjoy great beauty in the chancel and the wonderful Bedingfield monuments in their chapel. The rest was ruined when the tower and spire fell in 1948. All Saints *Foulden* also lost its tower, but not its fine and atmospheric interior.

GREAT YARMOUTH. A giant of a church is the parish church of St Nicholas, overlooking the Market Place. There are 25,023 square ft of it and it claims to be England's largest parish church. We see work of all periods here, but the most wonderful work is that of the 20th century because the church, having been gutted in 1942, was gloriously made to live again to the designs of S.E. Dykes Bower and reopened in 1961. It is the great width and bulk of this church, rather than its height, which impresses us.

North of Yarmouth we may visit interesting churches at Holy Trinity *Caister*, St Mary's *Hemsby*, *Great* and *Little Ormesby* (St Margaret's and St Michael's) and possibly end up at *Winterton*, where the 130 ft tower of Holy Trinity is one of the most spectacular (and the third highest) in the county.

223

HALES. One of the most delightful in this area of little rustic churches, which usually have round towers and Norman doorways. St Margaret's (RCF) is totally isolated and its round tower (possibly of Saxon origin) and thatched roofs enhance an exterior which is truly lovely – just a nave, chancel and rounded apse, with Norman, EE and early Dec windows and two splendid Norman doorways. Inside is an 18th century musicians gallery from which we can get a good view eastwards. The pretty 15th century font has a 17th century cover. The base of the screen remains, and the rood-loft stairs. Behind the 17th century pulpit is a 14th century wall-painting of St James, with his pilgrim staff. There is much more to see here, and such a wonderful atmosphere.

Tiny St Gregory's *Heckingham* is just as charming in its way, St Mary's *Norton Subcourse* is mainly 14th century, St Matthias *Thorpe next Haddiscoe* has a beautiful Saxon and Norman round tower and Holy Trinity *Loddon*, by contrast, has a stately Perp church, with a Seven Sacrament font, fine screen (showing the martyrdom of St William of Norwich) and much of interest.

HINGHAM. The little town is dominated by its mighty church of St Andrew, with a massive 120 ft tower. This church was built by Remigius of Hethersett who was rector here from 1319–59. It is 160 ft long and is largely Dec, with Perp chancel chapels. The nave has a hammer-beam roof and the east window is filled with imported German glass of c1500. Magnificently set against the chancel wall is one of England's grandest wall monuments – to Thomas Lord Morley, who died in 1435.

Hardingham has a noble church of St George, with a south porch tower, in a beautiful setting. *Deopham*'s 100 ft tower of St Andrew's is set high and is visible for miles around, but it is worth examining at close quarters also.

INGHAM. A 100 ft tower – one of the many to be seen on the skyline in this part of Norfolk. Again a small village with a vast church. The porch is three storeys high. Holy Trinity was built by the canons of the priory here in 1360 and the tower added c1488. There is much to see in the spacious and lofty interior, including a 13th century Purbeck marble font, remains of a stone screen, medieval benches and stalls and some superb monuments and brasses.

There are several wonderful churches in this part of Norfolk. St Michael's *Sutton* is attractive outside and in, St Mary's *Hickling* has a 90 ft tower and is mostly Dec, All Saints *Catfield* has a screen, an hourglass stand and a banner-stave locker, St Nicholas *Potter Heigham* has a round tower, a fine clerestory, a screen and a brick font, and to the north is the 110 ft tower of glorious St Mary's *Happisburgh*, which is visible (with the lighthouse) for miles from land and sea.

KINGS LYNN. There is so much history here, and many interesting buildings. Of the three medieval churches, All Saints' is towerless and has Norman remains and a medieval nave roof, but St Margaret's and St Nicholas' are both enormous buildings of premier interest and importance.

St Margaret's is cathedral-like, with two western towers, a noble exterior and much of interest inside, including 14th century screenwork, Georgian pulpit, fine Snetzler organ, medieval brass lectern, Bodley reredos and two of the largest monumental brasses in England, which may be Flemish and are truly amazing – they commemorate Adam de Walsokne (1349) and Robert Braunche (1364).

St Nicholas', although only a chapel of ease, is of tremendous length. Its EE tower has a lead-covered spire, but the church itself was rebuilt c1419. The west window has eleven lights and the east window nine. A superb two-storeyed porch shelters medieval traceried south doors. The architecture here is grand and the proportions of the barnlike interior are impressive. Here we see a font of 1627, a 15th century lectern, a reredos by Hardman and a wonderful angel roof. There are also several monuments here.

KNAPTON. This church of St Peter and St Paul has a delightful weathervane, thought to have been designed by John Sell Cotman, also a fine main porch and a beautiful smaller porch over the priest's door. Inside this mainly 14th century church the EE font and cover of 1704, the pulpit and some old benches will be noted, but here is a place where we *must* lie down and look up. Here is one of the grandest roofs in existence, covering an area of 70 ft by 30½ ft – a double hammerbeam construction, embellished with 138 representatives of the Heavenly Host – and we can date it to 1504; it was given by the rector.

Trunch St Botolph's church is superb (Perp, with fine tower and amazing font canopy of 15th century oak, also a screen of 1502 and a splendid roof), St Nicholas *Swafield* stands well and delights us with its painted screen, St Margaret's *Paston* has a fine St Christopher wall-painting and good Paston monuments. Remote, round-towered All Saints *Edingthorpe* has another St Christopher, also a pulpit (1632), reading desk (1587) and 14th century screen, and the 114 ft tower at St James *Southrepps* dominates the countryside hereabouts.

LITTLE SNORING. What could be more endearing than this fascinating church of St Andrew in its solitary setting. Who could not be tempted to stop the car here! The Saxon round tower with its conical tiled cap stands on its own, with evidence that it was once part of an earlier church. In the present church we have Norman, EE, Dec and Perp architecture and a most wonderful atmosphere. The font is Norman, the Royal Arms of James II (a very fine set) are dated 1686, the pulpit is 18th century, but what can be better than the light and airy EE chancel, with its lancet windows, and angle piscina.

Great Snoring St Mary's church (with 16th century rectory nearby), is bold, barnlike and beautiful, with a traceried door, a 15th century screen and benches and a 15th century brass. All Saints *Kettlestone* has an octagonal tower and a good Perp font. At Walsingham we have two medieval parish churches – St Peter's *Great Walsingham* with its beautiful Dec architecture and its complete set of exquisite 15th century benches, and St Mary's *Little Walsingham*'s delightfully set church, with its tapering spire, western porch, Seven Sacrament font (which is perhaps the most complete and beautiful of them all) and the many beautiful features of the rebuilding (to the designs of Laurence King) after the fire in 1961. St Peter and St Paul's *Fakenham* is an enormous church with a 115 ft tower and a fine screen.

MARSHLAND CHURCHES. This group of mighty and magnificent stone churches south and west of Kings Lynn and in the diocese of Ely include some of the finest in the county, although they are not at all typical of it. Every one of the following should be seen because each is a gem. St Germaine's *Wiggenhall St Germans*, *St Mary Magdalene* and *St Mary the Virgin* (RCF) are all the proud possessors of superb benches, the finest of all being in the latter church. *Tilney All Saints* has a fine tower and spire, Norman arcades, a wonderful double hammerbeam roof and a Jacobean screen. *Terrington St Clement*, with its mighty detached bell-tower, is 167 ft long and 47 ft wide, with wonderful Perp architecture and a fascinating 17th century font-cover. *Terrington St John* has an attractive exterior, with a priest's house linking the distinctive tower with the south aisle. Inside is a roof of c1688, a font of 1632 and much else of interest. All Saints *Walsoken* has a fine spire, sanctus bellcot, Norman arcades, some medieval stalls, benches and screenwork, fine roofs and also a superb Seven Sacrament font. St Mary's *West Walton* has a massive and magnificent detached tower – a feast of EE craftsmanship. There is superb EE craftsmanship in the church too, which has great atmosphere and charm. *Walpole St Andrew* (RCF) has a fine brick tower and large rood-staircase turrets at the east end of the nave, also an unusual chamber in the south-west buttress of the tower. There is much to see inside.

Grandest of all is *Walpole St Peter*, which is one of the finest churches in England. Its tower is Dec, the rest grew between c1370–1450. It is 161 ft long and its magnificent exterior has panelled parapets, handsome Perp windows, fine porches and marvellous proportions. Take time to stand back and enjoy it as a whole. We enter through the exquisitely vaulted porch, by means of traceried medieval doors into a treasure house, flooded with light and with so much to enjoy. There is a western screen of 1630, lovely benches in the aisles, font of 1532 with fine cover of c1600, medieval screenwork, lectern of c1500, misericord stalls and much, much more. The High Altar is raised 14 steps above the level of the nave, above a passage which passes beneath it. Everything is work of the highest quality and beauty and one could easily spend the best part of a day here.

NORTHWOLD. St Andrew's fine Perp tower was erected c1473, but inside are lovely EE arcades and the windows in the aisles and chancel are Dec. There is a 15th century nave roof and chief amongst the treasures here is the glorious Easter Sepulchre, with soldiers sitting between trees in its base, clad in uniforms of Richard II's reign, but of course guarding the sepulchre and reacting to the Resurrection. Note the unusual wooden memorial to Robert Burhill, set up in 1727.

Methwold St George's church has a magnificent tower and spire, a fine roof and the five ft nine inch armoured figure of Sir Adam de Clifton (1367) effigied in brass. Do find St Mary's *Cranwich*, so beautifully set, with its circular Saxon tower and its charming interior; also St Leonard's *Mundford*, which was so gloriously refitted by Sir Ninian Comper.

NORWICH. There are more medieval churches within the city walls here than in any other town in the United Kingdom. Today there are 31, in addition to the cathedral, the great Dominican church, now known as St Andrew's Hall, and the remains of three others. Of these ten are still in regular parochial use. What a paradise for the church enthusiast, because even those which are closed have interesting exteriors, with an array of towers and porches and fine (mostly Perp) windows. Facing one of the finest market places in the world is St Peter Mancroft in all its Perp splendour. It was erected c1430–55 and shows Perp architecture at its very best. Street restored the tower and added its elegant fleche (reaching 146 ft), but inside the magnificence of Norwich's Civic Church is breathtaking. It is 212 ft long and the eye is drawn upwards to the splendid 15th century roof, which runs unbroken from west to east, with elegant ribbed coving each side. Of special note is the carefully restored canopy over the font, the blaze of colour in the reredos and the wonderful array of glass in the mighty east window – all except seven of its 42 panels are original.

Other great and splendid churches include St Andrew's (still in use, and noted for its monuments). St Laurence's, St Gregory's, St Giles' (its 120 ft tower is a landmark and this church, still in use, has a wonderfully colourful and devotional interior) and St Stephen's (still in use and here again Perp par excellence). Other churches still in use and worth a visit include St George Tombland (atmospheric Anglo-Catholic interior, with lovely 17th and 18th century fittings), St George Colegate (fine Perp outside, but inside the 'feel' of a city church in the 18th century), St John Timberhill (devotional and colourful Anglo-Catholic interior) and St Julian's (gutted in the Second World War and rebuilt in the 1950s. Again Anglo-Catholic, but simple and very prayerful). St Clement's should be visited – it is always kept open for prayer, although now not in regular use by the Anglican Church. St John Maddermarket (RCF) is also regularly open and is a treasure house at the city's heart. St John de Sepulchre, with its lofty tower set in a prominent position, is now used by the Orthodox Church. Not far from it is St Mark's, which is one of the more interesting of the 19th century suburban churches. Originally designed by John Brown of Norwich and opened in 1841, it received a new chancel (designed by his son) in 1864, and now has a splendid interior, thanks to its transformation in 1910 by Temple Moore, who devised the magnificent screen and loft which stretches across the church.

PULHAM ST MARY. Approached by an avenue of lime trees this fine church has a tall and well-proportioned tower, good Dec and Perp windows and a lavish and very beautiful two-storeyed porch. Inside are excellent roofs, with much medieval timberwork and a 15th century font, with a cover by Bodley, who restored the church in 1886. Here also we see a screen of c1450, with paintings of the Apostles, medieval benches and some good medieval glass, including a 14th century Coronation of the Virgin and 15th century saints and Apostles.

Nearby St Mary Magdalene's *Pulham Market* has another good tower and splendid porch and at *Tivetshall St Margaret* is a magnificent and rare Royal Arms of Queen Elizabeth I. St Margaret's *Starston* has a pretty setting and a monument, whilst Harleston's mother church is St Mary's at *Redenhall* – and what a glorious place it is, with one of East Anglia's very finest towers, and many treasures to be seen inside and out.

RANWORTH.   Here in the heart of Broadland, and serving a tiny village, is one of the county's most visited churches. People come to obtain wonderful views from St Helen's 96 ft tower (which is always open for you to climb) and to marvel at its truly magnificent screen. The tall nave is Perp and the chancel Dec. There are old benches and stalls, an Easter Sepulchre, a cantor's desk and a rare and beautiful Service Book of c1400. Dominating the interior is one of the finest screens anywhere, complete with the reredoses for the side altars which flank it – a masterpiece of c1450, with wonderful original colour and displaying the Apostles and many saints in exquisite medieval painting.

Woodbastwick is a pretty village with a lovely church of St Fabian and St Sebastian, much restored by Sir Gilbert Scott; *South Walsham* has two medieval churches in one churchyard, St Mary's and St Lawrence's, and to the south we may discover *Hemblington*'s· remote and endearing round-towered church of All Saints, with its delightful interior, and *Blofield* St Andrew and St Peter's with its magnificent 110 ft tower. North of the Bure (but a little distance by car) is St Benedict's *Horning*, with its remarkable benches and St Catherine's *Ludham*, which is large and has one of Norfolk's most interesting interiors, with so much to see.

SALLE.   To many people this almighty church of St Peter and St Paul (serving less than 200 parishioners) is Norfolk's absolute finest. A wonderful exterior, dominated by the elegant 126 ft pinnacled tower, with two-storeyed and vaulted porches, glorious proportions, fine windows and immense size. Great medieval west doors admit us to the interior of the 170 ft long church – and what a treasure house, with soaring arcades, a mammoth east window, ancient roofs, 15th century ringers gallery, Seven Sacrament font and tall cover. We can go into the upper chambers of the porches (one is the Lady Chapel with its beautiful ceiling bosses).

Nearby is wonderful St Agnes *Cawston* – another treasure house which ranks high in this county of fine churches. Here is a 119 ft tower of tremendous beauty, also roofs, pulpit, ringers gallery and glorious screen – all of the 15th century. *Booton* St Michael and All Angels church (RCF) is the most amazing 19th century creation – it is totally eccentric and was designed by Whitwell Elwin, its rector. The stonework, glass and strange mixture of features (mostly copied from other churches) make this impressive building unforgettable.

Reepham has two medieval churches, St Mary's and St Michael's, (and the remains of a third) in the same churchyard, whilst *Heydon* is a beautiful picture-postcard village with a fine church of St Peter and St Paul (tower, screen, pulpit, pews, etc) and St Andrew's *Wood Dalling*, which stands high, has a fine tower and several brasses.

SAXLINGHAM NETHERGATE.   We will not forget the perfect setting for this village church of St Mary the Virgin. Its exterior, with slender tapering tower and elegant Perp windows, is delightful also. Inside is some of Norfolk's finest glass, dating from the 1200s to c1500. The oldest glass in Norfolk is in the south-east chancel window. The window to the west of it has 14th century glass with St Philip and St James the Less and later glass shows the Apostles at the Ascension and Pentecost, and several other saints.

Shotesham has two medieval churches, All Saints and St Mary's, and the ruined tower of a third, whilst St Mary's *Howe* has a low Saxon tower with a conical tiled cap. St Mary's *Tasburgh* has another Saxon round tower and St Margaret *Hempnall*'s much later square tower must be viewed for its splendid weathervane of 1727.

SHELTON.   Another grand Norfolk Perp church (with a 14th century tower) set in the middle of nowhere – and this time an essay in mellow Tudor brick of c1480. St Mary's exterior has fine windows and an eastern sacristy (as at St Peter Mancroft and St Peter Parmentergate Norwich). In the bright and elegantly proportioned interior is a lovely East Anglian font, stone angel corbels which once supported a lovely (but now lost) roof, panelling beneath the clerestory, a screen base, the Royal Arms of William III, original glass in the east window and the tombs of the Sheltons, who rebuilt the church and whose arms and rebus (a shell and a tun, or barrel) appear in several places here.

St Catherine's *Fritton* and St John the Baptist's *Morningthorpe* are rewarding round-towered churches, as is St Mary's *Long Stratton* (glass, Jacobean font cover, benches and rare sexton's wheel) and All Saints *Wacton* (good Dec, with screen and sturdy south door). Further west are two of the county's best Saxon round towers – at St Michael's *Aslacton* and *Forncett St Peter*.

SHERINGHAM.   The medieval church of All Saints is at Upper Sheringham – inland but in lovely scenery. Here we see good Dec and Perp work, also a wonderful screen which has retained its original rood-loft, several good medieval benches (look for the little chrisom child on one of the ends) and much more to see. St Peter's in the town, with its distinctive shingled bell-turret, is by St Aubyn & Wadling (1895–7).

Nearby is *Beeston Regis*, whose clifftop church of All Saints has a wonderful 15th century screen, painted with twelve saints, Holy Trinity *West Runton*, with a sturdy EE tower and devotional interior and then on to *Cromer*'s mighty Perp church of St Peter and St Paul, which is magnificent outside and in and has a soaring 160 ft tower, Norfolk's highest. Inland are pretty round-towered churches at All Saints *Gresham* (Seven Sacrament font), St John the Baptist's *Aylmerton*, St Peter and St Paul's *Sustead* and St Mary's *Bessingham* (a lovely Saxon example). The parkland church of St Margaret at *Felbrigg* has a delightfully atmospheric interior and a superb collection of fine brasses.

SNETTISHAM. A commanding position for a splendid and most ambitious Dec church (St Mary's was cruciform but now lacks its chancel), with a majestic tower and stone spire, reaching 175 ft in height. Lovely Dec architecture inside too, also a 15th century lectern, two excellent brasses, an ancient sanctus bell and a fireplace used for baking the wafer bread for Mass in medieval times.

St Michael and All Angels, *Ingoldisthorpe* also has Dec work, and a Norman font, whilst the great treasure in *Shernborne*'s rebuilt church of St Peter and St Paul (by H.J. Green, 1898) is one of Norfolk's finest Norman fonts. Not far away is St Mary Magdalene's *Sandringham*, with its lavish and very royal interior and *Dersingham*'s large Dec and Perp church of St Nicholas, with much to see, including a fascinating parish chest.

SOUTH CREAKE. To really feel the atmosphere of devotion in a medieval church, delightfully and colourfully furnished – you must come here. There is so much to see and such a wonderful and prayerful atmosphere. St Mary's long chancel is of c1300 or just after and the rest of the church is mostly Dec and Perp. The exterior is sturdy and venerable and the interior is all that a medieval church was designed to be. There are seats at the bases of the 14th century arcade piers, and fine 15th century roofs, also a 15th century pulpit and Seven Sacrament font. The chancel has some 15th century bench-ends and here we may admire two old chests (one totally ironbound), medieval glass, brasses and many later aids to devotion, with beautifully adorned altars and so much which makes this place a shrine where heaven and earth meet and not just an ancient building.

North Creake also has a fine church of St Mary, with much of interest, *Waterden*'s tiny All Saints church is Norman, EE and thoroughly delightful, and the three *Barshams (East, West and South)* have small churches of great character.

SWAFFHAM. A large stately and elegant cruciform market town church of St Peter and St Paul, with a fine stone-faced tower crowned by a distinctive lantern spire, 173 ft high, which is the same as the length of this very large church. There is much to admire here, including the superb proportions of the building, its fine clerestory of 13 triple windows each side and lofty arcades. The superb double-hammerbeam roof has 190 angels in all and the other roofs have medieval timberwork. There is interesting 15th century carving in the clergy stalls and in the sanctuary lies John Botwright, who was rector here from 1435–74. We also see in various places in this church the 'Pedlar of Swaffham' (John Chapman) and his dog. He was in fact very wealthy and gave money for the rebuilding of this church in the 15th century.

Necton All Saints' church has a superb tower, a glorious clerestory and a magnificent 15th century roof. In *South Pickenham*'s round-towered All Saints' church (what a lovely setting here) is the fine organ case from West Tofts church, which was designed by Pugin in collaboration with Sir John Sutton.

WILBY.   In this country church of All Saints we have lovely Dec work in the chancel, especially in the east window, with its Flowing tracery, a nave which is mostly Perp and a bold west tower. The interior is a 17th century period-piece, having been refurnished after a fire in 1633. Of the 17th century are the ringers gallery, the parish chest, the Royal Arms, the nave benches, the three-decker pulpit, the almsbox, box-pews, chancel-screen, rails and Communion table. Earlier work remains in the piscinae, aumbries, sedilia, font, St Christopher wall-painting and two 13th century coffin-lids.

The lonely round-towered church of St Mary at *Eccles* has its original medieval altar-slab, and *Quidenham*'s fine St Andrew's church (round tower, octagonal belfry and spire) has a beautiful setting and much of interest.

WORSTEAD.   Here they made the Worstead cloth and so we are not surprised that the village is dominated by a giant of a church. St Mary's exterior is graced with a stately 109 ft tower, a superb south porch (vaulted inside), a fine clerestory, supported by flying buttresses, much flint panelling on buttresses and parapets, fine windows, excellent proportions and considerable size. The length of the church is about 130 ft. Inside we are treated to good medieval roofs, a 15th century font-cover, four screens (the rood-screen has 16 painted figures of saints), poppyhead stalls and box-pews. John Alabastyr (died 1520) has a little brass effigy in front of the rood-screen, which he presented to the church.

Sloley St Bartholomew's church has a very fine Seven Sacrament font, whilst St Botolph's *Westwick* has a fine tower and a lovely screen. St Mary's *Tunstead* is a large and stately church, well away from its village.

It is 140 ft long, with a clerestory composed entirely of flushwork arcading, wonderful ironwork on the south door and much of beauty and interest inside. *North Walsham* St Nicholas' church is enormous – even for Norfolk – (160 ft long), with only the fragment of what must have been a mighty tower. There is much to see here.

WYMONDHAM. Two great towers with the roofline of the nave of the former abbey church between them – an unforgettble sight, set sedately and quietly away from the centre of a lovely market town. The great west tower rises 142 ft, whilst the east tower is elegant, octagonal at the top, and roofless. Its eastern arch is 60 ft tall. Outside we admire a beautiful flushwork clerestory and a handsome vaulted porch. Inside we take several steps towards heaven! The nave is tall and majestic, with sturdy Norman arcades. It is 112 ft long and, some 65 ft above us is a glorious single-hammerbeam roof, with angels and c45 bosses. The north aisle roof, also a single-hammerbeam, is panelled and its eastern bay forms a canopy of honour over what is now the Lady Chapel. The lovely 15th century font has a modern cover designed by Cecil Upcher (1962), the mighty organ was built by James Davis in 1793 and there are many other features of interest. The climax of this interior is Sir Ninian Comper's magnificent reredos, which is a mass of carving and a blaze of colour – blue and gold predominating. It is Wymondham's memorial to those who died in the First World War, and it is stunning in its beauty.

NORTHAMPTONSHIRE

Signboards as we enter introduce this county as 'The Rose of the Shires' – and there is certainly wonderful beauty and colour in this land of gentle hills, many trees, undulating pastures, parkland and country mansions. There are stone villages and the towns have many stone buildings which give them character. Certainly countless rose-petals must have been pressed between the pages of 19th century books of engravings of English architecture, which seem to feature more Northants examples than of any other county, because of the great beauty and quality of the architecture to be found in its churches – particularly the delectable carving of the Dec period. This is a premier county for quality churches and an oasis for the church enthusiast, who has nearly 300 medieval ones to discover although a few, once in the Soke of Peterborough, have now been taken into Cambridgeshire.

It is quality in abundance that we can enjoy here – Saxon at Brixworth and Earls Barton, which are nationally famous, and Norman work which appears in several of the churches but does not always make the textbooks. The EE and Dec periods produced the real glories in Northants churches and the exquisite architecture of c1250–1350 to be found here is unsurpassed in England – mouldings, carvings, gargoyles, window tracery, arcades, corbels – all textbook features, to be found in so many of the churches. Perp is not so universal or plentiful as in some counties, but when it does appear, it is usually remarkable, as in Titchmarsh tower (and other grand towers), or at Whiston or Fotheringhay. The county has its interesting post-Reformation churches – Classical at Stoke Doyle, Great Houghton, Daventry, Aynho, etc, and Gothic Revival at Benefield, Northampton, Orlingbury and others, and the 20th century is seen at its most worthy in Comper's St Mary's Wellingborough.

The county is blessed with building stone of a variety of hues, the most distinctive being the warm golden brown (or in places almost deep orange) ironstone, which makes churches here stand out so beautifully, yet blends so well with the greens of churchyards and countryside. This is the county for wonderful stone spires, of all sizes and heights. Every one is a masterpiece of design and construction and they punctuate the landscape.

There is plenty to tempt the lover of monuments in these churches, as we would expect in a county of country seats and manorial families. Many of its churches are open and usually the keys for locked ones are advertised. Here, however, there is so much usually to admire in structure and detail in the exterior of the churches that even if we cannot get in, we never lose out!

ALDWINCKLE. Two lovely churches in this village – St Peter's, with its perfectly proportioned tower and spire (not the highest but one of the very best), its 14th century glass and its lovely architecture, and All Saints' (RCF) with its superb Perp tower and exterior, but with fine 13th century arcades inside. Now most of its furnishings have been disposed of, we can stand in this almost empty church and really drink in the beauty of its architecture and proportions.

Within a few miles is stately and glorious St Peter's *Lowick* (tower, glass, monuments, etc), also *Wadenhoe* (lonely setting, saddleback tower, atmospheric interior), *Stoke Doyle* (1722, Classical, with original fittings) and St Mary the Virgin *Titchmarsh*, with its wonderful Perp tower. The spires at St Nicholas' *Islip*, St Mary's and All Souls *Pilton*, St John the Baptist *Thorpe Achurch*, St Andrew's *Barnwell* and magnificent *Oundle* will draw you to most rewarding churches.

AYNHO. Near the Oxfordshire border stands the church of St Michael and All Angels, which is Classical of 1725 but is attached to the graceful medieval tower of the original church. It is equipped with a gallery on Tuscan columns, box-pews, pulpit and font – all of 1725.

Nearby is St Peter and St Paul's *King's Sutton*, which has one of the county's most elegant and graceful spires.

ASHBY ST LEDGERS. A village of great charm, with a fascinating church of St Leodegarius, set near the manor house. The interior here is a treasure house, with medieval benches, a tall 15th century screen, a 17th century three-decker pulpit, 17th and 18th century pews (including a musicians pew) and faded, but very precious, wall-paintings, showing 18 scenes of the Passion, Death and Resurrection of Christ. There are excellent brasses here and, in a room over the gateway to the manor, it is said, the Gunpowder Plot was planned.

In this area near the Leicestershire border, we can visit St Margaret of Antioch *Crick* (good Dec, with fine spire) and the large Classical church of Holy Cross at *Daventry*, built in 1752–8.

BRIXWORTH. An incredible and fascinating Saxon minster church of All Saints, much of which may well be 1,300 years old – what an

Here at Aldwincle is a perfect stone spire, which is really the roof of the tower and blends perfectly with it.

amazing thought! The tower is unbuttressed and to it a big western staircase-turret was added about AD 900 and a belfry stage and spire c1340. There is a large nave, a chancel (or presbytery) and an apsidal sanctuary. When we think that the nave once had aisles and so the church was once even larger, it seems even more amazing. So much early craftsmanship here and on such a large scale. The 13th century Lady Chapel looks remarkably modern in comparison!

In pursuit of Saxon churches, do discover St Andrew's *Brigstock*, also All Saints *Earls Barton's* wonderful tower.

EDGCOTE's St James'. A very lovable little church, beside the 18th century Edgcote House. There is EE work in the doorway and south arcade and the nave is equipped with 18th century box-pews and pulpit. A set of interesting monuments to the Chauncey family (including four by Rysbrack) make this church worth the journey to visit.

Nearby St Leonard's *Aston le Walls* and St Nicholas' *Eydon* have Norman fonts, and St James the Less *Sulgrave* is a place of pilgrimage for Americans, not least to see the Washington pew and brass.

FOTHERINGHAY. St Mary and All Saints shows exquisite grandeur of Perp architecture in the heart of the country. An amazing exterior with grand stonework, large windows and flying buttresses, with a sturdy but elegantly and beautifully proportioned lantern tower. Do walk down to the stream to see it in its setting from the south. In this village, Mary Queen of Scots was executed and here we see Perp at its most gratifying, despite the lack of a chancel. The interior is light and airy, with a fine font and pulpit and a superbly vaulted tower ceiling.

A truly unforgettable Dec chancel awaits the lover of architecture at St Andrew's *Cotterstock*, and a charming and atmospheric church, showing all architectural periods at St Mary's *Tansor*. *Nassington's* All Saints church has everything from Saxon to Perp (and a wonderful spire) and St Mary the Virgin *Warmington*, with its superb spire and rare wood-vaulted roof, is mainly EE.

HIGHAM FERRERS. This must be one of the most exciting parish churches anywhere in England. We are drawn by its soaring 170 ft spire (visible for miles) to a limestone town of great character which is set high – then to a churchyard with a Bede House of 1428 (looking like a church), a Perp grammar school with exquisite stonework (looking like another tiny church) and the wonderful bulk of St Mary's, in all its glory, with its double nave, its superb EE and Dec architecture and its endearing character. We enter by means of a rare and beautiful double portal of

237

c1260. Inside, the width is amazing, the use of colour is perfect and the atmosphere of devotion is real and unavoidable! There are wonderful screens (enriched by Comper and Temple Moore), 20 misericord stalls, 14th century tiles, some fine brasses and much, much more. Here ancient and modern craftsmanship combine happily in this much cherished, much used and much prayed-in shrine.

The area here is so rich in wonderful churches. St Mary's *Raunds* tower, spire and EE and Dec architecture are well-nigh incomparable for their beauty, Holy Trinity *Denford* and St Mary's *Ringstead* have atmosphere, beauty and textbook architecture, St Mary's *Finedon* is large, elegant and full of interest, and St Peter's *Irthlingborough*, with its intriguing detached lantern tower, has a 15th century font and stalls. *Rushden*'s large town church of St Mary's has a handsome spire and much to admire, St Lawrence's *Stanwick*'s tall spire sits upon an octagonal tower and St John Baptist *Chelveston* is venerable, full of character and again so very devotional inside.

NORTHAMPTON.   The busy county town has five medieval parish churches. Of stately and 'civic' All Saints' only the medieval tower and crypt survived a nasty fire. The large Classical nave was rebuilt in 1676, it is square (70 ft × 70 ft) and has a central dome. The chancel was added in 1888. St Giles' is an imposing town church, with a noble central tower and some work dating from Norman times. The best Norman work is to be seen at St Peter's (the county's finest and most complete Norman church) where the carving is glorious. An impressive tower and spire beckon us to Holy Sepulchre, where we have one of England's four 'round churches'. Around the original circular nave, a much larger church, with work of several periods, has grown.

Northampton is the place to enjoy interesting Victorian churches, especially Christ Church, St Mary's (Far Coton), Holy Trinity and the truly magnificent St Matthew's (works by Graham Sutherland and Henry Moore may be seen in its cathedral-like interior). All these churches are by Matthew Holding.

ROTHWELL.   Holy Trinity is a vast, bulky church (173 ft long), of warm-coloured Northants stone. Most of what we see here is 13th century and the font of this date is very fine. There are two 13th century coffin-lids (each weighing about half a ton) which were found beneath the tower roof. There are misericord stalls, brasses and a fascinating crypt which is a charnel-house, full of skulls and human bones representing some 1,500 persons who lived between 1300 and 1500.

Desborough has an impressive church, St Giles, with a fine tower and spire. *Kettering*'s stately medieval church of St Peter and St Paul has a perfectly proportioned 179 ft tower and spire and superb Perp work. The smaller churches in the area have great character also. Pick any one and you will not be disappointed!

STANFORD ON AVON. This is one of the county's hidden gems. Near the Leicestershire border, set delightfully, and unforgettable in so many ways. St Nicholas' structure is almost entirely Dec and therefore possesses a satisfying unity of style. Its tower, clerestory and tiebeam roof are Perp. What an interior! There are hatchments on the walls, wonderful glass from the 1300s to the 1600s in the windows, medieval woodwork in the pulpit, screens and stalls, a west gallery with a rare and noble 17th century organ-case, and the most amazing array of monuments. Exploring its treasures could take hours.

WELLINGBOROUGH. Medieval All Hallows, with its Norman doorway, sturdy late 13th century tower and spire, Perp screenwork and stalls, and much more to see, is an oasis of peace in the centre of the busy town. It is St Mary's, which took shape between 1908–1930, which is the most memorable church here, because it is the incomparable Sir Ninian Comper at his very best. A bold Perp ironstone exterior, with a square western tower, and the interior full of majesty, beauty and colour. Here is heaven on earth beneath a wonderful vaulted ceiling with pendants, tall arcades, and light flooding in through the glass of large Perp windows – some of the glass being Comper's own very special design for stained glass, using delightful colours which do not block out the light.

Amongst the churches in the area St Mary's *Wilby* (steeple and 17th century pulpit), St Mary's *Wollaston* (spire and much rebuilding in the 18th century, but great atmosphere) and St Katherine's *Irchester* (striped tower, spire, and much of interest inside) are specially worth a visit.

WHISTON. Lonely, in the fields and on a hillside, but visible for miles, is St Mary's graceful Perp church, which was built in one piece and has altered little since. An elegant tower with pinnacles and gargoyles of great beauty graces its stately exterior. The interior is bright and full of atmosphere, with a 15th century font and benches and a fine monument (1700) to Thomas Catesby.

Charming churches may be seen at *Grendon* (St Mary's) and *Cogenhoe* (St Peter's) and the setting of *Castle Ashby* mansion and St Mary Magdalene's church is superb, as is its brass to William Ermyn (priest, 1401). *Easton Maudit*'s church of St Peter and St Paul has a magnificent spire and 17th century monuments to the Yelvertons.

NORTHUMBERLAND

This is very much the Border County – the scene of tussles of olden days with Scotland, and it is indeed an area steeped in history and mystery. The Roman Hadrian's Wall crosses the southern part of the county, running westwards from Newcastle, and what fascinating treasures and views this much visited feature has in store for us. Grand castles may be seen in Northumberland – Alnwick, Bamburgh, Warkworth and an assortment of others, also the smaller pele towers, which were built for defence. The 50 or so miles of Northumbrian coastline is extremely beautiful; much of the county is moors and hills, with the Cheviots in the north-west and the Pennines beneath them. There are lovely valleys and the scenery is delightful, with many of the villages, towns and churches being in the eastern part of the county and in the south, although the south-eastern section (containing Newcastle, where the cathedral is) has been joined with part of County Durham to form Tyne and Wear.

Northumberland is a great cradle of Christianity, with the Holy Island of Lindisfarne (and what a beautiful and moving place this is) having been a centre of Christian teaching since the 600s AD. Here we see a fair amount of early Saxon work, in Saxon towers and the remains of cross-shafts, also some interesting work from the Norman period and a remarkable amount of EE, although not a great deal of Dec and Perp, in its 70 or so medieval churches. Several towers contain Saxon work and some look very sturdy and fortified and were clearly built with defence in mind. Several churches have stone bellcots over their western gables.

There is much to be discovered in Northumberland and so much individuality in this county where the scenery encourages you to relax and to take your time. It is England's most northerly county and large areas of it are totally unspoilt.

ALNWICK. Well known for its castle, St Michael's church is also of interest. It is completely Perp, very rare in this county. The tower is at the W end of the S aisle and it is of sturdy Northumbrian style. There are large Perp windows, and the two chancel chapels have columns with foliage capitals and angels above. A 14th C Flemish chest with a chase.

ANCROFT. St Anne's is a Norm church with an original S doorway: above it and along the S wall is a corbel-table. The 13th C tower is like a vicar's pele. It is a fortified church tower with a tunnel-vaulted ground floor, a spiral stair and on the upper floor a room with three deeply splayed small windows.

BAMBOROUGH. The church and castle on the coast make a fine picture. St Aiden's tower is broad with lancet windows and battlements. The chancel is long, as often in the North, with lancets, three at the E end. There is an elaborate squint between the N transept and the church, piscina and sedilia, and a niche with the effigy of a cross-legged knight c1325.

BLANCHLAND. Well known as a model village, and a former abbey. The tower of St Mary's is at the N of the N transept: the top of the tower is 14th C. There are several coffin-lids.

BOLAM. St Andrew's has a late Sax tower, tall and unbuttressed, with belfry windows of two lights separated by a shaft, and small windows (three triangular-headed) above. The interior is Norm, the chancel arch is also Norm. The S doorway with dogtooth and E part of the chancel with lancets are EE. Sedilia, octagonal font, several coffin-lids and a cross-legged knight of 1342.

BRINKBURN PRIORY. A beautiful setting in a loop of the Coquet river. It is almost entirely EE with lancets – chancel, transepts with aisles, N aisle, low central tower, and nave. The E end has three tiers of lancets. Above the nave arcade is a triforium, there are round-headed clerestory windows, and the W end has three tall lancets. The finest doorway is on the N side – rich Norm, yet above in the gable is a Gothic arcade.

BYWELL. Two medieval churches stand close together near a 15th C tower-house, beautifully situated above the river Tyne. The church of St Andrew (RCF) has a Sax tower which is the best in the county. It is tall, narrow and unbuttressed and has belfry windows of two lights with a circle above.

St Peter's has a squat tower of the 13th C. The nave walls are Norm, and the fine chancel is 13th C, with its group of three lancets at the E end. The N chapel is 14th C. There is an incised slab to a knight, 15th C.

CHILLINGHAM. St Peter's has an 18th C bellcot. The chancel is built high above a crypt, probably 12th C, and the chapel is 13th C which has been converted into a family pew with a plaster vault. It has a magnificent monument to Sir Ralph Gray and wife, 1443; around it are 14 figures of saints separated by figures of angels. A Jac pulpit.

CORBRIDGE.   This was originally a Roman town. The lower part of the tower of St Andrew's is at least 8th C. It was a porch and the window above it and the entry to the nave are of that early date. The upper part of the tower is 11th C, with later belfry windows. The S doorway is Norm, and then mostly EE with the chancel with six lancets. A small chapel at the W end of the N aisle may have been the residence for the priest before he moved to his grander quarters S of the churchyard. This is the medieval vicarage, a tower-house known as the Vicar's Pele, c1300.

HALTWHISTLE.   Holy Cross is a complete EE church of Northumbrian style. The chancel has four lancets on each side and the usual group of three at the E end. The clerestorey of lancets is set above the spandrels, not above the apexes of the arcade. The aisle windows are restored lancets. At the W end are two tall lancets with renewed oculus and a bellcot. Piscina and sedilia, the font has carvings carved in 1676, and there are three 14th C coffin-lids.

HEXHAM ABBEY.   Of the first church of St Wilfrid, only the remarkable crypt remains, AD 680. The E end of the church of St Andrew dates from 1858, the nave (by Temple Moore) from 1909, and the remainder is EE. The central tower is mainly of that time. The chancel aisles are vaulted. In the S transept is the famous Monk's Night Stair. Both transepts have a 15th C timber roof. The N transept gives a good display of lancet windows. The church is rich in furnishings, but poor in monuments. It has a 13th C font and a 13th C pulpitum about four ft high. In the S transept is a Roman tombstone of Flavinus and in the slype (between the S transept and the chapter house) are two Roman altars. The vaulted rood-screen is c1510 with Flamboyant (French) tracery and paintings of bishops. The loft above is original: on the W front the parapet has 20 little niches, and on the E front is a projecting balcony with paintings of bishops, while in the centre passage are paintings of the Annunciation and Visitation.

MORPETH.   St Mary's is mainly 14th C with a low tower. The feature of the church is the fine 14th C E window which also fortunately contains its original bright glass of that period (though renewed) – a Jesse Tree; also Christ and two saints in the E window of the S aisle. Small piscina and rich sedilia with ogee arches and little figures. The vestry door and priest's door and the aumbry all have original doors with original ironwork. The S door has its original iron door-knocker. Original roofs in nave and aisles, and an octagonal font.

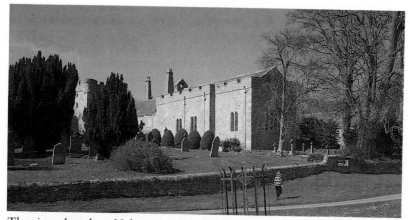

The tiny church at Halton near Corbridge, set beside the ancient Halton Tower. Visiting churches here in the North East brings many pleasant surprises.

NORHAM. The village green with the base of its cross, the castle (built by the Bishops of Durham) and the church of St Cuthbert are on a bend of the river Tweed. It was much rebuilt in the 19th C, but original Norm work remains in the chancel and the S arcade. The arcade has large massive piers (reminding one of Durham Castle) and moulded arches. The chancel has four windows on each side, with flat buttresses between the windows. The eaves rest on a corbel-table. There is a 17th C pulpit and stall, the Royal Arms of Charles II, and the effigy of a knight c1320.

OVINGHAM. St Mary's Sax tower is tall and narrow and unbuttressed as usual. The belfry windows are of two lights with a circle above. The church is mainly EE. The E end has three stepped lancets, and the transepts also have long lancets. Sedilia, a circular font on four shafts, and two fragments of Sax crosses.

WARKWORTH. The great castle, the church and the village are all on a loop of the picturesque Coquet river. St Lawrence's is splendid for studying Norm and Perp side by side. The nave and chancel are Norm, the latter very rich with a vault with zig-zag, all derived from Durham Cathedral. The tower is c1200 with a 14th C broach spire. The S aisle is Perp of c1500 with large windows. The S porch has a rib vault. There are 18th C wrought-iron altar rails, a Sax cross with interlace work, and a well-preserved cross-legged knight with a shield, c1330.

NOTTINGHAMSHIRE

Probably the most unvisited, untouristed and undiscovered of our counties. So many of our cathedrals are jam-packed with trippers and sightseers, but not Southwell, which is one of the most beautiful and memorable of them all. Do go and see it – the city is just about the right size!

Its scenery is lovely, if not always spectacular, and its many-faceted character is well worth getting to know. Its far north becomes one in landscape with Yorkshire and its eastern part looks across to Lincolnshire on the other side of the Trent (this is the 'A1' Nottinghamshire, which thousands rush through, bound for elsewhere). The southern part includes the charming Vale of Belvoir and the Wolds, whilst the west is where so much of the industry is, and the urban areas, and the pylons (but also several fine churches). Nottinghamshire is not all Basford and Arnold, Eastwood and Sutton in Ashfield. This is the county of the unique Dukeries, where four great estates stood together, leaving us with an area of forest and lovely parkland scenery, of the unspoilt country north of Southwell, of the strings of villages around the Trent valley to the south of it and of almost 200 medieval churches, of new red sandstone, magnesian limestone or blue lias – churches which are often wholesome and interesting, if unspectacular. There is spectacular architecture here, however – Saxon, for example, at Carlton in Lindrick and Stapleford, premier Norman at Blyth and Worksop or in Lenton's magnificent font, EE at Thurgarton and in bits of many Nottinghamshire churches. The county comes into its own in the Dec period and has craftsmanship of fine quality which would rival any county, seen in village churches like Hawton, Sibthorpe and Car Colston. Perp of course is widespread (as in most counties), but some of the predominantly Perp churches here are really superb, like Holme and East Markham and then Newark upon Trent and Nottingham St Mary's, which are among the finest churches in the land.

Amongst the 60 or so later churches are some real characters – like the Classical churches of West Stockwith (1722) and Milton, which is a real surprise, built in 1832 as church and mausoleum combined. Also delightfully eccentric is dear little Papplewick, down a rural lane and exquisite 'Strawberry Hill Gothick' of 1735. For the best Gothic Revival churches, Nottingham and environs must be visited (Pearson, Bodley and Caroe built good churches here), Temple Moore created St Mark's Mansfield with his usual taste and dignity whilst, superior amongst all the 19th century country churches, is Bodley's masterpiece at Clumber. So much is waiting to be discovered in this undiscovered county!

BLYTH PRIORY.   Only part of the W part of the priory remains, the nave and N aisle (both vaulted) and these are Norm, the S aisle being c1300 with large windows and S porch. The Norm work of St Mary and St Martin's follows the usual plan of ground storey, triforium and clerestory. The grand W tower of Notts-type is Perp and indicates civic pride instead of monastic pride. It has open-work battlements and eight pinnacles. The S aisle has its original wooden screen with vaulting, and the rood-screen remains, both with painted panels. There is a 17th C font with Jac cover and pulpit. Mon to Edward Mellish, semi-reclining, 1703.

BUNNY.   A tall tower and crocketed spire and an exterior with stone panelled parapets and pinnacles, Dec predominating. Inside St Mary's is also good Dec in the sedilia and piscina. Amongst the monuments of note we see Sir Thomas Parkyns (1741), standing braced for his wrestling match with Time – which (as we observe in the next compartment) he lost!

CAR COLSTON.   St Mary's has a Perp tower (13th C below) and a grand 14th C chancel (as in several other churches round here) with large windows of Flowing tracery and piscina and sedilia. The N aisle has similar windows, and a doorway with an ogee arch. Norm font, and altar-rails c1700. A large village green with attractive houses.
   Bingham has a venerable church of All Saints with a noble tower and spire of the late 1200s and early 1300s. St Peter's *East Bridgford* has several items of interest – beneath it are the foundations of its Saxon predecessor.

CARLTON IN LINDRICK.   We come to St John the Evangelist mainly to see its 11th century Saxon tower, with herringbone masonry and two-light belfry openings – made taller in the 15th century with a handsome belfry stage and pinnacled top. There is earlier Saxon work in the nave and chancel. Much Norman work here also, including the north arcade, chancel arch and font. The nave and north aisle roofs are 15th century, as is the alabaster carving of the Trinity over the north aisle altar.

CLIFTON.   A delightful riverside village with a large green and a dovecote. St Mary's is equally impressive with a central tower, 14th and 15th C. The N arcade is Trans and the S arcade 14th C. The clerestory is also 14th C. The chancel has a flat timbered roof with bosses, and sedilia. There is an old gable cross with the Crucifixion at the W end of the nave, and an old chest. Several notable mons; Sir Gervase Clifton (head on a peacock) late 14th C; Dame Alice Neville (lamb at feet) late 14th C; Sir Gervase Clifton and two wives and children (wearing 19 rings) 1587; Sir Gervase Clifton bust 1666; and his first three wives (he had seven) shown by coats of arms and as bones and skulls, 1631.

In *West Bridgford*'s largely rebuilt church of St Giles is a 14th century screen and a cross-legged knight of c1300.

CLUMBER. Deep in the Dukeries and in a serene setting rises this spectacular church, built as his chapel by the 7th Duke of Devonshire at vast expense (we think over £40,000) in 1886–9. Cruciform and 137 ft long, this cathedral-like building in red Runcorn stone and buff stone from nearby Steetley, has a magnificent central tower and spire, rising 180 ft into the air. The Duke was an Anglo-Catholic and inside all is designed to aid worship and to give a glimpse of divine splendour which is beyond human description. It is lofty and is vaulted throughout, with feasts of sumptuous stonecarving and magnificent woodcarving (particularly in the fine screen), with tasteful furnishings and adornments, also beautiful Kempe glass filling the majestic late Dec windows.

EAST MARKHAM. St John the Baptist's is a fine church, mainly Perp, with large windows. The tower is of that period with the usual eight pinnacles of Nottinghamshire. Clerestory and large E window of five lights. The gargoyles are notable, there is a S porch with an old timbered roof, a 17th C pulpit, font-cover and altar-rails and font bowl. Fragments of old glass. There is a tomb-chest of Sir John Markham with shields, but the figure is gone, 1409. Fine brass to Dame Millicent Meryng 1419, a dog at her feet with bells on its collar.

The Newcastle mausoleum/church at *Milton* (RCF) must be seen (1832 by Sir Robert Smirke), also the humble and delightful church at *West Markham* (Saxon work, Norman font, old benches and screen and much else, bathed in the atmosphere of antiquity).

EGMANTON. Here again at St Mary's we see the generosity of the 7th Duke of Devonshire, who turned the interior of a small medieval Nottinghamshire church (12th century arcade, 15th century tower and nave roof, also other medieval features) into a richly and colourfully adorned centre for Anglo-Catholic worship and a fitting home for the Shrine of Our Lady of Egmanton – the goal of many pilgrims both in medieval times and today. The architect was Sir Ninian Comper, who designed the organ-case, the magnificent screen, rood-loft and rood group, with canopy above, the hanging pyx for the Sacrament, the altars and their adornments, and much else in this wonderful and prayerful place.

Laxton St Michael's church has a noble Perp tower and clerestory and good Dec work in the sedilia and Easter Sepulchre. There are fine screens here and interesting monuments.

HAWTON. The chancel is the wonder of All Saints' church. It has rich work of c1330, Dec windows of three lights and the E window of seven lights. Inside on the N side is a group of door, founder's tomb recess, and Easter Sepulchre under a horizontal cornice. The Easter Sepulchre is the richest in the country. A niche in the centre is for the Blessed Sacrament, placed in it on Good Friday and remaining there until early on Easter Day (most churches must have had a temporary structure or used the top of an altar-tomb).

HOLME. St Giles' is a charming small church with a low 14th C stone broach spire, red pantile roofs and large Perp windows. The rebuilding in Perp times was due to a rich wool merchant, John Barton, who exclaimed 'I thank God and ever shall, it is the sheepe hath payed for all'. The monument to him and his wife has below it a cadaver or skeleton, 1491; his feet are on a tun with a bar across the top, for puns were popular. There is a two-storeyed S porch with a frieze of shields, simple screens and Jac altar-rails. Much old glass has now been set in the E windows. There are grotesques everywhere and the N door is old. The church is on the banks of the river Trent: formerly it was on the other side (it is the river that has changed its course!).

South Collingham St John the Baptist's has a stately Perp tower and good Norman and EE arcades, and a fine screen of 1940 by Martin Travers. All Saints *North Collingham*'s arcades are also noteworthy.

NEWARK. St Mary Magdalene's is among the two or three dozen grandest parish churches in England. The tower is EE with W portal in the lower stage and arcading, and a Dec belfrey storey with frieze and pinnacles and stone broach spire 252 ft high. A figure of St Mary Magdalene is in the niche above the E window. Fine clerestory and many quaint figures. The crossing piers are EE, and the S aisle is Dec, otherwise everything is Perp. Two-storeyed S porch, large windows and wide aisles. The High Altar reredos is by Comper, beautifully coloured, 1937. The rood-screen and choir stalls with 26 misericords are c1500. The transepts are the latest parts of the church: N and S windows of seven lights are as large as they could possibly be.

Balderton St Giles also has a fine spire and a grand Norman doorway, and medieval woodwork in its pulpit, screen and bench-ends (45 of them).

NORWELL. The S door and S arcade of St Lawrence's are late Norm but the lower part of the tower and the chancel are EE: in c1300 the E window with Geometric tracery was put in. The N arcade is 14th C. Perp nave with a fine clerestory (as often around here), and the upper part of the tower with pinnacles. The N transept roof is old and on an arch nearby is a grotesque with painted ears and three teeth.

NOTTINGHAM. The pride of this big and bustling east Midlands city is its mighty cruciform church of St Mary – bold, Perp, embattled and stately outside, with a massive central tower and fine windows. The interior is light, spacious and superbly proportioned, with much to enjoy. There are several monuments, also glass by Clayton & Bell, Hardman, Burlison & Grylls and others, a Bodley screen and reredos, and stately bronze south doors by Henry Wilson. Also in the city centre is medieval St Peter's (fine spire, roofs, etc) and the predominantly 17th and 18th century St Nicholas' – a building of considerable character. Other good churches away from the centre include St George's Kirkwhite Street (Bodley chancel and fittings of 1897), St Paul's Daybrook (Pearson, 1896, with splendid spire), St Stephen's Sneinton, (mostly rebuilt by Cecil Hare in 1912 and beautifully furnished) and Holy Trinity Lenton (a building of 1842, but containing the most amazing Norman font, which is regarded as one of the finest in England).

RATCLIFFE-ON-SOAR. Holy Trinity's tower is EE with a Dec broach spire and pinnacles. There are 14th C arcades and a 15th C roof in the nave and chancel. The chancel windows are EE, the E with fine Geometric tracery. The aisle windows are 14th C. EE sedilia and a 17th C Communion table and rails.

SIBTHORPE. Here is a 13th C W tower, an 18th C nave, and a grand 14th C chancel with Flowing tracery, three-lights N and S, and five in the E window. St Peter's has one of the few Easter Sepulchres: an ogee niche with the four sleeping soldiers at its sides and a steep crocketed canopy with Christ and two censing angels. Old benches and a 17th C font. Mon to Edward Burnell 1590, his feet on a skull. There is a 13th C dovecote nearby.

STRELLEY. At All Saints' the lower part of the tower is 13th C, and the upper part with battlements and eight pinnacles is 14th and 15th C. The 14th C is the date of the rest of the church except for the clerestory which is Perp. There is a Jac pulpit and tester, a 14th C font, some old fragments of glass and a fine tall Perp rood-screen with vaulting. The chancel is fine with notable monuments.

SUTTON-on-TRENT. The lower part tower is 13th C, and Perp in the upper part. The most glorious part of the church is the Mering chantry chapel 1525 with battlements and pinnacles and a frieze on the parapet and four-light windows. Inside there is an old roof, a piscina, a panelled pier, and an elaborate rood-screen with vaulted rood-loft with leaf friezes. The clerestory has six closely-set three-light windows and the E window of five lights is of the same date.

Carlton-on-Trent has an exciting Gothic Revival church of St Mary by G.G. Place, 1851, with a fine spire and a genuine 12th century doorway.

TEVERSALL. St Catherine's has a Perp tower, a Norm S doorway with medallions, and an old S door. The aisles and arcades are 13th C.

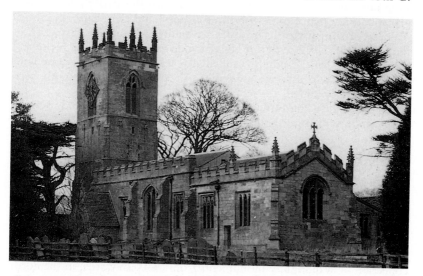

An embattled, pinnacled Nottinghamshire church now in the care of the Redundant churches fund. The tower is dated 1504 and there are monuments inside plus some lovely Kempe glass. Here is the place to see a really tasteful and sympathetic 19th century restoration.

There are 17th C furnishings – box-pews, Communion table, altar-rails, pulpit, reading desk, squire's pew with window openings, roof and W gallery. Norm font. Mons to Sir John Molyneux and wife 1691, two busts; Sir Francis Molyneux 1674, bust; Sir Francis Molyneux and wife 1741, busts; Sir Francis Molyneux 1817, bust in medallion framed by the Garter; and incised slabs to Roger Greenhalge and wife, 1563.

WOLLATON. This 14th C tower with recessed spire has a right-of-way through it. St Leonard's is mainly 14th C but the S doorway of the chancel is c1200. The N aisle is c1500, the Classical reredos c1660, also the date of the altar-rails in the S aisle. There are 14th C sedilia. Modern glass shows St Francis with 30 birds, English and foreign. Brass to Sir Richard Willoughby and wife 1471, on a stone slab beneath which lies a cadaver, with a lavish canopy and cresting. The mon to Sir Henry Willoughby and his four wives, three sons and three daughters, 1528, shows mourners and a cadaver.

WORKSOP PRIORY. St Mary and St Cuthbert's has two W Norm towers (of which the tower on the N is older by one hundred years) with Perp battlements and pinnacles. The interior has the usual three storeys – ground storey, triforium (with three arcades) and clerestory, and much nailhead ornamentation. The aisles are vaulted. The Lady Chapel (E of the S transept) is EE with fine lancet windows (a triplet at the E end and six on the S). The S porch (vaulted) has a fine late 12th C door with elaborate ironwork. Piscina and sedilia. A central tower has recently been very effectively added.

On the S side is the 14th C gate-house, vaulted: an oriel window and a Perp window of seven lights.

WYSALL. The tower is 13th C with lancet windows and a 14th C spire. On the N side is a small Norm window and doorway. Holy Trinity is 14th C. The S arcade is 15th C and also Perp are the chancel roof, clerestory, pulpit with Tracery panels and the rood-screen with four misericords at its back. A 14th C stoup in the chancel. The wooden altar below the tower is probably as old as the tower itself. Mon to Hugh Armstrong and his wife and seven children, 1572.

At St Mary and All Saints *Willoughby in the Wolds* is a wonderful collection of Willoughby monuments from c1300 onwards, in the north chapel of its fascinating church. *Widmerpool* church of St Peter and St Paul is mostly a late 19th century rebuild of great dignity, with a vaulted chancel of high quality.

OXFORDSHIRE

This county is bordered by six others and its varying but gentle scenery makes it rewarding to explore. To the west it becomes the edge of the Cotswolds (with the Cotswold town of Burford), whilst in the high country around Banbury we are almost in the Midlands. In parts of the east and south we are in the Home Counties, with Buckinghamshire and Berkshire nearby, the Chilterns penetrating the south-east corner and the lovely Thames taking us through Henley, Caversham and Goring. In the south-west it feels like Wiltshire-over-the-border. In 1974, Oxfordshire received a substantial area which was once Berkshire, including Abingdon, Faringdon, Wallingford and Wantage, also the Vale of the White Horse, which contained several of Berkshire's most interesting churches, adding about 60 to Oxfordshire's total of some 210 medieval ones. The heart of the county has its own individual identity – Oxford, the 'city of dreaming spires', is unique and has so much for the lover of architecture. There are pleasant market towns like Witney, Woodstock and Bicester and, to the north of the latter, the remote countryside immortalised by Flora Thompson's writings. There is the strange marshy area of Otmoor, the Forest of Wychwood and, in addition to the glorious Thames, there are rivers with deservedly lovely names, like the Windrush, the Evenlode and the Cherwell.

There are so many lovely churches, many in Cotswold stone, others in brown ironstone to the north, or flint to the south and east. Every period of architecture has fine examples here and they (like Northants churches) have provided illustrations for many an architectural textbook. There is interesting post-Reformation architecture here also, both the city and county of Oxford having interesting Classical work (as at Banbury and the exceedingly eccentric Nuneham Courtenay) and being a very popular territory for commissioning good Gothic Revival architects. There are fine furnishings and fittings in so many of the churches and this is a county in which to enjoy wall-paintings, medieval glass and splendid monuments, both inside the churches and in the lovely churchyards, with their mellow, lichen-covered headstones.

ABINGDON.   St Helen's fine tower and stone spire (rebuilt) are 13th C (the only other original stone spire in former Berkshire being at Shottesbrooke). The church is mainly 15th C with double aisles N and S which is most unusual. There are therefore four arcades. The font-cover

251

is dated 1634 and the pulpit two years later, the organ-case 1725, and the Mayor's seat with lion and unicorn, 1706. The most notable feature and unique is the painted roof panels of the inner N aisle c1390. They show kings and prophets and Christ crucified and the Annunciation. They were obviously a Tree of Jesse. There are two brasses and several tablets.

St Nicholas' church has Norman work and much of interest to see. St Leonard's *Sunningwell* is worth seeing if only for its unique octagonal porch of 1562.

ADDERBURY.   The tower with pinnacles of St Mary's and broach spire, are 14th C based on the earliest group of Oxford Cathedral, and others of a century earlier. There is a splendid cornice on both sides of the church – grotesque figures, humans, animals and birds. The S porch is 14th C. The magnificent chancel with six large windows and the piscina and sedilia show Perp work at its best, for which New College, Oxford was responsible. The nave roof is original, and also the rood-screen. The sacristy on the NE of the chancel has a charming (and rare) oriel window. A slab in the S transept records a death on the 30th February!

Milton church of St Mary (1856) is by Butterfield and there is much to enjoy in *Deddington*'s medieval church of St Peter and St Paul, whilst St Mary's *Banbury* (by S.P. Cockerell) is a Classical church of 1790.

BAMPTON.   A noble cruciform church, St Mary's broach spire is 13th C and is of the same date and style as the early cathedral group but taller. The saints on the little flying buttresses are original except St Andrew (19th century). The church is mainly 13th C but there are pieces of Norm work. Fine Dec W doorway. The E and W windows are early Dec. The S porch and a fine Easter Sepulchre are Perp. There is a 15th C reredos with Christ and the Twelve Apostles, and four misericords. Note the ironwork on the vestry door. Piscina and sedilia, and there are several brass effigies.

BLOXHAM.   This is one of our finest stone spires, rising from an octagon with pinnacles. It is 14th C. The W doorway of St Mary's is a setting for a carving of the Last Judgment with Christ enthroned. In the 15th C the splendid S chapel was built. A Norm doorway remains in the N wall of the chancel. Outside the N aisle is a lively corbel-table. A capital on the N side has human heads. There is much unusual Dec tracery, a Perp font and a Perp rood-screen with painted panels of the four Latin Doctors and Evangelists.

South Newington St Peter ad Vincula has the finest medieval wall-paintings in Oxfordshire. They date from the 14th and 15th centuries and they should not be missed.

BURFORD. One of our most picturesque Cotswold towns up a long hill (the church of St John the Baptist being at the bottom). The only Norm work remaining is the lower part of the central tower of the W wall of the nave. The belfry stage of the tower and the recessed spire are Perp, as also the W window of five lights and the S porch of three storeys, fan-vaulted, and with original doors and with a traceried front. The porch is wedged between two chapels. A 14th C font with the Crucifixion and St Mary and St John, and there are a number of wooden screens. Among several monuments and tomb-chests should be noted Edmund Harman, wife and children 1569, and Lord Chief Justice Tanfield and family 1628, a long canopied tomb with a skeleton below. In the churchyard are a number of Cotswold bale tombs c1700.

CASSINGTON. St Peter's is a complete tripartite Norm church (as at Iffley in this county and at Stewkley, Buckinghamshire). The tower is Norm with a 14th C broach spire. The two doorways are also Norm and a Norm corbel-table of carved heads runs round the church. The E and W windows are Norm. The S porch is of timber. The crossing tower arches are Norm. The chancel has a quadripartite vault and a Dec double piscina. Large Norm tub font. The Jac stalls are from Christ Church, Oxford. There are plain 15th C bench-ends with little buttresses. Brass to Thomas Neal, with an effigy in a shroud, 1590. Roger Cheyne has a foliated cross. Some 14th C and later roundels.

CHILDREY. St Mary's is an attractive cruciform church in a pretty village and there is so much to discover inside it. There are some old timbers in the roofs, screen and benches, the chancel has good late 13th century sedilia on one side and a 14th century Easter Sepulchre on the other. A little medieval glass remains and there is much atmosphere here. Above all are the superb brasses, especially that to John Kyngeston (1514) and his lady wife, which also has a charming brass showing the Holy Trinity. Don't miss the effigy of a cross-legged knight beneath his canopied recess.

Sparsholt's fine Holy Cross church also has an Easter Sepulchre and good monuments. St Andrew's *Letcombe Regis* and St Michael's *Letcombe Bassett* are both charming churches to visit and the noble cruciform church of St Peter and St Paul at *Wantage* has medieval screens and stalls, also good monuments and brasses.

CHISLEHAMPTON. A lovely Classical gem of 1762 (RCF), St Katherine's stuccoed exterior is delightful, with its curious two-staged bell-turret. The interior is a wonderful period-piece, with its original fittings – box-pews, reading and clerk's desks, three-sided rails, grand reredos, font and west gallery – the only exception is the pulpit and this is Jacobean and therefore older. Look for the children's benches near the altar rails.

Newington church of St Giles has a 14th century tower and spire, good 15th century glass and a 17th century monument. *Drayton St Leonard* has its patron saint in 14th century glass.

CHURCH HANDBOROUGH.   St Peter and St Paul's N doorway is splendid Norm work with a tympanum of St Peter, the Agnus Dei, and a lion. An EE piscina. The church was remodelled in the 15th C – the tower with a tall slender recessed spire and the nave with unusual concave columns. Perp font, and parts of the pulpit are 15th C. Fine 15th C screen carried across the chancel and both aisles: the vaulting remains in the aisles. Brasses to Jane Ford and two husbands c15th C, and to Dr Alexander Belsyre, figure in a shroud, 1567.

DORCHESTER ABBEY.   The N wall of the nave is Norm and is the oldest part that remains of St Peter and St Paul's. The most glorious part is, however, the 14th C sanctuary. The window tracery was extended over the whole window and is combined with figure sculpture. In the E window, the sculpture is the Passion and Resurrection of Christ. The N window is the Jesse window. The tracery is carved with foliage which forms a tree, springing from a figure of Jesse on the sill. On the branches are figures of the ancestors of Christ with the angel Gabriel and the three Wise Men: there were relevant figures in the glass. The S window transom has six stone figures carrying the bier of St Birinus (St Birinus was Bishop of Durham in AD 634; just after the Conquest the See was transferred to Lincoln.). The piscina and sedilia are equally beautiful and unusual. They have canopies with figures and a vault. Inside the sedilia are four small windows with ballflower, and still filled with their original 14th C glass. The piscina further W was of course in use before the chancel was extended. All the windows on the S side of the church have Intersecting tracery. The Perp S porch is of timber and the tower was rebuilt in the 17th C (but it has some medieval bells).

The Norm lead font is one of the best preserved, with figures of Apostles and bands of foliage. Early 16th C stalls. At the E end of the S aisle is a 14th C wall-painting of the Crucifixion, and there are also some modern paintings of interest. On a column of the nave is a large 14th C corbel of sleeping monks. The shrine of St Birinus has been reconstructed from fragments. Monuments include a fine 13th C cross-legged knight drawing his sword, Judge John de Stonor 1354, and an alabaster effigy of a knight c1400. Brass to Abbot Richard Beauforest c1510. The

14th C glass in the three eastern windows, and the E window of the N aisle and at the back of the sedilia should be studied in detail with the help of a guide-book.

Long Wittenham has an interesting church, with some fine Jacobean furnishings. Sir Gilbert Scott restored the medieval church of St Michael and All Angels at *Clifton Hampden*, which is beautifully positioned and well worth seeing.

EWELME. Could there be a more attractive group of buildings than the church, old red-brick almshouses, and the old red-brick school? The church of St Mary was rebuilt by the Earl and Countess of Suffolk in 1432 – hence a likeness to Suffolk churches. The Countess was Chaucer's granddaughter. The tower is low 14th C from the previous church. The S porch is of timber. The interior is unbroken by any chancel arch. The S chancel chapel roof is coloured and has angels with outspread wings, and the walls are diapered. On its N side is the tomb of the Duchess of Suffolk, 1475, perhaps the finest monument in England. She wears a coronet and the Order of the Garter (only three women do so): beneath is a cadaver and on the ceiling over it are painted St Mary Magdalene, St John the Baptist, and the Annunciation. Around the tomb are angels (feathered or in albs) with coloured shields, and as a frieze on the canopy are more angels. Four pinnacles on each side at the top bear wooden figures of angels (the monument and the effigy being of alabaster, and the canopy of stone). Brass to Thomas Chaucer and wife 1434, and there are also brasses to rectors and masters of the Hospital and some more monuments. There are some fragments of old glass. The font is Perp with a splendid tall tabernacle cover, again reminding one of Suffolk. It has a figure of St Michael at the apex, and the counterpoise is carved with a Tudor rose. There are 15th C screens, and the N and W doors and door to the vestry are old. Original roofs throughout.

HORLEY. A charming Cotswold village on a hill. Parts of the central tower and chancel of St Etheldreda's are Norm. The E and W belfry-windows are Norm, those on the N and S being Perp. The nave with tall piers is EE with three doorways. Some good Dec windows and clerestory. Norm piscina with zig-zag. The modern pulpit is brightly coloured with paintings of the life of St Etheldreda. The beautiful rood-loft with figures and canopy are also modern but continue the medieval tradition. An 18th C organ-case. On the N wall is one of the finest and best preserved St Christopher wall-paintings: there is an inscription and fishermen appear in the stream. There is also a painting of St Etheldreda. Fragments of old glass.

Wroxton is a pretty village with a church, All Saints, of considerable interest, not least for its woodwork and monuments. Do discover *Cropredy* (to the north-east) for a fine EE, Dec and Perp St Mary's church, with a 15th century lectern and plenty to enjoy inside.

IFFLEY. St Mary's is perhaps the most famous Norm church in England. It has a tripartite plan with the tower in the centre. The elaborate decoration indicates late 12th C work. The W front has three Norm windows with zig-zag and beakhead in the gable. A medieval circular window is in the centre, and at the base is a noble W doorway with zig-zag and beakheads and signs of the Zodiac and symbols of the Evangelists. The S doorway is even richer with beasts and zig-zag and interesting carved capitals. The N doorway is much plainer. A corbel-table runs round the nave – square blocks as the Norman mason only carved two of them (on the S side) as intended. The tower has two round-headed belfry windows on each side. The tower arches are richly decorated. The W bay of the chancel has a quadripartite vault with zig-zag as does its E bay which is 13th C. Norm piscina, sedilia and aumbry, and a square Norm font. Fragments of old brass.

J.H. Newman held the living of *Littlemore* and many devotees come to see his church there.

LANGFORD. The central tower of St Matthew's is Sax and here are three pieces of Sax sculpture. There is Christ (but headless) triumphant on the Cross on the E wall of the porch; on the S face of the same porch is a rood group with St Mary and St John – they now face outwards and Christ's arms are reversed; and on the S wall of the doorway are two figures in tunics with outstretched arms. The tower has two large belfry windows on each side. Inside the crossing arches are notable. The arcades are 13th C with foliage capitals. The N and S doorways are c1200. The windows of the nave are of the three Gothic periods. The chancel is 13th C with windows with unusual tracery of concave-sided lozenges. The aumbry is also 13th C with three gables and six compartments. A 15th C font, Jac pulpit and 15th C screens. Brass to Walter Prunes and wife 1609, and a monument to the Howse family 1691 – 'Within this little house three Howses lie'.

An area of delightful churches of great character. Do see St Peter and St Paul's *Broadwell* (a gem), St George's *Kencott* (Norman), St Peter's *Broughton Poggs* (Norman, rustic and atmospheric) and St George's *Kelmscot* (small and fascinating – William Morris lived nearby).

East and West Hendred, which were once in Berks both have charming villages and endearing churches. This is West Hendred, set beside its stream, rustic, unspoilt and beautiful.

MINSTER LOVELL. A cruciform Perp church with a central tower is very rare (Poynings, Sussex is another example). St Kenelm's was probably built on earlier foundations. The tower crossing is vaulted and all the roofs are old. Perp windows, a 15th C font and benches with simple mouldings. There is a 15th C alabaster tomb-chest with the effigy of a knight with figures on the sides – St Christopher, St Margaret, St Mary and female weepers. Fragments of old glass in tracery lights.

Leafield has a fine church of St Michael by Sir Gilbert Scott (1860) with a central tower and spire.

NORTH LEIGH. St Mary's W tower (formerly central) is late Sax with belfry windows of two lights divided by shafts. The round-headed arch of the former nave is c1200. The former chancel was made the nave and the N and S arcades were built. Dec windows in the S aisle and at the E end. The Wilcote Chapel at the E end of the N aisle is spectacular Perp – fan-vault and large Perp windows (with original glass including the alphabet). On the S of the chapel is a piscina and the ogee arch of the tomb-recess (opening to the chancel) with an elaborate finial of small angels with shields. The outer N aisle was added in the 18th C as a burial

257

chapel for the Perrot family. The stone chancel screen is modern. Above the screen is a splendid painting of the Last Judgment (or Doom) with the saved on one side and the damned on the other side (but an unusual way of dealing with the subject) – turn on the appropriate light switch to see it. Brass to Thomas Beckingham 1431 and mons to Sir William Wilcote and wife 1442 – two dogs at her feet and the knight's helmet has an eagle crest, and to William Lenthall and wife kneeling, 1596, a wall monument. There are a number of monuments to the Perrot family in the Perrot Chapel.

By contrast, *Freeland* has a fine Gothic Revival church of St Mary (1869–71) by J.L. Pearson which is worth seeing. It contains glass and paintings by Clayton & Bell.

NORTH MORETON. All Saints' round S arcade piers are Norm, but most of the church is EE and Dec with stiff-leaf foliage capitals. The large E window of the S chapel is early 14th C of five lights with unusual tracery. An angle piscina, and a frieze of beasts outside the chapel. Perp W tower with pierced parapet. Old glass – in the S chapel E window are 15 scenes in yellow, green and brown, c1300. The scenes are the life of Christ, and the death and burial of the Virgin, and St Nicholas, St Peter and St Paul.

Lovely churches hereabouts. Go south to St John the Baptist *South Moreton*, All Saints *Aston Upthorpe* and St Michael's *Aston Tirrold*, then west to St Michael's *Blewbury* and then north to St Andrew's *East Hagbourne*.

OXFORD. This wonderful city of towers and spires has nine medieval churches, also a fine (but refreshingly intimate) cathedral, which is also a college chapel. In addition the other college chapels have much to offer, as do the wealth of later churches. These buildings provide examples of all periods of architecture. Some of the best examples are as follows:

Saxon: St Michael's tower (there is late 13th century glass in the east window).

Norman: St Peter in the East, chancel and crypt.

EE: St Giles' (especially the tower), also the cathedral spire, said to be the earliest in England.

Dec: St Mary Magdalen (lovely Anglo-Catholic interior); St Mary the Virgin, tower and spire; and Merton College chapel (14th century glass here, a c1500 lectern, etc).

Perp: St Mary the Virgin (body of church); Merton tower; New College chapel; All Souls College chapel and Magdalen College chapel (also splendid tower). Each of the last three has a splendid stone reredos. Corpus Christi chapel is 16th century, with a medieval brass lectern and 17th century fittings.

17th C: St Mary the Virgin porch and the chapels of Brasenose, Jesus, Lincoln, Oriel and Trinity (the latter with exceptional furnishings).

18th C: All Saints' church (now Lincoln College Library) 1706–8, Pembroke, the Queen's and Worcester College chapels.

19th C: Amongst the best of many are St Barnabas', by Sir A. Blomfield (Italian romanesque, with a tall campanile and lovely Anglo-Catholic interior); St Margaret's, by H. Drinkwater, 1883, but with later fittings by Bodley and Cecil Hare; St Philip and St James – a stately church by Street, 1860–6, now used as a centre for mission studies, but still superb High Victorian EE, with a fine spire; and St John the Evangelist, Iffley Road (1894–6 and Bodley at his most uplifting and devotional in this lovely building, erected for the Cowley Fathers and now the chapel of St Stephen's House). Do also see Exeter College chapel (Sir Gilbert Scott), Balliol chapel (Butterfield), and above all the soaring and magnificent chapel of Keble College – a wonderful creation in brick and stone and one of William Butterfield's greatest works.

20th C: The chapel of Pusey House, in St Giles Street, is a hidden gem by Temple Moore (begun 1911) and Leslie Moore (1921–6). A mysterious and thrilling vaulted interior, splendidly adorned. Comper added the shimmering altar and baldacchino, also the glass in the east window.

RYCOTE CHAPEL. Begun in 1449 as a chantry chapel and never a parish church, but all church lovers must come here in order to luxuriate in its wonderful interior. The wagon roof, font, benches, stalls and lower part of the screen are the medieval originals. Nearly everything else here is 17th century – the west gallery, pulpit, reredos (1682), rails, upper parts of the screen and its huge flanking family pews.

The splendid cruciform church of St Mary at *Thame* is EE, Dec and Perp, and full of interest, with 16th century stalls and screen, pulpit and rails of c1700, several monuments and a fine collection of brasses.

SOMERTON. The greater part of St James' church is 14th C as is the tower, with Perp battlements and eight pinnacles and a crucifixion group on its N side. EE arcade and Dec S aisle. Dec E window, sedilia, an 18th C pulpit and a Perp rood-screen. A great treasure is the medieval reredos of the Last Supper with Christ and the apostles.

There is a low-side window with a seat, the nave is battlemented, and the Perp clerestory has square-headed windows (as so often in this area). Brass to William Fermor and wife 1552, and mons to Thomas Fermor and wife 1580, alabaster with figures; John Fermor 1625 and Richard Fermor 1643.

North Aston St Mary's church must be discovered – it is right against the mighty North Aston Hall.

SOUTH LEIGH. St James' is almost entirely Perp but there is a Norm pillar piscina. Perp font, 18th C pulpit, and the rood-screen is mostly Perp. The Perp wall-paintings are notable (though restored) – on the chancel arch the Last Judgment; on the S wall St Margaret weighing souls with the Virgin interceding; on the chancel S wall St Mary; and on the N aisle St Clement, and the Jaws of Hell with the Seven Deadly Sins (unrestored). Fragments of old glass.

STANTON HARCOURT.   There is a charming view from the E side of St Michael's church across the lake – we see the glorious triplet of lancets, a typical Perp window to its S, the sturdy central tower, Pope's Tower and the conical roof of the great medieval kitchen of the manor house. The N and S doorways are Norm, and the middle stage of the tower. The chancel was enlarged in EE times with lancets and this splendid triplet at the E end. Pillar piscina. The Harcourt Chapel and belfry-stage of the tower with battlements are Perp, as also the five-light window. The roofs of the nave and Harcourt Chapel are original. The rood-screen is mid-13th C with trefoiled openings, and is perhaps the earliest in the country. On its W side is a painting of a female saint. The little squints were made later.

On the N of the chancel is part of the shrine of St Edburgh (of Bicester Priory), with canopied figures. The gates of the Harcourt Chapel are 18th C. Mons to Maud Harcourt c1400; Sir Robert Harcourt and wife, both wearing the Garter (only three women do so) 1471; Sir Robert Harcourt with angels and bedesmen c1490; Sir Philip Harcourt and wife 1688, splendid portrait busts; and there are many later monuments. Brasses to Thomas Harcourt 1460, and Nicholas Atherton 1519, Ellen Cambry 1516 and Henry Dodschone in Mass vestments 1519. There is some 13th C grisaille glass in the S windows of the chancel.

Northmoor's cruciform church of St Denis is a gem – with so much to see and enjoy.

SWINBROOK.   St Mary's, in the valley of the river Windrush, has a small tower of 1822. Dec S porch, Trans arcades and chancel arch, and the E end of the chancel is filled with a large Perp window. The clerestory is also Perp. A 14th C font, altar-rails of c1700 and some 15th C misericords. There are two large Fettiplace monuments on the N side of the chancel: three figures in each leaning on the elbow, lying one above the other. One is to Sir Edmund Fettiplace 1613, with below him his father and grandfather, the other is of 1686 to another Sir Edmund Fettiplace and two predecessors, very similar to the last and adjoining it. Also monuments to Sir Edmund Fettiplace, bust, 1743, and Edward Fettiplace, cartouche, 1656. Brasses to John Croston and three wives 1470, and Anthony Fettiplace 1510. Some heads of angels in old glass, and some fine table-tombs in the churchyard.

Asthall has an interesting church, St Nicholas, in a pretty village. It is well worth stopping here.

UFFINGTON. St Mary's is a complete EE church with a central octagonal tower, the top added in the 18th C. The windows are mostly lancets. There are a number of blank circles for consecration crosses. The S porch is large and fine – vaulted and with stiff-leaf capitals. The tower is 13th C with original hinges. The transept E chapels are unusual – two on the N and one on the S, all with steep triangles, the mullions running into them. Each chapel has its own large piscina. Piscina and sedilia are also in the chancel. Mon to John Saunders 1638. The famous White Horse on the downs nearby is the only undoubted prehistoric hill figure in England.

The humble little churches of *Woolstone* and *Kingston Lisle* reward a visit, also idyllic and exquisite *Compton Beauchamp* (wonderful interior with furnishings by Martin Travers).

WIDFORD. St Oswald's is not on a road but isolated, in fields bordering the river Windrush, and a most pleasant walk from Swinbrook. It has a chancel and nave under one roof with a bell-turret. It is built on the site of a Roman villa, for the mosaic floor still remains and can be seen in the chancel. The church is 13th C with chancel arch and lancets. The S doorway is 17th C. Piscina, a 13th C font, old pulpit, Jac altar-rails and box-pews. A wall-painting of the Three Living and the Three Dead, also a part of a St Christopher. Royal Arms of the 17th C. Another little interesting detail – why the dedication to a Northern saint?

WITNEY. There is a fine view of St Mary's church with its majestic spire from the N across the green. The tower with three lancet belfry windows on each side and broach spire with dormer windows is early 13th C, and is of the same date and style as that of the cathedral, the earliest in England. The transepts have W aisles, which is very unusual. The 14th C added chantry chapels in the N transept and at the W end of the N aisles, with windows of Flowing tracery in the 15th C. The W doorway and window and clerestory were added with a parapet with gargoyles around the whole church. Norm N porch and doorway. Arcades in the tower arches are 13th C. There is a large Perp window of five lights and doorway, and on the N a large Flowing window of seven lights. In the N transept is a reredos with niches. The large S window is Perp. Mons include a 14th C effigy of an ecclesiastic, 14th C effigies of a man and woman, Sir Francis Wenman 1680 and Richard Ayschcone 1606. Brass on a tomb-chest to Richard Wenman and two wives, 1501.

The curious church of St Mary at *Cogges* is a real character – EE, Dec and Perp, with some old glass, monuments and a very odd little tower.

YARNTON. St Bartholomew's church and the Jac manor house make a splendid group. The nave and chancel with the chancel arch are 13th C, and also the E window. The nave windows are Perp. The clerestory and the roofs of the nave and aisle are early 17th C, as also the Spencer Chapel and SW tower, and S porch. The Spencer Chapel has its original roof, now beautifully coloured, and a large E window of five lights, all Perp in style. A fine Jac screen with obelisks and strapwork to the S chapel. Also a Jac pulpit and reading-desk. There are two fonts – Norm and Dec, and some poppyhead bench-ends. There are four alabaster panels of a medieval reredos presented in the late 18th C to the church by Alderman William Fletcher – the Adoration of the Magi (the Child has a very long arm), the Betrayal, Christ bearing the Cross, and a Pieta. Mon to Sir William Spencer and wife 1609, with recumbent effigies and kneeling children, and another to Sir Thomas Spencer. Here the father, wife and son are standing figures in classic attire, and the four daughters have to find such other positions on the monument as they can, 1709. The attitude of figures at this time did not produce humility or reverence, but rather self-glorification. Epitaphs also use the most pompous and verbose style to describe the merits of the deceased. Alderman William Fletcher has a revival in brass. The old glass is again largely from the collection of Alderman Fletcher. In the E window are two 15th C cherubim on red and blue backgrounds respectively and there are a number of early 16th C quarries of bears with scrolls (secular). The Spencer Chapel has early 17th C armorial glass: there are some Tudor badges and a number of saints including the Virgin and St Christopher.

The steps and a part of the shaft of the churchyard cross remain in the churchyard.

Begbroke has a Norman church of St Michael with a saddleback tower, but is also notable for its assortment of glass of different periods.

SHROPSHIRE

In its own very special way Shropshire is one of the most appealing counties of all. Its landscape is exciting and punctuated by hills which long remain in the memory – the Clee Hills in the south, the Clun Hills in the west, the beautiful slopes of the Long Mynd and of Wenlock Edge and the Wrekin which rises dramatically out of the landscape. There are plenty of trees and beautiful dales and valleys, not least the amazing Ironbridge Gorge, the pilgrim shrine for followers of Thomas Telford.

Shropshire churches are delightful and very varied, with good work of all medieval periods and several interesting examples of 17th century work. The 18th century provided some very interesting churches and in addition to those mentioned in our list, do find Whitchurch and Madeley. This is very much a county where the best way to see its richness and variety is to hunt out its churches (about 180 medieval ones await your visit). By going into the lanes, you will see the farmsteads, the meadows and the little undiscovered villages, also the splendid views available here – almost always with the near or distant sight of hills.

ACTON BURNELL.   St Mary's lies close to the castle, but is it thought to be slightly earlier, c1265. The chancel is particularly fine with a large E window and double piscina with foliage capitals: there is much ornament in foliage and quaint heads. The N porch is original and so are the roofs of the nave and chancel. Lancets abound and here they are cusped. EE font with Jac cover, and a Jac pulpit and Communion table. The N transept is paved with medieval tiles. A fine brass to Nicholas Burnell 1382. Mons to Sir Richard Lee, his wife and their nine daughters and three sons in alabaster, 1591, and to Sir Humphrey Lee and his wife at a prayer-desk with one son and five daughters below, 1632.

ASTON EYRE.   The tympanum over the S door is thought to be the best piece of Norm carving in the county. It shows Christ's entry into Jerusalem holding a palm branch and riding on an ass, while a bearded man spreads out palm branches, and there is another man with a young ass. There are Norm windows and a Trans chancel arch, an old door and a Jac pulpit.

There is good Norman work at St Gregory's *Morville*, which is delightfully set near the Hall, and a trip to remote St Michael and All Angels *Upton Cressett* (RCF) is well worthwhile.

BURFORD. Anyone interested in church monuments will come to St Mary's. The tower with double belfry windows is modern. The nave roof is original and also the priest's door with its hinges. Perp font. There is a brass to Elizabeth de Cornewayle c1370 and the monuments are notable. That to Princess Elizabeth, daughter of John of Gaunt and wife of Sir John Cornewayle 1426, is brightly coloured, as is Edmund Cornwall, knight 1508, made of wood. Outstanding is the coloured triptych 1588 of Richard Cornwall and his father and mother, shown as three large standing figures with the Apostles and shields on the wings. There are also two wall-monuments with couples at a prayer-desk, 1630. The superb 19th century work here was designed by Sir Aston Webb.

CLAVERLEY. All Saints' church groups well with its nearby black-and-white houses. It is of red sandstone. The lower part of the tower is late Norm and the upper part Perp. Some other parts are Norm, but all medieval periods make their contribution. Perp clerestory and two-storeyed S porch. The chancel roof is 1601, and there is a Norm font and a Jac pulpit. A wall-painting of c1200 shows, on the upper tier of the N wall of the nave, the battle of Virtues against Vices – a battle of armed knights on horseback: below are separate unconnected subjects. There is an incised slab to Richard Spicer and wife 1448, a monument to Sir Robert Broke and two wives and children 1558, and two incised plates of Elizabethan couples 1577 and 1599.

CLUN. St George's massive tower on the Welsh border was built for defence. It has the 17th C wooden pyramid on pyramid roof of this area. The tower is Norm but the nave W wall must be earlier, and the former W window looks into the tower. Late 12th C arcades, and an original clerestory. The N aisle roof with angels is also original. The E window has a canopy over the altar (for the pyx). Jac reredos and pulpit with tester, 13th C font and an 18th C lych-gate. The castle ruins by the river Clun are spectacular and to reach them from the church one crosses a medieval bridge.

DIDDLEBURY. St Peter's has a late Sax nave and a N wall with herringbone masonry, Sax doorway and Sax double-splayed window. The tower is Sax-Norm with a Norm string-course. The chancel is Norm and the S aisle 13th C. In the chancel are two 14th C recesses with ballflower and a two-light window. Perp font. Fragments of a Sax cross.

EATON UNDER HAYWOOD. Rural, secluded and beautifully set beneath the slopes of Wenlock Edge. A lovely spot, a lovely churchyard and an endearing church of St Edith of Wilton, with Norman nave and EE chancel and tower. Inside are many treasures, including ancient roofs, the Royal Arms painted upon a tympanum, a 17th century pulpit (using older timbers), reading desk, chancel panelling and rails and a 14th century wooden effigy beneath a canopied recess in the chancel.

St Peter's *Rushbury* has a lovely EE chancel of c1200 and good medieval roofs.

EDSTASTON. St Mary's has a 19th C bellcot, but its nave and chancel are Norm and there are three Norm doorways, the S one sumptuous with zig-zag. Also a Norm window in the chancel, S side, and two Norm string-courses. The chancel E window is Dec with Intersecting tracery. Original nave roof, Jac pulpit. Norm N & S doors with Norm ironwork and the priest's door has Norm ironwork on a medieval door. Fragments of old glass.

HEATH CHAPEL. A small Norm church lying on its own in a field – just nave and chancel and not even a bellcot. S doorway with chevron, small windows, a chancel arch and a tiebeam roof. There is a Norm font, a 17th C pulpit, a reader's desk, squire's pew, and box-pews and altar-rails. The ironwork on the S door could be 12th C.

Clee St Margaret has a Norman church, with 17th century pulpit and benches inside.

HOLDGATE. Holy Trinity's nave is Norm with a S doorway with beak-heads and zig-zag. The chancel is 13th C and the short sturdy tower is 13th C below and 15th C above. The fine font is Norm with a dragon and interlace. A misericord also has dragons. Old benches. Outside the S wall of the chancel is a stone carved with the head and shoulders of a human being.

HUGHLEY. St John the Baptist, under Wenlock Edge, has a timber and brick belfry and an EE nave and Dec chancel. In the chancel is a bracket for a figure above the head of lady. Pillar piscina, and Jac pulpit. The great treasure is the 15th C rood-screen, the finest in the county. The dado has pierced and unpierced tracery and quatrefoils: the tracery above is very dainty and the coving has lierne-vaults, and the cresting is very delicate. Fragments of old glass.

Kenley's small church of St John the Baptist has a lovely chancel roof and a Jacobean pulpit and reading desk.

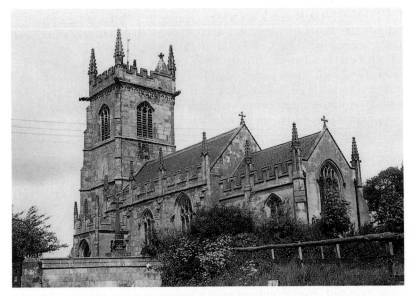

St John the Baptist, Ightfield, not far from the Cheshire border, shows the embattled and pinnacled exteriors which are so often found in Shropshire, Cheshire and Staffordshire.

KINLET. St John the Baptist's stands in the grounds of Kinlet Hall, but some way from the house. The N aisle is late Norm, and the S arcade, S porch and doorway are EE with stiff-leaf foliage. The brick W tower is also of that date with a Perp top with battlements and pinnacles. Fine tower arch. The chancel and transept are 14th C. The E window is of five lights with Intersected and cusped tracery. Timber-framed Perp clerestory, and also a figure of the Trinity.

LLAN-Y-BLODWELL. Wonderful scenery here near the Welsh border, amongst the hills – and a remarkable church of great character, Michael the Archangel with an octagonal tower and curiously convex-sided stone spire. Its priest, John Parker, gradually rebuilt and re-decorated most of it to his own designs between 1844–1860 – and what an eccentric and very satisfying building he created. He kept the Norman doorway, Perp arcade and screen and other survivals, also Rysbrack's memorial to Sir John Bridgman (1752). The wonderful decorations, painted texts and furnishings which he installed are imaginative and colourful.

LUDLOW.   St Lawrence's is one of England's greater churches. The fine S doorway is EE with a Dec hexagonal porch (the only other hexagonal porch being at St Mary Redcliffe, Bristol) with a vault. Dec are the N aisle and W window of four lights with ballflower. Perp are the W doorway, W window of seven lights and the fine tower with pinnacles and crossing arches inside. The tower is so tall that it serves as a landmark. Most of the roofs are original. The seats of the stalls are 15th C with entertaining misericords, including a fox as a bishop preaching to geese, a mermaid with a mirror, a pedlar with his pack putting on boots, a man in a comfortable chair warming his hands and feet in front of a fire with two sides of bacon hanging up and a kettle on the boil, two boys making fun of a woman with an ugly hat, the Devil carrying off the ale-wife for giving short measures while a demon reads out her sin and the mouth of Hell swallows her, wrestlers, an'ostler, birds and animals. A 15th C rood-screen with coving and cresting. There is much medieval glass, but restored.

MELVERLEY.   We come to this beautiful place, with its lovely views, set near the river Vyrnwy, to see one of Shropshire's two timber-framed churches (the other being the private chapel at Halston Hall) and how very special it is – an essay in black-and-white, all built in the early 16th century. A wonderful construction, which we can appreciate all the more inside. St Peter's is a rustic, single-celled, barnlike building with a timber belfry. What an interior – considerably restored, but still preserving its simple screen and west gallery (probably of 1588).

MINSTERLEY.   Holy Trinity is a period-piece of 1689 in a pretty setting, and a real individual, with its wooden belfry, Classical windows and pieces of Baroque detail. There are cherubs' heads above the windows and a rather eccentric but effective west front. Inside is splendid woodwork which is original, including the west gallery, pulpit with large tester, panelling and rails. A rare collection of maidens' garlands hangs beneath the gallery.

MORETON CORBET.   An unforgettable spot, dominated by the romantic and evocative ruins of the castle. There is much to see in the nearby church of St Bartholomew, with its Norman chancel and lovely Dec south aisle. The interior is truly beautiful. The pulpit and desk are Jacobean and the chancel was magnificently refurbished by Comper, who designed the east window in 1905. Above all we shall remember the monuments of the Corbets, who built the castle and gave their name to the village.

267

Stanton upon Hine Heath's St Andrew's is a Norman church with a later pinnacled tower. *Shawbury's* St Mary's has a Norman nave and font, a tall pinnacled Perp tower, a pretty 17th century porch and plenty to enjoy inside.

PITCHFORD.   St Michael's church and the manor house, as so often, are close together. Could there be a finer example than here, which enables us to see the magnificent medieval black-and-white Hall? The church has a wooden belfry-turret with pyramid roof. There are Norm and EE doorways and windows. The E gable with Classical details dates from 1719. Jac pulpit with tester, reading-desk and some benches. Mon to John de Pitchford, a cross-legged knight in wood, 1285, and four inscribed alabaster slabs to the Ottley family with 50 children, 1529, 1534, 1578 and 1587 with interesting changes in costume.

At *Cound's* St Peter's church we find a Norman font, Jacobean pulpit, Kempe glass in the east window, a 13th century ironbound chest and much else.

SHREWSBURY.   There are many churches in Shrewsbury, but the most interesting is St Mary's (RCF). The lower part of the tower is Norm and the upper part Perp with pinnacles and a tall recessed spire. Perp clerestory, two-storeyed S porch of c1200 and transepts and chancel of the late 12th C (but E window modern). There is a 13th C chancel arch and arcades with splendid stiff-leaf capitals, and a Perp font. Old glass, including a fine Dec Jesse glass in the E window, the donors below. In the chancel N windows and the middle window of the N aisle is imported 15th C German glass of the life of St Bernard of Clairvaux. There is also continental glass in some other windows.

The Norm abbey church (Holy Cross) should also be visited so that the splendid seven-light Perp W window can be seen. St Chad's church is a large and splendid Classical church (1790–2) with a circular nave and a wonderful feeling of space and grandeur inside. It should not be missed.

STOKESAY.   The church of St John the Baptist adjoins Stokesay Castle and gatehouse, one of our first fortified houses. It has a Norm S doorway and Perp tower and chancel but the chancel was largely rebuilt in the 17th C. Also 17th C roofs and a Jac pulpit with tester and canopied pew.

Do see *Onibury's* church of St Michael with its Norman chancel arch and sympathetic restoration by Detmar Blow (1902), also *Bromfield's* St Mary's with its beautiful setting, with Norman and EE work and 17th century painted chancel ceiling.

STOTTESTON. In St Mary's the oldest piece is the tympanum, Sax-Norm, with a head at the top and beasts on the lintel (now inside the door). The lower part of the tower is Norm, the upper part Perp. The interior with a Norm N arcade is mainly Dec with the E window of five lights with Intercepting and cusped tracery. Sedilia. The font is the most splendid Norm one in the county: it has scrolls and leaves, beasts and the Lamb and Cross. There is a Jac pulpit and fragments of old glass.

TONG. St Bartholomew's is all red sandstone and completely Perp with a crossing tower, square and then an octagon with battlements and pinnacles and a short spire (containing a particularly large bell). An E window of five lights. Old roofs and a Perp font and screens. A fine set of stalls with traceried backs (not canopies) with misericords – foliage, angels, an eagle, the Annunciation and Christ crucified on a lily. There is a pulpit of 1629, carved Royal Arms of 1814, an original door to the vestry, a vestment 1600 with the sun and I.H.S., and fragments of old glass.

WORFIELD. St Peter's has a handsome exterior with a grey recessed spire on a red sandstone tower. Dec predominates with Kent tracery in the windows. Dec arcades, a Perp font and the screen is partly old. Fragments of old glass, old doors with ironwork and an old chest also with ironwork. Mons to Sir George Bromley and wife 1588, alabaster, and Sir Edward Bromley and wife 1626, alabaster.

Bridgnorth St Leonard's (RCF) is large, grand and Gothic, with a magnificent tower – mostly by Slater, of 1860–2. St Mary's is large and Classical, by Thomas Telford, 1792.

WROXETER. Part of St Andrew's (RCF) N wall is Sax. The base of the tower is Norm, the upper part Perp. Norm clerestory with Perp E window. Large font with the base of a Roman column. Jac pulpit and box-pews and altar-rails. A 13th C chest with its ironwork, and part of a Sax cross-shaft high up on the S wall of the nave. Mons to Lord Chief Justice Bromley and wife, 1555 with their daughter in the middle panel; Sir Richard Newport and wife 1570, with children as mourners holding shields; John Barber and wife, 1618; and Francis Newport, Earl of Bradford 1708, with two kneeling putti.

Atcham St Eata's church stands beautifully beside the Severn. Here we see lovely 15th century glass in the east window.

SOMERSET

This county is always a joy to visit – so much of it is still unspoilt and it is incredibly rich in contrasting scenery. It is punctuated by several groups of hills, all noted for their beauty, from wild Exmoor in the west to the picturesque Quantocks above Taunton and the Mendips in the north-east. By contrast we have the fen-like marshes of Athelney and Sedgemoor. It is a county of many trees, of green valleys and of delightful villages with fascinating place-names. Its coastline is splendid, especially around Porlock, Minehead and Watchet.

Its churches are glorious, thanks to the prosperity of the wool-trade combined with the availability of superb building stone on the spot. Beneath Somerset soil is Doulting stone and golden Ham Hill stone, with limestone from the Mendips, also blue lias and red sandstone – all marvellous for creating churches, and it is their exquisite stonework which is surely the most memorable feature of Somerset churches. Stone is seen beautifully fashioned in arcades, parapets, panelling and above all in Somerset's magnificent towers. A group of about 60 of these towers are without doubt the grandest and most perfect in England. Not only are these the most amazing combinations of buttresses, pinnacles, arrays of windows and noble proportions, but some are vaulted internally and are divided from the nave by panelled arches.

The churches of Somerset have fine interiors which are rich in wood-carving of very high quality. Here we may look up to see sumptuous panelled roofs, often of the tiebeam variety. Martock's roof has 768 carved panels and Shepton Mallet's wagon roof has 350 carved panels, 306 bosses, 90 half-bosses and 1,400 leaves – all different! In this county of about 450 old churches, we may see 70 or so medieval screens, several pre-Reformation wood (and stone) pulpits, marvellous arrays of carved bench-ends and other fine woodwork.

Much church building was carried out here in the 15th and early 16th centuries, although work of most other periods is represented, especially Norman work in doorways, fonts, and a few churches which were not totally remodelled later.

But back to those wonderful towers. Here is a list of the very best of these, so that you may hunt them out (not a difficult task, as they are very prominent):– Batcombe, Bruton, Bishops Lydeard, Chewton Mendip, Evercreech, Huish Episcopi, Isle Abbots, Glastonbury St John,

Ilminster, Kingsbury Episcopi, Kingston St Mary, Leigh on Mendip, Mells, North Petherton, Staple Fitzpaine, Taunton St Mary and St James, Wells St Cuthbert, Weston Zoyland, Winscombe and Wrington. But you will discover others and wonder why these are not listed – or you may discover some earlier towers which are octagonal, or have octagonal tops, like North Curry, Somerton or Stoke St Gregory.

AXBRIDGE. Everybody goes to Cheddar, which has a fine church, but do also find Axbridge, just to the west, and enjoy its stately cruciform church. There is grand Perp work outside, with large windows, openwork parapets, pinnacles and a lofty central tower. Inside, we are treated to a beautiful and rare plaster ceiling over the nave, made in 1636 by George Drayton, a local man, for ten shillings. The aisle roofs are a century older. Here we may also discover a squint through one of the tower piers, a chandelier of 1729, a rare altar frontal of 1610 in the Lady Chapel (the handiwork of a Bishop's daughter) and a host of other items of interest.

In the area is St Leonard's *Rodney Stoke*, with its remarkable series of monuments, including the shrouded George Rodney (1651) rising from his coffin!

BRUTON. There are two towers here at St Mary's – a splendidly-proportioned Somerset west tower (104 ft tall) and a three-storeyed north porch tower. Here again Perp predominates, although earlier work may be seen. The chancel, however, is a Classical period-piece of 1743 and contains its original fittings, including box-pews, rails and altar-piece. The tower screen is dignified work of 1620, but the chancel screen dates only from 1938 – and very fine it is. The nave has a tiebeam roof; and there are also the Royal Arms of Charles II, a Jacobean pulpit and a fine monument of 1585, showing Sir Maurice Berkeley and his two wives.

Redlynch church of St Peter (SE of Bruton) dates from 1750 and is worth a visit. There are glorious towers to the north, at *Batcombe* and St Peter's *Evercreech*.

BRYMPTON D'EVERCY. What could be more delightful than this perfect combination of church and manor house standing together, both built of Ham Hill stone. The little church of St Andrew has a perky stone bell-turret, of a most unusual design and, although one of the county's more humble churches, this building is well worth penetrating. The 15th century screen here is of stone. The font is a century older and a priest, who is believed to have caught the Black Death whilst saying Mass in 1346, has a beautiful effigy here.

271

The area around Yeovil has several noteworthy churches, not least *Yeovil*'s parish church of St John – known, because of its array of splendid windows, as the 'Lantern of the West'.

NORTH AND SOUTH CADBURY. Two lovely villages near the Dorset border – both with delightful churches. North Cadbury St Michael's (which is the larger church) stands beside the manor house. Inside it we may admire eight blue-robed saints in 15th century glass in the west window, including St Apollonia, the patron saint of toothache sufferers. A fascinating series of benches, made in 1538, show a flute-player, various Christian symbols and mythological creatures, a face in pain, and what must be the only carving in existence of a Tudor cat and mousetrap.

South Cadbury St Thomas a Becket's is smaller, but stands in a pretty churchyard near the foot of Cadbury Hill. It has an arcade of c1280, a 15th century nave roof and a wall-painting of a coped and mitred bishop.

CROSCOMBE. A good Perp exterior, with a stone spire – but what splendour inside! This church was refurnished in the 1600s and has the most glorious 17th century woodwork of very high quality, including a magnificent screen, a canopied Jacobean pulpit (1616) and box-pews. The chancel roof is dated 1664 and there are two 18th century chandeliers.

Shepton Mallet is nearby, with a fine church noted for its tower, its medieval pulpit of stone and its amazing panelled roof.

CULBONE. It requires a cliff walk from Porlock to reach it, but how very worthwhile. Splendid north Somerset coastal scenery here, and this adorable tiny shrine in its sylvan setting. St Culbone's is England's smallest church to possess a structural nave, chancel and porch and there is even a cheeky-looking spire over the nave's west end. Its Norman walls shelter a screen of c1380, simple 15th century benches, a family box-pew, a very early font and a reredos of 1927 by C.F.A. Voysey.

Here we are on the edge of Exmoor. Nearby is Lorna Doone's haunting little church of St Mary at *Oare*, also the Exmoor churches of St Mary *Luccombe* and *Stoke Pero*. *Porlock* has an atmospheric church of St Dubricius, with a truncated spire and splendid Harlington monument.

EAST BRENT. Set on the eastern side of Brent Knoll Hill is this charming village with a fascinating and unforgettable church. St Mary's elegant stone spire crowns a tower where original statues are preserved in its western niches. Inside we are in for a feast! Beneath an amazing plaster ceiling of 1637 stands a pulpit which was made three years earlier. The wooden eagle lectern is a rare 15th century survival and the benches have poppyhead ends. Above all, we may admire the rich medieval glass in the north aisle's east window, with nine scenes of Christian teaching about Christ's passion, death, resurrection and ascension. It is everything put together here which really creates a wonderful atmosphere of devotion and antiquity.

Brent Knoll St Michael's church, on the other side of the hill, must be visited, if only to see its remarkable bench-ends, especially the three which hilariously depict the fable of Reynard the Fox.

GLASTONBURY. In this ancient place of pilgrimage, history, legend and sanctity meet and we are in touch with Christianity at its earliest. Did Joseph of Arimathaea come here with the Faith? If he did, he could not have come to a more lovely part of England's green and pleasant land. Now we have the remains of the great abbey, the bold Somerset tower which crowns the strange 500 ft Tor, and two medieval churches. St Benignus (Benedict), rebuilt in 1520, is smaller but worth a visit. People are drawn to the mighty (134 ft) tower of glorious St John's, which has a palatial Perp exterior of very high quality architecture. Inside is one of Somerset's most lavish roofs, a fine collection of old glass assembled in a chancel window, 15th century tomb-chests and a host of interesting things, ancient and modern, including a chest of 1421, the Royal Arms of Charles II and a German painting of the Crucifixion.

ILMINSTER. A lively and pleasant market town, dominated by its noble cruciform church of St Mary with a stately central tower – all in beautiful golden Ham Hill stone. This is a fine essay in Perp architecture, of which the north chapel (once described as a glass-house) is the climax. There are fine roofs and the tower has a fan-vaulted ceiling. All here is lofty and dignified, with excellent 19th and 20th century glass and two good monuments to members of the Wadham family – one to Sir William (1452) and the other to his grandson, Nicholas (1609) who founded Wadham College Oxford.

This is a lovely area to explore for countryside and churches. Inviting lanes lead to *Dowlish Wake* and *the Crickets*, to *Hinton St George* with its fine tower and to *Kingstone*'s delightful church of St Mary (all to the south and east). To the north-east is St Mary Magdalene *Stocklinch* with its 13th century work and the lonely and idyllic St Mary's *Stocklinch Ottersey* (RCF) in its delightful hillside setting; also lovely St Michael's *Shepton Beauchamp*, with its fine tower and devotional interior.

LEIGH ON MENDIP AND MELLS. Two of our best Somerset towers, within a few miles of each other. Leigh's is 91½ ft tall and a mass of stonecarving. St Giles' has a superb Somerset roof and a complete set of medieval benches to enjoy here.

At St Andrew's *Mells* (about four miles NE) we are treated to one of Somerset's most beautiful villages and the wonderful sight of a Tudor manor house and church (this tower is 104 ft high) forming a perfect and memorable group. The font inside is Norman and the equestrian statue in bronze to Edward Horner (1917) was designed and made by that great painter of horses – Sir Alfred Munnings.

LONG SUTTON. A village of stone houses, dominated by the 96 ft tower of 15th century Holy Trinity church. Original doors admit us to enjoy another glorious tiebeam roof in the nave and a wagon roof in the chancel, also a magnificent screen and what must be one of the best medieval pulpits in England – a wonderful tribute to the skill of its 15th century woodcarver. So much of the woodwork here has been given colour, as it would certainly have had originally. The lierne-vaulting beneath the tower and the panelled tower arch should not be missed.

Within a few miles are the fine towers of St Mary's *Huish Episcopi* and All Saints' *Langport*; also St Peter and St Paul's *Muchelney*, where angels in 17th century dress (and undress) peer down at us from their clouds in the wagon roof.

NETTLECOMBE. Amazingly awkward to find, but so well worth the effort. Here the red sandstone church of St Mary and red sandstone Court (1599) almost touch each other. A superb setting – sylvan, peaceful and rural. Not a vast church, but one of great character. Inside we have early 16th century benches, a handsome 18th century pulpit, original glass in the north chapel (including St Catherine with her wheel and St Sidwell carrying her head) and very deep, vaulted tomb-recesses in the south chapel. The great treasure here is the 15th century font – one of only two outside East Anglia which show the seven Sacraments of the Church.

Nearby All Saints *Monksilver*, with its leering gargoyles and lovely woodwork (in screen, benches, roofs, pulpit and lectern), is also worth finding.

SELWORTHY. A much visited picture-postcard village with thatched and whitened cottages and a whitened church on the hillside, with glorious views inland towards Exmoor and Dunkery Beacon. The church of All Saints is mostly Perp (look for the date 1538 on the respond at the west end of the south arcade). The south aisle is hailed as a masterpiece of design. Inside, old wagon roofs, studded with bosses, crown this light and airy church, which is entered through a two-storeyed porch and by means of an original door. From the 1300s remain the tower base and sturdy chest.

In the vicinity are lovely villages and grand scenery and along the coast is *Minehead*, whose fine church of St Michael is dramatically set near pretty cottages and reached by a climb up a series of steps, *Carhampton* St John the Baptist, with its lovely screen and, just inland, unforgettable *Dunster*, whose noble cruciform church of St George is straddled by one of the finest screens in the land, made in 1499.

STOKE SUB HAMDEN.   Not the usual Somerset church, but fascinating because we have work of most medieval periods here. The core of St Mary's nave and chancel are Norman, with two Norman doorways, one having a tympanum with fascinating carving. The tower and south transept are EE and many of the windows were made c1300. The lovely west window is Dec, and the east window is Perp. A treasure house inside, with a Norman font, a double piscina (c1300), a Perp stone screen to the north transept, 15th century woodwork in the benches and nave roof, and 17th century woodwork in the pulpit and Communion rails. The seeker after monuments will not be disappointed here, and do not miss the lovely 15th century cross in the churchyard.

Nearby *Tintinhull* St Margaret's church has much 13th century work and visitors to *Montacute House* must go to the church of St Catherine as well, where the chancel arch is 500 years older than the house and there are several good monuments to the Phelips. *Martock* All Saints' tiebeam roof, with its 768 carved panels, must be the finest of all Somerset roofs.

SWELL.   This little-known, tiny, towerless St Catherine's church, approached through a farmyard and set near the manor house – all at the end of a narrow lane, is a little hidden gem, well worth finding. The core is Norman, remodelled in the 1400s – the former period seen in the fine south doorway, the latter in the windows and panelled chancel arch. The interior is memorable for its atmosphere – fragments of medieval glass punctuating the clear glass of the windows, plain benches going silver with age, 17th century altar-rails, pulpit and font-cover, also 18th century box-pews. How lovely!

Not far away are the interesting churches of St Andrew's *Curry Rivel* and St James' *Curry Mallet*, also glorious St Mary's *Isle Abbots*, with its sumptuous tower and lovely stonework, which must not be missed.

275

TAUNTON. The skyline of Somerset's county town is punctuated by two elegant towers. St James' tower is 120 ft tall and the church has a Perp font bowl, adorned with carved figures, and a pulpit of 1633. St Mary Magdalene's tower is the tallest and most ambitious of all the Somerset parish church towers – 163 ft of it, rebuilt with care in 1863, an exact replica of the original. Approaching the church along Hammett Street the view is breathtaking – an intricate essay in golden Ham Hill stone from Montacute and pink sandstone from the Quantocks. It makes the body of the church seem rather low and insignificant, but it is a mighty building, with double aisles each side of the nave and a grand two-storeyed porch. Inside there are arches everywhere, and the patron saint (given in 1871) presides over the nave from her mighty niche. There are niches between the clerestory windows, above which rises the tiebeam roof, resplendent with its gilded angels. Many more treasures may be discovered in this church of many vistas – clearly the pride of Taunton!

Do also find St John's, with its tower and spire – designed by Sir Gilbert Scott and built in 1863. It has a majestic and devotional Anglo-Catholic interior.

WELLS. If only all cathedral cities were this size, and had this charm! The cathedral and its environs deservedly draw the visitors, but the majestic town church of St Cuthbert deserves a visit also. We are drawn there by its mighty tower (122 ft tall and massive as well). This is the largest church in the county, its exterior graced by huge Perp windows, openwork parapets and pinnacles. The arcade piers remain from the 13th century church, but most of what we see is Perp, including one of Somerset's most glorious tiebeam roofs and a mutilated (but still beautiful) stone reredos in each transept – the southern one, of 1470, having a Tree of Jesse. The Royal Arms of 1631 and fine pulpit (of 1636 and carved with Old Testament characters) are most worthy of an important town church. This is another church of vistas – and don't forget to look westwards, to the tall and elegant tower arch and then go beneath to look up to the tower's vaulted ceiling and its bosses.

S.S. Teulon's (1856) church of St Thomas, with its streaky tower and tall spire, is an interesting legacy from the 19th century, which has undergone sensitive treatment in recent years and deserves a visit.

WESTON ZOYLAND. From the flat land of Sedgemoor (which has an atmosphere of its very own) rises this magnificent 125 ft tower, beckoning us to admire a most rewarding church. The Perp architecture in the nave, aisles and south chapel is worth examining.

Some of the finest towers in England are in Somerset. This is the view towards St Mary's Taunton.

STAFFORDSHIRE

Here we are in the middle of England and as far as any county from the sea, and in an area which is underrated by those who have never taken time to explore Staffordshire's many faces. In the north are the Potteries (no other group of English towns are quite like these) and the wild places around Biddulph and Leek. In the north-east, the county borders some of the loveliest parts of Derbyshire and here we are in the Peak District, with the lovely river Dove forming the county boundary. The south-eastern part, where some of the finest churches are, has a character of its very own, with Needwood Forest, the Trent Valley and Cannock Chase. Its Black Country part (around Wolverhampton, Wednesbury, Willenhall and Walsall) has been lost to the West Midlands, although a finger of Staffordshire still reaches into Worcestershire around Kinver, and east of the M6 is pretty and undulating country which in time turns into Shropshire.

Staffordshire is not famed for its notable churches, neither can we find many features which are peculiar to the county alone, yet there are several really splendid churches if only we hunt them out and many more which are less noteworthy but have tremendous character. In all, about 120 medieval churches await our visit, although this is an area where so many are locked. The lovely cathedral at Lichfield (often underrated because it underwent thorough 19th century restoration) is one of England's most memorable – its three spires, sumptuous west front and its glorious EE and Dec architecture make it a real individual, and in a fine setting. Premier Norman work awaits the visitor to Tutbury and Stafford St Chad, EE at Coppenhall, Breward and the superb tower at Weston on Trent, glorious Dec at Clifton Campville, Checkley, Norbury and Tamworth and Perp at Penkridge and Barton under Needwood.

Post-medieval churches (about 250 in all) are well represented and at Ingestre, St Modwen Burton upon Trent, Marchington, Patshull and Elkstone we see 17th and 18th century Classical architecture, whilst Broughton, Stone and Cotton have Gothic work of the period. The Gothic Revival gave the county several monumental churches. No church lover should miss Pugin's magnificent St Giles Cheadle (RC), Bodley's Hoar Cross and St Chad Burton upon Trent, Norman Shaw's All Saints Leek, Oldrid Scott's fine church at Newborough or Street's lovely church at Denstone.

ALSTONEFIELD. A picturesque village in beautiful Peak District countryside, with a delightful church, steeped in beauty and interest. St Peter's chancel arch is Norman (as is the south doorway) and most medieval periods are represented here. The 1630s woodwork will be remembered too – the two-decker pulpit, the Cotton family pew, the other box-pews, the lectern and the western screen in the south aisle.

Further south and still near beautiful Dovedale is *Ilam*, where Scott's restoration of 1855, Watts' memorial chapel of 1831 and part of the shrine of St Bertelin add to the interest of Holy Cross church, which may have stood since Saxon times, also St Bartholomew's *Blore*, where lovely Jacobean woodwork may be admired.

BARTON UNDER NEEDWOOD. John Taylor – sometime Chaplain to Henry VIII – built this church from c1517 onwards. St James' is remarkable because it was built in one piece (although the aisles were cleverly widened in the 1860s) and it is a lovely example of late Perp which has great unity of style. It is a large building, with an embattled exterior, culminating in a polygonal apse, where an original 16th century crucifixion scene is surrounded by glass of the 1860s.

BREWOOD. St Mary and St Chad's is a large and venerable church, with a fine EE chancel, Dec windows in the aisles (although the south aisle was given a new character by Street in 1878–80) and a sturdy Perp tower with a lofty spire (168 ft). Inside are fine arcades, superb proportions, a reredos of 1911 by Caroe and four splendid Giffard monuments in the chancel. That to Sir John (1556) and his two wives, also shows their one son, four daughters, and 13 little babies in swaddling clothes.

BROUGHTON. A most fascinating and atmospheric little church, on its own, opposite the attractive black-and-white hall. Built as a private chapel in 1630–4 and made into a parish church in 1711, this gothic building has delightful characteristics like a font set in a recess at the west end, a window above the chancel arch, box-pews which are remarkably tall and the glass in the east window which is earlier than the building itself. This shows members of the Broughton family. St Peter's is a real character.

CHECKLEY. A wonderful Norman tower here at St Mary's, and a glorious Dec chancel, with superb windows. Amongst the treasures inside are a Norman font, stalls of c1535 and a fine array of 14th century glass in some of the windows which grace this stately chancel. There is a 17th century roof and Comper designed the south chapel screen, the

High Altar and a window showing St George.

Leigh has a fine cruciform church of All Saints of 1846 by Thomas Johnson of Lichfield, with good Dec architecture, rich floor tiles and glass by 14th century craftsmen, also by Morris and Burne Jones.

CLIFTON CAMPVILLE.   St Andrew's is perhaps the county's most notable church, its soaring spire (189 ft) guarded by pinnacles and flying buttresses and forming an elegant landmark in this land of meadows in the county's south-eastern extremity. A monumental building with fine Dec architecture and stately proportions, which grew during the first half of the 14th century. There is so much to enjoy here, including the 15th century rood-screen, the chapel screens (one 14th century and the other of 1634), 14th century stalls with misericords, a 14th century painting of Christ in Majesty, with two donors on their knees, a brass of c1360, the superb monument of Sir John Vernon (1545) and much else besides.

ECCLESHALL.   A noble town church of the 13th century in a pleasant market town. Holy Trinity's arcades are EE and Perp craftsmen added the clerestory, the upper stage of the stately tower and the vaulted porch. Street restored the building in 1866–9, Basil Champneys designed the reredos in 1898, and Caroe designed the organ case, also the screen and altar for the Lady Chapel, in 1931. To this mixture of high-quality work, we can add glass by Clayton & Bell. The Bishops of Lichfield lived at the castle here and some are commemorated by monuments in the church.

Chebsey has an interesting church of All Saints in a fine position, whilst *Slindon*'s St Chad's church of 1894, by Basil Champneys, is delightful of its period.

FORTON.   A charming spot, not far from the hall, for this distinctive church of All Saints, whose low and sturdy pinnacled medieval tower contrasts with the south face of the nave and chancel, which are Classical work of 1723. The medieval east wall and north aisle have survived. The arcade of 1723 has Tuscan columns and semicircular arches and the font and pulpit are also 18th century. Here also we see the effigies of Sir Thomas Skrymsher (1633) and his wife, fashioned in alabaster on their monument.

Another Skrymsher may be seen in *Norbury*'s lovely Dec St Peter's church (with a tower of 1759) also other good monuments and much of interest. Superb Norman, EE and Perp architecture awaits us at *Gnosall*'s cruciform church of St Laurence.

Here is a classical country church at Patshull, built in 1743 and designed by James Gibbs.

HAMSTALL RIDWARE. The setting is unforgettable, with the gaunt 16th century brick watch tower and the other remains of Hamstall Hall. A haunting place, and a church of great character, with a 14th century tower and spire and a long clerestoried body. An exterior to be enjoyed as a whole in its setting. Inside, St Michael's reredos has medieval painted panels with scenes from Our Lord's life, there are parclose screens to the side chapels, traceried bench-ends and a monument to Richard and John Cotton (1502), also some medieval glass. The west wall of the nave is Norman.

Mavesyn Ridware has an odd but fascinating St Nicholas' church, whose tower and north aisle are medieval and the rest a square preaching auditorium of 1782, which has real atmosphere and some interesting memorials.

HOAR CROSS. Here in the heart of rural Staffordshire rises, in all its majesty and splendour, a wonderful shrine, created between 1872–6 (with later additions) to the designs of G.F. Bodley, as Mrs Meynell Ingram's memorial to her husband. Here at Holy Angels Bodley has created the glory and dignity of a church of the 14th century. Outside, the solemn cruciform church is presided over by a tall and stately central tower. The noble interior, bathed in subdued light, gives us a glimpse of heaven on earth, through the richly coloured glass of Burlison & Grylls. Here we view, through rich and sumptuous screenwork, a vaulted chancel with its wonderful stalls, stately organ-case and magnificently adorned High Altar and reredos. There are so many lovely things to see here – the tall font-cover, the quiet chapels, the statues and aids to devotion, the tombs of the foundress and her husband, and much else – but above all, this 'modern' church is such a Holy Place, as all our churches should be.

Newborough All Saints' church (1901) is also very striking Gothic Revival work, by John Oldrid Scott. Its octagonal tower and spire rise for 120 ft. *Hanbury* St Werburgh's church, with its lovely position and stately tower, has a good selection of monuments.

INGESTRE. The great house of the Chetwynds and remarkable St Mary's church of 1676 stand near to each other in a sequestered spot. Wonderful Classical architecture here, and almost certainly the work of Sir Christopher Wren (although we cannot prove it). Externally we admire the bold west tower and a building of Classical correctness. Inside is splendour, with wonderful plaster ceilings, glorious woodcarving in the screen (surmounted by the Royal Arms), the pulpit and tester, also the panelled chancel and reredos. This memorable period-piece also contains several Chetwynd memorials.

LICHFIELD. When you have seen the cathedral, do go to St Mary's and admire Street's grand spire and Fowler of Louth's church. Go inside to visit the Heritage Centre here and discover how a great Victorian church can be given a new lease of life. There is EE work and much of interest at St Chad's, whilst St Michael's has a medieval tower and spire and its elevated position affords good views over the city.

PENKRIDGE. The grand embattled and pinnacled exterior of the large church of St Michael looks predominantly Perp, but closer inspection reveals earlier work, particularly in the lovely Dec east window. Inside are 13th century arcades, lofty and noble proportions and a great deal of interest. The chancel screen is wrought-ironwork, made in 1778. The medieval stalls in the collegiate chancel have misericords and the font was fashioned in 1688. The monuments to the Littleton family are well worth travelling miles to see. Above all, this red sandstone church needs to be enjoyed as a whole, both outside and inside.

Coppenhall St Lawrence's church is a small and unspoilt piece of EE architecture, which is well worth visiting.

RUSHTON SPENCER.   A real character this – so distinctive and so very attractive, with its quaint saddleback timber belfry and its dormer windows. St Lawrence's stands alone in the fields, along a track and well away from its village. What we see outside is mostly of the 17th and 19th centuries, but inside we are aware of the original timber-framed medieval church. A narrow north aisle has been added outside the original timber posts. There are sturdy tiebeams, one of which supports the later west gallery, also a commodious squire's pew, a 17th century pulpit, several hatchments and much which makes this little church ooze charm and curiosity.

Here we are not very far from *Leek*, with its fine medieval church of St Edward the Confessor and Norman Shaw's beautiful church of All Saints (1885–7), which is a 'must'.

STAFFORD.   Two lovely medieval churches await us in the centre of this busy town. One is regal and cruciform St Mary's, with its elegant octagonal central tower, where good EE, Dec and Perp architecture blend superbly. In its spacious interior, a fine Perp roof shelters a fascinating Norman font. West of this church are the interesting foundations of the lost Saxon church of St Bertelin. To enjoy a really superb Norman church, we must go to St Chad's, which was restored (1874) by Sir Gilbert Scott, but delights us with original Norman arcades, chancel arch and chancel wall-arcading. Much has happened to this cruciform church since the Normans first built it, but its core is certainly the genuine article!

TUTBURY.   A very distinctive little town overlooking the river Dove and Derbyshire, with a ruined castle and an unusual church (with a low tower on the south side) presiding over the town from above. St Mary's priory church, founded in the 1080s, has left us some Norman architecture of astonishing quality. We see this in the western portal, with its truly enormous doorway, in the south doorway, with a boar-hunt portrayed on its lintel and in the splendid nave, with its sturdy Norman piers. Street restored the church and created its present east end in 1866.

Rolleston has a mainly Dec church, St Mary's, with excellent Kempe glass and several monuments to the Mosley family, whilst *Marchington*'s delightful church of St Peter (by R. Trubshaw, 1742) is a period-piece of great charm.

SUFFOLK

The infinite variety of Suffolk's churches ranges from the might and grandeur of Long Melford, Lavenham, Southwold and Stoke by Nayland to the rustic charm of tiny unspoilt shrines like Badley, Withersdale and Thornham Parva with a host of permutations in between! Flint is the major building material, either as flint rubble or knapped flints which expose their shiny cores, which are often used with dressed stone to form the exquisite 'flushwork' panelling which adorns many Suffolk exteriors. Although work of all periods is well represented here, Suffolk churches excel in their 15th century Perpendicular architecture, which predominates. Here we discover large, light and airy interiors, with grand vistas and stately windows, as the designers went as far as they could to create walls of glass. This period produced splendid towers, clerestories and porches, which are masterpieces of craftsmanship. Earlier periods produced Suffolk's 42 round towers, of which more than half are of Saxon origin and the rest mostly Norman. It seems that the lack of stone for corners did not deter these early builders. This is also a county where Tudor brick is used in towers, porches and elsewhere.

Woodwork (mostly of the 15th century) abounds in Suffolk churches and may be enjoyed in a host of fine roofs, culminating in the lovely hammerbeam roofs which are plentiful here, in exquisitely carved bench-ends and in about 150 screens, of which 60 or more are just about complete and several are still painted with Apostles and saints. With pulpits, Suffolk comes into its own in the 17th century, of which about 117 examples remain. Suffolk fonts represent several periods, but the majority follow the typical East Anglian 15th century pattern, with the Evangelists and other emblems around the bowl and lions, or wild and hairy 'wodewoses' round the stem. Suffolk possesses 14 of the beautiful Seven Sacrament fonts of the period. The county is rich in monuments and over 100 of its churches possess brasses.

Sadly space does not allow the following notes to do real justice to Suffolk's array of churches, although as many as possible have been at least mentioned. Every one is of interest and should be visited.

BADLEY. A remote and unspoilt little gem (RCF) in a meadow, a mile down an unmade road. St Mary's tower has a Tudor brick top and a great Perp west window. Inside, beneath a king-post roof, are 15th century benches and other woodwork, also 17th century box-pews and pulpit – all mellowed to a silvery grey. Unforgettably quaint and rustic. Memorials to the Poleys who lived at the nearby Hall.

Needham Market St John the Baptist's has one of the most amazing 15th century roofs in any English church, whilst *Combs* has a fine (but remote) church of St Mary with glorious 15th century glass. *Barking* St Mary's church is full of treasures and is a 'must' to visit.

BARSHAM. A pretty pastoral setting for this little shrine of Holy Trinity, with its Saxon round tower and unique east window of lozenge trellis-work. Much 17th century woodwork (including the screen) and remarkably tasteful early 20th century restoration by F.C. Eden, with much glass by him. Devotional Anglo-Catholic interior of great character, wonderfully made to live again after a fire in 1979.

Nearby *Beccles* has a vast barn-like church of St Michael, with two splendid porches and a massive (97 ft) detached bell-tower. *Bungay's* two churches are both worth seeing. Holy Trinity has an early round tower and St Mary's (RCF) is fine Perp, with a spectacular 90 ft tower.

BLYTHBURGH. Perhaps the most lovable of the great Suffolk churches. Holy Trinity is glorious Perp inside and out, with great windows, superb clerestory and parapets and fine original doors. It dominates the heathland and the Blyth estuary and looks marvellous floodlit. The interior is lofty, light and largely unspoilt, with soaring arcades and fine vistas. Long unbroken angel roof with original colour, intriguing bench-ends with the Seven Deadly Sins and the seasons of the year, stall-fronts, screenwork, lectern of c1450, Hopton Monument, Jack O'Clock of c1652 and much else in this wonderful 128 ft long church.

Southwold's mighty church of St Edmund is one of Suffolk's best (100 ft tower), with roof, screen, flushwork, etc of the highest quality. St Andrew's *Walberswick* (95 ft tower) is a fragment of a once mighty building, *Wenhaston* St Peter's has a rare and beautiful Doom painting and St Andrew's *Bramfield* has one of Suffolk's finest screens (also a detached round tower and much else).

BRIGHTWELL. A tiny church in an idyllic setting, St John the Baptist's is c1300, but was remodelled in 1656–7. Its little brick tower rests upon a massive Tuscan arch. Lovely 14th century font with 17th century cover, also a splendid 14th century door with sanctuary ring. The atmospheric interior has been made beautiful in the 20th century.

Nearby St Peter's *Levington* also has great atmosphere, All Saints'

Waldringfield and All Saints' *Hemley* have Tudor brick towers, St Mary's *Martlesham* has a lovely setting, and much of interest, whilst *Kesgrave*'s tiny EE All Saints' church was tastefully enlarged and transformed in 1980 to the designs of Derek Woodley of Felixstowe.

BURY ST EDMUNDS. Two gigantic churches stand within yards of each other. St James' is now the cathedral and St Mary's, which is 213 ft long, has a magnificent Perp exterior and wonderful 15th century roofs inside, which shelter so many items of beauty and interest. St John's (by W. Ranger, 1841), with its 178 ft spire, is of 'white' Suffolk brick and has a devotional Anglo-Catholic interior.

Within a few miles of Bury are All Saints *Hawstead*, with its array of monuments, St Nicholas' *Rushbrooke*, with its unforgettable interior and St Nicholas *Little Saxham*, with one of our best Norman round towers.

CAVENDISH. A lovely picture-postcard setting across the green towards St Mary's tower with big staircase-turret and beautiful clerestory with flushwork. Full of interest inside and we are immediately aware of its enormous east window. Amongst the treasures here are two lecterns – a 15th century brass eagle and a 16th century wooden one – also a sumptuous 15th century south chapel reredos (restored by Comper) which came from Athelston Riley's London home.

Nearby is the lovely market town of *Clare* and there is another 16th century lectern in its glorious church of St Peter and St Paul. Panoramic views may be enjoyed from *Glemsford*'s high-set St Mary's churchyard – and another wonderful Suffolk church.

COTTON. St Andrew's is a large and gloriously rural church of great interest and character. Superb 14th century work in the chancel, the bold tower (with unusual western arch) and in the sumptuous south doorway with traceried doors. Inside, look for the other old door, carved into a bench-end. The 15th century gave it a noble clerestory and a superb double hammerbeam roof. The pulpit and rails are 17th century.

Bacton St Mary's church also has a fine clerestory and roof, and traces of a Doom painting. St Bartholomew's *Finningham's* great treasure is its medieval font cover, and *Westhorpe* St Margaret's is one of those delightfully devotional and unspoilt gems with a list of interesting features as long as your arm!

COVEHITHE. The vast ruin of what was a huge late 15th century church, with lofty 14th century tower (RCF). A tiny thatched church replaced this (built inside the ruins) in 1672. St Andrew's contains the font, 15th century pulpit and some bench-ends from the old church. This is indeed a church within a church – it is unforgettable.

Hereabouts is *Wrentham*'s fine church of St Nicholas, St Lawrence's *South Cove*, with its rood-door painted with a 15th century St Michael, St Michael's *Benacre*, with its Georgian interior and hatchments and *Kessingland* St Edmund's soaring 98 ft tower.

COWLINGE. Largely Decorated architecture here, and a brick tower of 1733. St Margaret's unspoilt and atmospheric interior offers us a 14th century crown-post roof, a rood-screen of c1400, a 15th century parclose screen, squints, old glass and a huge monument (1747) by Scheemakers.

Go northwards to discover the treasures in *Lydgate*'s delightful church and to admire *Ousden*'s Norman St Peter's church, with its central tower; then on to St Mary's *Dalham* and All Saints *Gazeley*.

CRETINGHAM. This must be everybody's ideal small Suffolk church. St Peter's is a simple and atmospheric exterior – but the flint tower is nevertheless very lovely and it has a most adorable interior, with hammerbeam roof, Royal Arms of Charles II, box-pews, three-decker pulpit, three-sided Communion rails and a pretty monument. Lovely!

What an area for churches here – and most of them little known. Space does not permit what they deserve, but just go to All Saints *Brandeston*, St Mary's *Framsden*, St Andrew's *Kettleburgh*, St Andrew and St Eustachius *Hoo*, All Saints *Easton*, St Mary's *Letheringham* and St Mary's *Earl Soham* and you will soon see why they are mentioned!

DENNINGTON. Incomparable Dennington – St Mary's is a treasure house which has so much. Wonderful late Dec architecture in the chancel, medieval two-storeyed sacristy, noble tower of c1383, seven medieval doors and an interior which is unrivalled anywhere for its features and treasures. There are sturdy medieval roofs, which shelter 76 bench-ends (exquisitely carved and all different), a 15th century font-cover, parclose screens complete with their lofts, 17th and 18th century box-pews, and a three-decker pulpit.

Unique in England is the Sciapod on one of the bench-ends, also the lovely pyx-canopy of c1500. So we go on to admire the massive ironbound chest, the Peter's Pence box, the scholars' sand-table (also unique) and the wonderful alabaster effigies of Lord and Lady Bardolph – and that is just for starters. Lovely 20th century work here too, designed by Randoll Blacking in the 1950s and by Eric Sandon in the 1960s.

What an area for churches hereabouts. They are all of well above average interest and every one should be visited. There is *Framlingham*, with its wonderful Perp St Michael's church containing many monuments to the Howards (the Dukes of Norfolk). There is St John the Baptist's *Badingham*, with its hammerbeam roof, superb Seven Sacrament font, and much else, also St Lawrence's *Brundish* (brasses and furnishings), St Mary's *Worlingworth* (of premier interest and importance), All Saints *Laxfield* (superb 100 ft tower, Seven Sacrament font, furnishings) and St Ethelbert's *Tannington* (bench-ends, roof, atmosphere).

DENSTON. Tiny village, but a most ambitious 15th century church of St Nicholas which is largely unaltered and when we enter it is like stepping back into the past. Roofs, screens, rood-beam, stalls and glass all survive from before the Reformation, also the lovely Seven Sacrament font. The pulpit is Elizabethan, the Communion rails and some box-pews are 18th century, there are shrouded Tudor effigies and brasses also, but above all it is the whole, all put together, which is so memorable.

All Saints *Stansfield* has a fine tower, St Mary's *Hawkedon*, with its lovely benches, is set beside a large green and *Wickhambrook* has a church of All Saints which is full of character.

ELVEDEN. A remarkable estate church at the edge of its park. The small Norman and 14th century church of St Andrew and St Patrick, with tower of 1421 (restored by the Maharajah Duleep Singh in 1869) was given a sumptuous new nave and chancel on the north side, with splendid woodwork in roofs and benches and a glorious alabaster reredos. This lavish work was designed by W.D. Caroe.

Eriswell St Laurence's has beautiful EE and Dec work and an interior of great beauty and interest. *Icklingham* has two churches, of which All Saints (RCF) is thatched, unspoilt and of premier importance, especially for its Dec architecture, its array of medieval encaustic tiles and its delectably unspoilt interior. *Euston*'s parkland church of St Genevieve shows superb Classical work of 1676.

FELIXSTOWE. The medieval churches of St Peter and St Paul Felixstowe and St Mary Walton were greatly altered in the 19th century. St John's, with its prominent spire, is a fine building by Sir A.W. Blomfield (1895–9) and completed by his son with the tower in 1914. Seaside High Church here, with dim and devotional interior of great beauty. Screen by Gerald Cogswell; reredos and much glass by J. Powell & Sons. St Andrew's is Suffolk Perp developed to its natural conclusion in concrete by Hilda Mason and Raymond Erith in 1929–31. It has a light and spacious interior which is Conservative Evangelical, with twin pulpits and a 16th century style Holy Table. A distinctive and most interesting church, built to thank God for the rejection of the 1928 Prayer Book!

Nearby *Trimley* has two churches, St Martin's and St Mary's, in one churchyard – both worth seeing.

FRESSINGFIELD. St Peter and St Paul's is an impressively-situated church with a handsome porch (c1420) and an ornate sanctus-bell turret. Grand 15th century roofs inside and a complete set of benches (c1470), with 36 carved ends. There is a fine ironbound chest, also a portrait of Archbishop Sancroft (died 1693) who was a native of this village.

Nearby *Wingfield* has the glorious St Andrew's church of the de la Poles, with their superb monuments. St Mary's *Cratfield* has one of our finest Seven Sacrament fonts and amongst the features in *Metfield* church of St John the Baptist is the canopy of honour over the former rood. Above all, do find *Withersdale*'s adorable unspoilt wooden-turreted Norman church of St Mary Magdalene, with its lovely atmospheric interior – so rustic and so memorable.

GIPPING. The exquisite 15th century chapel of the Tyrell family, idyllically set and with beautiful Perp windows and flushwork motifs. Its bright interior has 15th and 18th century furnishings (including altar and frontal of the latter period) and the east window is filled with glass of c1494–1513.

Nearby *Mendlesham* has an amazing church, St Mary's, with a glorious tower which is a treasure house of beautiful things, some from other churches now disused. Over its porch is a unique parish armoury. Ancient and modern combine here to create a beautiful and devotional shrine which is much prayed in.

GISLINGHAM. Simple in plan, but large (120 ft long), St Mary's has a superb double hammerbeam roof, sturdy brick tower of 1639 and embattled 15th century porch. The interior is a treasure house, with 15th century font and benches, 17th century font-cover, 18th century west gallery, box-pews and three-decker pulpit and amazing medieval glass, including early pictures of British wild flowers.

North of Gislingham is *Burgate*, whose Dec church of St Mary contains a magnificent military brass to Sir William Burgate (1409) and his lady.

HADLEIGH. The 15th century Guildhall, Tudor brick Deanery Tower and the massive flint church of St Mary make a picturesque group. The 135 ft lead-covered spire of c1300 carries a 13th century clock bell.

Sturdy Perp at Hitcham, with venerable flint walls and a fine porch.

The big-boned church (163 ft by 64 ft) has a wide and spacious interior, with a good chancel roof, 14th century font (tall 1925 cover by Charles Spooner), 15th century chapel screens, bench-end with the wolf guarding the head of St Edmund, and a palimpsest brass to Rowland Taylor, martyred in 1555.

Nearby is the picture-postcard village of *Kersey*, which is dominated by its hilltop St Mary's church, of great interest, also St Mary's *Boxford*, with its two grand porches and remarkable font-cover, but do find quiet, little known All Saints *Shelley*, because that is extra-special.

HESSETT.   St Ethelbert's is a church of tremendous interest, with a noble exterior graced by fine 15th century stonework and much of beauty inside, including medieval roofs, font, benches and stalls, a fine screen and a medieval sacristy. The wall-paintings include St Christopher, the Seven Deadly Sins and Christ of the Trades. There is much 15th century glass.

IPSWICH.   Twelve medieval churches here, of which six are still in parochial use. Grandest of all is St Margaret's, with its lavish clerestory and fine porch, also one of Suffolk's most wonderful double hammer-beam roofs, given painted panels in the 17th century. The dockland church of St Peter, associated with Cardinal Wolsey, has a bold 93 ft tower and some good 14th century work, also a massive square font-bowl (c1100) of black Tournai marble. There are Saxon carvings at St Nicholas', also much else of interest, whilst St Mary at the Elms, with its beautiful Tudor brick tower, has a Norman doorway and possibly also its door. The Anglo-Catholic interior here is much prayed in and the Acton monument is worth seeing. The 'civic church' of St Mary le Tower is mostly a stately gothic rebuild (1850–70) by R.M. Phipson, with a 176 ft spire. Inside there is much to see of the 19th century and earlier. Nearby St Lawrence has a fine 97 ft tower and down in the heart of Dockland is St Mary at the Quay (RCF) a complete Perp late 15th century church with an amazing double hammerbeam roof. The finest of the later churches is St Bartholomew's – a lofty towerless Anglo-Catholic shrine by Charles Spooner, consecrated in 1895. Its grand and spacious interior is furnished upon a large, lavish, but very tasteful scale and style.

KEDINGTON. St Peter and St Paul's is a memorable church for atmosphere and furnishings, untouched by Victorian alteration. Dignified exterior, with good Dec chancel. Inside it is a church-crawler's Aladdin's Cave, with 16th century roofs, medieval benches, and 17th–19th century box-pews, with children's seats in tiers each side of the c1750 singers gallery. A wonderful three-decker pulpit stands opposite the commodious and canopied Manor Pew (1610) which incorporates medieval screenwork. The present screen is of 1619, the three-sided rails 1707, but over the reredos is a Saxon stone crucifix. The incredible array of Barnardiston monuments of the 16th, 17th and 18th centuries (also several hatchments) have caused this church to be called the Westminster Abbey of Suffolk!

Hundon, nearby, has a venerable church of All Saints which was refitted after a fire in 1914 – all very tastefully done by Detmar Blow. *Little Wratting*'s tiny Holy Trinity church is Saxon and Norman, with much of interest. Further north are *Great* and *Little Bradley* (St Mary's and All Saints) and *Great* and *Little Thurlow* (All Saints and St Peter's), all lovely churches.

KETTLEBASTON. A tiny village set high, with endearing and atmospheric St Mary's church, where we see Norman work (including a square font), lovely 14th century windows, sedilia and piscina and one of the most devotional and colourful Anglo-Catholic interiors to be found in any of our village churches. The screen and reredos are by Ernest Geldart, the priest-architect. Again it is the feel of everything put together which moves us here.

Bildeston and *Hitcham* have fine churches (St Mary's and All Saints) and another Norman font awaits us at *Preston St Mary*. St Peter's *Monks Eleigh* and All Saints *Chelsworth* are in pretty villages with much to reward the church enthusiast, but it is St Mary's church *Brent Eleigh* with its marvellous 17th and 18th century furnishings and 14th century wall-paintings which will really remain in the memory.

LAVENHAM. This was a 'wool' town and hence many fine half timbered houses remain. The glorious church has so much written about it so suffice it here to mention just a couple of its glories – the huge tower 141 ft high and its nave with fine clerestory (Perp) and chancel (Dec).

LONG MELFORD. Long it most certainly is! Three miles of village street and 268 ft of village church! A superb situation for this giant amongst churches, which is regal and of cathedral proportions. Holy Trinity is Suffolk Perp at its very best. The exterior is a mass of flushwork and great windows, with a large, three-gabled eastern Lady Chapel. The brick tower was encased in flint by Bodley in 1903. A vast, long, light and airy interior with a long unbroken arch-braced cambered tiebeam 15th century roof. The north aisle windows display an amazing array of 15th century glass (find the three rabbits). There is so much here.

LOWESTOFT. England's most easterly point. Much fresh air here, which may be why its mighty parish church of St Margaret was built well to the north-west of the town. It is a beauty and is mostly elegant Perp, although the tower is older. It stretches 184 ft in length and its tower has a very tall and slender copper spire. A fine interior, with handsome proportions and much of beauty and interest, including a lectern of 1504 and early 20th century work by Comper. Do find St Peter's Kirkley on the south side of the town – a grand flint church by the local J.L. Clemence, begun in 1874, keeping the medieval tower. The interior is impressive and is noted for its splendid wrought iron screen-work, font-cover and clock all by Hart & Peard. The painted reredos, by Canon Gordon Roe, was installed in 1927.

Above Lowestoft, the Lothingland peninsula juts into Norfolk. The Lothingland churches are all worth a visit, including St Mary's *Somerleyton* (screen), St Mary's *Blundeston* (round tower and 14th century work), St Mary's *Ashby* (lonely, thatched and just lovely in every way), St Margaret's *Herringfleet* (Saxon tower and fine glass) and glorious St John the Baptist's *Lound* (enriched by rood-loft, font-cover and organ-case by Comper, who restored the church and turned it into one of the most memorable interiors in the county). *Fritton* St Edmund's church is a treasure house of ancient things, although it went into Norfolk for some reason!

MILDENHALL. St Mary's enormous church (168 ft long) has high quality work of many periods from the 13th century onwards. Its mighty (112 ft) tower is seen for miles across the Fens. Most glorious of all inside are the roofs, not only for their wonderful construction, but for their amazing wealth of carving – the north aisle roof being particularly outstanding and worthy of careful examination.

There is good 14th century work (including glass) at St Mary's *Barton Mills* and a trip to St Mary's *Lakenheath* (via Eriswell) is worthwhile; here are superb benches, a fine 13th century font, and another superb roof.

ORFORD. An atmospheric little town, with a sturdy 14th century church of St Bartholomew whose tower, having been long in ruins, was partly rebuilt between 1962 and 1971. The ruined chancel is Norman and has remains of lovely Norman arcades. The lofty interior is full of interest, including a 15th century font, three bells on the floor, 18th century woodwork and eleven brasses. A good restoration here by J.T. Micklethwaite (1897–1900), also screen and stalls by S. Tugwell (1921).

Delightful churches in this area include All Saints *Sudbourne* (Norman work and monument), St Botolph's *Iken* (wonderful site, Saxon carving and associations with St Botolph), St Peter's *Chillesford* (setting, tower of coralline crag and atmospheric interior) and St Michael's *Tunstall* (fine tower, 18th century furnishings and remarkable graffiti).

POLSTEAD. One of Suffolk's most beautiful settings for a church, and here we see the county's only medieval stone spire. St Mary's church is a real character, with Norman arcades and clerestory windows, incorporating 12th century brickwork. This atmospheric interior has a king-post roof and some good 17th century woodwork, also brasses.

Across the valley is *Stoke by Nayland*, where we see one of Suffolk's great churches. St Mary's is 168 ft long and its magnificent tower is 120 ft high. It is full of treasures.

RAMSHOLT. An idyllically set church, remote and overlooking the Deben estuary. All Saints' round tower (made to look oval by later buttresses) has stood for a thousand years. Its humble and rustic interior is furnished with box-pews and a two-decker pulpit of c1857.

REDGRAVE.   St Mary the Virgin is a substantial church, well away from its village with a grand 14th century chancel, fine Perp clerestory and an 18th century tower. There are important monuments here, including two by Nicholas Stone and one of 1710 showing Sir John Holt, seated and wearing his long wig.

Rickinghall Superior (RCF) and Inferior both have interesting churches (both St Mary's), whilst Botesdale has a fascinating chapel of ease, attached to a house. St Mary's Wortham has the shell of England's largest round tower and St Peter's Palgrave has a superb hammerbeam roof.

RUMBURGH.   A former priory church in a beautiful setting, with a curious wooden belfry stage to its massive rectangular EE tower. Inside St Michael and St Felix's is a medieval screen, 17th century pulpit and some old benches, also bags of character.

In the neighbourhood are the six South Elmhams and four Ilketshalls – all named after saints and providing ten little churches to occupy a day's church-crawling.

STONHAM ASPAL.   A large village church, St Mary and St Lambert's, with a wooden top stage to its south porch tower, made in 1742 to accommodate the ten bells. A magnificent 15th century stone-faced clerestory here and much of interest inside, including medieval roofs to aisles and chancel, 15th century bench-ends and some fascinating medieval glass. A judicious restoration took place here in 1871–3 under the direction of E.C. Hakewill, when Lavers, Barraud & Westlake made the east window, showing over 60 figures.

St Mary's Earl Stonham and Stonham Parva (RCF) both have handsome towers and magnificent hammerbeam roofs, and much else to see. The tiny church of All Saints at Crowfield has a medieval timber-framed chancel.

STOWLANGTOFT.   St George's church is simple in plan but lofty and impressive in structure, all built c1370–1400. Outside are tall windows, fine gargoyles, an elegant tower and a flushwork porch. Inside are fine proportions, with splendid roofs, font and array of benches. The chancel stalls are complete and are probably the finest in East Anglia.

Pakenham St Mary's church is cruciform, with an octagonal top to its tower. St Andrew's Norton is full of treasures, including misericord stalls showing a lad having his bottom smacked, old glass and a lovely font. All Saints Great Ashfield has one of Suffolk's grandest pulpits, dated 1619.

SUDBURY. This busy market town has three magnificent medieval churches – each one large and full of interest. All Saints' has a stately Perp exterior, with a beautiful tower, two beautifully traceried medieval doors, good roofs, a medieval pulpit and chapel screens. St Gregory's also has a fine tower and elegant Perp windows. The roofs are splendid here also, but the real treasures are the misericord stalls and the superb medieval font-cover. St Peter's (RCF) dominates the Market Hill and again we must stand back to admire a magnificent exterior. More lovely traceried doors here and fine roofs. Butterfield restored this church in 1854–8 and Bodley designed its handsome reredos in 1898. There is good 19th century glass by John Hardman.

THORNHAM PARVA. St Mary's is a tiny thatched gem in a meadow (even the truncated tower is thatched). One of Suffolk's smallest, but one of the most interesting of all its churches. Here we see craftsmanship of most periods from Saxon times to the present day in a wealth of features. Superb wall-paintings inside, also a 15th century screen, 14th century chest and, above all, the beautiful retable (c1300) with its exquisitely painted figures. There is engraved glass by Lawrence Whistler and Sir Basil Spence (who designed Coventry Cathedral) is buried in the churchyard. A prize example of 'Small is Beautiful'.

Not far away is the magnificent church at *Eye*, which is also one of Suffolk's finest. The tower (101 ft) is covered in flushwork panelling and inside we marvel at a host of beautiful things – most wonderful of all being the 15th century screen with its painted panels, which was given a magnificent new loft and rood by Sir Ninian Comper in 1929.

UFFORD. Lovely approach along an attractive street towards its noble tower. St Mary's is a real treasure house, with 11th century herringbone masonry in the nave wall and a fine Perp south porch. The interior here is wonderful – lovely roofs and benches, Comper reredos and window in the south chapel, exquisite adornments and aids to devotion. But we come here especially to stand back in amazement and behold the most beautiful font-cover in the world. Here it rests, still fulfilling its original purpose – a mass of 15th century woodcarving, rising 18 ft above the font.

Woodbridge St Mary's is one of Suffolk's most spectacular Perp churches, with its breathtaking 108 ft tower, its glorious flushwork porch and its lofty interior, with a Seven Sacrament font and glass in the east window by Martin Travers, amongst many other items of beauty and interest. *Wickham Market* All Saints' church must be visited, if only to enjoy its curiously positioned octagonal tower and tall spire. There is as much to interest us in the exterior here as there is inside.

WESTHALL. There is so much to admire in this remote but truly wonderful church. The original and superb western portal of the Norman St Andrew's church can be seen from beneath the tower, which was added c1300. Then a new nave and chancel were built on the north side. The chancel has grand windows of c1330. A treasure house inside, with 14th and 15th century arch-braced roofs, a Seven Sacrament font with its original colour, a screen-base with 16 painted panels, a Jacobean pulpit, and much else, not least the atmosphere here.

WILBY. We are drawn by the tall and elegant Perp tower of St Mary's and through a beautiful 15th century flushwork porch into a glorious church where, beneath medieval roofs to nave and aisle, we may admire a fine East Anglian font, a set of 15th century benches carved with the Sacraments, the Acts of Mercy and the Seven Deadly Sins, an elaborate Jacobean pulpit with sounding-board, a St Christopher wall-painting and a great deal more.

All Saints *Stradbroke*'s 100 ft tower guards a church with good Dec and Perp work, although much restored in the days when J.C. Ryle was vicar (he was later Bishop of Liverpool). St Mary's *Horham* has a beautiful Suffolk tower and much to see inside, whilst tiny St Peter's *Athelington* surprises us with a lovely set of 15th century benches.

WOOLPIT. The elegant tower and spire of St Mary's remind us of Lincolnshire, but they are in fact by Phipson (1854). In the stately exterior we see good Dec windows, a superb Perp clerestory and a truly magnificent south porch, faced with stone. Inside we marvel at one of the county's best double hammerbeam roofs, also a lovely set of benches, a 16th century lectern and a Perp screen.

Elmswell St John the Baptist's church has a commanding position which sets off its superb tower. St Nicholas *Rattlesden* is beautifully set in its village; this fine church has good architecture and many treasures. St Mary's *Wetherden* is another treasure house, but dear little *Shelland*, so simple and rustic, captivates everybody. Dedicated to King Charles the Martyr, it was reordered in 1767 and most of its furnishings from that date remain, also a barrel organ of c1820.

SURREY

Surrey has some of the grandest scenery in southern England – more spectacular in places even than Kent. The wonderful Surrey Hills and valleys; the North Downs to the east, Box Hill and Leith Hill with their panoramic views, the Hog's Back and the spectacular scenery around Hindhead, are some of the better-known spots. Finding the churches will reveal many others as we explore the lanes and discover so many villages which are beauty spots in themselves, and old towns like Reigate, Godalming and Farnham.

True, many little rustic Surrey churches have been altered and enlarged out of all recognition by the Victorians, but still Surrey has so much to offer and so much of the Victorian work is of considerable beauty and the product of architects of national repute, like J.L. Pearson, G.E. Street (who built the lovely church at Holmbury St Mary, where his second wife is buried and where he was churchwarden) and especially Henry Woodyer, who lies buried near the little church at Grafham, which he designed and paid for.

There are about 110 medieval churches here and what gems some of these are, from Compton, with its rare and remarkable Norman work, through all periods to Guildford Cathedral – that high and holy place created in the 20th century – so sturdy and imposing, yet lacking in silly fussy detail and embellishments, and that ugliness which so often spoils modern church design. The Surrey churches are remembered for their beautiful settings – like Tatsfield which is 788 ft up on the downs, Ockham and Albury in their lush parkland, Wotton with the incomparable backcloth which Nature has provided, Holmbury St Mary beneath a wood, Oakwood isolated and in a wood and, for a village setting, what could beat Alfold, with its tile-hung houses guarding the lane to the church, the little green, and the stocks by the churchyard gate. This is a county of timber bell-turrets, with pretty shingled spirelets, of delightful timberwork in roofs and sometimes porches, of fine monuments and brasses, of churches which are real individuals, with walls of flint or Bargate stone.

The best selection of Victorian churches are in the parts of the county which are now officially Greater London Boroughs (but are still treated as Surrey here). These should be explored, especially Croydon, Sutton, Merton and Kingston – there is much beauty and history in them as well.

ALBURY. (RCF) A sylvan spot in the Tillingbourne valley, with its square-towered neo-Perp Catholic Apostolic church and its brick Romanesque church in the village, both 19th century and by William McIntosh Brookes. Idyllically set in the park, near the great house (which Pugin remodelled for Henry Drummond) is Albury's medieval church of St Peter and St Paul, whose central tower has Saxon and Norman work and is capped by a strange shingled dome.

High on the hills is St Martha's *Chilworth*, which is Norman and cruciform, but was largely rebuilt by Woodyer. We see it from afar and the views back are splendid. At St Martin's *Blackheath* is an eccentric little Arts and Crafts church of 1895, by C. Harrison Townsend, which is rather special and is worth a visit.

BURSTOW. St Bartholomew's has a remarkable 16th C timber tower, belfry with pinnacles, and spire, quite in the Essex tradition. The beams inside the tower supporting the belfry are amazing. Just think that when those trees were planted, the Weald was still largely forest. The church still retains two Norm windows, but is mostly Perp. The font is Perp and more elaborate than most in Surrey. Note the piscina and large ironbound chest.

Horley St Bartholomew's church is pleasantly set at one end of its large village. It has a curious tower with a shingled belfry and thin spire. Inside are two interesting brasses and a life-sized 14th century effigy of a knight. *Horne*'s pretty church of St Mary has a Perp screen and a monument of 1618.

CHALDON. The small tower and timber spire are 19th C, otherwise it is completely 12th and 13th C. There is a Perp Easter Sepulchre on the N side of the chancel, and a pulpit dated 1657. The feature of St Peter and St Paul's is, however, the wall-painting on the W wall of c1200. It is called the Ladder of Salvation. The colouring is dark red and yellow ochre. Little figures climb up the ladder or fall down. In the upper half (Purgatory) they ascend towards Heaven, shown by a demi-figure of Christ: also shown in this half is St Michael weighing souls in scales which a devil is trying to pull down (but unsuccessfully), and Christ trampling on Satan (known as the Harrowing of Hell). The lower half represents Hell. Two devils stir up a big cauldron above a fire with many figures. Another two devils hold up a big saw across which cheating tradespeople have to walk. At the foot of the picture are shown the Seven Deadly Sins (Avarice with money-bags round his neck and seated in flames, is clear). On the extreme right is the Tree of Good and Evil with the serpent climbing around it. Incidentally, the Ladder and the cloudy

The atmospheric church and churchyard at Crowhurst, with its tall timber belfry and spire.

division between the two tiers make a Cross. Below the painting is a consecration cross.

At *Caterham* two churches face each other across the road – the tiny and lovable St Lawrence's which is Norman and has medieval roofs, and Victorian St Mary's, by W. Bassett Smith. *Chipstead*'s cruciform church of St Margaret is squat but beautifully set and contains much of interest.

CHARLWOOD. A most attractive place and the church of St Nicholas is a mixture of several periods, with a central tower. Inside are treasures indeed, set beneath king-post roofs. Here we have a superb 15th century screen – Surrey's best medieval woodwork, also a little brass of 1553 and a set of wall-paintings of c1350, showing St Margaret of Antioch and the story of the Three Living and the Three Dead.

Go to St Peter's *Newdigate* to see the 15th century tower, which is entirely of timber, and have a look inside to see its timber construction, also a beautiful church.

COMPTON. The large timber-shingled spire attracts us to this interesting church in a charming setting. The tower is 11th C and the nave and chancel are c1180. The unique feature of St Nicholas' is the two-storeyed sanctuary, a vaulted chamber below, and a chapel above with a Norm wooden screen as hard as iron, and the oldest piece of woodwork in the county. The upper chapel has a piscina and is reached by a wooden staircase which also gives access to a cell. It may be that this upper chapel was used by pilgrims on the nearby Pilgrims Way to venerate a relic: the wooden stairs are very worn.

The capitals of the arcades have scallops or stylised foliage, and the chancel arch has an early use of dog-tooth. The altar-rails, pulpit with sounding-board and tower screen are all Jac. The small E window has a tiny piece of 13th C glass of the Virgin and Child. On the wall near the pulpit is a scratching of a Norman knight. Most of the roofs are old. There was an Anchorite's cell on the N side of the chancel.

CROYDON. St John's is Surrey's largest medieval church (but largely rebuilt by Sir Gilbert Scott in 1870). It has a stately flint exterior and a fine 124 ft tower. There is great majesty inside, with noble proportions and much to see, including a medieval lectern, brasses and monuments. Archbishop Whitgift (1604) has his hands folded in prayer, whilst Archbishop Sheldon (1677) lolls wearily amidst emblems of mortality (could this be the C of E – or possibly the Bench of Bishops – at rest?). St Michael's, with its turrets and fleche, is one of the finest of Pearson's vaulted EE churches, built in 1871. This is a beauty and even the brick exterior is glorious, although its tower was never finished. The interior is so inspiring, with furnishings also by Bodley and Temple Moore. Here architecture, craftsmanship, colour and atmosphere all contribute to inspire worship and devotion. (Do find other churches by Pearson in Surrey, including St John's *Upper Norwood*, St John's *Redhill* and the delightful village church at *Titsey*).

ESHER. St George's (RCF) with its perky little timber belfry, cannot fail to delight you. Its core is of c1540, but much has happened to it since then. The brick transept with the totally self-contained Newcastle Pew was added (to Vanbrough's designs) in 1725 and the north aisle in 1812. What a surprise awaits us inside – a wonderful ensemble of old roofs, two western galleries, one above the other, a very tall and commodious three-decker pulpit, a fine altarpiece of 1722, hatchments, memorials and so much else in this small church, all of which the inhabitants of Claremont could view through the pedimented opening from their very private pew on the south side – in the congregation, but certainly not of it!

Go west from Esher to see the churches at St Peter's *Hersham* (1887) and St James *Weybridge* (1848 and with interesting earlier brasses) – two more churches by J.L. Pearson.

GATTON. If you would like to see how the Squire worshipped in comfort, then come to this church in the park. It is most remarkable. Most of the woodwork and glass have been collected from abroad. St Andrew's itself was originally Perp. The N transept has a family pew; it has a fireplace, panelled overmantel, padded benches and comfortable chairs, and there is a complete covered way from this pew to the house (so that the lord of the manor did not have to meet any villagers). Most of the glass has come from the Continent – armorial glass (and Arms of Henry VII), and saints. The pulpit is suspended level with the family pew. The chancel panelling, altar-rails, lectern, doors, chair, and Communion table are all Continental of the 16th and 17th centuries.

Merstham church of St Katherine has a sturdy EE tower and shingled spire and interesting 13th century work inside. An atmospheric place, with much to see, and a picturesque setting, shaded by trees.

GODALMING. The exterior of St Peter and St Paul's is impressive with its tall large 13th C lead spire on a Norman central tower. The chancel is also Norm, and other parts of the church are of the succeeding styles, particularly Dec, one window (E of the S chancel chapel) being an excellent example of Geometric tracery. The sedilia are Dec, and the interesting piscina in the S chancel chapel is 13th C. The nave roof has heraldic bosses. There is a Jac pulpit and a 14th C tomb-chest with roundels. Brass to Thomas Purvoche and wife 1509.

Busbridge has an attractive church of St John the Baptist by Sir Gilbert Scott (1865–7), with a central shingled belfry and spire. Burne Jones designed the east and west windows and Sir Edwin Lutyens designed the chancel screen and rood, also the war memorial in the churchyard.

GREAT BOOKHAM. St Nicholas' has a remarkable and very picturesque timber belfry and spire, supported inside on massive beams and struts. This might have been part of a Sax wooden church. The S arcade is Norm and the N arcade slightly later, and there are two blocked Norm windows. The chancel is Dec, and the Slyford Chapel (E of the S aisle) is Perp. There is 15th C Continental glass in the E window showing scenes from the life of Christ. Brasses to Elizabeth Slyford 1443; Henry Slyford and his wife and ten children 1598; and Robert Shiers, Bencher of the Inner Temple, 1668. There are mons to Robert Shiers, wife and son (busts) 1668; Arthur Moore 1735, an early example of a military man with trophies etc; William Moore 1746; and Cornet Geary 1776 with bust and showing his death in ambush. The monument to Elizabeth Andrewes and relatives in the chancel 1816, has a weeping willow tree at the back rising the whole height of the chancel (and taking in a lancet and iron railing at the base).

Little Bookham is tiny, Norman and lovable, with a wooden belfry. There is Norman work at St Mary's *Fetcham* too, also EE of interest.

HASCOMBE. Surrey at its most lovely – a lovely village in the hills and one of the most memorable village churches by Henry Woodyer, built in 1864. St Peter's is attractive outside, with its steeply pitched roof gables, shingled belfry and spire and small rounded apse. It is so beautiful and devotional inside, where the old screen has been restored and given new colour by Hardman & Powell. In fact there is colour everywhere and particularly adorning the little sanctuary, and in the Hardman glass. What atmosphere here – it must be seen and experienced. (To see Woodyer's work on a very different scale, do visit his majestic church of St Martin at *Dorking*.)

Whilst in this lovely area, go south to St Mary and All Saints *Dunsfold*, where we have a church of c1270–90 furnished with benches of that date, which must be among our very oldest. Then find *Alfold*'s St Nicholas church in its perfect setting – and lovely and atmospheric outside and in.

LINGFIELD. St Peter and St Paul's stands at the end of a picturesque village street. The tower of the church is at its SW corner and is 14th C with a timber spire, otherwise the whole church is Perp – the only one in Surrey. The font and cover and the screens are all Perp, and there is a double-sided lectern and stalls with carvings and misericords.

The monuments are notable. That of Reginald, 1st Lord Cobham, 1361 is coloured with his coat of arms on his surcoat; his head rests on a Moor's-head helm supported by two angels while his feet rest on a marvellous fierce-looking Saracen. He wears the Garter and was one of the first to do so. Sir Reginald, 3rd Lord Cobham and wife 1446 have at the head a Moor's-head helm and a pair of angels, at the feet a sea wolf and a wyvern. There are also two fine cartouches on the S wall of the chancel.

Crowhurst St George's church, with its tall wooden belfry and spire, is attractive and well worth seeing. EE, Dec and Perp here, also a little 15th century glass, some brasses and a cast iron burial slab in the chancel floor of 1591.

OCKHAM.　All Saints' has a famous E window of seven 13th C lancets (the only other one in England being at Blakeney, Norfolk). Inside the windows are separated by columns with stiff-leaf capitals. There are two windows with fine Flowing tracery in the S wall of the nave. The tower is Perp and there is a wagon roof with bosses in the nave and a panelled roof in the aisle. There is a double piscina and fragments of old glass. The King Chapel on the N side is 1735. Brasses to Walter Frilende, priest 1370, a demi-figure; and to John Weston and wife 1483. Mon to Peter, 1st Lord King and wife, 1734.

Do see the little churches at *Wisley* and St Nicholas' *Pyrford* – both with timber belfries, both Norman and both delightful. Many Surrey churches were once like this.

SHERE.　This is one of the prettiest villages in England, with St James' completing the picture. The central tower is Norm and with its fine timber spire dominates the church. The belfry windows are three tall single lights. The two E windows of c1300 are almost identical, but not quite, the E window of the chancel, a little later, having an ogee arch.

The N window of the N transept is still later and is a good example of Flowing tracery. A beautiful W doorway and door, and old roofs throughout. There is definite evidence of an Anchorite's cell on the N side of the chancel. The S doorway is Norm, and there is a fine early 13th C font with stiff-leaf capitals, a 13th C chest and fragments of old glass. Brasses to Robert Scarcliff, rector 1412, and John, Lord Audley 1491.

STOKE D'ABERNON.　St Mary's church is by the manor house and the river Wey, and is crammed full of interest. It is Norm and 13th C (but part of the S wall is Sax) with a modern W end with timber bell-turret and containing the recent organ. The chancel is vaulted, of c1250. The Norbury Chapel (N of the chancel) is of c1490: it contains a fireplace, which is rare before the Reformation. There is a magnificent Jac pulpit 1620 with a sounding-board held by Sussex ironwork and supported on monsters. It states 'Fides ex Auditu' ('Faith comes from hearing'), and it still has its hour-glass attached. Eagle lectern, 17th C altar-rails, and a wall-painting on the E wall – the Adoration of the Lamb. In the E window, Continental glass and also in the N windows of the nave. There is a fine 13th C wooden chest. There has been much Victorian restoration. The church is world-famous for having, supposedly, the oldest brass in England, Sir John D'Abernon, knight, in chain armour 1277 with a lance and a shield which still has its blue enamel. Sir John his son, 1327, is shown in plate armour and already slightly smaller. Both knights tread on a lion. These dates have always been the accepted ones, but modern scholarship now fixes the dates as 1327 and 1340, with the oldest brass in England at Buslingthorpe, Lincs 1290.

Cobham church of St Andrew has a Norman tower and south doorway, also some interesting brasses. *Leatherhead*'s noble church of St Mary and St Nicholas has a sturdy Perp tower and arcades of c1200.

WEST HORSLEY.   The church and manor house are on their own, almost a mile E of the village. All mainly 13th C, but the tower of St Mary's is partly 11th C, with a timber spire. The W porch is 15th C and also of timber. The rood-screen is partly old, and there is a small 14th C alabaster panel of the Nativity. Small 13th C medallions of old glass in the N and central lancets at the E end, show the anointing of Christ's feet by St Mary Magdalene and the deliverance of St Catherine from her executioners. There is also glass of Sir James Berners kneeling 1388, in the N chancel window. Look out too for the 13th C chest, and a fine 15th C wall-painting of St Christopher on the W wall. On the mon to Ralph Berners, rector 1348, the cusps of the monument are monkey heads – the badge of the Berners family (a Flowing window above). Other monuments to Sir Edward Nicholas 1669; Sir John Nicholas 1704; John Kendal aged 23, 1750; and John Read 18th C.

East Horsley is an eccentric place, greatly influenced by East Horsley Towers. St Martin's church contains some 15th century brasses and the monument of Thomas Cornwallis (died 1626). *East Clandon*'s little church of St Thomas is small and lovely, with a simple EE chancel and much charm both outside and in.

SUSSEX

What character Sussex has – and what charm (and churches) awaits our discovery, in lovely towns (often set high) like Petworth, Midhurst, Arundel, Mayfield, Battle and Rye, or in historic Lewes or the cathedral city of Chichester, where the roads still meet at the market cross. And yes – do find the seaside towns, many of which have tremendous character and grand architecture, also a superb array of 19th century churches (Brighton and Hove having probably the best selection of Gothic Revival churches in southern England). Sussex villages are lovely and there are few of these which do not have pretty scenery and attractive houses.

Sussex churches (of which some 280 medieval ones remain) form a wonderful selection of tremendous interest, yet it is in the smaller churches where the greatest fascination and value lies. Because there was not the prosperity here in the 1400s as there was in many other counties, Sussex seems to have avoided all those Perp rebuilds and enlargements of its churches. This has left us with many where we see mainly Norman, Transitional and EE work, and maybe some Dec, although this is not widespread. Even when the Victorians replaced the furnishings in a church and restored it, they so often left its ancient structure, with the 12th and 13th century features. Several Sussex churches have good Saxon or early Norman work (Worth, Sompting and Bosham showing premier Saxon craftsmanship) and others clearly have Saxon cores, or chancel arches, or doorways. Three of the five round towers outside East Anglia and Essex are in the valley of the Ouse (Lewes St Michael, Piddinghoe and Southease). Great stunning Perp towers are not usually found here, but a profusion of shingled chamfered spires (only four stone spires), towers with pyramid caps (often called 'Sussex Caps'), wooden belfries and simple and venerable towers of flint or local brown stone, may be enjoyed in Sussex churches. Another feature of so many is the great, all-embracing roof, which covers in a single sweep both nave and aisles and reaches down to a very low level. Internally, many 13th or 14th century simple trussed-rafter roofs remain. Sussex has many wall-paintings or traces of them (go to Clayton, Hardham and elsewhere to see premier examples) and the seeker after monuments and brasses will not be disappointed here.

The 19th and 20th century churches of Sussex should not be dismissed, especially in the seaside resorts, where many are by good architects and several have glorious, adorned interiors, often reflecting the Anglo-Catholic tradition which was, after all, once described as the 'London, Brighton and South Coast Religion'!

AMBERLEY. One of those delightful villages and churches which could only be in Sussex. The church of St Michael, set beside the castle walls, has fine Norman work (especially the chancel arch) and much EE (don't miss the south doorway). There are wall-paintings, a consecration cross, simple medieval roofs and much atmosphere.

Tiny cruciform *North Stoke*, at the end of a road which leads nowhere else, is lovable and totally unspoilt. St John the Evangelist *Bury* has a shingled spire, sweeping roof, screen and 17th century pulpit, whilst the nearest town is glorious *Arundel* in its incomparable setting, with castle, RC cathedral and venerable St Nicholas' church which has so much to see.

ASHBURNHAM. How lovely this substantial building looks in its parkland setting. St Peter's is a Gothic church, but rebuilt in 1663, retaining its Tudor tower. The interior is wonderful and set beneath panelled wagon roofs are all the 17th century furnishings – gallery, pulpit, box-pews, font-cover and altarpiece of 1676 where the Commandments are flanked by Moses and Aaron, also two magnificent memorials to the Ashburnham family.

Go to nearby St Michael's *Penhurst*, which is delightful for roofs, screen, 17th century furnishings and unspoilt atmosphere. *Battle*'s large church of St Mary has 12th century arcades and fine brasses.

BERWICK. This tiny village at the foot of the Downs has a church with a shingled spire and a sweeping roof, much restored in 1856, but containing exquisite beauty from our own century. In 1942–3 the interior was covered with wall-paintings (mostly on plaster-board fixed to the walls) which really show how our churches must have inspired people in medieval times. They are wonderful – from Christ in Majesty over the chancel arch, to the four seasons, dawn and sunset, depicted on the screen. The people seem so real and the scenes so typical of the locality. Bishop Bell of Chichester commissioned them and Quentin Bell, Vanessa Bell and Duncan Grant carried out the work.

There are so many endearing churches around here – *Alciston*, St Mary and St Peter's *Wilmington* and dear little St Peter's *Folkington* are charming bell-turreted churches off the A27 and to the south are *Litlington*, *Lullington* (a contender for England's smallest church), also St Andrew's

Alfriston (superbly set across its green, cruciform and of c1360). Anglo-Saxon St Pancras *Arlington*, to the north-east, is also worth discovering.

BOXGROVE. Amazing EE architecture in this glorious priory church of St Mary and St Blaise, with its vaulted and exquisitely painted ceiling, its arcades set in pairs and its bold and distinctive exterior, with a low Norman tower and pyramid cap. The magnificent de la Warr Chantry (1532) has to be seen to be believed – no wonder they call it a church within a church.

Nearby St Andrew's *Tangmere* is delightful Norman and EE, whilst at St Andrew's *Oving* we have a complete EE church.

BRIGHTON AND HOVE. How do we even begin to point you to the wonderful variety of 19th century churches here? The medieval church of St Nicholas was much rebuilt by R.C. Carpenter in 1852. He also created the magnificent St Paul's in 1846. The stately 'Parish Church' of St Peter (by Sir Charles Barry 1824–8, with chancel of 1906 by Somers Clarke) stands in splendour in Victoria Gardens. St Martin's (also by Somers Clarke, 1873–5) is enormous and magnificent inside, whilst St Mary's is also mighty, but is rather eccentric and French-looking in design (by Sir W. Emerson, 1877–9). Nothing however can compare with the breathtaking bulk of St Bartholomew's (Edmund Scott 1872–4) – a towerless barn of a church which rises taller (135 ft) than any other English parish church. Its interior and sumptuous furnishings (all larger than life) are unforgettable. Equally unforgettable, however, is the tiny church of the Annunciation in Washington Street – so simple and basic in structure (William Dancy, 1864), but inside it is Brighton's hidden gem – colourful, prayerful and devotional. At St Michael's we have a Bodley church of 1858 dwarfed by a larger Burges church of 1893.

Hove has two fine churches by Pearson – All Saints (1890–1) which is stately and cathedral-like and St Barnabas (1882) which is less magnificent, but still very imposing.

BURTON. This very special little gem is worth finding. Its parkland setting near the big house is lovely. The church itself is as memorable as many of the better-known churches because it is unspoilt, mellow and has tremendous charm. Herringbone masonry in the walls takes us back to the 11th century, although great alterations took place in 1636. Inside we find old linenfold work in the benches, and a 15th century screen and rood-beam, above which are the Commandments painted upon a tympanum. Painted in one of the window-splays is a much older picture of a

307

female martyr, while upside down and painted upon plaster on the nave wall is a fine Royal Arms of Charles I (1636), with a scripture text above, telling us to obey those who rule over us. Some interesting monuments here, including 16th century brasses.

Delightful small churches in the area include St Agatha's *Coates* and St Mary's *Barlavington*; *Selham* has a fascinating 11th century church of St James, whilst *Petworth* has a fine church of St Mary with much to enjoy.

COOMBES. So humble, unassuming and rustic – this single-celled exterior, built on a sloping hillside and approached across a meadow at the end of a cul-de-sac on the west side of the river Adur. Little shrines like this make church-crawling so very thrilling. A mixture of windows (including a low-side window) punctuate its flint walls; there is a little red-tiled bell-turret, a Norman doorway with pilgrims' crosses and an old door with a grille admits us down steps and into a little taste of paradise! Here are brick and tile floors, simple medieval roof-timbers, an 11th century chancel arch and enough remains of wall-paintings to show us that not only was the interior absolutely covered with them, but also that their artistry was of the highest quality.

The road northwards takes us to *Botolph*'s Saxon church of St Botolph, to *Bramber*'s castle and curious high-set St Nicholas' church and to the fine Norman church of St Andrew at *Steyning*, where Norman arcades, chancel arch and clerestory grace its lofty interior.

EASTBOURNE. In the old town is the large medieval church of St Mary, with its massive tower and with much of interest to see inside, including fine arcades of c1200, a triple sedilia, piscina and Easter Sepulchre, also medieval screens. Amongst the fine Victorian churches are St Saviour's (by Street, 1867) with its tall spire and colourful Anglo-Catholic interior, All Saints (by T.E.C. Streatfield, 1878) and All Souls (by A.P. Strong, 1882), which is like an Italian basilica, complete with campanile.

ETCHINGHAM. A distinctive and venerable church of the Assumption and St Nicholas, with a prominent tile-capped central tower, built by Sir William de Etchingham (died 1387) and showing high quality Dec architecture. Amongst the many treasures inside are medieval tiles and screen, stalls with misericords which have fascinating carvings, medieval glass and fine brasses, including that of the church's donor.

Interesting churches in the neighbourhood include St Bartholomew's *Burwash* (Norman tower and 14th century tomb-slab in cast iron), St Mary's *Salehurst* (large, with west porch and font with salamanders) and St Mary's *Ticehurst* (fine font-cover and 15th century glass).

Tiny Tortington, with its timber belfry and all embracing roof to nave and aisle.

LEWES.   Six churches of medieval foundation in this hillside town which is so full of character. St John's Southover, at the foot of the hill, was associated with the priory and has interesting early monuments. St John sub Castro (rebuilt 1839) incorporates the Saxon doorway and chancel arch of its predecessor. St Thomas at Cliffe has 14th century arcades, a 15th century tower and a pleasing exterior. St Anne's is Norman and EE, with a Transitional arcade and Norman font. St Michael's (apart from its round tower and shingled spire) was rebuilt in 1749 and altered in the 19th century. Its interior is devotional and atmospheric and the reredos is by Pearson.

St Peter's *Hamsey*, to the north, is a memorable church in the middle of nowhere, which is well worth finding. The churches between Lewes and Newhaven are all worth seeing. St John's *Piddinghoe* and delightful little *Southease* both have round towers, St Peter's *Rodmell* and St Nicholas' *Iford* have Norman work of interest, but even better Norman may be admired in St Michael *Newhaven*'s central tower and apse.

THE MARDENS.   Three little churches – all humble and unassuming and all little gems. St Mary's North Marden is Norman, tiny single-celled and apsed, and we get to it through a farmyard. St Peter's East

Marden is also single-celled but is EE. St Michael's Up Marden is a real treasure, remote and rural, entirely EE and the centuries have given its unspoilt interior an atmosphere which is rare and precious. All is so simple and rustic – brick floors, box-pews, triangular headed (16th century) chancel arch, all set beneath plastered wagon roofs and within 13th century walls. A most memorable church.

SHOREHAM.   It is Old and New Shoreham, but both churches are old and both of tremendous interest. St Mary's New Shoreham rises gloriously above the town centre, its stately tower, transepts and aisled chancel, with flying buttresses (but only the stump of the former nave) showing the gradual evolution from Norman to EE. To think that all this wonderful architecture was fashioned by hand 800 years ago. St Nicholas Old Shoreham is quietly set to the north of the town. It is cruciform, with Norman work of high quality, but the nave has Saxon evidence and 14th century craftsmen left their contribution also. Their screen survives, also some of their glass, showing the coronation of the Virgin, in the east window. Outside we enjoy grand views across the Adur to the wonderful chapel of Lancing College (by R.C. Carpenter) rising like part of a great French cathedral from its glorious position.

Further west is St Mary's *Sompting*, with its unique and famous Saxon tower. To the east we must find *Kingston Buci*, whose odd little church of St Julian has lovely woodwork and an Easter Sepulchre.

SOUTH HARTING.   We are drawn by the tall copper spire to this cruciform church of St Mary and St Gabriel near the Hampshire border, splendidly placed in its lovely village and showing good EE and Dec work. Inside we look up to the roofs, which were made following a fire here in 1576 – especially the chancel roof, where the craftsmanship is superb. Amongst the monuments is a fine one to the Cowper and Coles families.

Do take the road westwards to find the tiny Shepherd's Church at St Andrew's *Didling*, with its old benches and wonderful rustic atmosphere, also the carefully restored Saxon church of St Paul at *Elsted*.

TROTTON.   Here the river Rother is crossed by a grand medieval bridge. St George's is a single-celled church of c1300, with an oblong EE tower, and may be mistaken as 'ordinary', until we get inside and discover that the west wall is covered with 14th century wall-paintings of the Last Judgement, the Seven Deadly Sins and Acts of Mercy. Also here are superb brasses – that to Lady Margaret Camoys (1310) being the oldest brass to a female in England. Here also is a Norman font, 17th century rails and font-cover, a 14th century roof, benches and box-pews. There is no such thing as an 'ordinary' church!

Tiny *Chithurst*, in its delightful setting, has not grown at all since it was built in the 11th century. *Woolbeding* All Hallows rewards us with interesting Saxon work.

WEST CHILTINGTON. St Mary's has a most attractive exterior, with central wooden turret and spire, gracing a very pretty village, and there is so much charm and interest in this church of many periods. Norman, Transitional, EE and Dec are well represented here. There is a king-post roof of 1602 and a fine pulpit, but it is the array of wonderful 13th century wall-paintings which we will remember most of all in this marvellous unspoilt place.

Within a few miles we may enjoy Holy Sepulchre *Warminghurst* (RCF), with its interior completely refurnished in 1770, St Mary's *Thakeham*, with its 15th century porch and font and Apsley monuments, *Pulborough*'s Perp St Mary's church, with EE chancel, and *Hardham*'s tiny 11th century shrine of St Botolph, which is adorned with the most wonderful 12th century wall-paintings.

WINCHELSEA. Both town and St Thomas' church are 'one-offs' and very memorable. What we have here is the chancel and side chapels of a once mighty church, but still resplendent with superb Dec work in its large windows, sedilia and piscina in the chancel and south chapel and magnificent 14th century monuments. This is just a taster – there is much more to see here.

In this far eastern corner of Sussex, near the Kent border, nearly every church is well above average and St George's *Brede*, All Saints *Icklesham*, St Mary's *Udimore*, St Mary's *East Guldeford* and St Michael's *Playden* should be specially visited, also *Rye*'s grand church of St Mary, which is full of interest.

WARWICKSHIRE AND THE WEST MIDLANDS

'Leafy Warwick', as this county is called, is at the very centre of England and here, at England's heart, are some lovely aspects of the English scene, as well as about 190 medieval churches. There are larger towns of great interest, like Coventry, Rugby, Stratford upon Avon and Warwick itself, also smaller and more intimate country towns like Alcester and Henley in Arden. Warwickshire villages are on the whole very picturesque and greatly cared for. They are set in rich agricultural, wooded and pleasantly undulating countryside. Birmingham's mighty conurbation, together with small adjacent parts of Worcestershire and Staffordshire have been formed into the new 'county' of West Midlands, which reaches eastwards to embrace Coventry and, as most of it was once Warwickshire, we include it here.

Warwickshire has some lovely churches, although it is difficult to classify them – they are very varied and are full of surprises. This is a very good county for Dec architecture and there are some splendid large Perp churches. Here we find several Classical churches of great character and, especially in the West Midlands, 19th and 20th century churches abound. Warwickshire churches usually have a live, cared for and homely feel about them, but sadly so many have to be locked. Sandstone predominates here – reddish brown, and often rather blackened (for contrasting colours, look at the use of different types of stone in the tower at Dunchurch). There are some very spectacular towers and spires, especially around Birmingham.

ASTLEY. There is something very intriguing about a church which has been altered as this one has. St Mary the Virgin's splendid nave was the Dec chancel of a collegiate church, built in 1433. After a period of post Reformation neglect and the fall of the tower in about 1600, the chancel became the nave of a re-ordering in 1608, when a new Perp tower was added, also a new Perp chancel – both very authentic-looking. The pulpit and lectern are 17th century and beautifully carved, but thank goodness they preserved the wonderful 15th century stalls, with their paintings of prophets and Apostles and carved misericords. There is much of interest here.

Another good church is St Lawrence's at nearby *Ansley*, which is Norman. *Nuneaton* has two medieval churches – the large parish church of St Nicholas, also St Mary's – a fascinating fragment of the nunnery which gave the 'nun' part to Nuneaton!

BIRMINGHAM.   A Classical cathedral of St Philip, Classical St Paul's (1779) and early Gothic Revival St George's (by Rickman, 1822). The old parish church of St Martin in the Bull Ring with its 200 ft spire, was largely rebuilt by J.A. Chatwin in 1873–5, but preserves some older work, including monuments.

There are fine soaring towers and spires at the ancient suburban churches of Aston, King's Norton and Yardley. Edgbaston St Bartholomew, Handsworth St Mary, Northfield St Lawrence and Sheldon should be hunted out for their medieval work. Supreme amongst the many 19th and 20th century churches are Pearson's St Alban's Bordesley (1879–81), Bidlake's St Agatha's Sparkbrook (1899 and post-war) and Bishop Latimer in Handsworth (1913), Chatwin's St Augustine's Edgbaston (1868), R.C. Hussey's St Saviour's Saltley (1849) and T. Proud's St Aidan's Small Heath (1893).

BRAILES.   Stately Dec and Perp here in the village church of St George which they call the 'Cathedral of the Felden'. Of the latter period the stately tower and the porch; of the former the lovely chancel and the delightful sanctus bell-turret remain in the memory.

In this area near the Oxfordshire border is *Tysoe*, with its church of the Assumption of the Blessed Virgin, which is of great interest, St Martin's *Barcheston*, which is attractive and atmospheric, *Long Compton* St Peter and St Paul's, which is elegant, well-set and has a two-storeyed lychgate, also the rare and unforgettable chapel (c1665 and full of atmosphere) near the great house at *Compton Wynyates*.

COLESHILL.   St Peter and St Paul's wonderful spire, set high, is a landmark which dominates the skyline to the east of Birmingham and looks grand from the M6. Of red sandstone, it is perhaps the finest of all the Black Country spires. Here we may also enjoy a remarkable Norman font and a superb collection of monuments.

It is worth finding *Great Packington*'s amazing 18th century St James' church (by Joseph Bonomi, 1790) set deep in the park. A trip across the M6 to *Castle Bromwich* is a must – to the church within a church of St Mary and St Margaret. Here a Classical shell of the 1720s encloses (and hides) a medieval timber-framed church. Good Classical furnishings here.

313

COUGHTON.   A delightful setting beside the noble Coughton Court for this Perp church of St Peter with its wonderful array of furnishings (pulpit, reredos, screens, stalls, etc), its unusual Dole-Bread basket and inscription (1717), its glorious medieval glass and its array of Throckmorton monuments.

Alcester's St Nicholas church of 1729, with a medieval tower, should also be visited.

COVENTRY.   Three breathtaking spires – The Cathedral of St Michael (295 ft) Holy Trinity (237 ft) and the former Greyfriars church (230 ft).

Holy Trinity is an important cruciform church of the finest Perp, but with earlier craftsmanship also. In its stately sandstone interior are noble tiebeam roofs, misericord stalls, a 15th century stone pulpit, a medieval brass eagle lectern and much more. St John's church is smaller, but also has good Perp architecture and an attractive central tower.

HAMPTON LUCY.   This mighty building of St Peter ad Vincula (by Rickman & Hutchinson 1822–6, with a chancel by Sir G.G. Scott 1856) is like a mini-cathedral in the heart of the country, beside Charlecote Park and the river Avon. The tower is magnificent and the interior rich with sumptuous stonecarving.

Charlecote St Leonard's church (by John Gibson 1851) has three good monuments to members of the Lucy family.

LAPWORTH.   St Mary the Virgin's is an embattled and pinnacled church of great character, in a charming setting. Much Perp to be seen externally, including a western porch, which has processional arches and two spiral staircases. There is EE and Dec work inside, also Norman remains. Human heads peer out from the 14th century font and a wooden staircase leads to a delightful chantry chapel. The clerestory and roof of the nave are noteworthy, but most memorable of all is the fine tower and spire, once detached, but now connected to the north side of the church by a vestibule.

There are some pretty churches in this canal area, including St Lawrence's *Rowington*, which is a treasure-house.

LEAMINGTON SPA.   A well-appointed town with some very good 19th century churches. All Saints is stately and magnificent – the brainchild of John Craig, the vicar, who collaborated with J.C. Jackson, the architect (1843). It was extended by Blomfield (1898–1902), who added the sumptuous 145 ft tower. Jackson also designed St Mary's (1839),

The tall Black Country sandstone tower and spire at Coleshill.

which is Evangelical and has great character. St John's (1877, by J. Cundall) is Anglo-Catholic and has a tall spire, as does Cundall's other church of St Paul. St Mark's is a stately building of brick and stone (1879) by George Gilbert Scott Junior.

MEREVALE.   What a delightful spot for this church of Our Lady, which stood by the gate of the great abbey. This church is a real individual, with unusual dimensions. There is superb craftsmanship here – in the 15th century screen, in the early 14th century east window glass, showing the Tree of Jesse, in the 13th century knight with his chain mail, the Ferrers brass (1412) and the alabaster effigies of a knight of c1440 and his lady. All living history – and what atmosphere here!

Atherstone St Mary's church is also distinctive and unusual, St Peter's Mancetter has a good tower, roof and 14th century glass, and Polesworth has an abbey church dedicated to St Editha.

SOLIHULL.   A massive tower and spire (168 ft) rise from the centre of this great cruciform church of red sandstone. It is very much a town church, full of life, colour and devotion. There is excellent architecture here, especially in the early Dec chancel and north chapel, with their delightful window tracery. The south aisle and west end were renewed in 1535. There is so much to discover here, including a vaulted crypt chapel, a 17th century pulpit and reredos, a medieval reredos and screenwork, and elaborate 17th century Communion rails.

To the south-east is Knowle, whose fine Perp church, dedicated to St John, St Lawrence and St Anne, has superb woodwork in its screen and stalls, also a feast of Dec architecture may be seen in the Knights Templars church of St Mary at Temple Balsall.

STONELEIGH IN ARDEN.   A most beautiful setting for the church here, where we find marvellous Norman work in its doorway, chancel arch and font (carved with the Twelve Apostles). St Mary's box-pews and gallery were made in 1821 – these and other furnishings of note enhance the character of the interior. The monuments include the shrouded figures of Alice, Duchess of Derby (1668) and her daughter.

Do visit nearby Kenilworth, which possesses one of our finest ruined castles and the remains of an abbey, also one of Warwickshire's most ambitious Norman doorways at the church of St Nicholas.

STRATFORD UPON AVON.   Its mighty and magnificent church of the Holy Trinity is idyllically set away from the town centre, amongst trees by the river (the view of it from the other side of the Avon is perfect). We see EE, Dec and Perp in this cruciform building (crowned by a 183 ft spire) which, we are told, has 56 windows. Externally, the Perp stonework in the clerestory and the mighty chancel windows is noteworthy. Internally the spaciousness, grandeur and colour are superb, where the stone-panelled clerestory, tiebeam roofs, splendid organ case (by Bodley, who restored the church) set high above the arch of the crossing, and an array of tasteful furnishings join with a wonderful collection of monuments (including one to W. Shakespeare) to make this church well worth a long and absorbing visit.

The Guild Chapel in the town has good Perp windows, also a fine Doom painting over its chancel arch.

WARWICK. A town steeped in history and with so many historic buildings. Its mighty collegiate church of St Mary is magnificent. Much of it was rebuilt (by William Wilson) after a fire in 1694. His are the nave, aisles, transepts and tower, in a distinctive and pleasant form of Gothic. The tower, with its huge pinnacles reaches a height of 174 ft. The great nave, with its tall arcades and vaulted ceiling, is superb, but the collegiate chancel is real Perp – a mass of stone panelling and vaulting, and glorious windows – some containing Kempe glass.

WOLFHAMPCOTE. The fascinating church (RCF) of a long-deserted village, set in the middle of nowhere near the county's eastern border. St Peter's takes some finding, but is well worth the effort. Here is an example of how the Friends of Friendless Churches and the Redundant Churches Fund have saved a gem of a church from dereliction. The squat 13th century tower sits at the west end of the north aisle.

WOOTTON WAWEN. A dignified setting overlooking fields, for a grand church. Outside St Peter's we admire the embattled Perp clerestory and a noble central tower with double belfry windows. It is only when we go inside and stand beneath it that we see that the tower base is in fact Saxon, the rest of the church having grown up around it at different times. We can also identify Norman, EE, Dec and Perp work here. Lovely furnishings also, including a 14th century font and chest, 15th century pulpit, bench-ends and two parclose screens. There are interesting monuments and brasses, also a rare 17th century chained library.

To the north is *Henley in Arden*, with its 15th century church of St John the Baptist, with *Beaudesert*'s Norman church of St Nicholas down a lane eastwards from Henley High Street.

317

WILTSHIRE

There is so much for the searcher after beauty and history to see in this fascinating county, roughly oblong in shape, which is punctuated by chalk downland and green river valleys, with the barren uplands of Salisbury Plain in its centre, the Marlborough Downs in the north and the Vale of Pewsey between them. Above all, Wiltshire is still wonderfully rural and largely unspoilt. Many of its towns and villages retain so much of the atmosphere of the past, conserved and cared for by the present. Towns like Malmesbury, Devizes, Marlborough, Chippenham and Amesbury and villages like Lacock, Castle Combe and hundreds of others which are less well-known and little visited. Some of the church lover's routes, if he so wishes, have been mapped out by Nature here, with strings of lovely villages and churches distributed along the river valleys, especially if he uses the city of Salisbury as his centre. He can follow the Bourne valley through the Winterbournes, Idmiston and Cholderton, or the Avon valley past Durnford and Wishford to Amesbury and further up through Bulford, Netheravon and Upavon to Pewsey, or the Wylye valley to Heytesbury and Warminster, or the Ebble valley through lovely villages to Ebbesbourne Wake. Salisbury is one of our most lovely English cities, with its fine old buildings, its meadows and its breathtakingly beautiful cathedral, set in a cathedral close which is unrivalled anywhere.

What a county also for the very ancient places – Stonehenge, Avebury and Silbury Hill are all here, also a host of lesser-known ancient sites, hill forts, earthworks, barrows, etc. Here also we see England's best preserved Saxon church, at Bradford on Avon. Norman is also well represented – it has been splendidly preserved at Manningford Bruce and is seen in great glory at Devizes St John and Malmesbury Abbey. EE appears at Bishops Cannings, Potterne and many Wiltshire churches, Dec in all its beauty at Bishopstone and in lovely windows and stonecarving in many other Wiltshire churches. Perp appears at its best in some of the greater churches, like Steeple Ashton, Cricklade, Salisbury St Thomas and Lacock. There is fine Classical at Farleigh and Hardenhuish and very early Gothic Revival in Charles Fowler's remarkable estate church at Teffont Evias (1824). The Gothic Revival churches and restorations occur mostly in the villages. Butterfield, Pearson, Street and others are represented here, as is a great deal of work by the Salisbury Diocesan

Architect, Thomas Henry Wyatt.

Over 270 churches have medieval work and it is very much the smaller churches which remain in the memory here (although there are some grand churches, many built of Cotswold limestone). There are shoals of smaller churches, usually set in pretty villages and built of flint from the chalk downs, or Wiltshire's own grey Chilmark stone. Every one is very much a character and the interiors are soaked in atmosphere, with a wealth of fittings and furnishings of interest, also many monuments. This is also a county where cruciform churches abound. Although people think of churches as being cruciform, in most areas they are usually the exception rather than the rule.

AVEBURY. Quite rightly a tourist centre, the charming village, manor house and church of St James are set in the middle of England's oldest stone circle, which is about 4,000 years old. Although the church is Saxon, it is really quite modern in comparison! There is a fine Perp tower with pinnacles and higher stair-turret. Two Sax windows can be seen high up in the nave walls and three circular Norm clerestory windows. The unusual Tuscan columns belong to the 19th century. The Norm font is a fine piece with intersecting arches and two serpents with twisted tails and a small figure of a bishop with his crozier. The rood-screen is Perp with a restored lower part and coving, but the parapet of the loft is original and a very rare treasure, now beautifully coloured.

BISHOPS CANNINGS. St Mary's, a large church, is almost entirely EE with a central tower and a Perp stone spire. Most of the windows are therefore lancets. There is, however, Norm work in the N aisle W window and in the S doorway in an early 14th C vaulted porch. Inside, it is apparent that the arcades are late Norm. The vaults are quadripartite or lierne. The sedilia are 14th C and the piscina in the S transept should be noted. The penitential seat is very curious: a large hand is painted with thumb and fingers having admonitory inscriptions in Latin about Sin and Death, presumably 17th C.

All Cannings has a large church of All Saints with a tall central tower and much to see, and further west are the pretty churches of St Mary's *Alton Barnes* (Saxon and unspoilt) and All Saints *Alton Priors* (RCF, Norman chancel arch, 17th and 18th century woodwork).

BISHOPSTONE (near Salisbury). A lovely setting for a jewel of a church, where we may luxuriate in the exquisite beauty of 14th century Decorated architecture, seen in the wonderful window tracery, the

319

vaulted chancel and south transept, the sedilia and piscina and the glorious tomb-recess in the north transept. St John the Baptist's south transept has a 19th century tomb by Pugin. All this and much more must be seen here – such quality!

Do see the nearby churches of St Mary and St Lawrence *Stratford Tony* and All Saints *Broad Chalke* – also very rewarding.

BRADFORD-ON-AVON. St Lawrence's is one of our most important Saxon churches. It consists of nave, N porticus, and chancel. What will at once be noticed is its great height. The date is thought to be 10th C. There are two flying angels over the chancel arch.

There is much to enjoy in Holy Trinity church, nearby.

BROMHAM. To prove that there was a Norm church, see the blocked windows in the N wall and a doorway in the W wall. The central tower of St Nicholas' was begun in the 14th C and it has a recessed Perp spire. There is a two-storeyed S porch. One comes here, however, to see the Tocotes and Beauchamp Chantry Chapel. It forms the S chancel chapel and is exceedingly ornate, with large windows and numbers of pinnacles, and it shows Perp work at its best. The roofs of the aisle are a tierceron-vault and a painted ceiling. Perp font, 15th C door to the tower, and in the tracery of the SE window are fragments of medieval glass, canopies and figures. Mons to Sir Richard Tocotes 1457, and Elizabeth Beauchamp 1492, with a brass at the back. Brass to John Baynton 1516. Also a monument to Sir Edward Baynton 1593 with two wives and children, again with brasses at the back. Ferdinand Hughes, with a skeleton in a shroud 1640, is under the tower.

CLYFFE PYPARD. St Peter's church is in a wonderful setting, at the bottom of a steep hill. The charming Perp tower has pinnacles and a stair-turret continued above. The church is also Perp, with a rebuilt chancel. Nice wagon roof with tiebeams, on the easternmost of them the base for the former Rood. Medieval font, a fine pulpit dated 1629, a Perp rood-screen and N and S parclose screens, all coloured. Fragments of old glass. Mons to a 14th C cross-legged knight, and to Elizabeth Goddard 1605, a painted board with a coat of arms. The monument of Thomas Spackman, a carpenter, 1786, shows tools of his trade, and below are two children reading and writing, for whom the deceased provided a schoolmaster to teach them. Two figures peeping out of the rood-loft doors are also from a monument. A fine 14th C brass of a knight. The churchyard will be a place of pilgrimage for church enthusiasts – it has the grave of Sir Nikolaus Pevsner and his wife.

At St Katherine's *Winterbourne Bassett* we see exquisite Dec architecture in a delightful church, also 17th century woodwork and a 13th century husband and wife holding hands on their burial slab. There are fascinating monuments at St Peter ad Vincula *Broad Hinton*.

CRICKLADE. St Sampson's amazing central tower will certainly attract notice. It was built just after the Reformation. Outside there are polygonal buttresses, openwork battlements and very large pinnacles. Inside, the tower is elaborately ornamented with a lierne-vault with over 60 bosses: also many shields and niches with canopies. The church, however, dates back to Sax times, as the Normans left some Sax walling when they made their arcades. The W bays are 13th C, as also the chancel and the three doorways. Perp font. Some Sax and Norm sculptures remain.

St Mary's church is small and has a Norman chancel arch, medieval roofs, a Jacobean pulpit and a lovely 14th century churchyard cross.

DAUNTSEY. St James' has Norm N and S doorways and an early 14th C E window, but much is 17th C – the tower (but with Gothic gargoyles and pinnacles), and the N chapel. Low Perp arcades. The lower parts of the rood-screen are Laudian and the upper part 14th C. The stalls are partly medieval and partly later. Jac box-pews, and a 16th C pulpit. The great interest of the church is the wooden tympanum painted with the Last Judgment. This was formerly above the rood-loft and formed a background to the Rood itself with Heaven on one side and Hell on the other side, the artist usually enjoying himself more on the latter side. There is only one other such board in the whole country, namely at Wenhaston, Suffolk, although Penn in Buckinghamshire has something somewhat similar. Fragments of old glass, and a rood celure. Mons to Sir John Stradling and wife, a 15th C incised slab, and Sir John Danvers and wife 1514. Brasses to Ann Danvers 1539, a brass plate with kneeling figure and Trinity, and the 1st Earl of Danby 1643, very large but without ornament.

A lovely little church of St John the Baptist at *Little Somerford*, with a 15th century screen and 17th century fittings.

DEVIZES. The fine central tower of St John's is Norm with much ornamentation and a higher round stair-turret. The tower is oblong. The Beauchamp Chapel on the S shows Perp at its best and is most ornate. What a wonderful comparison between Norm and Perp, side by side. The crossing arches are round on the E and W and pointed on the N and S (an early example). The chancel has a rib-vault and the Beauchamp

321

Chapel a ceiling of hundreds of traceried panels. The Lamb Chapel on the N is not so elaborate, but it has a ceiling of traceried panels. The Beauchamp Chapel has a tall canopied niche at the E end outside. The E bay of the chancel has intersected arches with zig-zag. Perp pulpit, 17th C organ-case. The modern font-cover is beautifully coloured.

St Mary's is a splendid Perp church with a Norman chancel. It has a fine tower, as does also the church of St James.

DURNFORD. St Andrew's is a Norm church rich in furnishings. Both doorways are Norm and also the chancel arch. Lancet windows indicate 13th C work which is also the date of the tower. Perp S porch of timber. Single-framed nave roof. A Norm font, Jac pulpit, lectern, family pew and altar-rails, and an 18th C W gallery. There are some medieval bench-ends and some fragments of old glass. There have been extensive wall-paintings, including a Doom and St Christopher. There are several Mass-dials. Brass to Edward Younge and wife and their 14 children, 1607.

Nearby All Saints *Woodford*, although much renewed by Wyatt, is lovely and has 17th century woodwork and Comper glass. *Amesbury* has a grand cruciform church of St Mary and St Helor, with much EE and excellent 15th century roofs and screen.

EDINGTON. This is a magnificent embattled church, dedicated to St Mary, St Katherine and All Saints, with a somewhat low central tower and three-storeyed S porch all of c1361, and showing the change from Dec to Perp. The E window itself shows such changes. The clerestory is Dec and the W window is Perp. The S porch is vaulted. The plaster roofs will at once be noted – in the chancel c1789, and in the tower, transept and nave c1663. There are several canopied niches in the chancel supported on figures, two still retaining their original figures. The font base is Perp, the cover Jac. There is also a 17th C pulpit with tester, two misericords – a dragon and a griffin, and a Jac altar-rail. Some fragments of old glass and some consecration crosses remain. There are two early 14th C figures of cross-legged knights and monuments to Sir Ralph Cheney and wife 1401; one of the medieval canons, who has a tun with a sprig issuing from it (ie 'Beechington' referring to John Beckington) on a little vault inside, all beautifully coloured; and Sir Edward Lewys, his wife and their four sons and daughter, 1630.

Bratton has an endearing church of St James, beautifully set, mainly Perp and atmospheric. *Erlestoke* St Saviour's church is by Street (1880), and All Saints *Westbury* is an imposing Perp church which is worth a visit.

FARLEY. An extremely satisfying brick Classical church of 1688–90 and almost certainly by Sir Christopher Wren. All Saints has a charming exterior, with a square tower crowned by urns, and a wonderful interior, with many of its original fittings – font, pulpit, screens, pews, etc. There are also monuments to the Fox family, who built it.

GREAT CHALFIELD. What could be more wonderful than a small ancient church in the lovely gardens of a perfect late medieval English manor house? This is Great Chalfield. The manor house has two oriel windows and is now vested in the National Trust. The church, All Saints, has a small square stone bellcot projecting a little and crowned by a small crocketed spire. The Tropenell Chapel built c1480 has a wagon roof. The chapel to the E was built in 1775. There is a stone screen (common in Wiltshire) to the Tropenell Chapel, and a Perp wood screen to the organ-chamber. There are some old stalls with poppyheads, 17th C three-decker pulpit, reader's and clerk's desks and altar-rails, six panels of the life of St Catherine, and some fragments of old glass.

South Wraxall St James' church has a pretty saddleback tower and some monuments to the Long family.

INGLESHAM. St John the Baptist (RCF), in a delightful situation and equally delightful inside, is one of those rare churches that have escaped the restorer. It has a 13th C double bellcot and this is mainly the date of the church and its windows and doorways. Old roofs, a Perp font, an Elizabethan pulpit with tester, Perp parclose screens, Jac pews, box-pews, and pews for the squire and vicar. The N door is medieval with long hinges. Fragments of old glass. There is an exceptionally interesting Sax sculpture of the Virgin and Child with the Hand of God above. Also the base and shaft of a churchyard cross.

LACOCK. A wonderfully conserved and cared for village with a predominantly Perp church, dedicated to St Cyriac. A stone spire here and a vaulted western porch. Wonderful stonecarving in the north-east chapel – magnificent outside and gloriously vaulted inside. There is so much to see in this church, not least Sir William Sharington's monument (c1553), which is one of the best of its period in England.

LYDIARD TREGOZE. St Mary's is mostly Perp with a fine tower and sanctus-bell turret. The nave has a wagon roof and the chancel a ceiling c1633 of coved blue sky with sun, moon and stars. A 13th C font, and a Jac pulpit, family pews and a screen with the Royal Arms of James I. The reredos is 18th century and the altar-rails are superb wrought-iron work c1700. Some wall-paintings may be made out – St Thomas of Canterbury, St Christopher, and Christ of the Trades, the Resurrection on a pillar, and Christ Crowned in the S porch. Remains of 15th C glass, and Flemish glass of c1633 with St John the Baptist and St John the Evangelist. The church is, however, really noted for its monuments: Nicholas St John and wife 1592; a family triptych with large figures inside and a family tree outside – the kneeling couple are Sir John and wife 1594 and the standing figure is their son who put up the triptych in 1615; Sir John and two wives 1634 and children (those who had died, shown in medallions); Sir Giles and Lady Mompesson 1633, seated as if carrying on a conversation; Edward St John 1645, a standing gilt figure in armour.

MALMESBURY ABBEY. Only the W half of the abbey church remains, dedicated to St Peter and St Paul, but fortunately it contains the magnificent Norm S porch, quite the finest in England. The Old and New Testaments are completely shown in the outer shafts, with six Apostles with flying angels above facing the other six on the other side inside the porch, and Christ in Majesty with angels above the doorway. The interior of the church is the usual three storeys, ground-storey, triforium and clerestory c1170 with a 14th C vault. The aisles have rib-vaults of c1170. Altar-rails of c1700, two Perp stone screens, and a Perp tomb-chest with an effigy of King Athelstan. There is a watching-chamber in the S triforium. The detached 14th C tower with a broach spire now does duty for the church. The Perp market cross in the town is a fine piece of work.

In *Sherston's* fine Holy Cross church, with its tall central tower (mostly of 1730) and lovely Perp porch, we see Norman and EE work, a Jacobean pulpit, and several monuments.

MERE. St Michael's fine Perp tower with prominent pinnacles domi-nates the church. The church is of the three Gothic periods and provided two chantry chapels. There is a fine Dec two-storyed N porch with a figure of St Michael. Perp clerestory and chancel arch, an Easter Sepul-chre, a rood-celure, Perp font and tall Perp rood-screen. The side chapels also have their screens. Some stalls have misericords, and there are some 17th C benches. Some Dec glass of 1398. An alabaster panel of the Magi. Brass to Sir John Betteshorne 1398.

MILDENHALL. A small village church of many periods with its Georgian furnishings preserved, the tower of St John the Baptist's is Sax, Norm and Perp. The roofs of the nave and chancel are Jac. The chancel arch has the Royal Arms of George III. The furnishings are reredos, pulpit with tester, reader's desk, pews for the incumbent and squire, box-pews, and a W gallery. The font is also of that period. There are 17th C altar-rails, fragments of old glass, and two 19th C Gothick monuments.

Marlborough has two medieval churches – one at each end of its grand High Street. St Mary's has Norman work, whilst St Peter and St Paul's has a fine tower, a Perp chancel which is vaulted, and a new lease of life.

OAKSEY. All Saints' church of the three Gothic periods should be visited to see the fine wall-paintings of St Christopher (there is a mermaid with a looking-glass and comb and one foot of the saint is bitten by a fish: the foot seems to have plenty of toes), and Christ of the Trades. Also some 15th C glass including whole figures.

Minety has a delightful church of St Leonard with lovely woodwork inside, including a magnificent pulpit of 1627.

OLD DILTON. St Mary's (RCF) is a small Perp church with a bell-turret with a spire. The interior is charming with plenty of clear glass, so that one can see all its original furnishings – three-decker pulpit, box-pews, family pews, and N and W galleries. The view through the E window is particularly attractive.

Warminster's grand Perp cruciform church of St Denys is worth a visit, although Sir Arthur Blomfield restored it very thoroughly in 1887–9. It contains the organ case (1792) from Salisbury Cathedral.

POTTERNE. On a hill above the village, St Mary's is a complete EE church with lancets. The only piece later is the Perp top of the central tower with pinnacles. Sax font, Perp wood pulpit, a painting of Moses and Aaron, and the original N door.

PURTON. Beautifully placed near the manor house, St Mary's has a W tower and a central tower with a stone spire (there are only a very few like this in the whole country). The central tower (vaulted) came first, in the 14th C. The W tower is Perp with pierced parapet, pinnacles and niches. Niches are certainly favoured at this church! There is some Norm work and also of the three Gothic periods, with a Perp two-storeyed S porch and chancel with Easter Sepulchre and sedilia. Some wall-paintings, including the Death of the Virgin, 14th C, and fragments of old glass.

About four miles east of Swindon you will discover St Andrew's *Wanborough*, which also has two towers (one hexagonal and with a spire), and much else of interest.

SALISBURY.   St Thomas of Canterbury's is almost completely Perp. The tower has clock-jacks below the clock of 1582. Large windows and clerestory. The E window has five lights and the W window seven lights. There is a fine nave roof of the Somerset type. On the chancel arch is a 16th C Doom wall-painting showing the Rising of the Dead and the Fate of the Damned, with the Mouth of Hell. At the top is Christ on a rainbow with the Virgin and St John the Evangelist. Below, most unusually, a town is also shown. There is a 15th C tomb-chest, and two 17th C monuments to the Eyre family. The 15th C Poultry Cross in Butcher Row should be seen, and also the beautiful close of the cathedral with England's highest spire, 404 ft. Do also find the medieval churches of St Martin (stone spire, good wagon roofs and medieval brass eagle lectern) and St Edmund (Perp, with tower of 1653).

STANTON FITZWARREN.   St Leonard's has much Norm work, with a tower dated from 1631, but one comes here to see the Norm font with eight Virtues trampling on eight Vices. All are named, with the names of the Vices upside down, and there is also Ecclesia and the Devil and a seraph with six wings.

William Butterfield's work may be seen at nearby St Leonard's *Broad Blunsdon* and *Blunsdon St Andrew* – two medieval churches which he almost entirely rebuilt.

STEEPLE ASHTON.   St Mary's is a fine complete Perp church, all due to cloth-weaving, and in a most picturesque village. The tower is superb, and the whole church abounds in windows, pinnacles, battlements and gargoyles. The S porch has a vault (a boss showing the Assumption). A vault in the nave is of wood, all the other roofs are lierne-vaults of stone. In the N chapel the E vault has the Assumption surrounded by the signs of the Evangelists, and the W vault has Christ surrounded by prophets and sybils. The vaulting shafts stand on busts with niches. Fragments of old glass. A brass plate has a palimpsest: on the front a deceased of 1730, and on the reverse a Frenchman, the Pope and the Devil outweighed in a balance by the Bible, Queen Anne looking on.

On the village green, side by side are the lock-up and village cross with a sundial on the top.

Some lovely churches in this area, including St Leonard's *Keevil* (tower, roof and 12th century sanctus bell), St Nicholas *North Bradley* (good Perp tower, font and north chapel) and the large Perp church of St James at *Trowbridge*.

STOCKTON. What an incredibly beautiful corner of England – and what a fascinating church of St John the Baptist, with Norman, EE, Dec, Perp and c1600 work to discover. The great rarity here is the stone wall dividing nave and chancel (the fine screen is of 1910). The font is Norman and its cover is 17th century. There are also interesting monuments to enjoy here.

Sherrington has an adorable little church of St Cosmas and St Damian, much rebuilt in 1624, with a delightful interior which is a period-piece of the 17th century. There is fine EE work at *Boyton*, dedicated to the same two saints, (especially in its south chapel) and St Mary's *Wylye* must be seen for its wonderful 1628 pulpit and its EE east window.

STOURTON. This lovely little Perp church of St Peter is in the beautiful gardens of Stourhead House (National Trust). It has a simple tower and pierced parapets round the church. There is a family pew with fire-place. Mons to Lady Stourton 1403; the 5th Lord Stourton and wife

Broad Chalke is a lovely village with thatched houses and a sturdy cruciform church of the 1200s and 1300s with 13th century roof timbers and a grand vaulted ceiling beneath the central tower. The painter, Christopher Wood, who died in 1930 is commemorated in the churchyard.

327

and three children, 1536; Henry Hoare (who built the house), a bust of 1725; Henry Hoare (who made the gardens) 1785; and Hester Colt Hoare 1785.

It is worth travelling north to All Saints *Maiden Bradley* to see some lovely Jacobean woodwork and the Rysbrack monument to Sir Edward Seymour, who died in 1707.

URCHFONT. Amongst a host of features to enjoy in this interesting church of St Michael is its memorable Dec chancel, with sturdy gabled buttresses outside and vaulted interior. The porch is Perp and the nave roof was renewed in 1631. A real character this, and set in a beautiful village.

WESTWOOD. St Mary's has a fine Perp tower with a prominent stair-turret crowned by a dome. The top stage is panelled (as in other small towers in this area and a style which was favoured in Gloucestershire). Perp nave, a good ceiling in the N aisle, a 13th C chancel, a Perp font-cover, suspended from an iron bracket, a pulpit of 1607 and Perp stall-fronts with poppyheads. Much Perp glass: in the E window, Christ crucified on a lily plant with the Instruments of the Passion and surrounded by angels. The church adjoins Westwood Manor, a perfect Wiltshire manor house.

WILTON. The mighty parish church of St Mary and St Nicholas is compelling, but is anything but English! It is in the Romanesque style which we would find in Italy and it cost an amazing £20,000 when it was built in 1843 to the designs of Thomas Wyatt and David Brandon – but it is great fun and is certainly impressive, its tall campanile reaching 108 ft. Inside it is vast, colourful and glorious. It is embellished with much marble and beautiful mosaics which were imported from Italy (together with some genuine 2nd century columns from ancient Rome). There is wonderful glass here, but again imported, and including 12th and 13th century French, 14th century German, 15th and 16th century English and 17th century Flemish, also good Victorian glass which was made for it. There are notable monuments also in this church, which is undescribable, but rather must be experienced.

To sober up afterwards, why not visit its medieval predecessor (RCF) in the square, of which only the chancel is roofed. Why not also make a pilgrimage to the tiny bell-turreted church of St Andrew, *Bemerton*, where the saintly George Herbert was parish priest, and its impressive daughter church of St John, built in 1861 to the designs of T.H. Wyatt.

YORKSHIRE

What was England's largest county was divided up in 1974. A small corner in the north-east went into Cleveland, whilst a larger area in the south-east (containing some of its finest churches) became part of Humberside. The churches in this section are divided into the new Yorkshire's three regions – north, south and west.

The north has the incomparable scenery of the Dales, with their delightful villages, the City of York (second only to Norwich in the number of its medieval churches) and lovely market towns like Skipton, Bedale, Thirsk and Northallerton. The south has much of the county's industry, with collieries and steelworks. The scenery here is very different and large industrial towns, like Sheffield, Barnsley, Rotherham and Doncaster, have made parts of the area very urban. Industrial towns do however have much to interest the church enthusiast. West Yorkshire has the Pennines at its west and here is great variety, with barren moors, lush valleys, trees, arable land and several industrial towns and cities, like Leeds and Bradford. Here man's craftsmanship reveals itself in dry stone walls and great woollen mills and chimneys – in Adel's small Norman church and in great Victorian temples like Scott's All Souls, Haley Hill, Halifax.

This little pen-portrait cannot begin to do the county or its churches justice (before the 1974 division there were about 540 medieval and a similar number of later ones). Suffice it to say that one is never bored here, with the varied coastline, the rugged moors, the Dales and valleys which are as lovely as anywhere in England and the many tangible links with ancient and modern Christianity. In Yorkshire we now have five cathedrals (York, Ripon, Bradford, Sheffield and Wakefield), a host of romantic ruined abbeys (with splendid architecture which is usually unaltered by later restoration – see Rievaulx, Byland, Whitby and others), plenty of castles and historic houses, and so much to see in the churches – from Saxon Kirkdale in its sylvan setting, to mighty Perp at Halifax or Tickhill, from Classical Horbury to Gothic Revival seaside splendour at St Martin's Scarborough, from hunting out the abundance of Saxon crosses which abound in the north to searching for the little mice which lurk on the lovely 20th century woodwork of Robert Thompson of Kilburn.

NORTH YORKSHIRE

BEDALE. St Gregory's large tower is Dec below and Perp above with two square-headed belfry windows on each side. Attached to it is the S porch and both are vaulted. That the tower was used for defence is proved by the grooves of the portcullis. The fine broad Geometric window at the E end of the S aisle is original. Perp clerestory and S chapel. The N arcade is 13th C and the S arcade c1300; the columns of the N arcade all differ. Under the chancel is a vaulted crypt, containing a 9th C cross-shaft and a 9th C hogback and a carving of the Virgin. There are also some Danish fragments and 16th C wooden panelling with profile heads and small 16th C figures of the Apostles. Sedilia. Wall-paintings on the chancel arch of the Angel of Annunciation (14th C), and on the N aisle wall of St George and the Dragon (also 14th C). Of the mon to Sir Brian Fitzalan and his wife, early 14th C, his effigy is of alabaster, hers of stone. There are also two effigies of knights of the 14th C, an effigy of a priest in Mass vestments 1343, and Thomas Jackson 1529, in black marble.

BIRKIN. Here we have a complete and very impressive Norman church of St Mary, with tower, nave, chancel and apse – all of which show lovely work of this period. The Decorated period added the south aisle, the 17th century the font and the 18th century the beautiful pulpit.

BRAYTON. St Wilfrid's has a Norm tower with twin bell-openings and a corbel-table above which is a Perp octagon and spire which is a local landmark. The S doorway of three orders is also Norm, and the tower arch and chancel arch are of the same date. All the capitals of the arches should be noted. The chancel is Dec with fine windows, the E window having Flowing tracery. Piscina and sedilia, 14th C arcades, and a Perp square-headed clerestory.

COXWOLD. In this picturesque village, St Michael's is a complete Perp church distinguished by its tower being octagonal all the way up: tall belfry windows, pierced parapet and eight pinnacles. The nave ceiling has bosses. There are 18th C altar-rails, box-pews and W gallery. Fragments of old glass and the monuments are numerous. There is Sir William Bellasyse with his wife and children, 1603; Thomas Bellasyse, Viscount Fauconberg, and wife 1632; and Thomas Bellasyse, Earl of Fauconberg, the father in Roman dress and his son wearing a wig and carrying a coronet, 1700.

Do go on to *Kilburn*, where Robert Thompson (the 'mouse' man) created lovely woodwork. The chapel of St Thomas in the lovely church of St Mary was refurnished in 1958 as a memorial to him.

CROFT. St Peter's stands by the river Tees, which is the boundary with County Durham. The lower part of the tower is Norm. There is a low nave with clerestory and a long chancel. The S arcade is 13th C and the N arcade 14th C. Piscina with frieze and the sedilia has two figures to support the frieze which has interesting carvings, as also its spandrels. The family pew is a show-piece. This, a raised double box with a long staircase, is 17th C as are also the altar-rails. There is a 9th C cross-shaft, and by the door an ancient human figure. Mons to Sir Richard Clervaux 1490, and Sir Mark Milbanke 1680 (with original railing).

GIGGLESWICK. St Alkelda's is a Perp church with straight-headed windows, the E window being of six lights uncusped. There is a clerestory, but there is no chancel arch, as usual in Craven. An ornate pulpit with tester and reading-desk dates from 1680, as do the altar-rails. Almsbox of 1684.

GRINTON. A real Dales church this – St Andrew's is grey, austere and broad, as if clamped upon Swaledale for all time! The exterior is mostly Perp, but inside is a Norman font with 15th century cover, a 15th century parclose screen and some glass, a pulpit of 1718 and other interesting features, also much atmosphere.

For another Dales church of great character, go to St Oswald's *Askrigg* in Wensleydale – again mostly Perp. Anywhere in the Dales of course rewards us with wonderful views.

HEMINGBROUGH. The glorious spire of c1446 is 189 ft high, and is much higher than the tower, which breaks all rules but is most effective. This was due to the Prior of Durham. The nave and aisles of St Mary's are 13th C and the chancel late 13th C. The E window has five stepped lancets and the S transept window and the clerestory are Perp. The font is c1200, and the pulpit 18th C. There are stalls with poppy-heads and one misericord with stiff-leaf foliage which must be c1200 and is possibly the earliest in England. A number of 15th C bench-ends with figures. The S porch is 14th C and the aisle roofs are original and also some doors. A mon shows a skeleton in a shroud.

HORNBY.   St Mary's is situated in the gardens of Hornby Castle. The lower part of the tower has twin bell-openings with a mid-wall shaft, probably Sax or very early Norm. The top stage and battlements are Perp. Inside the N arcade and the chancel are late 12th C, the N aisle windows and S doorway are 14th C, and the S arcade and S aisle windows are Perp. There is an 18th C font and a Perp rood-screen with delightful paintings in the rood and screen of birds in thick foliage.

HUBBERHOLME.   The church is very isolated and beautifully situated at the upper end of Upper Wharfedale, but it is well worth finding. The nave and aisles are under one large roof. There is a Perp font. The feature of St Michael's is the screen with a rood-loft. There are only about twelve original ones in the whole of England (Flamborough being another in Yorkshire). It is dated 1558 and is very late, being after the Reformation. The E parapet is pierced with tracery (as often in Wales) and is coloured pink, yellow and black. There is an old door. The modern woodwork is equally beautiful, by Thompson of Kilburn, with the carved mouse emblem.

KIRK HAMMERTON.   Truly remarkable – a tiny but complete Saxon church of St John the Baptist, tower, nave and chancel, which is now the south aisle of Hodgson Fowler's new church of 1911, replacing a 13th century north aisle, whose arcade survives. A visit to *Nun Monkton*'s wonderful St Mary's church (formerly monastic with Trans and EE work) is well worthwhile.

KIRKDALE.   St Gregory's is as secluded as it has been since Sax times. The small tower is 19th C added to a Sax church. The narrow but tall arch at the W end (now leading into the tower) was formerly the W doorway to the Sax church. The famous Sax sundial is above the S doorway. There are only about 20 Sax sundials in the whole country and, as usual, the dial is enclosed within a double circle. It has an inscription (there are only one or two Sax inscriptions in the country) which briefly translated reads 'Orm son of Gamal built St Gregory's Minster when it was ruined and rebuilt it in the days of King Edward and Earl Tosti' (ie 1060). The chancel arch is of the same date, but the chancel is mainly 19th C. The N aisle is c1200. There is a 14th C stone figure of the Virgin, a Sax cross with a crucifix, and two Sax coffin-tops.
   Kirkby Moorside All Saints church, although medieval (fine south porch) was restored by Sir Gilbert Scott and has a lovely altar, reredos and screen by Temple Moore (1919).

LASTINGHAM. At St Mary's, the crypt must be mentioned first. Its date is about 1080 and it is divided by four thick columns into nine compartments with groined roofs. In the crypt are the head of a Sax cross, a hogback gravestone with a bear, and coffin-lids with an incised sword, and with a cross and chalice. The apse and bay adjoining are the original Sax church. The tower is Perp.

At *Appleton le Moors* is fascinating Christ church by J.L. Pearson (1863–5), where we have French Gothic in the Yorkshire Moors!

LEAD. (RCF) A tiny 14th century church isolated in the middle of a field. Single-celled, rustic and thoroughly adorable! Inside we find the simplest of benches, a three-decker pulpit, godly texts upon the walls and ancient grave-slabs in the floor.

All Saints' *Saxton* has Norman features and at All Saints *Sherburn in Elmet* (lovely elevated position) are Norman arcades, an EE chancel and much of interest.

NEWBALD. St Nicholas' is a fine Norm church. The central tower top has two lancets on each side. There are four Norm doorways, the corbel-table is well-preserved and the chancel is Perp with a five-light E window. The crossing arches are fine, the W and E ones with zig-zag, and all have scalloped capitals. There is a Norm font, a 13th C chest with ironwork, and the vesica encloses a seated figure, a big cartouche, for William Gill 1723.

Sancton, to the north, has one of Yorkshire's two delightful octagonal towers.

PICKERING. St Peter and St Paul's N arcade is 12th C and the S arcade a little later. The tower is 13th C with a 14th C belfry storey and a Perp recessed spire. The chancel is Dec with sedilia, the S porch and clerestory are Perp and there is an 18th C pulpit. The church is of course noted for its 15th C wall-paintings, the most complete in England, but restored. They give a good idea of what every church in England would have been like before the Reformation. On the N side from the W are St George, St Christopher, Herod's Feast, the Coronation of the Virgin, and the Martyrdom of St Edmund and St Thomas of Canterbury. On the S side from the E are shown the life of St Catherine, the Seven Acts of Mercy, the Annunciation, the death and burial of the Virgin, some Passion scenes, the Descent into Hell, the Resurrection, and the Apostles. The church also has a 14th C cross-legged knight holding a heart, and the effigy of a knight of c1400.

333

At *Middleton* St Andrew's we see a Saxon tower and three splendid Saxon crosses. More may be seen at *Ellerburn*'s delightful little church of St Hilda, in its sylvan setting.

ROBIN HOOD'S BAY. The 'old' church of St Stephen at Fylingdales (RCF) has a lovely position and is an atmospheric period-piece of 1821, showing how a church was furnished in the years before the Oxford Movement, with box-pews everywhere, and galleries, all gathered around the towering three-decker pulpit. What atmosphere here! The 'New Church' could not be a greater contrast. It is fine Gothic Revival work by G.E. Street (1870), with a saddleback tower and a noble interior with high quality glass by Henry Holiday.

SCARBOROUGH. The medieval St Mary's is beautifully set near the castle. It is part of what was a great church, with two west towers and a chancel to the east of the present tower. There is good 12th and 13th century stonework inside, also two unusual chapels east of the porch which, like the porch itself, are tunnel-vaulted. Interesting memorials here include many small brass plates from 18th century headstones. Anne Bronte's grave, much visited by devotees, is in the churchyard.

St Martin's is a masterpiece by Bodley (1860–3). In the EE style, it is tall, dark and devotional, with a distinctive saddleback tower. It is full of magnificent craftsmanship, including work by William Morris, Philip Webb, Ford Madox Brown and Edward Burne Jones. The reredos, screen and organ-case, by Bodley, are splendid.

SELBY ABBEY. St Mary and St German's nave and transepts are Norm and the chancel Dec. The central tower was rebuilt after a fire in 1906, and the tops of the two western towers were added in 1935. The large W doorway is Norm, above which are EE lancets and a Perp window. The N doorway is similar to the W doorway but its porch is a little later with a vault. The N aisle windows have old Geometric tracery. The S aisle windows are early Dec, while the clerestory is just single lancets. The N transept has a Dec clerestory and a seven-light Perp N window, but the S transept suffered from the collapse of the former central tower. The Latham Chapel has five-light Perp windows. The base of the central tower is original Norm. The glorious E window of seven lights shows Flowing tracery to perfection, the chancel windows show Dec tracery in slightly different forms and the clerestory is of that period. The aisles are vaulted. The nave ceiling was damaged in the fire, but many bosses (the mermaid, elephant and castle etc) were rescued and have been reinstated. The capitals of the chancel have natural foliage.

Such a variety here, in villages and churches. Here is Coxwold, where the pinnacled church has a fine octagonal tower.

There is a tall tabernacle Perp font cover. The Dec sedilia have four seats, and a Dec stone screen is behind the altar. The gorgeous bright glass of the late 14th C is well seen in the E window, a Jesse window, with numbers of small figures. There is also a mon to a 14th C cross-legged knight.

SKELTON (near York).   A gem of EE work, all about 1250, with the original double bellcot. There is a stiff-leaf cross on the gable. At the W end is one lancet with a circular window above. The S doorway of St Giles' has dogtooth and stiff-leaf capitals. The E window has three lancets of equal height with a vesica above. There is a rich piscina and an octagonal font.

SKIPWITH.   It is the fine chancel of St Helen's which first attracts attention – all square-headed windows c1300. The tower was a Sax porch with long-and-short work, with a later Sax stage and Perp top stage. The tower arch is a splendid example of Sax work. The N aisle is c1190 and the S aisle a little later. There is a fine piscina, beautiful 13th C ironwork on the S door, Norm carving of figures and an animal, an almsbox of 1615 and fragments of old glass.

   Riccall church was restored by J.L. Pearson, but preserves its magnificent Norman doorway.

335

STILLINGFLEET. St Helen's S Norm doorway is notable, with five orders with intricate carving. The door has very early ironwork with two hinges and two figures and a boat with a typical stern. The N doorway and door are simpler. The tower is 13th C with a Perp top. The Moreby Chapel is 14th C, with foliage capitals and figures, and its W window is circular. There is some heraldic glass. Mons to a 14th C cross-legged knight and to John Acclom, which has four kneeling figures facing one another, 1611.

THIRSK. A completely Perp church of the 15th C, St Mary's tower has openwork battlements, as also the clerestory, S porch, aisles and chancel with pinnacles. The clerestory has six broad windows on each side. There is a fine wagon roof with bosses, sedilia and two screens. The S door has tracery, the N door is also Perp. Above the W window is a seated figure of the Virgin. Fragments of old glass, and a fine restored Perp tabernacle font-cover. Brass to Robert Thirske 1419, a demi-figure with angels.

WENSLEY. Situated by the river Ure, Holy Trinity's tower was rebuilt in 1719. The chancel is EE with an E window of five stepped lancets in one arch: piscina and sedilia and low-side window. Dec arcades, a tower arch, a chancel arch and aisle windows, and a Perp two-storeyed vestry. The W window is post-Reformation. The font, with font-cover with pineapple, is of 1662. There is a wooden box with a Gothic panel (perhaps a reliquary) with an almsbox attached, and 18th C pulpit and box-pews. The Scrope family pew is late 17th C with part of the medieval rood-screen behind. Eight stall-ends have poppyheads and little animals; two ends have shields. The benches and altar-rails are 17th C. There are some pieces of Sax sculpture and on the N wall remains of the lower part of a wall-painting of the Three Living and Three Dead, also the murder of a saint. The Royal Arms of George III hang in the N chapel. The large brass to Sir Simon de Wensley, priest, 1375, shows him with his head on a pillow supported by two angels and a chalice on his breast – this is a Flemish brass plate. The mon to Henry and Richard, children of Lord Scrope 1525, is a black marble plate with two figures in relief.

WEST TANFIELD. This is an unforgettable scene – St Nicholas' church tower, Marmion's Tower, and the red pantiled cottages of the village perched above the river Ure. Marmion's Tower (note the oriel window) was the 15th C gatehouse of the castle and the only part of the castle that now remains.

The oldest part of the church is the S doorway c1200, then the N arcade 13th C and the rest is Perp with a typical tower of that period. The N chapel has a small recess on its S wall with a two-light opening to the chancel and a single light above the two-light opening to the E. Its purpose does not seem to be known but it might possibly have been a small chantry chapel. There are two pieces of Sax sculpture and fragments of old glass. The mon to Sir John Marmion and his wife 1387 shows two angels at her head and a dog with a long tail at her feet. There are several other figures but they are badly worn. The monument is placed under an iron hearse with sconces for candles. Brass to Thomas Sutton, rector in a cope, c1490.

Several interesting churches in the area, including St Michael the Archangel *Well* (font-cover, chapel reredos and monuments) and St Mary's *Masham* (fine tower and spire, Saxon cross-shaft and fine monument to Sir Marmaduke Wyvill 1613).

WHARRAM-le-STREET. St Mary's has a Sax nave and tower (its arch horseshoe-shaped) and rebuilt chancel. The former W doorway and tower arch are also both Sax with Norm additions. The tower is of Sax proportions with its top stage added c1066. Norm S doorway and chancel arch. The N aisle is 14th C and there is a Norm font.

It is worth the journey to see the nearby deserted village of *Wharram Percy*, with Saxon and Norman work in its ruined church.

WHITBY. There is a magnificent view of the coast and an equally fine view of the church and abbey over the red roofs of the old town. The church and abbey ruins (lancets predominate) are high above the town, 199 steps up. St Mary's has a Norm tower, EE belfry windows and a Georgian nave of 1764, with large windows. There is a S Norm doorway in a later porch and the chancel is also Norm, with three stepped E windows.

There are no interior furnishings in any church in England to compare with Whitby. Galleries are everywhere. Instead of a rood-screen there is the Cholmeley Pew, late 17th C, painted white on four twisted columns. There are box-pews of the 17th or 18th C throughout, and above everything is the three-decker pulpit with tester 1778; attached to it are two vamping horns, thought to be ear trumpets.

Of the later churches the Proprietory Chapel of St Ninian, Baxtergate is an atmospheric building of 1776–8, and bold, massive and cruciform St Hilda's (by R.S. Johnson 1884–6) looks tempting as we view it from St Mary's – and is well worth the journey to see it.

337

YORK.   York Minister has more medieval glass than all the churches in England put together. Most of the parish churches of York also have their original glass. Here are two such churches of the greatest possible interest.

All Saints, North Street, has a Perp tower with octagon with an open parapet and a stone spire, all most effective. Hammerbeam roofs in the chancel and chancel aisles. A 17th C pulpit and some Perp stalls with misericords. It is for its medieval glass that the church is noted, all 15th C unless otherwise mentioned. In the E window is St John the Baptist, St Anne teaching the Virgin to read, and St Christopher: below are Nicholas Blackburn junior and wife, the Trinity, and Nicholas Blackburn senior and wife. The N aisle E window (14th C) has the Magi, Crucifixion, and Coronation of the Virgin above with Annunciation, Nativity and Resurrection below.

Holy Trinity, Goodramgate (RCF) has a Perp tower and charming unrestored interior, mainly Dec. There is an 18th C two-decker pulpit, font-cover, reredos, box-pews, and three-sided altar-rails. Again it is the medieval glass that is the feature of the church. That in the E window is 15th C – above, St George and the Dragon, St John the Baptist, the Trinity, St John the Evangelist, and St Christopher: below Mary Cleophas, Alphaeus and their four children; St Anne, Joachim, and the young Virgin Child; the Trinity; Salome, Zebedee and John the Evangelist as a child holding a book and eagle; St Ursula and her Companions.

The N aisle E window has 14th and 15th C fragments – the Virgin crowned and an Archbishop. The S aisle E window, also 14th and 15th C fragments, depicts St Paulinus and St Olave.

York has 19 medieval churches, several of which serve very useful new lives. All are worth seeing, but some interesting examples include:
All Saints Pavement – lantern tower, 13th century door knocker, 15th century lectern, glass.
St Cuthbert Peasholme Green – 15th century roof and door, Saxon remains.
St Helen Stonegate – 12th century font, glass, lovely interior.
St Martin cum Gregory – fine Perp church, partly ruined, glass, distinctive clock.
St Mary Bishophill Junior – Saxon tower, Temple Moore reredos.
St Mary Castlegate – fine tower and spire, glass, Heritage Centre.
St Michael le Belfry – splendid late Perp (1525–35) with marvellous interior, glass.
St Michael Spurriergate – fascinating interior, glass, 18th century reredos.
St Olave Marygate – glass, monuments, impressive font-cover by George Pace 1963.

WEST YORKSHIRE

ADEL. St John the Baptist's is a complete Norm church of about 1160, and still in unspoilt country. There is a small bellcot, and a corbel-frieze with faces and beasts. A sumptuous S doorway. Christ in Majesty and the Lamb of God, and symbols of the Evangelists are on the gable, and there are four orders of arches with zig-zag and animals. The original door-ring is a monster swallowing a man. The chancel arch is equally splendid. The capitals should be noted: on the N is the Baptism of Christ with a flying angel holding His clothes, and on the S the Crucifixion, and the other capitals have beasts. The arches have beak-heads and zig-zag.

HALIFAX. Adjoining the Ring O'Bells inn, and surrounded by high hills, St John the Baptist's could be said to be in the country. The N aisle is early 14th C, otherwise all is Perp, giving a handsome church. The tower is a splendid example of that style with eight pinnacles and eight merlons. The church is crowned by a cresting and pinnacles. Fine 17th C wooden ceilings in the chancel and nave. A soaring Perp tabernacle font-cover, and three stalls used as sedilia. Fine late 17th C altar-rails and Communion table, and the box-pews are complete and also 17th C. Also of that date is the almsbox held by an over-lifesized coloured bearded man.

All Souls, Haley Hill (RCF) by Sir Gilbert Scott (1856–9) dominates its area of the town and is a magnificent building, grandly set, and with a magnificent spire 236 ft high.

LEEDS. A vast and overpowering town, but a great oasis for churches. The parish church of St Peter is unique because of its cathedral-type musical tradition – and what a place it is, rebuilt in 1841 for its famous vicar, W.F. Hook, to the designs of R.D. Chantrell. The exterior is massive, with a stately (144 ft) tower. The interior is mighty and dignified, built to accommodate 2,000 and full of seating and commodious galleries, but with the clear early Tractarian feel that it is not just a preaching house. All Soul's, Blackman Lane, is a fine building by Sir Gilbert Scott, with a devotional Anglo-Catholic interior. St Saviour's, Ellerby Road (1842–5) was founded by Dr Pusey and is a noble building in a commanding position, whilst St Aidan's, Roundhay Road (1891–4) is Romanesque, with wonderful mosaics by Frank Brangwyn. Mighty St Michael's, Headingley (1885) is by Pearson and St Matthew's chapel Allerton is by Bodley. Holy Trinity, Boar Lane (1721–7) is Classical, with a handsome 'city church' interior. St John's, New Briggate (RCF) is probably the most precious of all the Leeds churches. It was built in 1632–4 and is gothic, but contains so many of its original furnishings – a wonderful screen and pulpit, an almost complete set of benches and a wooden Royal Arms. A wonderful 17th century interior here.

SOUTH YORKSHIRE

ARKSEY. All Saints is a real oasis in an area of colliery villages and a wonderful cruciform church, with central tower and spire, which is still substantially a Norman building, with interesting Norman features, in addition to fine EE and Perp work. Inside are 17th century furnishings, including pews, pulpit (1634) and font-cover (1662).

Sir Gilbert Scott, who tastefully restored Arksey, created the mighty and magnificent St George's *Doncaster* after the destruction of the medieval church by fire in 1853. A wonderful, cathedral-like building this, with a glorious 170 ft central tower and a splendid lofty interior. The east window (44 ft tall) is filled with Hardman glass and the work of other good 19th century glassmakers may be seen here.

CAMPSALL. St Mary Magdalene's tower is a fine example of Norm. Its W doorway has three orders of zig-zag and the upper part of the doorway has two twin belfry windows on each side and Perp battlements and four pinnacles. The church is mainly Dec with a beautiful S doorway. Perp aisle windows, clerestory, battlements and pinnacles, and the S porch vaulted and with arcades. Also a Perp roof-screen with vaulting and a rhymed inscription. The pulpit is Jac.

Burghwallis St Helen's has 11th century herringbone masonry, also a lovely interior with a medieval screen and a good brass (1554) to Thomas Gascoigne.

DRAX. It is easy to detect the styles here. The tower and N arcade of St Peter and St Paul's are Norm, the church and S arcade are EE, the N chapel is Dec and the fine clerestory with eight windows on each side with gargoyles, and the belfry storey and recessed spire, are Perp. The bench-ends have Renaissance heads and Instruments of the Passion. Note the roof figures of Apostles and saints. There is a Norm tower arch and chancel arch and the W window is also Norm. The chancel has lancets (the three lancets at the E end being modern) and there is a Dec S doorway.

ECCLESFIELD. St Mary's is mainly Perp with a central tower with eight pinnacles. A peculiarity of this church is its half-detached buttresses and pinnacles, connected to the church by small flying buttresses. The chapels have original roofs. The font is dated 1662. Rood-screen with vault and parclose screens, stalls with two misericords and heads on the benches in front. Two small figures of Christ and St Anne and the Virgin. In the S chapel are more benches with little figures. There is a Sax cross-shaft and fragments of old glass. The mon to Sir Richard Scott, 1640, has its original grille.

Wentworth is worth visiting, for its old church (RCF) with excellent monuments, and Holy Trinity church – a magnificent building by J.L. Pearson, vaulted throughout and with a central tower and spire.

FISHLAKE. The lower part of St Cuthbert's tower and the nave arcades are 13th C. Then there is Dec work, including the E window of seven lights with Flowing tracery, and the chancel arch. Perp upper part of the tower with two-light belfry windows each side and battlements and eight pinnacles. Perp upper part of the tower with eight pinnacles. The five-light W window has a figure of St Cuthbert above. Also Perp is the clerestory with battlements and pinnacles. Old nave roof. Even so, the real glory of the church is the Norm S doorway with four orders of columns with capitals of animals and human figures, arches of Virtues fighting Vices, and medallions with pairs of seated figures, animals in profile, and leaves with human heads. There is a late 14th C font with eight figures of saints, a Jac font-cover and three screens.

LAUGHTON-on-the-MORTHEN. At the belfry storey the tower of All Saints turns octagonal with battlements behind, which is a recessed spire: in the diagonals the battlements have pinnacles and this is connected with the spire by flying buttresses. Where these flying buttresses touch the spire, another set of shafts start and end with pinnacles and are again linked to the spire by flying buttresses. All is Perp. This is an ingenious arrangement. The height is 185 ft, and the tower is vaulted. The N doorway of the church is Sax – pilaster strips and blocks instead of capitals. A smaller Norm doorway has been set in this doorway. The N arcade is late Norm and the S arcade Perp. Perp chancel E window, and a Dec S doorway. The head-moulds of the windows rest on figures. Perp font. There is also the base of a stone rood-screen, and a piscina.

ROTHERHAM. All Saints is a large and stately town church, with a central tower and spire, rising 180 ft. The exterior is noble and stately Perp and inside is fine craftsmanship, seen in the fan-vaulted crossing roof, the nave roof, the 15th century south chapel screen, chancel stalls and south chapel bench-ends. The 1604 pulpit has an 18th century sounding-board and the organ, by Snetzler, has a fine case. Much beauty and quality here.

Do find the little Bridge Chapel, built in c1483.

THORPE SALVIN. There is much Norm work in St Peter's – windows in the tower and S aisle, the tower arch, arcades, chancel arch and S doorway. Dec chancel with Flowing E window. Sedilia and low-side window. The S aisle windows are Dec and the N aisle windows Perp, as also the top of the tower and the clerestory. The Norm font is the feature of interest. Under two arches is a scene of a baptism, under four arches are the Four Seasons – sowing for Spring, harvesting for Summer, hunting for Autumn, and a man warming his legs before a fire for Winter. The mon to Katherine Sandford shows her with 17 children incised on her dress, an incised slab of 1461. Other monuments to Henry Sandford, his wife and three children and an infant, 1582, and Sir Roger Partington and wife, 1604.

TICKHILL. St Mary's W doorway and the lower part of the tower are EE, otherwise it is Perp. The upper part of the tower has two belfry windows of three lights on each side with battlements with crocketed arches over each embrasure and eight pinnacles. The tower has a W window of five lights and shields and three figures – a knight with a little son, a saint, and the knight's wife. There is one canopied niche on each of the S and E sides. Battlements and pinnacles are everywhere. A large clerestory has twice as many windows as bays and above the chancel arch is a five-light window and a demi-figure of an angel. The capitals have natural foliage. Perp font, screen to the N chapel and fragments of old glass. A tomb-chest of Thomas Fitzum and wife, 1478.

INDEX

343